2

3

Bo
abc
ww

ι

Critical Conflict

Critical Conflict

THE ROYAL NAVY'S MEDITERRANEAN CAMPAIGN IN 1940

Peter C. Smith

Pen & Sword
MARITIME

First published as Action Imminent in 1980 by William Kimber & Co Ltd.

This edition published in Great Britain in 2011 by
Pen & Sword Maritime
An imprint of
Pen & Sword Books Ltd
47 Church Street
Barnsley
South Yorkshire
S70 2AS

Printed in Great Britain by
CPI Antony Rowe, Chippenham and Eastbourne

Pen & Sword Books Ltd incorporates the Imprints of Pen & Sword Aviation,
Pen & Sword Family History, Pen & Sword Maritime, Pen & Sword Military,
Wharncliffe Local History, Pen & Sword Select, Pen & Sword Military Classics,
Leo Cooper, Remember When, Seaforth Publishing and Frontline Publishing

For a complete list of Pen & Sword titles please contact
PEN & SWORD BOOKS LIMITED
47 Church Street, Barnsley, South Yorkshire, S70 2AS, England
E-mail: enquiries@pen-and-sword.co.uk
Website: www.pen-and-sword.co.uk

for

CAPTAIN CLAUDE HUAN

with thanks for an entente cordiale

Contents

PART THREE
'Run, Rabbit, Run'

Maps and diagrams in the text

List of Illustrations

Foreword

The degree with which Winston Churchill, while First Lord of the Admiralty between September 1939 and May 1940, and again as Premier and Minister of Defence from May 1940 onward, directly intervened in the normal running of the Admiralty, and the effects, good or bad, that this interference had on the day-to-day conduct of the war at sea, have raised a considerable amount of controversy among the naval historians of the period. In particular the two foremost historians on naval affairs Captain S. W. Roskill and Professor Arthur J. Marder, arrived at rather different conclusions on these points.

There seems little doubt that Churchill's personal influence and intervention were strong, as would be expected from so forceful a personality, although, learning his lessons from World War One and the Admiral Fisher debacle over the Dardanelles, Winston's methods were, on the whole, more subtle. They appear to have taken the form and method of continued pressure on the Board of Admiralty, and in particular on the First Sea Lord, Admiral of the Fleet Sir Dudley Pound, and the later First Lord, A.V. Alexander, to force his own particular viewpoint or desire upon the Board, often against their sounder judgement and professional advice. The degree with which these two held out against such constant pressure and the degree to which Churchill overrode their advice is the subject of contention. Perhaps the most spectacular event for which this policy was largely responsible was the despatch, and consequent loss, of the *Prince of Wales* and *Repulse* to Singapore and the resulting disaster in *South East* Asia in 1941-42.

However the pressure started much earlier than this and in this book we examine the results of Whitehall interference in the actions of the three principal naval commanders in the Mediterranean Theatre in 1940. Admiral A.B. Cunningham was just as forceful a character as the Premier and the apparent lack of confidence shown in his early plans was surely the most unfounded of all. As we see in Part One, Cunningham was able to refute such criticism early on with an object lesson in the correct use of sea power, at the Battle of Calabria. The criticism of Admiral Sir Dudley North, the Flag Officer Commanding, North Atlantic, at Gibraltar, stemmed mainly from his revulsion at the action taken against the French Fleet at Mers-el-Kebir. His stand on that issue raised doubts at home as to his fighting spirit and when a second incident was considered to have been mishandled by him, despite the fact that his orders were far from clear, he was removed from his command. He was never able to redeem himself by action and fought a long post-war campaign to clear his name. We examine in depth in Part Two the naval operation that led to his removal, the passage of Force 'V'. Finally the Flag Officer, Force 'H', Admiral Sir James Somerville, was another forceful person with a style of his own. Retired before the war, he had been recalled to service and built up a superb reputation and partnership with Admiral Cunningham. However, he was a forthright character, fearless and outspoken and his similar criticism of the operations against the French, his defence of Admiral North and his condemnation of what he considered foolhardy plans from London, marked him down for the same treatment meted out to North. At the Battle of Spartivento, with which Part Three is concerned, his action in breaking off combat was taken, *before* all the true facts had come to light, as a sign of weakness and his subsequent treatment, at the instigation of Whitehall, aroused perhaps the greatest ire of all in the Service.

The purpose of this book is to examine these three incidents in depth as *naval actions*, and give fresh insight into what really happened. Only with clear knowledge of the incidents themselves can the political intervention be seen in its true light.

Peter C. Smith

Acknowledgements

I owe a particular debt of gratitude to the following persons who extended help, advice and assistance during my research for this book, and who tolerated my endless questions with patience and kindness: The Lady North for permission to use the papers held at Churchill College, Cambridge under the North archives and for the two photographs of Admiral North; Commander J. Somerville for permission to use the papers held at Churchill College, Cambridge under the Somerville archives. Correlli Barnett, for access to the Alexander, North, Somerville and Grenfell papers at the Archives Centre, Churchill College and special thanks to Clare Stephens and also Victor Brown of the Archives Centre for their help in tracking down documents I required; Rear Admiral A.S. Bolt, CB, DSO, DSC, RN, for his wise discourse on Fleet Air Arm matters; Mrs G. Cooper (her husband, Commander B.T. Cooper, CBE, DSO, commanded the destroyer *Wishart*); Dean C. Allard, Head of the Operational Archives Branch, Department of the Navy, Washington, DC; Monsieur J. Audouy, Conservateur d'Archives en Chef, Service Historique de la Marine, Paris; Mr P. Buckley, Army Historical Branch, London; Comte Guillaume Harcourt, for sending copies of his father's diaries and papers; Brigadier R.J. Lewendon, Assistant Secretary (Historical), Royal Artillery Institution, Woolwich, London; Dr Jurgen Röhwer, Bibliothek für Zeitgeschichte, Stuttgart; Robert Wolfe, Chief, Modern Military Records, Military Archives Division, National Archives, Washington, DC; Mrs Mollie Travis, Broadlands Archives; Captain Hervé Cras, Musée de la Marine, Paris; my old friend John R. Dominy for again contributing clear and precise diagrams to my work; Squadron Leader G.R. Spate MA, No 202 Squadron Archives, RAF; Mrs Anne Hewitt and Mrs René Petche, for the French translation work, which was considerable. Chris Ashworth; Chaz Bowyer; General Rinaldo Cruccui, Stato Maggiore Dell'Esercito, Ufficio Storico, Rome; Herr H.H. Hildebran, Hamburg; Rear Admiral Hans Mirow, Bremen; R.

Simpson, Department of Archives and Aviation Records, RAF Museum, Hendon, London.

I would especially like to thank the officers and men on the spot who were kind enough to give me their own viewpoints of the incidents here related; particularly valuable are these for they have hitherto been generally ignored. So my thanks to Admiral of the Fleet, Baron Fraser of North Cape (Third Sea Lord); Admiral Sir Manley Power, GCB, CBE, DSO, RN (Staff Officer, Operations, *Warspite*); Vice Admiral Gabriel Rebuffel (Chief-of-Staff, Force 'Y', *Georges Leygues*); Rear Admiral J. Broussignac (commanded the cruiser *Gloire*); Rear Admiral E.N.V. Currey (commanded the destroyer *Wrestler*); Rear Admiral R. Delaye (French Naval Attaché, Madrid); Rear Admiral J. Lee Barber (commanded the destroyer *Griffin*); Rear Admiral W.T.C. Ridley (Engineering Officer of the destroyer *Firedrake*); Rear Admiral J.H. Walwyn (Gunnery Officer in the battle-cruiser *Renown*); Captain F.M. Costet (Chief-of-Staff, Casablanca); Captain F.S. De Winton (Captain (D), 13th Flotilla); Captain M.J. Evans (Navigation Officer of the battle-cruiser *Renown*); Captain J.O.H. Gairdner (Engineering Officer of the destroyer *Faulknor*); Captain H.F.H. Layman (commanded the destroyer *Hotspur*); Captain J.S.S. Litchfield (Joint Planning Staff); Captain J. Osborne (Engineering Officer of the destroyer *Hotspur*); Captain A.W. Gray (Chief Engineering Officer, Force 'H', *Renown*); Captain E.V. St J. Morgan (commanded the destroyer *Encounter*); Captain René Chaix (Chief-of-Staff, Operations, Casablanca); Captain R.E.D. Ryder (commanded the 'Q' Ship *Willamette Valley*); Commander C.P.F. Brown (commanded the destroyer *Gallant*); Commander J.P. Parker (Rate Officer of the cruiser *Neptune*); Commander G. Cobb, OBE (Navigation Officer of the battleship *Malaya*); Commander John B. Murray (Swordfish pilot, *Eagle*); Commander W.A. Juniper (First Lieutenant of the destroyer *Griffin*); Commander E.N. Walmsley (commanded the destroyer *Vidette*); Commander Hugh Haggard, DSO, DSC, RN (commanded the submarine *Truant*); Commander T.F. Hallifax, (First Lieutenant of the destroyer *Velox*); Group Captain T.Q. Horner, RAF (commanded No. 202 Squadron, Gibraltar); Lieutenant Commander C. Mc D. Stuart (midshipman in the battle-cruiser *Renown*); Brigadier G.G. Wainwright (commanded the 4th Heavy Battery, RA, Gibraltar); A.H. Trignell (P.O. in battleship *Malaya*); E.B. Mackenzie, (AB in carrier *Eagle*); L. Griffin (Boy Seaman in cruiser *Neptune*); and D. Clare, (Signal Boy on carrier *Eagle*).

Finally a very special thank you to Captain Stephen Roskill for his particularly kind hospitality and wisdom; Professor Arthur J. Marder, for sustained interest, help and advice and to Captain Claude Huan, for whose work on my behalf in Paris I am deeply indebted. I am very grateful to all these most kind and helpful people and wish to point out that, unless quoted, all conclusions and opinions are mine and mine alone.

Notes on Sources, Ranks and Times

All my sources are annoted by superior figures in the text and are listed, chapter by chapter, at the end of the book. The North (NRTH), Somerville (SMVL), Alexander (AVAR) and Roskill (ROSK) papers are held at the Archives Centre, Churchill College, Cambridge and are reproduced by permission of the Trustees. The Admiralty (ADM), Air Ministry (AIR) and War Office (WO), along with the Cabinet Office (CAB) papers and documents are held at the Public Record Office, Kew, London, and are Crown Copyright, Controller of HM Stationery Office. Direct quotations from published sources are by permission of the authors, agents and publishers concerned.

For permission to quote brief extracts from the underlisted published works I would like to thank the following:

Churchill and the Admirals by Captain S.W. Roskill and *Ambassador on a Special Mission* by Viscount Templewood, to Collins Publishers; *A Sailor's Odyssey* by Viscount Cunningham of Hyndhope, to A.P. Watt & Son; *Sea Warfare* by Vice-Admiral Fredrich Ruge to Cassell Ltd; *The Second World War: Their Finest Hour*, by W.S. Churchill, to Cassell Ltd; *Destroyers' War* by A.D. Divine, to David Higham Associates Ltd; *Ark Royal 1939-41* by William James to Granada Publishing Ltd; *Pierre Laval and the Eclipse of France* by Geoffrey Warner, to Eyre & Spottiswoode (Publishers) Ltd; *The Vichy Regime* by Robert Aron to The Bodley Head; *The Italian Navy in World War II* by Marc Bragadin, to Naval Institute Press, Annapolis; *Operation*

Menace by Professor Arthur J. Marder, to Oxford University Press; and *Fighting Admiral* by Captain Donald Macintyre to the author and Evans.

Foreign ranks have, in general, been translated into the nearest British equivalents, which are, French: *Contre-Admiral* (Rear Admiral); *Capitaine de Vaisseau* (Captain); *Capitaine de Frégate* (Commander); *Lieutenant de Vaisseau* (Lieutenant); and Italian: *Ammiraglio di Armata* (Admiral); *Ammiraglio di Squadra* (Vice Admiral); *Ammiraglio di Divisione* (Rear Admiral); *Capitano di Vascello* (Captain); *Capitano di Fregata* (Commander); *Capitano di Corvetta* (Lieutenant Commander).

The times used throughout the text are the British Zonal Times. The French times are one hour in advance of these throughout (GMT) but, like the Italian, have been brought into line for clarity and are usually so noted in the text. Similarly distances are expressed English miles, yards and feet. The only exceptions to this practice have been in the case of quoted signals, where the original time of origin, or distance, has been preserved in context to keep the historical record accurate.

Admiral North's title is variously written in official documents as FOCNAS (Flag Officer Commanding, North Atlantic Station) ACNAS (Admiral Commanding North Atlantic Station) etc; and the original quotation has been followed in each case, but no change in rank or designation change is indicated by this.

I

The Action Off Calabria
9th July 1940

A SINGLE SHELL

CHAPTER ONE

Against the Odds

Ever since the rise of Fascism in Italy in the 1920s the prospects of a direct clash of interests between the upsurging power of that state and the long-established presence of Great Britain in the Mediterranean had been increasingly likely. Although Benito Mussolini initially was frequently regarded as a beneficial influence in the area, in that his dictatorial methods removed Britain's First War ally from the chaos into which she had sunk, it was fairly obvious that such a proudly nationalistic leader would, sooner or later, seek to usurp the colonial power on the borders of his expanding influence.

Dictators, once the initial momentum internally has worn off, can only thrive on success, and that success, as the Duce made increasingly clear, would be the re-establishment of the former Roman Empire across the narrow seas. The Italian people had taken him to their hearts but they were soon not content merely that their 'trains ran on time'. Bolstered by promises of a dizzy future as a major power again, they expected more and more of their new leader, and he was born along on the path of his own wild ambition and the need to prove himself over and over again to his followers.

There was already a legacy of bitterness in Italy towards her former friends arising from the outcome of the Great War, which Italy had entered on the Allies' side only after receiving promises of territory upon victory, promises in which the United States would have no part when she later joined in that great struggle. Italian colonial expansion in the Mediterranean area had already begun in the earlier years of the century with the occupation of Libya, Cyrenaica and the Dodecanese islands and Rhodes from Turkey as well as possessions in Africa itself. The Duce planned to use his Libyan bridgehead as a base for further expansion both eastward and westward, although initially it was against France that his venom was mainly directed, through his parrot calls of 'Corsica, Tunisia and Nice' from the balcony of the Palazzo Venezia. In the Adriatic his ambitions were reflected in the naming of a class of heavy cruisers, *Fiume, Pola, Trieste* etc and his ministers schemed and plotted their way across the Balkans with long-term ambitions against Albania (which was occupied in 1939), Yugoslavia and Greece.[1]

Britain's influence in the area was considerable, and had been for over a century, but her only actual possessions were Gibraltar to the west, Malta in the centre and Cyprus in the east. There was however the neutral nation of Egypt and the treaties which permitted the stationing of our forces there to protect the Suez Canal and keep watch over the Anglo-Egyptian Sudan to the south. This enabled the British to build up an important naval base at Alexandria which was less vulnerable than Malta, hitherto the lynchpin of British military planning in that area. The dominant factor in the British position in the Mediterranean was of course the Mediterranean Fleet, second in size only to the Home Fleet. Despite the fact that, for almost two decades following the termination of the Great War, Japan had been the most obvious naval threat, the bulk of the Royal Navy remained firmly based in the Atlantic and Mediterranean, and its constant existence in the latter was a continual irritation to Mussolini busy proclaiming himself as master of that particular stretch of water. '*Il Mare Nostrum – No!*' he shouted. The British Mediterranean Fleet silently gave the answer to this boast merely by its presence, – No!!

Nonetheless Mussolini gave free rein to his armed forces to build up their strength in the 1930's in order to challenge the domination of the British and the French fleets and armies, which, combined, far outnumbered his strength. As the decade rolled on more and more factors emerged to swing the balance in the Duce's favour. We shall examine them briefly one by one.

In the first place Anglo-French accord was not backed up by any particular treaty, or indeed, any firm commitment to help each other against Italy. France tended to arm herself with a possible conflict with Italy in mind, in particular with respect to her naval and aeronautical forces. Germany did not arouse too much concern in the early 1930's, disarmed as she was and with the Maginot Line felt by many to be impregnable. But the emergence of Hitler and the Nazi party, loosely modelled on Mussolini's own movement but with far greater potential behind it, tended to give the French other things to preoccupy them which could only be good for Italy.

Britain was still nominally friendly with both powers, but suspicious of anything that would shackle her own freedom of movement, and so at sea Anglo-French co-operation was friendly but minimal and planning was almost non-existent. Thus the Naval Armaments' Race in the Mediterranean tended, in the 1930s, to come down to a two-horse race, with Italy and France building battleships in a growing tit-for-tat momentum that gathered pace as the decade rolled on. Britain tended to look on things with a more comprehensive view and had meanwhile shackled herself more and more with various Naval treaties that steadily reduced the number of fighting ships she herself maintained, while the Treasury gripped the pursestrings tighter and tighter, preventing any replacement of the old units still left to her. Although the Royal Navy's position in the Mediterranean remained an impressive one on paper, it was a steadily declining asset in terms of fighting power.[2]

In strict contrast Italy gave her armed forces every opportunity to build themselves up fully to Treaty limits and to do so with the most modern equipment available. In naval terms this meant the laying down of four brand-new 35,000-ton battleships to replace her four old vessels of that type, and, in the interim, of fully modernising these latter. This was supplemented by a large-scale building programme of other classes of warship, 8-inch and 6-inch cruisers, large flotilla leaders and destroyers and the construction of one of the largest submarine fleets in the world.[3]

In material terms the new fleet of Italy was most impressive. The new battleships were armed with 15-inch guns and building had commenced at a time when Britain was still haggling over the ships of her new programme and asking for a 14-inch limit in gun calibres. The Italian 8-inch cruisers were fewer in number than the fifteen 'Treaty' ships of the same type built for the Royal and Commonwealth navies, but being laid down later, they benefited by this fact and, far more, by the fact that Italian Naval constructors were not encouraged to bind themselves very tightly to the tonnage restrictions which British warships were designed. This came very dramatically to light during the Spanish Civil War when the Italian heavy cruiser *Gorizia* was towed into Gibraltar dockyard for repairs and found to be at least ten per cent higher in displacement than the 10,000 tons accredited to her.[4]

Italy's light cruisers and destroyers were reputed to be very fast, although not as powerfully armed as their British equivalents. This fact tended to be discounted as it was claimed that the sensational trial figures were only achieved by 'cheating' (running without full armament etc. embarked and the like), but the realities of war showed that they could normally show a clean pair of heels to British units. They lacked armour though, and this too was to be put to the test ere long.

Their naval tradition was not strong and their outlook, being solely concerned with the maintaining of their short-sea routes from Italy and Sicily to Libya, was entirely different. At a time when radar was not a factor in sea warfare the enclosed, bullet-proof bridges of Italian destroyers, for example, tended to restrict visibility at night to a fatal extent, a factor not found in the open bridges of the contemporary British ships of that type.[5]

Her absolute priority on submarine building gave greater concern and with over one hundred such vessels on her strength it was thought that the domination of the Central Mediterranean Basin was within her reach, especially as these would be backed up by intensive mining of the shallow waters of that region and by the huge bomber force accredited to the Regia Aeronautica.

Altogether, then, by the later 1930's, Italy's military position looked quite strong, coupled as it was with her physical position centrally astride the Mediterranean, which cut Allied forces effectively in half. It was certainly powerful enough an influence to dominate British political thinking at the time of the Abyssinian invasion, when calls for something more positive than the patently ineffective 'sanctions' were made. Fear of large casualties from the air and sea on British surface forces was widespread and, although naval reinforcements were moved into the area from Home Waters, Mussolini called the bluff and got away with another addition to his colonial empire. He also, naturally, drew further away from Britain and France and into the welcoming arms of his fellow dictator in Germany, a movement which was accelerated by the Spanish Civil War in which Italy was by far the largest interventionist in terms of military hardware.[6]

Britain had already, by 1937, decided that Malta would be untenable to all but light forces in event of war with Italy, and the bulk of the Mediterranean Fleet lay concentrated at Alexandria. A small force of one destroyer flotilla and a few auxiliaries was based on Gibraltar and this was supported by a pitifully small army in the Egyptian desert and an almost non-existent air component of a few obsolete biplanes, plus a limited number of AA guns.

The position was made tolerable on the outbreak of war in 1939, by the fact that the main strength of the French Navy lay in the Mediterranean, at their major bases of Toulon in southern France and Mers-el-Kebir in Algeria, close to Oran. Further naval bases were strung along the northern coast of Africa as far as Bizerta. The balance still lay, nominally, at sea, with the Allies. Moreover Italy was in such a poor state economically that the Duce, eager as he was to join Hitler in the showdown with the Western Democracies, had little choice but to fretfully hold back and wait and watch for a better opportunity. The imposition of a blockade of coal from Germany by the Allies did nothing to lessen his feelings of hatred toward Allied seapower but, for the moment, he was impotent.

With the fall of France in June 1940 the Duce felt his moment had come, and, with a great fanfare, Italy entered the war on the 10th of that month. Within a few weeks enormous changes had been made to the map of Europe and the balance of power in the Mediterranean now swung dramatically away from the British; so far indeed did it swing that for a time her whole position there appeared completely untenable.

With the French surrender and the signing of the Armistice with the Axis powers, Britain straight away lost the benefit of the powerful and modern French fleet, the French air force in the area and all military and naval bases in the Western Basin save Gibraltar itself. In the central basin only Malta stood, virtually undefended, against all that Italy chose to send against it, while in the Western Basin the main Mediterranean Fleet was based over a thousand miles away from the main Italian supply lines into Africa.

Nor was this fleet the compact and highly drilled fleet of pre-war days. Then indeed it was the envy of the world, despite its old ships, for it was a finely honed force in which the cream of the Royal Navy sought to serve. There was no fear of Italy in the pre-war Mediterranean Fleet under Admirals Fisher and Pound, and nor was there any under Admiral Sir Andrew Cunningham, its Commander-in-Chief in June 1940. But during the early months of the war this highly skilled force had been whittled away on other duties in other parts of the globe. Its 1st Cruiser Squadron, 8-inch ships in a high pitch of readiness,[7] had been dispersed among the world's trade routes hunting raiders. Its unrivalled destroyer flotilla had been flung into the cauldrons of Narvik and Dunkirk and decimated, its old battleships, with their proud and highly trained gun crews, had been taken away to Arctic Waters, until only a mere skeleton of that once feared fleet remained.

Not until May 1940 did this fleet gradually receive reinforcements from all the scattered stations; by then of course, many had been sunk or damaged, and with the German army and air force at the gates of Britain many more had to be retained at home to face the threat of invasion. The force which re-assembled at Alexandria was therefore both smaller and less a whole than the one that had watched over the Mediterranean ten months earlier.

What was life aboard the ships of the Mediterranean Fleet at this time? Let Mr D. Clare give his recollections:

I joined the *Eagle* on 4th May 1940 from the *Ramillies*, just prior to her entering the Mediterranean, a few days before my seventeenth birthday. I think I can honestly say I really enjoyed my time aboard her – though I would have much preferred a smaller ship at the time (I was itching to get on a destroyer). The living conditions were average for an old ship of that period I suppose, but most certainly rugged in extreme compared to the present day, or even the more modern ships of that time. As usual there was never enough fresh water at sea; everyone needed a bucket in which to retain his ration for the day. But in those days it was all happily (!) accepted as part and parcel of a sailor's life. Drinking water usually hung in canvas bags to cool for we had no mess fridges of course.

However, I still consider we were all one family, and no matter how much one might squabble aboard just let someone from another ship or whatever talk disparagingly of our ship while on leave in Alexandria and all 'Eagles' would soon become one. As a signal boy, ordinary seaman, signalman and leading signalman, certainly all the officers I had contact with on the bridge were first class. The Captain, as was usual, was rather an aloof figure, but quite fatherly, particularly to us boys (there were several younger than myself aboard).

To my mind, as a signalman, *Eagle* was quite outstanding in that she had a signal bosun who, though being a driver as far as work was concerned, was very interested in his signalmen gaining promotion, and to that end was always on the go, cajoling, questioning, imparting his knowledge, and I most certainly have him to thank for myself becoming a Yeoman of Signals at just nineteen years of age. His name was Mr Godden.

When I joined her her crew were almost all long serving members of the Royal Navy. But on entering the Med we were joined by many short-service ratings and hostilities only ratings. This turned out to our advantage of course; we had been highly trained, the newcomers had not, so that we found ourselves doing the more responsible jobs and our poor unfortunate SS and HOs having to do the menial tasks which would rightly have been ours![8]

Another description of the Mediterranean Fleet's ships is given by the Rate Officer aboard the *Neptune* at this time:

The first seven months of the war had been spent in the South Atlantic searching for German raiders, on our own, sometimes with the *Ark Royal* and *Renown* and once with a French squadron. We spent only the odd day in Freetown or Dakar, intercepted and sank the *Ihn* on the second day of the war and the *Adolph Woerman* a few weeks later. When *Graf Spee* was sighted we were detached from the French squadron to join Commodore Harwood but had to refuel in Rio and while waiting for our turn heard that the *Graf Spee* had scuttled.

The ship was transferred to the Mediterranean just before the Italian war was declared. At about that time a number of officers were changed including Captain Morse who was replaced by Rory O'Connor. Rory O'Connor was undoubtedly a great captain, who soon knew everyone in the ship, but later on, when we left the Mediterranean Fleet again to go to the Indian Ocean for raider chasing again, things did not go too well. We kept thinking we were going home but were continually being diverted for one last task; another raider to chase, the Southern Islands, including Kerguelen, to search; the flag of Admiral J.D. Cunningham to be flown just after the abortive Dakar operation, when the ship had to lurk around between Lagos and the Cameroons as encouragement to the Free French, a hot and dreary job. The ship's company and some of the officers began to feel that Rory was more interested in fighting the war than in their welfare. Most of them had left the UK in September 1937 and had not seen their families since then and they were worried about the Blitz.

While in the Med. *Neptune* had bombarded Bardia with the Anglo-French force. We started off from Alexandria with our French allies to steam through the Straits of Messina but the operation was called off because of the French attitude and they pulled out of the war. We spent most of one day in Alexandria with our guns trained on a French cruiser in the next berth. We took part with the rest of our squadron in the interception of three Italian destroyers of which we sank one and we went up into the Aegean one Sunday afternoon to intercept an Italian ship carrying petrol, which we sank and were ourselves heavily bombed without damage.[9]

The 'Neptunes', by the time of Calabria, could therefore consider themselves a very efficient and full worked up company.

There was little else to spare for the Alexandrian force: no modern fighters, no tanks, no modern equipment of any kind on land, sea or air. In contrast the whole weight of the re-built Italian military might could be thrown against them with no fear of complications and endless scope for reinforcement. It is true that the Admiralty at once reinforced the Western Basin with a new striking force, Force H, but they were initially tied down in the complicated and repugnant task of reducing the fleet of their former ally to impotence to prevent the Axis laying their hands on it, and their contribution to the defence of the Mediterranean was reduced to holding the Straits of Gibraltar and a few brief sorties into the western basin towards Sardinia to create diversions. It was upon Cunningham's shoulders mainly, therefore, that the whole initiative fell, and upon his small fleet.

Fortunately the right man was in the right place. Andrew B., as he was known, was one of the greatest sailors of modern times, fearless in the face of such odds, and confident in the future outcome, no matter what, and this attitude was, happily, the norm amongst his men. Despite the squawkings of the Jeremiahs back home, who ruefully predicted defeat and annihilation should the Navy venture out into the submarine- and bomber-infested waters of the central Mediterranean, Cunningham's first move was to do just that, to test the mettle of his opponents. Holding that the British seaman was more than a match for his Italian opposite number, Cunningham's philosophy was to *seek* combat, whether at sea or from the air, rather than hide from it.[10]

The Duce had laid down his grand policy for his commanders as a general offensive throughout the Mediterranean area, but in truth it was another futile gesture. The main concern of his military chiefs was to cautiously build up their strength in Libya while they could during the summer months, in preparation for a probe at the British defences in Egypt with a view to a limited autumn offensive. To do this it was essential that regular convoys of fuel, munitions and troops got safely across the narrows between the ports of Italy and Tripoli, Benghazi and Tobruk. No 'grand offensive' was envisaged by the Italian Naval High Command, Supermarina, other than by massive submarine patrols in both basins under cover of which the convoys would move, covered by the full strength of main Italian Fleet.[11] The High Command of the Regia Aeronautica was eager to test its long-held theories of the invincibility of the heavy bomber over the battleship, and Superaero conducted long-range searches throughout the area to locate the British fleet in order to destroy it wholesale. They had large numbers of highly skilled bombers on hand at bases in the Dodecanese, Libya and Italy itself all within easy flying distance of the main sea routes and were confident of success.[12] However direct contact between Supermarina and Superaero was minimal, in contrast to the British practice, whereby, although the forces available were tiny, co-operation was much more prevalent.

The Italian fleet was commanded by Admiral Inigo Campioni,

who was very conscious that the Duce expected great things of him and his fleet. But Campioni also knew that his fleet was far from ready for a major encounter with the British. The new battleships although almost ready, had not yet joined the fleet. Until they did his old ships would be at a disadvantage against the larger-gunned ships of Cunningham. He therefore rejected any wild schemes to provoke a general action at this time, relying instead on his minefields and submarines to protect his flanks and the air force to provide him with ample warning to avoid any such encounter.

Thus the stage was set for the first major clash of fleets in the Mediterranean since the Battle of the Nile a century and half earlier, or Navarino a hundred years before. Let us now examine in more detail the forces available to both Commanders-in-Chief at this time.

For a start, as we have stated, Cunningham relied for his main base on a port in a country by no means wholeheartedly behind Britain in its fight. Since the events of the bombardment of Alexandria and the Battle of Tel-el-Kebir at the tail-end of the nineteenth century Britain's military presence and her overriding influence in running affairs had been the dominant feature of Egyptian life, but Egypt did not pretend to enjoy it. There was certainly little enthusiasm for war with Italy on Egypt's part and in 1940, as at an earlier period, 'sulky acquiescence' was the most that could be hoped for in that quarter, in spite of the Anglo-Egyptian Treaty of 1936 which gave Britain the right to maintain Alexandria and the Canal Zone garrisons and to reinforce these in an emergency.

With Malta the main fleet base for decades the facilities at Alexandria left a great deal to be desired. Pre-war plans to establish a Mobile Naval Base Defence Organisation at either Navarino in Greece, or at Suda Bay in Crete to set up a more advanced fleet base, came to little through lack of money, as had requests by Sir William Fisher and other Commanders-in-Chief to improve the defences of Malta, including the building of bomb-proof submarine pens. All these urgent needs had been thrown out by the limited amount of funding allowed to the services and the question of Alexandria had gone largely down the same road. The limited MNBDO equipment sent out to the Mediterranean in 1935 was used, instead, to supplement Alexandria's sparse utilities.

By the summer of 1939 the base was a little improved but not, by any stretch of the imagination, an adequate fleet base for a major war. There were pitifully few AA guns, the coastal defences were manned by the Egyptians themselves, there were no fighters to speak of and an airstrip close by was only in the initial stages of construction and was designed for use by Fleet Air Arm aircraft when disembarked ashore from their carriers. There was no balloon barrage, no safe munitions' storage, no floating dock able to take battleships and indeed, precious little else to support a main fleet.

The largest dock could only take warships up to the size of small cruisers, the workshops of the Khedivial Steamship Line had to be utilised for the smallest repairs. Deep water berths were under construction along with a new wharf and storehouses.

Although by June 1940 further improvements had been made, Alexandria was described by the C-in-C as poorly defended and a bad substitute as a fleet base. The large floating dock based at Portsmouth was finally sent out but, in the main, the fleet had to be made as self-sufficient as possible. The large repair ship *Resource* (12,300 tons) was sent out, as were the destroyer depot ship *Woolwich* (8,750 tons) and the submarine depot ship *Maidstone* (8,900 tons) and various other essential auxiliaries like netlayers and boom defence vessels, water carriers and small fuel and ammunition carriers. A few Hurricane fighters were promised, and additional AA guns at the expense of Malta. These latter duly arrived but were never very efficient. The searchlight batteries were equally poor and both units suffered from a mixed British and Egyptian control that left them very much out of touch with each other.

The Italians of course were relying on their own home bases from the outset and these were well-placed, well-protected and fully efficient. Taranto was the main fleet base set in the natural haven of the heel of Italy and surrounded by land which guarded approaches from three sides. Here were based a division of two old battleships, a division of 8-inch cruisers, two divisions of light cruisers and four divisions of destroyers plus lesser vessels. Italy's control of Albania and the mine and submarine blockade across the straits of Otranto gave the Italians, in theory and practice, complete and secure control of the whole of the Adriatic. They also had the major base at Naples far up the west coast from which to menace the western basin. Far from the immediate potential battlefield two light cruiser divisions and one destroyer division lay here as the main units, while further up the coast at Spezia lay another old battleship and three divisions of escort destroyers (torpedo boats as the Italians classified them). The fourth old battleship was in the Adriatic on the outbreak of war. The two new battleships were completing at Taranto and Naples respectively, but would not be ready for combat until August, while two others were still building.

Watching over the Straits between Sicily and Tunisia, Italy had important bases at Messina and Augusta and here were based one heavy cruiser division, one light cruiser division and four divisions of destroyers. These latter could quickly concentrate with the ships at Taranto. In North Africa itself two destroyer divisions were based on Tripoli with escort divisions there and at Tobruk.

The Dodecanese islands and Rhodes blocked the Aegean and were utilised by light forces, but their main menace to Cunningham lay in the fact that from the airfields of the latter island long-range bombers could outflank him for any sortie he made into the Central Basin, while similar large concentrations on the airfields of Calabria and Sicily dominated the central basin. In addition, the overwhelming Italian submarine strength was deployed to give maximum warning of any penetration westward by Cunningham's fleet, whereas his own limited strength in that category was thinly spread from its Malta base.

So much for base organisation; what of the actual ships themselves? In the main units Cunningham could deploy four battleships. His flagship, the famous *Warspite*, had been modernised between the wars, although, like the others in the Mediterranean, British and Italian, she dated back to the First World War. Of 30,600 tons displacement, she mounted eight 15-inch guns which had been given a maximum elevation of 30° during her rebuilding which gave her weapons a range of 32,200 yards. Her former sister ship, the *Malaya*, had received no such complete reconstruction, and although she carried the same main armament their maximum elevation of 20° gave them a range of only 23,400 yards. On her pre-war trials she was credited with a little over 23 knots maximum speed, whereas *Warspite* was marginally faster by almost a knot. By 1940, however, the *Malaya* was not capable of keeping up with her sister by at least a two knot margin. The other two battleships with the Mediterranean fleet were the *Royal Sovereign* and *Ramillies* (29,150 tons), which although built later than the former two had not been modernised to any great extent. They also carried the 15-inch gun in four twin turrets but their best speeds hardly exceeded 20 knots at this time. The machinery of the *Malaya*, *Royal Sovereign* and *Ramillies* was old and prone to breakdowns; the first suffered trouble with her condensors while the latter two had boiler trouble which made them unreliable.

On the Italian side the four old battleships ready for action were the *Conte di Cavour, Guilio Cesare, Caio Duilio* and *Andrea Doria*. They too had been extensively modernised between the wars. Their main armament consisted of ten 12.6-inch guns, a smaller calibre than the British ships but one which, in practice was able to outrange them all save the *Warspite*. They were credited with speeds of 27 knots giving them a decisive margin over the British vessels of that type.

As we have seen Cunningham's 8-inch cruiser strength, once a major factor in the Mediterranean Fleet's power, had been taken away from him completely, and had not been replaced. He thus had no heavy cruisers at all to oppose the seven such ships which the Italians could deploy. These were the *Gorizia, Fiume, Pola, Bolzano* and *Zara* (12,000 tons) and the older *Trento* and *Trieste* (10,000 tons), all armed with eight 8-inch guns and speeds of 32 knots.

In light cruisers too the British were heavily at a disadvantage for they could only muster nine of these, the modern *Gloucester* and *Liverpool* (10,000 tons), armed with twelve 6-inch guns, the slightly older and smaller *Neptune* and *Orion* (7,270 tons) armed with eight 6-inch guns, and the Australian *Sydney* (6,830 tons) with the same main armament. All these ships had speeds of around 32 knots, and they formed the 7th Cruiser Squadron.

Backing these up were the older ships of the 3rd Cruiser Squadron, the *Delhi*, (4,850 tons) armed with six old 6-inch guns, dated back to 1920, while the smaller and older *Capetown, Caledon* and *Calypso* were built in the Great War and had not been modernised at all. They displaced 4,290 tons and were armed with five 6-inch guns. These old ships were credited with top speeds of 29 knots. In fact they operated only in the second division, the *Delhi* going to refit at Gibraltar in May and the *Calypso* being an early loss when she was sunk by the Italian submarine *Bagnolini* on 12th June.

Against five modern light cruisers then the Italians could range a force of twelve such vessels, all credited with speed of up to 37 knots. These were the *Abruzzi* and *Garibaldi* (7,874 tons, ten 6-inch guns), *D'Aosta, Attendolo* (7,283 tons, eight 6-inch guns), *Diaz, Di Guissano* and *Savoia* (5,050 tons, eight 6-inch guns), *Montecuccoli* and *Colleoni* (5,050 tons, eight 6-inch guns), and *Da Barbiano, Bande Nere* and *Cadorna* (5,000 tons, eight 6-inch guns).

In destroyers the difference in numbers was even more striking. Cunningham had a nominal strength of 20 such vessels in three flotillas. These were the 2nd Flotilla, *Hyperion, Havock, Hero, Hereward, Hostile, Hasty, Ilex* and *Imperial* (1,360 tons, four 4.7-inch guns, four 21-inch torpedo tubes, the latter two five) credited with speeds of 35 knots; the 14th Flotilla, *Mohawk* and *Nubian* (1,870 tons, eight 4.7-inch guns, 4 21-inch torpedo tubes, 37 knots), *Jervis, Janus* and *Juno* (1,690 tons, six 4.7-inch guns, five 21-inch torpedo tubes, 36 knots); and the 10th Flotilla, *Stuart* (1,530 tons, five 4.7-inch guns, six 21-inch torpedo tubes, 35 knots), *Vendetta, Waterhen, Vampire* and *Voyager* (1,100 tons, four 4.7-inch guns, 4-inch in latter two, six 21-inch torpedo tubes, 34 knots), *Dainty, Diamond, Decoy* and *Defender* (1,400 tons, four 4.7-inch guns, four 21-inch torpedo tubes, 35 knots). In addition the destroyer *Garland* was refitting at Alexandria; she had been sold to the Polish Navy and was due to transfer to the United Kingdom when ready. All were fairly modern ships, which, after war experience at home, had their after set of tubes replaced by a 3-inch HA gun. The only exceptions were the four old destroyers of the Australian Navy, *Stuart, Vampire, Voyager* and *Waterhen*, which dated back to 1917-20 and were unmodernised, they were affectionately known as the 'Scrap-Iron Flotilla' and they performed valiantly despite their age.

Against this score of flotilla vessels the Italians had some 57 fleet destroyers and 67 escort destroyers available, most of them equally as powerfully armed, but, in most cases, much faster ships.

Submarine strengths were 115 Italian against 12 British, the latter being the old, large boats from the China Station, *Odin, Olympus, Otus, Grampus* and *Rorqual* being based at Malta in June, with *Osiris, Oswald, Pandora, Parthian, Phoenix* and *Proteus* being based initially at Alexandria. All dated back to 1929-32 and were armed with a single 4-inch gun and six 21-inch torpedo tubes, except the more modern *Grampus* and *Rorqual*, which were minelayers.

The one ship which the British had and to which the Italians had no equivalent, was the aircraft carrier *Eagle*. She was old, having originally been the Chilean battleship *Almirante Cochrane* building on the Clyde during the First World War. Her uncompleted hull was taken over by the Royal Navy but instead of completing her as a battleship, as was done with a sister, she was suspended until 1918 and then completed as an aircraft-carrier, joining the Navy in 1923. She was slow for a carrier, 24 knots was her maximum speed, and she had poor stowage of aircraft, only being able to take 21 to sea. Of 22,600 tons and armed with nine 6-inch guns, and four 4-inch guns, she reflected her age for these weapons were of no use to her and only added weight.

Although the Italians had wanted their own carriers, Mussolini scorned the idea of any such ship in the land-locked waters of the Mediterranean, dominated, as he confidently expected them to be, by his hordes of long-range bombers. Even some British experts expected the carrier to be quickly annihilated by these but they proved tougher than expected in the event. Their greatest vulnerability, as with most warships, lay in dive-bombing, but the Italians only had one experimental group of these and posed no real threat. Torpedo bombers were the major threat to the British and Italian battleships, but again, Italy had very few of these aircraft operational in June 1940, although development was going ahead fast, while Britain only had the obsolete Fairey Swordfish TSR's of the *Eagle*'s squadrons, 17 of which were operational at this time. She carried no fighter aircraft at all for protection of herself and the fleet at this time.

In addition to the above vessels Cunningham had the old monitor *Terror*, based at Malta (7,200 tons, 2 15-inch guns, 12 knots), the netlayer *Protector*, four Fleet minesweepers, *Abingdon*, *Bagshot*, *Fareham* and *Fermoy*, two armed boarding vessels, *Chakla* and *Fiona*, ten trawlers and lesser vessels including oilers and suchlike. Thus the situation was not good in terms of pure hardware.

Nor was the geographical position very bright either. With France gone the whole of the coastline of the Mediterranean was either enemy-held or neutral, and in many cases hostile to Britain or surly, as Egypt and Mandated Palestine. Save for Gibraltar, Malta and Cyprus, the British toe-hold was slender.

However, once the initial thoughts of abandoning the whole area had been put aside Admiral Cunningham was ready to put into play his one trump card, the *morale* of his command. Despite some unnecessary and unhelpful prompting from Churchill, the C-in-C had no intention of taking a defensive line at all and the feelings of his command were reflected in his letter to Admiral Pound at the time, his fleet was, he told the First Sea Lord, '... imbued with a burning desire to get at the Italian fleet ...'.[13] Within a month of war opening in the Mediterranean they were to get that sought-after opportunity.

Admiral Sir Manley Power, at that time Cunningham's new Staff Officer, Operations, makes the following points regarding the condition of the Mediterranean Fleet at this time.

The old Med Fleet, at the beginning of the war in '39, had been the biggest and most highly trained of the Royal Navy. This had been dispersed during the period of 'phoney war'. The Fleet which was eventually assembled in May '40 was all dribs and drabs scratched up pretty much haphazardly and had had no opportunity for combined training. They were seasoned ships and in fact worked together pretty well when the crunch came, which says much for the ingrained common doctrine built up pre-war.

The same is really true of the C-in-C's Staff. Most of them had been there some time before the war, but I (in some respects a key member) had only joined after the outbreak of war. As a submariner I had virtually no knowledge of fleet work and none at all of the action organisation of a C-in-C's staff. We were then very shortly grounded in Malta and became absorbed in a host of activities far removed from problems of fleet action. When we did get afloat again we continued to be absorbed in activities relating to the station as a whole and had no time to work up an action organisation.[14]

CHAPTER TWO

Opening Moves

Early in July 1940 the main preoccupation with both commanders at sea was the passage of vital convoys. For the Italians it was the need to further build up their land forces on the Libyan border in readiness for the long-awaited assault on Egypt. Here a large Italian army under the command of Marshal Rodolfo Graziani, Marquis of Neghelli, the so-called Viceroy of Ethiopia in 1936-37, was not showing very much enthusiasm for its task, despite the fact that the Marshal himself was one of the leading voices for Italy joining in the war. His constant refrain was for supplies, and yet more supplies. He also recommended postponing the invasion until the spring because of the heat, advice that infuriated the Duce who was seeking an early success in North Africa to balance the German victories in Western Europe and the poor showing of his own troops against France on that Alpine Front in June.[1]

Among his demands were an extra 13,000 troops, 40,000 tons of supplies, and so on and so forth of which the Navy had only been able to transport a fraction by single merchant ships and submarines so far. Accordingly the risk of running a major convoy was accepted and preparations began at Naples to organise this. 2,200 troops, 300 armoured vehicles and trucks and some 16,000 tons of essential supplies were loaded onto the liner *Esperia* (11,398 tons), the freighters *Calitea* (4,013 tons), *Marco Foscarini* (6,342 tons) and *Vettor Pisani* (6,339 tons). To provide the close escort for this convoy were allocated the escort destroyers of the 4th Division, *Orione, Orsa, Pegaso* and *Procione* (855 tons, two 3.9-inch guns, 28 knots). This group was to be joined at sea by the freighter *Francesco Barbero* (6,343 tons) which was to sail from Catania escorted by the escort destroyers *Abba* and *Pilo* (615 tons, five 4-inch guns, 32 knots), and the combined convoy was to be given close cover by the 2nd Light Cruiser Division commanded by Admiral Ferdinando Casardi with the 6-inch cruisers *Bande Nere* (Captain Franco Maugeri) and *Colleoni* (Captain Umberto Novaro), with the 10th Destroyer Division, commanded by Captain Franco Garofalo in the destroyer *Maestrale,* with the *Libeccio* (Commander Enrico Simola), *Grecale* (Commander

Eduardo Cacace) and *Scirocco* (Commander Francesco Gatteschi).

It was recognised that the British Fleet might catch wind of this important convoy and further emphasis that its protection would need to be enhanced was given by a reconnaissance report received on 7th July that a British cruiser squadron had arrived at Malta. In fact this report was false; only the destroyers *Jervis* and *Diamond* had reached that island as we shall see, but it was enough to make Supermarina take far-reaching steps to reinforce the convoy's protection.

The convoy sailed from Naples on 6th July and was joined by the *Francesco Barbero* the next day. The 2nd Division and its escorting destroyers sailed from Augusta just after midday, the destroyers at 1215 and the cruisers at 1325 to provide immediate cover.

Meanwhile the Supermarina had instructed Admiral Riccardo Paladini to sail with his cruisers in order to give stronger protection against the British cruisers, and his forces began to put to sea the same day. Paladini himself flew his flag in the heavy cruiser *Pola* (Captain Manlio De Pisa), escorted by the 12th Destroyer Squadron, led by Captain Carmine D'Arienzo in the *Lanciere*, with the *Carabiniere* (Commander Alberto Battaglia), *Corazziere* (Commander Carlo Avegno) and *Ascari* (Commander Sabato Bottiglieri). This force sailed from Augusta at 1840 on the 7th, some hours after the 1st Division. Commanded by Admiral Pellegrino Matteucci flying his flag in the heavy cruiser *Zara* (Captain Luigi Corsi), this comprised the 8-inch cruisers *Gorizia* (Captain Giuseppe Manfredi) and *Fiume* (Captain Giorgio Giorgis), escorted by the destroyers of the 9th Squadron under Captain Lorenzo Daretti in the *Alfieri*, with the *Oriani* (Commander Mario Panzani), *Carducci* (Commander Vincenzo Novari) and *Gioberti* (Commander Marco Aurelio Raggio). This group had sailed at 1410 on the 7th.

From Messina to join Paladini's force sailed the 3rd Division under Admiral Carlo Cattaneo with his flag in the heavy cruiser *Trento* (Captain Alberto Parmigiano) and the *Bolzano* (Captain Gaetano Catalano Gonzaga di Cirella), escorted by the 11th Destroyer Squadron under Captain Carlo Margottini in the *Artigliere*, with the *Camicia Nera* (Commander Giovanni Oliva), *Aviere* (Commander Carlo Tallarigo) and *Geniere* (Commander Giovanni Bonetti). They left harbour at 1545 on the 7th.

Yet another force was added to this powerful array with the sailing from Palermo at 1235 on the 7th of the 7th Division, led by Admiral Luigi Sansonetti with his flag in the 6-inch cruiser *Eugenio di Savoia*

(Captain Calo De Angelis) with the *Duca d'Aosta* (Captain Franco Rogadeo), *Attendolo* (Captain Federico Martinengo) and *Montecuccoli* (Captain Francesco Zannoni), escorted by the destroyers of the 13th Squadron under Captain Gerardo Galati aboard the *Granatiere*, with the *Fuciliere* (Commander Alfredo Viglieri), *Bersagliere* (Commander Candido Bigliardi) and *Alpino* (Commander Giuseppe Marini).

Nor was the purpose of the Italian concentration to cover the five vital merchant ships. The Fleet Commander himself, Admiral Inigo Campioni, sailed from Taranto around the same time with the 5th Division, flying his flag aboard the battleship *Giulio Cesare* (Captain Angelo Varoli Piazza) with the *Cavour* (Captain Ernesto Ciurlo), escorted by the destroyers of the 7th Squadron under Captain Amleto Baldo in the *Freccia*, with the *Dardo* (Commander Bruno Salvatori), *Saetta* (Commander Carlo Unger di Lowemberg) and *Strale* (Commander Andrew De' D'Ostiani), and the 8th Destroyer Squadron led by Captain Carlo Liannazza aboard the *Folgore*, with the *Fulmine* (Commander Leonardo Gramaglia), *Baleno* (Commander Carlo Maffei) and *Lampo* (Commander Luigi Guida). This force sailed at 1410 on the 7th at the same time as the 4th Division commanded by Admiral Alberto Marceno Di Moriondo flying his flag in the light cruiser *Da Barbiano* (Captain Mario Azzi) with the 6-inch cruisers *Cadorna* (Captain Romolo Polacchini), *Di Giussano* (Captain Giuseppe Maroni) and *Diaz* (Captain Francesco Mazzola), and also by 8th Division under Admiral Antonio Legnani flying his flag in the light cruiser *Duca Degli Abruzzi* (Captain Pietro Parenti) with the *Garibaldi* (Captain Stanislao Caraciotti) and escorted by the 16th Squadron of destroyers under Captain Ugo Salvadori in the *Da Recco*, with the *Usodimare* (Commander Sante Bondi) and the *Pessagno* (Commander Carlo Giordano).

The 14th Destroyer Squadron sailed much later, at 0618 on the 9th, to reinforce this group for the expected battle, under Captain

Table 1: Italian Forces at Sea.				
	Battleships	8-inch cruisers	6-inch cruisers	Destroyers
From Naples:	–	–	–	4
From Catania:	–	–	–	2
From Augusta:	–	4	2	12
From Messina:	–	2	–	4
From Palermo:	–	–	4	4
From Taranto:	2	–	6	16
In Total:	2	6	12	42

Giovanni Galati in the *Vivaldi*, with the *Da Noli* (Commander Achille Zoli) and *Pancaldo* (Commander Luigi Merini).

Meanwhile Supermarina had alerted all submarines on patrol in the Eastern Basin to be on special alert for the British battle fleet. Off Malta were patrolling the *Capponi* and *Durbo*, in the Ionian Sea were deployed the *Brin*, *Sciesa*, *Settimo* and *Settembrini*. In the central area patrolled the *Beilul*, *Tricheco*, *Lafolè* and *Smeraldo*. It was from one of these latter submarines, the *Beilul*, that the Italians first received confirmation of their fears that the British fleet was out and heading their way. The *Beilul* made her sighting report just before midnight but was unable to get in an attack.

The British plans and preparations were also brought on by the need to cover convoys, in this case two from Malta to Alexandria. A large quantity of urgently required stores was still at the island and it was planned to bring them away while there was still time to further reinforce the Fleet's main operational base. The splendid dockyard at Malta itself was still being used, but only by destroyers and submarines in limited numbers. Secondly, as it was only a few minutes' flying time from the main airfields in Sicily, it was expected that the island would be subjected to prolonged and heavy air assault, and such proved the case. A large number of civilians and other unnecessary mouths remained there and with an acute food shortage already beginning to make itself manifest, it was also decided to evacuate as many of these as could be embarked in the ships available there. There were also, already, quite a large number of Italian prisoners of war and the like, who were taking up valuable space and supplies.[2]

Accordingly the personnel were embarked in the Egyptian ship *El Nil*, the ex-Italian vessel *Rodi* and the British *Knight of Malta* and designated as the fast convoy, MF1. The supplies were loaded on the British vessels *Kirkland*, *Masirah* and *Zeeland*, and the Norwegian vessel *Novasli*, and these were designated as the slow convoy, MS1. The destroyers *Jervis* and *Diamond* arrived at Malta on the 7th to help escort these ships, along with the *Vendetta*, already at the island. Further destroyers were to be detached from the main fleet which was to take up a covering position east of Cape Passero on the afternoon of 9th July, to refuel and either rejoin the fleet or escort the slow convoy eastward.[3]

Submarines based at Malta were sent out to their covering patrol areas and long-range reconnaissance patrols were arranged with No 201 Group (RAF) with their old London flying boats. These flying boat patrols were arranged for 9th, 10th and 11th July to provide continuous cover along lines from Malta to Cape Spartivento and Cape Colonne to Corfu, which, it was hoped, would give early warning of any hostile move by the Italian main fleet.

Admiral Cunningham put to sea with his main force on the evening of 7th July, all ships being clear of the harbour by 0001 on the 8th. The force was divided into three groups for the initial stage of the sortie. Force A comprised the 7th Cruiser Squadron under the command of Vice-Admiral John C. Tovey CB, DSO, the Vice-Admiral (D) flying his flag in the light cruiser *Orion* (Captain G.R.B. Back), with the 6-inch cruisers *Neptune* (Captain R.C. O'Connor), *Sydney* (Captain J.A. Collins) and *Gloucester* (Captain F.R. Garside CBE), along with the flotilla leader *Stuart* (Commander H.M.L. Waller, RAN-D.10). They were joined at sea by the light cruiser *Liverpool* (Captain P.A. Read) which had sailed from Port Said after a transport run down to Aden earlier.

Force B consisted of the Commander-in-Chief, Admiral Andrew Cunningham, flying his flag in the battleship *Warspite* (Captain D.B. Fisher, CBE) and escorted by the destroyers *Nubian* (Captain Philip J. Mack, D.14), *Mohawk* (Commander J.W.M. Eaton), *Hero* (Commander H.W. Biggs), *Decoy* (Commander E.G. McGregor) and *Hereward* (Lieutenant Commander C.W. Greening).

Force C was built up around the battleships *Royal Sovereign* (Captain L.V. Morgan CBE, MVO, DSC) in which Rear Admiral H.D. Pridham-Wippell, BS1) was flying his flag, and *Malaya* (Captain I.B.B. Tower), with the aircraft carrier *Eagle* (Captain A.M. Bridge) and escorted by the destroyers *Hyperion* (Commander H. St L. Nicholson, D.2), *Hostile* (Commander J.P. Wright), *Dainty* (Commander M.S. Thomas), *Juno* (Commander W.E. Wilson), *Janus* (Commander J.A.W. Tothill), *Vampire* (Commander J.A. Walsh), *Voyager* (Commander J.C. Morrow DSO), *Hasty* (Lieutenant Commander L.R.K. Tyrwhitt), *Ilex* (Lieutenant Commander P.L.

Table 2: British Forces as Sea.				
	Battleships	Carrier	6-inch cruisers	Destroyers
Force A :	–	–	5	1
Force B :	1	–	–	5
Force C :	2	1	–	11
At Malta :	–	–	–	3
In Total :	3	1	5	20

Saumarez), *Imperial* (Lieutenant Commander C.A. de W. Kitcat), *Defender* (Lieutenant Commander St J.R.J. Tyrwhitt).

Their outward routes were designed as follows:

Force A to pass through position 35°00′ N, 21°30′ E.
Force B to pass through position 34°15′ N, 24°50′ E.
Force C to pass through position 27°20′ N, 27°50′ E.

Further flying boat patrols from Malta were established on the 8th to cover the line Malta-Zante. The rendezvous for the fleet was 120 miles east of Cape Passero, and 150 miles from Malta. The whole operation was codenamed MA5, and just about every fit ship was involved; only the *Ramillies* and the *Capetown* and *Caledon* remained behind, for the time being.

Although Cunningham's principal task was to cover the two convoys, he was in no way adverse to stumbling across the Italian main fleet, and, like the Italians, his first news that it was in fact out, came from his submarine patrols.

The British forces were very soon made aware that their movements were under close scrutiny. The destroyer *Hasty*, screening Force C in position 32°35′ N, 28°30′ E, at 2339 on the 7th, sighted an Italian submarine on the surface at a range of 1,000 yards. Although the submarine dived very quickly *Hasty* was able to get in one very accurate depth charge attack on a good echo with a full pattern of charges. Nor was this all, for on her way back to rejoin the 1st Battle Squadron's screen, she gained another firm submerged contact which she also duly attacked. In her estimation the first submarine had been sunk and the second damaged by these attacks, but post-war examination of the records offers no confirmation of this.

By early morning all three British forces were steering north-west by west at twenty knots towards the rendezvous. The only mishap occurred in the destroyer *Imperial* which suffered a burst feed tank during the night and had to return to Alexandria to effect repairs, passing the *Warspite* on opposite course at 0800 that morning.

As part of the overall plan Force H based at Gibraltar under Vice-Admiral Sir James Somerville, was to sortie into the Western Basin and launch an air attack on Cagliari airfield in Sardinia as a diversion. It was hoped that this might draw off a portion of the enemy's air strength. Accordingly on the morning of the 8th Force H also put to sea with Somerville flying his flag in the battle-cruiser, *Hood*, with the battleships *Valiant* and *Resolution*, the aircraft-carrier

Ark Royal, light cruisers *Arethusa*, *Enterprise* and *Delhi* and the destroyers *Faulknor, Forester, Foresight, Foxhound, Fearless* and *Escort*, of the 8th Flotilla and *Keppel, Douglas, Vortigern, Wishart* and *Watchman* of the 13th Flotilla.

It was felt that such a powerful force would have little to fear from any Italian reaction and Admiral Cunningham's original suggestions were far more bold in that he thought Force H could effectively operate against Naples or ports like Augusta in Sicily. This latter target would have been useful enough, but, as we have seen, the main Italian units based there had already sailed on the 7th. In any event Somerville was not prepared to adopt such a policy, holding that the Italian air bases around the Tyrrhenian Sea meant that his ships would be too exposed to bombing to justify the risk. So he put forward the air strike by twelve Swordfish on Cagliari as a safer alternative.

Reaction to this was strong in London, and it was suggested that the battleships might also lend a hand by bombarding the naval base, but again Somerville rejected this, fearing minefields and submarine traps, and so the smaller diversion was settled for.

Being mainly concerned with the safe arrival of their own convoy in Libya the Italians had no intentions of being diverted by Force H unless they came much further east than this and they left it to their local air units and submarine patrols to fend off Somerville's ships. The submarines *Emo, Marconi, Dandolo* and *Barbarigo* were in position off Gibraltar, the *Argo, Iride, Sciré* and *Diaspro* to the north-west of Sardinia guarding the approach route to Genoa and Naples and the submarines *Ascianghi, Axum, Turchese, Glauco, Manara* and *Menotti* had set up a patrol line south of Sardinia to block any movement towards Sicily. In the unlikely event of Force H penetrating that far east the submarine *Santarosa* patrolled the Sicilian Channel itself.

Meanwhile the Italian convoy had proceeded unmolested across the Central Mediterranean at a steady 14 knots with the heavy covering forces maintaining themselves north and east of them. They steered a direct course for Tobruk until they reached a position some 245 miles north-west of Benghazi whereupon they changed course directly for that port. When about a hundred miles from their destination the *Esperia* and *Calitea* pushed on at their best speed of 18 knots with their troops, leaving the slower freighters to follow them in at 14.

The Regia Aeronautica was also astir, their aircraft providing patrol cover over both convoy and battle fleet, mounting bombing attacks on Malta and Alexandria and extending patrols between the whole area from Cape Passero to Cape Matapan. On their airstrips hundreds of tri-engined bombers, SM 78s and SM 84s, stood confident, ready to demonstrate the power of the heavy bomber against the battleships should the British venture forth.

It was at 0807 on the morning of the 8th that Admiral Cunningham received the first positive news that the Italian battle fleet was at sea. A sighting report was picked up from the submarine *Phoenix*. She stated that she had sighted two enemy battleships and four destroyers in position 35°36′ N, 18°28′ E, steering 180 degrees at 0515 that morning. She carried out a torpedo attack at extreme range but this proved unsuccessful. Alas for the little *Phoenix* this vital report was just about the last received from her for she never returned from her patrol. On 16th July she was attacked and sunk by the Italian submarine chaser *Albatros* off Sicily.

However her news was electrifying. On the *Warspite*'s bridge Admiral Cunningham and his staff plotted the reported enemy's course. This was Campioni's force from Taranto and it was estimated to be some 180 miles east of Malta and some 500 miles west of the *Warspite*. Accordingly Admiral Cunningham signalled to the Vice-Admiral Malta, to arrange for an air search by the Londons to try and locate these enemy ships and shadow them. If they held their course south they might so expose themselves that the Mediterranean Fleet would be able to interpose themselves between the enemy and his base.

Until the enemy force could be firmly located and its composition and course firmly plotted the British fleet held its original course. Further confirmation that the enemy was by now fully aware of Cunningham's own movements came with the sighting during the morning of two more Italian submarines by *Eagle*'s patrolling Swordfish, both of which were attacked and driven off by the old biplanes. Nor were the Regia Aeronautica long in putting in their expected appearance.

The Mediterranean Fleet was by now well within range of the Dodecanese-based aircraft and heavy bombing was not unexpected. Indeed on their earlier foray into this area considerable surprise had been expressed that no such action had taken place but very soon it became apparent that the Italians had been saving their Sunday punch for just such an opportunity.

The main types of heavy bombers available to the Italians at this time were the Savoia Marchetti Sm 79 and the Savoia Marchetti Sm

81. For short-range reconnaissance they relied principally on the Creda Cz 506 floatplanes and the like. For the main they devoted themselves to precision, formation high-level bombing, with considerable skill. This type of attack by aircraft enabled the bomb aimer in the lead plane of each group to select his target while flying on a straight, steady course, far beyond the range of the multiple pom-poms and the like. On release of his bombs the whole section of four or five bombers also released, and thus, in theory, the target would be completely bracketed by heavy bombs no matter which way she might take evasive action.

Success of such bombing had been demonstrated time and time again in pre-war exercises and with large numbers of aircraft on hand to deliver mass attacks of such nature against such slow-moving targets as battleships, the Italians felt every confidence in themselves. Their immaculate formations could only be broken up by either fighter attack or heavy and accurate anti-aircraft fire. The British fleet, in this instance, was able to provide little of either to distract them.

As we have seen, the old *Eagle* normally carried no fighters and it was fortunate that on this occasion they had the foresight to embark two old Sea Gladiator fighters from the very limited Fleet Air Arm reserve ashore in Egypt before she sailed. There were of course no fighter pilots in *Eagle*'s air complement, but two Swordfish pilots volunteered to fly them and performed wonders during the five-day period. Nor was the fleet's anti-aircraft fire as accurate or successful as hoped for from pre-war exercises.

As Admiral Power recalls:

It must be remembered that at this stage we had no radar and relied entirely on visual sighting. At the outset the lookouts were pretty useless, but fear soon sharpened their eyesight and they quickly became very good. It was surprising how often the planet Venus was sighted at high noon in bright sunlight, and reported as 'aircraft in sight'.

It is only fair to say that the Italians did not have much luck in these operations. Their bombing was unpleasantly accurate and it was sheer luck that our ships always fitted into the gaps in the sticks. Our AA control systems were shown to be very inadequate. They did knock down one or two, as far as I recollect, which actually went on fire and crashed in sight of the fleet and we occasionally saw parachutes coming down in the very far distance which indicated aircraft in trouble. One felt pretty cross that our Gunnery Division had taken the wrong turning pre-war in turning down the Vickers Tachymetric System which was subsequently largely adopted by the US Navy and was very effective. It was not until the advent of *Illustrious* with her fighters that we had any sort of answer to the High Level bomber.

One of the minor irritations of this bombing was that we got dowsed with black water, which didn't go well with white uniform! But the only bomb damage had been that to the *Gloucester*. She, with *Liverpool*, had been detached during our westward passage to bombard Tobruk. She received a hit on the compass platform, destroying the navigational and gunnery control equipment and killing her Captain and Commander. In passing it is interesting to recall that we afterwards heard that a patrol of Hussars sat on the beach near Tobruk and watched this bombardment. They were well over 100 miles inside the enemy lines.[4]

The first aerial attacks began at 0951 and were directed at Force C, and five other such attacks were delivered against this force between then and 1749 that evening. Force A was steaming in line abreast early on the 8th, with the *Stuart* placed ahead of the line, and the first attacking group of Savoias arrived overhead without being sighted at all. The first indication that they were there was just after 1000 when a stick of three heavy bombs exploded astern of the Australian flotilla leader and ahead of the cruisers.

'The attacking aircraft were so high as to be tiny shining specks against the blue sky', read one report of this incident.[5]

Seven high-level attacks were also directed against the flagship and her screen between 1205 and 1812; some 50 bombs were aimed at them, none of which hit her. Cunningham himself was to write:

Here let me settle once and for all the question of the efficiency of the Italian bombing and general air work over the sea experienced by the fleet in 1940-41. To us at the time it appeared that they had some squadrons specially trained for anti-ship work. Their reconnaissance was highly efficient, and seldom failed to find and report our ships at sea. The bombers invariably arrived within an hour or two. They carried out high-level attacks from about 12,000 feet, pressed home in formation in the face of the heavy anti-aircraft fire of the fleet, and for this type of attack their accuracy was very good. We were fortunate to escape being hit.

It is not too much to say of those early months that the Italian high-level bombing was the best I have ever seen, far better than the German. Later, when our anti-aircraft fire improved and the trained squadrons of the Regia Aeronautica came to be knocked about by our fleet fighters, their air work over the sea deteriorated. But I shall always remember it with respect. There was some consolation in realizing that there was always more water than ship. Nevertheless, one felt very naked and unprotected.[6]

About eighty bombs were aimed at Force C this day, and again none hit, although Cunningham later confessed that:

> I was seriously alarmed for the old ships *Royal Sovereign* and *Eagle*, which were not well protected. A clutch of those eggs hitting either must have sent her to the bottom.[7]

The *Eagle* was one of the major targets for the Italian bombers, as E.B. Mackenzie describes:

> We soon learned the pattern of these air attacks. First we heard, in the distance, the guns of our destroyer screen. This heralded the approach of the Italian air force, which came in very high up. The cruisers and big ships opened up next, letting the formations of Savoia-Marchetti bombers have a sky-full of bursting AA. The Gladiators were away, but the specks in the sky got bigger and our Captain watched through his binoculars as the bombs were released. He would bring the ship round in a swaying throbbing turn to an estimated course parallel, rather than through, the lines of falling bombs. He never failed, but we had some shower-baths.
>
> We watched the battleships swing round as the towering columns of water erupted in fascinating rhythm, one after the other, or sometimes in great clumps, making vast walls of water. This was spectacular to say the least. For us, the lurch of the ship, straining with thumping engines to change course, the crash and splash were enough to make you duck involuntarily, and the shower of dirty water sweeping over the ship. There was the incredible racket of the multiple pom-poms pumping away just overhead and the shattering intrusion of the 4-inchers, together making a complicated drumbeat. The sharp smell of cordite smoke drifting past, and the clatter of empty shell cases tumbling from the deck above, bouncing and rolling around.
>
> I remember going to pick one up and getting burnt fingers – I still have that empty brass case. I saw one of the planes circling round this seeming confusion, waiting to land on. I thought, what a reception for the poor chap returning home to this, having already faced more than his share of danger in his own sortie.
>
> It was on this occasion that the weight and frequency of near misses damaged the old *Eagle* to such an extent that she had to miss Taranto, although her squadrons took part to great effect. When the smoke cleared, there was a return to reasonable normality for a while. There was the usual chatter, inevitable funny remarks and the chuckles of relief. Then the clearing up and preparations for the next go.[8]

What the Italian bomber crews were, in fact, trying to achieve, was the near impossible task of hitting moving targets with only one salvo by their methods. No matter how skilled the pilot and the discipline of the whole bomber group in bombing together on his signal, the fact that few ranging shots would be attempted meant that their job was far more difficult than they had realised. Naval gunnery never scored hits with just one salvo; the range had to be found from the shell splashes, and adjustment made for course, speed and deflection, whether the initial salvos were 'over' or 'under' and so on. So it was hardly likely that the incredible number of direct hits forecast pre-war by the highly vociferous air factions of all nations, would, in fact, be achieved. From 12,000 feet the time of flight of the bombs would always enable even a slow-moving ship to make some alteration in her course to avoid the worst concentration.

In point of fact the bombing achieved only one such result during the whole five-day operation, as we have seen, and this took place during the very last attack of the day, against the 7th Cruiser Squadron again. This seems to have been very much an individual effort rather than a result of setpiece pattern bombing as was customary:

> The last attack of the day – it interrupted a game of Mah Jong on the watch keeper's mess deck of *Stuart* – was aimed at the cruiser squadron. One aircraft tracked *Gloucester* from astern, and its stick of bombs crept along the cruiser's wake in successive lofty plumes of water until the final bomb overtook its target and scored a direct hit on the compass platform.[9]

As well as killing Captain Garside and six other officers and eleven ratings, this bomb wounded a further three officers and six ratings and damaged the Director Control Tower. All gun control and steering had to be immediately switched aft which reduced the cruiser efficiency in a surface fight considerably. The fire was quickly got under control and the *Gloucester* stayed in line, but as a passenger for the most part during the rest of the operation.

The whole series of bombing attacks in fact took place outside the range of what limited RAF help was available, and, on the 8th the two Gladiators aboard the *Eagle* were husbanded and the fleet relied on AA fire only for its defence. Although the Italians' success was limited to this one hit, it was a valuable one, for it reduced the already inadequate British cruiser strength by one of its most powerful vessels. In addition the strain on personnel as a whole from this type of prolonged bombardment was very great. For the most part, with the exception of the AA gunners themselves, the fleet had to sit and take it, which was not only totally alien to them but frustrating as well. The two-shift system already in force for the gunners in the larger ships was found to be some help in combating this fatigue, but of course the smaller vessels were allowed no such refinements by their limited complement. In addition of course the destroyers themselves were woefully equipped to combat such high level bombing. Their main armaments had, for the most part, an elevation of only 40° which was useless save to engage the enemy at long-range for a short while. The D class destroyers had come from the China Station, the V and Ws from Australia and neither had had time to land their after banks of torpedo tubes and embark a solitary 3-inch HA gun as had their sisters who had come from Home Waters. Even this gun was no sinecure, its value being of more moral effect than accuracy.

In all the Italians had employed a total of 61 SM 79 'Sparrows' from bases in the Aegean to attack Cunningham's fleet on 8th July, drawn from 10, 11, 12, 14 and 15 *Stormo* based at Leros and Rhodes. But despite this scale of attack, which was in fact to grow during the succeeding days of the operation, Cunningham remained completely undeterred and the fleet held on west-by-northwest, straining to place itself behind the Italian heavy units before they could gain the shelter of their base at Taranto.

In this aim the British desires in many ways matched those of the Italians. Although fully informed at the size of the British fleet and its possible intentions, Campioni decided that he could perhaps offer limited battle close in to the Italian coast, with his bases and his powerful air force at his back, and his submarine trap spread ahead of him. Here, nicely tucked in, he could lure the British on and hope that, well before they closed with his own superior forces, the Mediterranean Fleet would have been even further whittled down by bomb and torpedo, as in the case of the *Gloucester*.

His confidence was probably added to by the highly exaggerated reports flowing into his flagship's bridge from the Italian pilots who returned to their bases full of accounts of hits and heavy damage being inflicted on the British warships. One such incident received wide publicity. The Italian press printed across their front pages an impressive shot of a British battleship smoking, it was claimed, from bomb hits. On close study it turned out to be a view of the old *Royal Sovereign* steaming flat-out under a pall of her own funnel smoke printed upside down, and caused enormous hilarity in the wardrooms of the fleet later. But of course such claims could not be initially checked out by Campioni or, indeed, the air staffs back at the bomber bases, and so much of it was taken seriously; after all it was only what the airmen had been claiming would happen for years. Moreover the very accuracy of their bombing, which quite often straddled the target ship, made exact definition hard, a near-miss and a hit being difficult to assess from such heights. It was to be a common factor in all air forces which utilised this method of attacking ships; the Royal Air Force and the United States Army Air Force were even more prone to such misinterpretation than the Axis airmen when it came to such totally inaccurate claims. And so, like the case of the 'sinking' of the *Ark Royal* in 1939 by the Luftwaffe, the totals of ships sunk or badly knocked about steadily mounted up and must have given Campioni, just as it did Mussolini, a highly satisfactory picture of how Cunningham was taking punishment at this stage of the proceedings.

Dusk on the evening of 8th July, brought some temporary relief to the British seamen but all the while they were drawing steadily further into the central Mediterranean and closer to the home airfields where new and fresh groups of Savoias stood ready and waiting to renew the assault at daybreak. The Italians knew that the shorter distances involved would mean they could mount a larger number of sorties and even Italy's solitary dive bomber formation, 96° *Gruppo*, under Captain Ercolani, with nineteen of the home-built twin-engined SM 85 and 86 dive bombers, was placed on full alert at its base on Pantellaria in the middle of the Sicilian Channel, in case it too, might have the opportunity of fulfilling the destiny planned for it by the Duce himself, of '... sweeping the English warships from the sea ...'

CHAPTER THREE

Closing the Enemy

While the Mediterranean Fleet had been undergoing its aerial baptism of fire during the afternoon of 8th July, the Sunderland flying boats from Malta had been sent out to try and locate the enemy reported in the *Phoenix*'s fleeting contact. As we have noted, a series of standing air patrols had already been requested for the 9th through the 11th July to cover the area Malta-Cape Spartivento-Cape Colinne-Corfu and this was extending the limited resources of No 202 Squadron considerably, under-equipped as it was.

However, London L5803 was airborne from Malta that afternoon, scouring the area of the submarine's sighting and attack. This same aircraft and crew had, just a few days before, showed their worth by leading the 7th Cruiser Squadron onto an Italian destroyer squadron of three ships, one of which was sunk. Now she repeated her excellent service by locating Campioni's main force, which she reported as comprising two battleships, six cruisers and seven destroyers, in position 33°35′ N, 19°40′ E, steering 340 degrees. She stayed in contact, and thus was able to report, at 1610, that this group had changed course to 070 degrees, some 220 miles north of Benghazi.

The fact that the battleship group and the cruiser group reported earlier had now joined forces, and that they had reversed course from south, to north-north-west and then to east-north-east, coupled with the prolonged bombing, led the C-in-C's Staff to conclude from their plotting table and charts that the Italians had some very special reason for keeping Cunningham's fleet out of the Central Mediterranean. With Benghazi as the obvious termination for movements covering a potential convoy it was easy to deduce just what this reason was. If a supply convoy to Libya was being run in covered by the main fleet, then it was felt that the opportunity to engage that fleet should take priority over the planned British convoy movements and so Cunningham temporarily abandoned his own convoy sailings and moved his ships more directly towards Taranto. Initially, despite the accuracy of L5803's reports, it was suspected

that her reported battleships might in fact be 8-inch cruisers. Nonetheless Force B maintained its mean line of advance as 310 degrees at twenty knots throughout the night of 8th/9th July. That night passed without incident as the gap steadily closed.

The Italian convoy had now safely arrived at Benghazi, at noon on the 8th for the fast section, and Campioni was left to decide what to do about Cunningham who, when last sighted by his aircraft, was still holding steadfastly westward in the waters south of Crete despite his reported losses due to bombing.

He initially decided to concentrate in the Ionian Sea as we have seen, and, at 0330 in the early hours of the 9th, he received a message from Supermarina (despatched 2200/8th) giving him more detailed, information of the British movements and dispositions and their own intended back up for his action. It estimated that by 1800 on the 9th, the British forces could be as far west as A, the cruisers 37°20′ N, 16°45′ E, B, a battleship, 37°20′ N, 16°45′ E and C, two battleships, an aircraft carrier and destroyers, 37°00′ N, 17°00′ E. Five Italian submarines were in position to form the submarine trap in the area bounded by 35°50′-37° N and 17°00′-17°40′ E. Air Command Sicily and Puglia had been ordered to ready all available bomber groups and reconnaissance aircraft were standing by to locate and track all these British forces. The floatplanes were also standing by to carry out aerial torpedo attacks should the British cross the line 35°40′ N, 18°05′ E.

As Campioni had plenty of time to wait for Cunningham to enter the waters of his own choosing, the morning of the 9th was spent forming this formidable force up off the coast of Calabria and with refuelling and reinforcing his destroyers to ensure he was at maximum strength by the early forenoon. The first destroyer squadrons were sent in to top up with oil at 0600, these being the 8th (*Folgore, Fulmine, Baleno* and *Lampo*), the 15th (*Pigafetta* and *Zeno*) and the 16th (*Da Recco, Usodimare* and *Pessagno*). Meanwhile the 14th Squadron sailed from Taranto under the command of Captain Giovanni Galati in the *Vivaldi*, with the *Da Noli* (Commander Achille Zoli) and *Pancaldo* (Commander Luigi Merini) to reinforce the fleet.

At this time the British fleet had effected its dawn concentration in readiness for the fight in 36°55′ N, 20°30′ E in cruising position No 1 in the classic style, rehearsed so often during the two decades between the world wars.

The 7th Cruiser Squadron was spread ahead of the fleet in line abreast to form the standard search disposition, the 'A-K' line, some eight miles ahead of the main fleet together with the flotilla leader *Stuart* who was to act as a link between the probing cruisers and the C-in-C. The Fleet flagship, *Warspite*, because of her five knot margin of speed over the other two battleships, was being utilised by the C-in-C in effect as a battle-cruiser, to support her heavily outnumbered and outgunned light cruisers. Accompanying her as her screen were the destroyers of the 14th Flotilla, *Nubian*, *Mohawk*, *Hero*, *Hereward* and *Decoy*, spread in a V-shaped arrowhead in front of her. Rear-Admiral Pridham-Wippell's main force pounded along some eight miles astern of the *Warspite*, with the *Royal Sovereign*, the slowest ship, leading the *Malaya*, and with the aircraft-carrier *Eagle* tucked in astern of the two heavyweights, but free to conduct her operational pattern according to the vagaries of the wind.

The screen was the 10th Flotilla, and the 2nd Flotilla, *Hyperion*, *Hostile*, *Hasty*, *Ilex*, *Dainty*, *Defender*, *Juno*, *Janus*, *Vampire* and *Voyager*. The mean line of advance of the whole concourse of vessels was 260 degrees at a speed of fifteen knots.

Eagle herself had been early astir in order to launch her own reconnaissance flight of three Swordfish to probe ahead of the fleet for the enemy to a depth of sixty miles between 180 and 300 degrees, but of course Campioni was far to the west of these searches and they came back empty-handed after being flown off at 0440 that morning.

As the dawn rose on the morning of the 9th the Mediterranean Fleet was thus fully ready for the Italians should they choose to stand their ground and expectations were high. A passenger on his way to Malta aboard the Australian destroyer *Vampire* recorded the following impressions of that sunrise:

In the Royal Australian Navy things are slightly different to what they are in the Royal Navy. The Captain's servant was a very pally sort of cove, and woke me the following morning with a cup of tea and the remark: 'I shouldn't lie around all day if I was you. Get up on deck. You'll like it. There's going to be a battle.'

'A battle!' I echoed stupidly, 'What sort of battle?'

'Just an ordinary bloody battle,' he replied. 'The sea's lousy with ships. Looks like all the Med Fleet's here.'

I went on deck as I was, in a pair of pyjama-trousers, with a cup of tea in my hand. Remember it was mid-July in the Mediterranean. The morning was fresh and glorious, with a brilliant young sun still painting the new sky with the effulgence of his coming. The sea was sapphire, set with diamonds. The wake of *Vampire's* passing was like coiled ropes of pearls. It was a morning for poesy. It was also a morning for something grimmer. The young Australian rating was right. The sea was lousy with ships.[1]

The Italian Fleet was also concentrating and at 0640 the 3rd Division (*Bolzano*, *Trento* and four destroyers) rendezvoused with the other two heavy cruiser groups, the 1st Division (*Fiume*, *Gorizia*, *Zara* and four destroyers) and the flagship of Admiral Paladini, the *Pola*, and her four destroyers. At the same time Campioni was steering with his two battleships and their screen to make contact with this force. In the interim Paladini had signalled the 7th Division (*Savoia*, *D'Aosta*, *Attendolo* and *Montecuccoli* and four destroyers) to cancel their return to Palermo and also join the concentration.

Campioni, who had expected to be well-served by the Regia Aeronautica and hoped for both frequent sightings reports, air cover for his own ships and massive attacks on the British fleet before they got within gun range was now experiencing the first of his bitter disillusionments that day. Far from feeding the Italian C-in-C with a continuous flow of information about Cunningham's movements and whittling away at his margin of strength in heavy ships, the Italian air force proved itself entirely impotent during the crucial build-up phase of that morning. Only a single sighting report did Campioni get while he awaited the oncoming enemy. Nor was this the only disappointment.

In strict contrast to the legions of aircraft at the Italians' disposal the solitary Sunderland flying boat which No 202 Squadron was able to launch from Malta that morning L5807, quickly found his main force of battleships, and hung in the sky reporting the Italians' every movement despite all that they could do by way of heavy anti-aircraft fire, to drive him away.

It was thus that Sunderland L5807's first sighting report was picked up on the *Warspite*'s bridge. Her first report stated that two battleships, four cruisers and ten destroyers were in position 37°14' N, 16°51' E, steering 330 degrees at fifteen knots, at 0732. Seven minutes later she had also picked up the Italian heavy cruisers steering to join their battleships, reporting at 0739 a force of six cruisers and eight destroyers stationed 080 degrees some 20 miles from the main fleet, steering 360 degrees.

Campioni was furious at this shadowing when his own reports were nil and made repeated requests to the Italian air forces at Messina for fighters to either shoot down or drive off the Sunderland

and provide an umbrella over his ships against further snoopers and the expected British torpedo bomber assault. Despite his requests nothing stirred and the sky above his ships remained empty that morning of all save British aircraft, despite the fact that he was never much more than fifty miles from the Italian mainland.

At 0805 the Sunderland sent in a further report that the Italian battleships had changed course to 360 degrees. This placed the Italian fleet about 145 miles, 280 degrees west of the *Warspite*. Admiral Cunningham studied these reports and, at 0810, changed his own line of advance to 305 degrees and increased speed to eighteen knots in order to continue his policy of working around between the Italians and Taranto to cut off their escape should they lose their nerve at the last moment.

An eyewitness described the scene on the *Warspite*'s bridge as the gap narrowed between the two fleets that beautiful sunlit morning.

> The *Warspite* had been designed as a Fleet flagship, with an admiral's bridge one deck below the compass platform and the view from it was somewhat constricted. In the middle of it, in the armoured structure, was the admiral's chart house and an operational plot with an ARL table with voicepipes and armoured shutters communicating with the outside. The equipment was of course primitive compared to what came later but, under cruising conditions, the set-up sufficed.
>
> In the plot Tom Brownrigg (the Master of the Fleet) and I had quite a good picture of the situation from the reports of other ships, but getting nothing from our own. What we got through made us both exclaim simultaneously, 'this is exactly like a game on the tactical table' – we had it all there, the cruisers on the A-K line reporting, then concentrating to engage opposing cruisers, the destroyers concentrating in the van to attack, and *Warspite* acting as a battle-cruiser in support. Astern, and oh how slowly!, came our battle fleet, *Royal Sovereign* and *Malaya*.[2]

Away to the west Admiral Campioni, despite the unexpected handicap that the lack of information was causing him, still hoped that things might yet develop as he had planned, was still determined to offer battle on his own terms. At 0900 he sent out a long signal to Supermarina detailing his concentration.

He intended to arrange his fleet in four columns at intervals of five miles in preparation, should he receive precise information of the British in time, for engaging them at about 1400 that afternoon, in position 37°40′ N, 17°20′ E. The *Cesare* would be on a course of 120° at 18 knots, with the *Cavour* astern, and this, the 5th Division, would have the 8-inch cruisers placed five miles to the south-east of them with the left hand column formed by the 6-inch cruisers of the 4th Division (*Barbiano, Cadorna, Giussano, Diaz*) and 8th Division (*Abruzzi* and *Garibaldi*) and the right hand column formed by the 6-inch cruisers of the 7th Division (*Savoia, D'Aosta, Attendolo* and *Montecuccoli*). Once formed up he planned to keep his entire fleet marking time in the broad area between the coast of Calabria to his north, and the submarine trap to his south.

However the Italian Commander-in-Chief was soon faced with other problems than lack of reconnaissance and air cover. One after another destroyers of his force began reporting mechanical faults in their engines which were by no means used to such prolonged activities and sorties as this one was turning out to be.

Between 1030 and 120 the destroyers *Dardo, Da Noli* and *Strale* all reported defects of one kind or another and asked for permission to return to Taranto to carry out repairs. This left the Commander-in-Chief for a short time with only two destroyers (*Freccia* and *Saetta*) of his original screen but this dangerous situation was resolved by the arrival of the 14th Squadron and the return of the 8th and 15th Squadrons after refuelling later. During this time he had been heading due north but, at 1125, on sighting the mountains of Punto Stilo to his front, Campioni reversed course due south and steered for a position sixty miles offshore to await clarification of the position.

During this period of march and counter-march the Italian fleet had been constantly under aerial surveillance. Sunderlands L5807 and L9020 kept watch being joined from time to time by scouting planes from the *Eagle* herself, and there was still no sign of Italian fighter cover. Admiral Cunningham therefore continued to receive a stream of update signals while Campioni remained unaware of the British dispositions.

Eagle had launched a further three Swordfish on reconnaissance patrols at 0858 to search as far west as they could in a sector between 260 and 300 degrees. Their sightings amplified those of the Sunderlands, although the locations and references given differed by a considerable margin. Still plotting all these on *Warspite*'s bridge the British staff were able to draw a pretty comprehensive picture of Campioni's 'run to the north'. At 1105 *Eagle*'s Swordfish 'D' reported two battleships and one cruiser in position 38°07′ N, 16°57′ E with four more cruisers close by. Ten minutes later Sunderland L5807 reported the Italians' main force in position 38°06′ N, 17°48′ E, steering 360 degrees.

As the Italians were steering north at this time it was felt that they might yet evade the intercepting movement of the main British fleet and it was therefore decided to launch *Eagle*'s torpedo bomber striking force without further delay to slow them down. Accordingly, at 1145, the *Eagle* hauled out of line into the wind and nine of No 813 Squadron FAA's old 'Stringbags' lumbered into the air, each with a 21-inch torpedo slung beneath its frail body and headed out towards the Italians, which, at this time, were thought to be some ninety miles from the *Warspite* at 295 degrees. Ninety miles sounds a small distance for the aircraft of the day, but for the Swordfish, it was quite a way. These old biplanes, flying antiques, had a top speed of only 139 mph at best, and with their 1,695-lb torpedo slung below them they could only manage about 100 mph.

It therefore took the Swordfish the best part of an hour to close the distance. As the last sighting report received aboard the *Eagle* had given the Italians' course as due north it is not very surprising that this aerial strike force failed to locate the *Cavour* and *Cesare* when they reached their expected location, for the two battleships were by that time well to the south and continuing in that direction. Contact by *Eagle*'s own shadowing planes had been lost with the main Italian force at this time nor was there a Sunderland report again until 1215 when L5803 made a signal stating that six cruisers and ten destroyers were in position 37°56′ N, 17°48′ E, steering 220 degrees at a speed of 25 knots. This was followed five minutes later by a second report of three 8-inch cruisers in position 37°55′ N, 17°55′ E, steering 225 degrees.

It was upon the Italian heavy cruiser divisions that the Fleet Air Arm Swordfish stumbled at 1252. They were still astern of the Italian battleships but, because of their more northerly position, they were taken for the battleships by the attacking airmen throughout their assault, although there was in fact little resemblance in the physical outlines of the ships.

The Swordfish therefore worked their way slowly round to the westward of this force and delivered a concerted attack against the rear ships at 1330, still under the impression that it was a battleship force they were up against. A withering hail of flak from the cruisers and destroyers met the aircraft but despite this, and their slow relative rate of approach due to the cruisers' high speed and the fact that the torpedo bombers were approaching them from the right hand side of their formation, none of the Swordfish was lost in this attack and they only suffered slight superficial damage.

The Italian position at this time was that the 4th and 8th

Divisions, (6-inch cruisers) with the 9th and 14th destroyer squadrons coming up late from Taranto (due to the *Da Noli*'s breakdown and return to that base earlier) had already formed the left-hand column to the east of the battleships of the 5th Division together with the 7th Destroyer Squadron, which was steering 168° at 18 knots towards the rendezvous point which it was to reach at 1400. The heavy cruiser group, led by *Pola*, with the 11th and 12th Destroyer Squadrons were still astern of the 5th Division battleships and at full speed were closing the distance to form the western column, while the other light cruisers of the 7th Division with the 13th Destroyer Squadron, were still far away from the main concentration.

The attack broke over the 8-inch cruisers between 1315 and 1326. The Swordfish according to the Italian accounts, approached at a height of about 80 feet and dropping from a distance of 3,000 feet after being engaged by the destroyers on the stern side of the screen and the cruisers themselves. Their main targets during this attack seem to have been the *Trento*, *Fiume*, *Zara* and *Pola*, all of which had torpedoes launched at them, but avoided them successfully by their high speed and a quick turn away. Admiral Paladini, aboard his flagship *Pola*, described their attack thus:

> Two of the aircraft made a determined effort to attack the head of our line, coming up from astern, and one of these, having penetrated our destroyer screen and avoided the fire of all our escorts, unleashed a torpedo in a beautiful manoeuvre against the *Pola* from the left at an angle of about 70°, and at a distance of between 1,000 to 1,500 metres. The *Pola* turned left at maximum speed and engaged this aircraft with every weapon that would bear.[3]

As in all the other attacks, which the Italians say were pressed home with absolute bravery and disregard for safety, no torpedo hits were made on any Italian vessel. The striking force itself was unharmed, re-assembled and made its way back to the *Eagle*, landing on around 1434 that afternoon. One of the young Swordfish pilots that day describes the attack in typical modest fashion thus:

> Briefing for the attack was elementary as far as I remember; it just reiterated the standard squadron attack, which was to approach the target at reasonable height, about 8,000 feet, split into three sub-flights when in position, and co-ordinate the attack so that each sub-flight made its final dive to dropping position from a different sector on the target at

the same time, this procedure had been practised *ad infinitum* over the years, always against a specified target ship.

The final dropping conditions were a height of 50 feet, a range of 1,000 yards and a maximum speed of 90 knots. To achieve these conditions after a near vertical dive from 8-10,000 feet required practice, too low was dangerous, too fast and the torpedo would not enter the water correctly and would not run properly and too high would again cause damage to the torpedoes.

In the event we took off in brilliant cloudless weather with unlimited visibility, possibly 50 or so miles from the Italian fleet and clambered laboriously to gain sufficient height (a Swordfish with a torpedo climbs very slowly at about 60 knots). The Italians put up a heavy barrage well before we were in range and kept this up during the approach and dive to dropping position. I think we were all a bit confused with the large number of enemy ships, and this no doubt led to aircraft attacking different targets instead of concentrating on one specific ship. Low down on the water at 50 feet the barrage was very heavy and came from all angles as we were by then in the middle of the fleet. One factor which disturbed our aim was the disturbing use by the enemy ships of their main armaments firing at very low angle, the splashes made by these projectiles was most disconcerting. We obtained no hits and none of our aircraft was damaged.

After the attack, on our way to rejoin the *Eagle*, we were able to watch as the two fleets joined action, a unique experience to sit at 2,000 feet and watch the fireworks from between the two battle lines. The Italians did not stick it out for long and soon altered course and, with their greater speed, set off for home.[4]

Meanwhile a search by another of *Eagle*'s Swordfish, Duty C, reported no enemy ships could be located anywhere in her search area which was bounded by bearings 334 and 291 degrees at a depth of 60 miles from 38° N, 18° E, at 1330. Although the first aerial attack reported they had struck at battleships, an analysis of their speed and rapid turning indicated that these were, in fact, cruisers, and this sighting report confirmed the C-in-C's feelings that the Italians *had* in fact, turned south around 1200 and that the cruiser forces which had been reported earlier were effecting a concentration with them in approximately 37°45' N, 17°20' E. This deduction was further strengthened at 1340 when Sunderland L9020 reported three battleships and a large number of cruisers and destroyers steering 220 degrees in position 37° N, 58' N, 17°55' E. She followed this up at 1415 with confirmation that this large concentration was now on course 020 degrees at 18 knots. From this the plot on *Warspite*'s bridge showed the enemy main force all together in strength superior to their own and again heading northward but that the British forces were now rapidly closing with them. Cunningham assumed from this that the enemy indeed intended to stand and fight, '... albeit on his own ground and with more than one road of escape left open to him.'⁵

The British fleet therefore maintained their north-westward course to cut off Campioni from his main base at Taranto and, at 1400, when from further reports it was clear this objective had been achieved, came round to 270 degrees for the final run-in to their target.

The weather during the forenoon of the approach was good for a fleet action. The wind veered from north-west to north by west, force 5, and back to north-west again. This would clear the smoke from the guns of the British ships while obscuring that of the Italians; on the other hand it would facilitate any covering smoke screen they cared to lay down should they decide to retreat. The sea was calm and the sky 2/10ths cloud at noon, but the Regia Aeronautica remained conspicuous by its absence during the morning and failed to take any advantage of clearer skies earlier on during the day to effect the heavy bombing of the previous day which might have further seriously hampered the British movements and inflicted the further casualties that Campioni had hoped for. Visibility was fifteen to twenty miles, which was good and necessary in those pre-radar days.

The 7th Cruiser Squadron was spread on line of bearing still eight miles ahead of the Fleet flagship which at 1430 was in position 38°02′ N, 18°25′ E, steering 270 degrees at 22 knots. The *Royal Sovereign* and *Malaya*, with *Eagle*, were then some ten miles astern due to their slower speed. *Eagle* completed the landing on of her striking force at 1435 which confirmed Cunningham's dispositions were entirely correct; the main Italian force were reported steaming at 15 knots 360 degrees. Four minutes later she reported the centre of the enemy fleet as being 260 degrees, thirty miles from the *Warspite*.

However, soon after the failure of the Swordfish attack on the 8-inch cruisers astern of him, Campioni finally received a sighting report from the air force for which he had been waiting all morning. It did not make for good reading, stating at 1330 an aircraft from 142 Squadron had sighted two battleships and eight destroyers on a course of 330° at a speed of 22 knots about 80 miles from his own force. This sighting, of what was the *Royal Sovereign* and *Malaya* and their destroyers while *Eagle* was away recovering her planes, coupled with the recent aerial attack by what could only be carrier-based aircraft, showed the Italian C-in-C exactly how well informed the British were of his own movements, and how well Cunningham had already succeeded in interposing himself between the Italians and their main base. Campioni therefore decided to reverse course at once before the advanced British forces he had plotted the day before should cut him off completely. It was clear that the Regia Aeronautica by their failure to attack in force that morning, had not weakened the British force or their resolve, and also, that if they maintained their course they were going to miss the submarine trap also, by passing far to the north of it. This would leave the Italian and British fleets to slug it out on their own, which was not what Campioni had in mind at all. By pulling back north he could perhaps lure the British, who seemed determined on a fight, within even closer range of the massed Italian bomber formations ashore.

The importance of that one aerial sighting report is hard to exaggerate, for, had he *not* received it, Campioni would have continued to the south with his full force and Cunningham would have been well behind him within a very short time. As it was his immediate reversal was now to save him from a very difficult situation and a lucky escape.

At this point events were already piling up on Campioni: not only was the turn in column a difficult manoeuvre to perform with the enemy known to be close at hand to the north-east of him, but not all his ships had yet joined up, the 7th Division still being some way astern. However in the latter respect the turn north facilitated their rendezvous. The two 6-inch cruisers of the 4th Division, *Diaz* and *Cardorna*, had meanwhile been experiencing similar engine difficulties to the three destroyers sent back earlier, but their request to return to base because of this was postponed and they held their places in line.

By 1405 the Italian force had sorted itself out on a course 010° converging with the British fleet heading north-west, with the 4th and 8th Divisions five miles east of the two battleships of the 5th Division in the centre, and the heavy cruisers of the 1st and 3rd Divisions with the *Pola*, some three miles to the west of the Italian flagship. The 7th Division was still badly adrift however, closing at its best speed from the south-south-west.

At 1415 the cruisers of the 4th and 8th Divisions were instructed to send off their catapult aircraft from the *Barbiano*, *Guissano* and *Abruzzi* to conduct a search across the front of the Italian fleet for the enemy and a repeated demand was made to the army bomber squadrons ashore for their maximum intervention in a preventive attack on the British fleet, an attack which Campioni had been awaiting in vain all morning.

He also received a message from Supermarina which did little to arouse his enthusiasm for the coming clash and one which indicated a distinct feeling of cold feet for Campioni's apparent temerity in seeking a battle at all with the Royal Navy. He was told to avoid engagements with even isolated groups of British battleships, to delay any exchange of gunfire or contact until such time as the bombers of the air force had made their attacks and crippled the British ships. At sunset he was to make a withdrawal towards his bases, and draw the British towards his submarine trap. If things appeared favourable he might then make night torpedo attacks on the enemy with his light forces but that was as far as they wished to go.

This instruction was not only somewhat disheartening for Campioni, it was also far too late for him to adopt such a course of action for within a few minutes of its receipt the two opposing fleets were in sight of each other and there was not an Italian bomber in the sky. Campioni therefore had no choice other to fight a holding action at extreme range until they duly arrived. This limited objective should not have been beyond him for he had the superiority in speed and numbers to be able still to dictate the course of action so as to avoid getting too embroiled with the British.

On the British side the Mediterranean Fleet was approaching the battle with far more confidence, despite the obvious disparity in strength. As Cunningham was to recall later:

> It was not quite the moment I would have chosen to give battle. They had a large number of cruisers, and we, because the damaged *Gloucester* was not fit to engage in serious fighting, had no more than four, which had little more than 50 per cent of their ammunition remaining. Moreover, the speed of approach was limited by the maximum speed of the *Royal Sovereign*. However, any opportunity was welcome, and the *Warspite* was soon pushing on in support of our cruisers, which, with no 8-inch gun ships, were heavily outgunned and outnumbered by the Italians.[6]

CHAPTER FOUR

'Enemy Battle Fleet in Sight'

Out ahead of the British fleet the five light cruisers of the 7th Squadron were steaming in line abreast. Flying his flag in the *Orion* was Vice-Admiral John Tovey, CB, DSO, one of the war's outstanding officers, and later to be C-in-C of the Home Fleet. One who knew him well described him to this author as 'a fine officer to serve under, completely straight, forthright, honest, and always ready to commend any worthy action and to tell you when you had done something wrong without rancour.'[1] He had been an outstanding destroyer officer during the First World War, utterly fearless in action and had won his special promotion to the rank of commander at the Battle of Jutland in 1916 while commanding the *Onslow* with the 13th Flotilla, screening Beatty and the battle-cruiser force. His citation recorded the 'persistent and determined manner in which he attacked enemy ships ...' at that encounter. Now his squadron of light cruisers was to be the first to sight an enemy battle fleet since that far-off day in the North Sea.

An eyewitness aboard the *Stuart* recalled the final impressions before the battle was joined:

> In the perfect visibility, blue sea and cloudless sky, the cruisers on the wing, and the destroyers in semi-circular formation screening in front of the battleships, made a picture no one who saw it can ever forget ... A few flags would flutter up to the flagship's yardarm and answering pendants to the yardarms of the other ships. Then, in unison, down would come the flagship's signal and the answering pendants and over all helms would go together, and the fleet would alter course like so many well drilled soldiers, the destroyers leaning over with the sea creaming from their bows, the battleships, more ponderous, but not the less spectacular, moving more slowly around in their constricted circle to take up their new course.[2]

With the enemy just over the horizon Cunningham made his final dispositions. The *Eagle* was ordered to act independently to fly off further spotters and hopefully get in another torpedo attack. She was to keep well clear of the main fleets, as she was very vulnerable on her own, and the destroyers *Vampire* and *Voyager* were detached to provide her anti-submarine screen, as they were the oldest ships present. The *Stuart* was pulled back from ahead of the light cruisers at 1435 and took her station ahead of the *Royal Sovereign* as leader of the 10th flotilla, ready to lead them in any torpedo attacks that might be ordered.

The five light cruisers moved confidently ahead seeking the enemy, knowing that when they found them they would be heavily outnumbered, and also knowing that their shell rooms were far from full.

> One of our handicaps in the Calabria operation was that our cruisers were very short of 6-inch ammunition. There had been a heavy expenditure a week or two earlier when they had chased two Italian destroyers at very long range. The trouble was that the original 1939 Mediterranean Fleet had had 8-inch cruisers in the majority, whereas now we had none. The reconstructed fleet had been assembled at short notice and the necessary ammunition reserves had not come round the Cape, though we got a small amount from Aden. It was a considerable anxiety until stocks were built up. Anyhow it had proved in practice that the standard reserve of 1½ outfits per ship was quite inadequate.[3]

It was at 1415 when the Italians had launched their three floatplanes from their light cruisers of the 4th and 8th Divisions and fifteen minutes later one of these reported back that they had sighted a suspicious vessel to the south-east of where they were searching ahead of the Italian fleet.

On the British side the Australian cruiser *Sydney* first sighted smoke broad on the port bow at 1445 and two minutes later the *Orion* also sighted the enemy. At the same time on the bridge of the Italian flagship Campioni received another signal from the catapult aircraft stating that the enemy were spread over a large area some thirty miles from the Italian fleet. This was followed by another aerial sighting from a Regia Aeronautica plane that the British were approaching him very close steering north-north-west.

At 1452 the *Neptune* sent in the first sighting report to the *Warspite* reporting two enemy vessels in sight bearing 238 degrees distance about sixteen miles. Three minutes later the *Orion* reported three destroyers at 31,000 yards, bearing 234 degrees and followed this up at 1500 with a report of three destroyers and four cruisers between 240 and 270 degrees. At the same time *Sydney* logged five enemy cruisers in sight at 1501. There were now only four British cruisers in company, the damaged *Gloucester* having been sent back earlier to join the *Eagle*, as she was in no condition to engage in a main fleet action, but might provide some help should any of the enemy cruisers work their way round to catch the old carrier unawares. The remaining four ships were ten miles ahead of the *Warspite* and were formed on a line of bearing 320 degrees and steering 270 degrees at eighteen knots, and rapidly closing the Italian ships which appeared between twelve and eighteen miles distant in several groups.

Tovey kept pressing in against this mass seeking the main quarry and at 1508 he was duly rewarded with the first sighting of the Italian battleships bearing 250 degrees at fifteen miles range. Captain R.C. O'Connor at once made the historic signal, 'Enemy battle fleet in sight', which was the first time this signal had been made in the Mediterranean since the days of Nelson. Everyone in the British fleet was elated at this news and scanned the western horizon avidly hoping themselves to catch a glimpse of their opponents.

On sighting the heavyweights Tovey at once brought his four ships round on course 000 degrees in line ahead, increasing his speed and two minutes later veered slightly away, to avoid getting too involved with the various groups of Italian ships that were in sight to his left, to 045 degrees. On this course he was ready to engage and keep in touch while heavy support in the form of the *Warspite* could come up from astern.

On the Italian side the 4th Division held their course northwards but the 8th Division under Admiral Legnani with *Abruzzi* and *Garibaldi* altered course towards the British cruisers on course 070 degrees and rapidly worked up to thirty knots, and opened fire at 23,600 yards with their main armament. These ships were mistaken for 8-inch cruisers by the British and Tovey prepared to take them on, ordering, at 1512, his cruisers, *Orion*, *Neptune*, *Liverpool* and *Sydney*, to engage an equal number of enemy ships. At 1514 the British cruisers altered course to 025 degrees and four minutes later to 030 degrees to open their 'A' arcs, on which bearing all their guns could engage the enemy with salvos or full broadsides. The cruiser slugging match had begun.

Considerable confusion has resulted from the various accounts hitherto published of this battle about both the number and types of ships actually involved and it will perhaps be convenient at this point to analyse the actual combatants on the field as the battle opened. Here it will be noticed that there is a considerable difference between

the ships that sailed to take part in the operation and those which
actually came to grips in the fight. At this juncture the actual ships
on or near the field of battle were as follows:

Italian	British
2 Battleships	3 Battleships
–	1 Aircraft Carrier
6 Heavy Cruisers	–
8 Light Cruisers	5 Light Cruisers
16 Destroyers	14 Destroyers

Contemporary British accounts also over-estimated the numbers
of Italian destroyers present, a fault which has never been rectified in
post-war versions of the battle. Of the thirty-two destroyers with
which Campioni is always credited with in British versions, only half
were actually on the field of combat at the *onset* of the action.
Likewise through the period of combat Italian light cruisers were
often reported as heavy cruisers and the number of the latter has
always been grossly inflated. Of the thirty-two destroyers which
Campioni started the operation with, half were absent at 1520. The
two light cruisers of the 2nd Division, (*Bande Nere* and *Colleoni*) had
been sent to Tripoli with the four destroyers of the 10th Squadron
(*Maestrale, Libeccio, Grecale* and *Scirocco*). Three more destroyers had
been sent back to Taranto with engine trouble as we have seen,
(*Dardo, Da Noli* and *Strale*) while the nine destroyers sent in to refuel
earlier that morning had still not rejoined him (*Folgore, Fulmine,
Baleno, Lampo, Pigafetta, Zeno, Da Recco, Usodimare, Pessagno*) and nor
had the *Vivaldi* and *Pancaldo* which sailed to reinforce him. These
latter ships did not again rejoin Campioni until 1930 that evening,
with the expectation of the 13th Destroyer Squadron which rejoined
the 7th Division during the afternoon.

On the British side the *Gloucester* of the cruisers, and the *Vampire*
and *Voyager* of the destroyers took no part in the main battle, while
the *Malaya* and *Royal Sovereign* never got into the actual fight,
especially the latter with her slower speed, despite valiant efforts by
her engine-room personnel. So a fairer assessment of the odds is two
Italian battleships, six heavy cruisers, eight light cruisers and sixteen
destroyers against one battleship, four light cruisers and twelve
destroyers on the British side. Intervention from the air on both sides
came later on and was not effective in either case.

The main difference which could have swayed the issue is the
proximity of the Italians to their main fleet base at Taranto.

Knowing that the British were pressing on seeking an engagement there should have been ample time for the Italians to heavily reinforce Campioni so as to place the issue beyond any reasonable doubt. Instead they relied solely on the intervention of the air force and their own limited numbers of naval air arm torpedo-bomber floatplanes to back him up, along with the submarines, and these all let them down completely.

It is thought that strong disapproval of this cautious line was much in evidence at the time at Taranto among the more offensively-minded Italian commanders. Admiral Bergamini, for example, commanding the most powerful division in the Italian fleet, was most upset by his passive role. When he learned from sighting reports that two Italian battleships were about to come up against three British vessels of that type on his very doorstep, he made strenuous efforts to get permission to sail with his ships to give assistance, and in this he had the full backing of the captains of the two brand-new battleships of his force, Girosi and Sparzani. Their commands both lay at Taranto almost ready for action, the *Littorio* and *Vittorio Veneto*. Nominally 35,000 tonners to comply with Treaty regulations, they both in fact had a standard displacement of over 43,000 tons and were powerfully armed with nine 15-inch guns, and were heavily protected and fast vessels which could both outpace and outrange the *Warspite* and her companions and were far more heavily protected than either *Warspite* or *Malaya*. *Littorio* had run her sea trials in the Gulf of Genoa in December 1939 and *Vittorio Veneto* completed in June 1940, but neither were declared fully operational until 2nd August. Despite this their commanders all felt that they could have played a decisive part in the battle developing a few miles from their anchorages, but in this they were overruled by Supermarina, partly on account of the fact that by the time they had got themselves to sea it would have been too late anyway.

At 1522 the four British cruisers opened fire in return at the Italian units nearest to them. The *Neptune* was the first to engage, with *Liverpool*, at a range of 22,100 yards at enemy cruisers, followed at 1523 by *Sydney* who took as her target what she thought to be a cruiser of the 'Zara' Class at 23,000 yards range. The *Orion* commenced firing at 1526 and chose as her target initially, a destroyer ahead of the Italian cruisers, which was in fact the *Alfieri* of the 9th Squadron. This squadron of destroyers, under Captain Daretti, had pushed out to the right and ahead of the 1st Division and in such an exposed position was soon steaming strongly through the shell splashes of the *Orion*'s 6-inch guns. Although the *Orion* only engaged this squadron for about three minutes, before switching her target to a cruiser bearing 249 degrees at a range of 23,700 yards, it was a hot three minutes for *Alfieri*, as her captain later recalled:

> When first seen the enemy cruisers were approaching bows-on in our direction, (1508). *Alfieri*'s squadron turned towards them at 1512 and closed them until the range was down to 18,000 metres; behind us the 4th Division (*Barbiano* and *Cadorna*) had also turned their bows towards the enemy in a like manner while 8th Division (*Abruzzi* and *Garibaldi*) were giving us close support and closing the enemy to bring maximum fire to bear, with their 6-inch guns. The enemy turned broadside to us and also opened a heavy fire but we continued to close to perform our task of identification of the enemy units. At 1519 when very close we caught a glimpse behind the enemy cruisers of a larger ship which we could not clearly identify. This scouting phase saw us closing to within 16,000 metres of the enemy when we received the recall from the commander of the 8th Division ordering us to resume our screening positions on him.[4]

The 9th Squadron turned north-west at 1523 and after surviving *Orion*'s salvos for a short period again took station on the 8th Division which had turned sharply away to the west at 1530 after receiving the full attentions of the British cruisers. The two cruisers of the 4th Division had feinted astern of the British squadron but were also driven off by concentrated fire and took no further effective part in the action, steering away on the disengaged side of the fleet, first north-north-west and then, just after 1611, sharply west to follow the main fleet's movements. Nonetheless their fire and that of the 8th Division had been reasonably accurate in the opening stages. The Italian ships had the advantage of having the sun behind them and were quickly achieving straddles. The British return fire against both Italian light cruiser divisions was also fierce and accurate however, although no ship on either side was hit at this juncture. The only casualty was the *Neptune* when shell splinters from a near miss came aboard at 1525 damaging the aircraft and its catapult. The Sea Fox was later jettisoned overboard to avoid the risk of fire from its reserve aviation fuel tanks.

Commander J.P. Parker describes for us the feelings aboard the *Neptune* at this time:

> During the Battle of Calabria, I was the Rate Officer in the six-inch Director of HMS *Neptune*. I was a paymaster lieutenant but for most of

the war had been 6-inch control officer during cruising and defence stations and rate officer during action. On the day of the battle we were stationed on the port wing of the cruiser screen ahead of the Fleet. The ship was at action stations and because of my seat in the director I was one of the first to see the enemy.

The three officers in the 6-inch director, above and behind the bridge, sat in a row, the gunnery officer who controlled the main armament in the middle, with the spotting officer on his starboard side (a lieutenant commander) and the rate officer, myself, on the port side. We each had powered fixed binoculars which trained with the director. My job was to estimate the speed of the target and its course in relation to my own ship expressed for example as 'Speed 28, Inclination, Green 120'. I passed this information through the headset I wore, to the transmitting station plot in the bowels of the ship. I had to keep this information up to date and make certain that new information was due to alterations of course or re-estimation on my part. From this information, deflection was automatically passed to the gun-trainers.

Neptune signalled 'Enemy in Sight' and this was the first time this had been done in the Mediterranean since the days of Nelson. Visibility was extreme and the first thing I saw was the masts of a great number of ships which were below the horizon. There were so many that I thought they must have been those of MTBs, but it soon became clear that we were approaching a large fleet of destroyers, cruisers and battleships.

It took some time to get within range and I think that the enemy battleships must have opened fire some time before we could. Once battle was joined everything became very confusing and visibility was obscured by cordite smoke, smoke screens and cascades of water from bursting shells. The approaching shells sounded like express trains and the confusion was added to by the need to keep shifting target as cruisers and destroyers appeared through the smoke.

The director team wrongly believed at the time that we had scored a direct hit, but we must have confused enemy gun flashes with our own fall of shot. We gained great confidence when we saw HMS *Warspite* opening fire and the Italians breaking off the action as their flagship was hit.

Considering the amount of hardware that was being thrown between the fleets, it was astonishing that the only people who got hurt were the few Italians when *Warspite* scored her hit. From my seat I had a very good view of the rest of the British fleet and watched with great excitement as the destroyers formed up to carry out a mass torpedo attack which was unfortunately cancelled shortly afterwards. I could also see *Eagle* operating her Swordfish. *Neptune* tried to catapult one of her two Sea Fox aircraft before, or rather at the beginning of the battle, but the petrol tank was punctured by a near miss and the aircraft tipped over the side to avoid a fire. I do not think any effort was made to catapult the second aircraft.[5]

A young seaman aboard the *Neptune* also recalls the excitement of that action:

> My action station was in 'Y' turret's 6-inch magazine. I was only a boy at the time, but I can remember those hatch clips being shot on the hatch cover entombing us in the bowels of the ship. Of course we were too busy keeping 'Y' turret supplied with cordite. All we could hear was the explosions of enemy shells all around us. The Padre was on the bridge giving a running account of what was happening over the ship's Tannoy system.
>
> Although we didn't have much time to worry I do remember some of those enemy shells were falling very close to us. Our guns did inflict damage on the enemy but to what degree I forget. I know the enemy fleet was chased back into their harbours and I believe we waited outside for a long while for them to come back out, but they never did.[6]

So far then the four 6-inch cruisers of Admiral Tovey had more than held their own against the four 6-inch Italian cruisers and forced both these and the 9th Destroyer Squadron to turn away. A more decisive factor was now to enter onto the scene, however, in the form of the 7th Italian Division (*Savoia*, *D'Aosta*, *Attendolo* and *Montecuccoli*) under Admiral Sansonetti. They turned towards the British cruisers at 1520 and were mistaken by them for heavy cruisers. The two Italian battleships and the two heavy cruiser divisions (*Pola*, *Zara*, *Gorizia*, *Fiume*, *Trento* and *Trieste*) which remained on their left, or disengaged side at this time, at first held their course northward. Campioni steered a slightly diverging course north-west until the battleships and heavy cruisers were in an extended line with their broadsides open and then, at 1523, both groups of the Italian main force turned on course 060 degrees towards the British ships but at a converging angle. Meanwhile Admiral Sansonetti had sighted the *Warspite* coming up in support of the British cruisers and duly signalled this news to Campioni.

The intervention of the *Warspite* was a blessed relief for Tovey's gallant four ships, who, with the whole of the western horizon alive with smoke and gun flashes and with the water around them churned up by near-misses from all calibres of weapons, most of which outranged their own main armaments, were hard-pressed.

When the *Warspite* came into action she chose for her initial target, an 8-inch cruiser bearing 265 degrees and engaged her at a range of 26,400 yards, and was in fact probably Sansonetti's flagship *Eugenio di Savoia*, leading her division of four 6-inch cruisers and hotly engaged with Tovey's four ships at this time. *Warspite* opened fire at this target at 1526 with shattering effect, and not just on the enemy, as Admiral Power, watching the plot picture, recalls:

> As we were admiring this picture, quite unexpectedly *Warspite* opened fire. Our picture disintegrated as the ARL table shattered with the blast of 'X' turret firing on her war limits. Tom Brownrigg became the first, and, I think, only casualty of the action when his nose was scratched by his dividers leaping off the table. I left Tom to try and piece together a manual plot and went onto the compass platform to try and keep some sort of record on a pad. The illusion of the tactical table became even stronger with shell splashes all over the place looking like the cotton wool plumes that used to be stuck about with varying significance on the table. I also found William Carne (F.T.O.) had possessed himself of a stop watch, was watching the enemy gun flashes and in due course saying 'Falling – Splash'. As he seemed to be doing this entirely for his own amusement, and as the said splashes were unhealthily close, I took his watch away and felt better.
>
> It must be remembered that for nearly all of us it was the first time we had been under fire. As staff and therefore having no part in fighting the ship it was quite alarming at first.[7]

They were not the only ones caught by surprise when the 'Old Lady' first let fly at the enemy.

> At the beginning of the action there was a collection of senior Admin Staff officers on the quarterdeck. The Fleet Medical, Accountant, Educational, Engineering officers etc. – all of Captain's rank. I heard afterwards that they were caught napping when 'Y' turret opened fire and nearly blown overboard – certainly considerably inconvenienced! They had of course, no action station in the ship's operation.
>
> It is remarkable to think that we had the entire Admin Staff of the Mediterranean on board which would have caused quite a hiatus if we had got sunk; but this situation persisted for many months until a shore H.Q. was set up at Gabbasi.[8]

Nobody was happier at his juncture than A.B.C. himself of course!

> When the action became imminent Admiral Cunningham found he couldn't see well enough and, with the COS went onto the compass platform followed by the Fleet Gunnery Officer and the Fleet Telegraphic Officer, thus severing all connection with the Plot. He conducted the whole business in his own inimitable style, roaring with laughter and saying, 'Shoot that bugger up! ... That's enough for him, now that bugger', and so on.[9]

The C-in-C obviously felt he was back on the bridge of his destroyer but others were rather more hesitant about joining in quite so enthusiastically in the fun! One of these was an American reporter who had a horror of action, and during bombing crouched inside the armoured structure.

> One of us, going in and seeing him there, said, 'Come on, you'd better come outside, there's a lot of news value out there'. He said, 'No, I'm not going outside. My group of newspapers wants live news, not a dead reporter.' This man by the way was in his own way one of the bravest men I have met. He became physically terrified, to an extent I have never seen in another man when any rough stuff was in progress; but he always turned up for the next operation. To the best of my recollection he was sunk at least twice and carried on regardless.[10]

Warspite loosened off some ten salvos at these cruiser targets which had the satisfying effect of causing them to break off under cover of smoke. Many of her one-ton projectiles fell close to the ships of the 4th and 8th Divisions and hastened their departure from the battle scene as they took refuge astern and to the west of the two battleships and the heavy cruiser divisions which Campioni was herding in battle formation hastily and steering north-east to gain contact with the advanced British forces. Although a hit was claimed on one of the Italian cruisers during this first stage there is no confirmation of this from their records. The blast from her own guns damaged *Warspite*'s floatplane which was on its catapult, and, like *Neptune*'s, it had to be ditched.

It was at 1530 that the Italian light cruisers finally vanished for a time behind a smokescreen laid by the 9th Squadron and time was taken to briefly take stock of the situation. The Italian battleships were obviously close at hand as well as numerous heavy cruisers so Cunningham decided to mark time and give *Malaya* a chance to come up and join him before the next stage of the battle. Accordingly, and with memories of Jutland when she had done the same thing in front of the whole High Seas Fleet, unintentionally, *Warspite* made an complete circle at 24½ knots. The four light cruisers of the 7th Squadron which had been tearing along ahead at 29 knots, did the same so as not to get too far out of touch again, and for a little period there was a lull in events.

Within three minutes, however, further glimpses of the Italian ships were obtained and the *Warspite* let go another eight salvos at these targets, again the two light cruisers of the 8th Division.

Cunningham gave these two ships four salvos each as he assumed that they were trying to work their way east to get at the *Eagle*. This had the effect of making Admiral Legnani turn sharply, and finally, due west ahead of the 5th Division and he maintained this position ahead and to the west of the main Italian fleet for the rest of the action.

Meanwhile, far astern, *Eagle* had managed to assemble a second torpedo bomber striking force. One eyewitness aboard the *Eagle* described his experiences as follows:

My own action station was with a medical aid party in the island on the flight deck. From there you could see what went on all round, but it was certainly not the quietest place in the world – planes were running up engines, squadrons coming and going in action, the pom-poms and four-inch guns blasting away. You could see the salvos of bombs sending up huge forests of water spouts, often blotting out the sight of our escorting battleships. It was quite incredible seeing them emerging again from the curtain of falling water.

Before the action, the big ships were all together quietly steaming through the Med, with our screen of destroyers and cruisers all round, and our Swordfish ranging far out on A/S patrols. Suddenly the urgent repetitive call to action stations sounding on the Marine bugle. Then the excitement of seeing the battle ensign flying, men rushing to their action stations, the flight deck clearing and the planes taking off.

The steady, pulsating beat of the engines increased, urging extra speed and the sound of swishing water frothing by took on a new note. Then came the heavy thud of the big guns and the news of what it was all about. We watched the *Warspite* and her escorts gradually draw away from us – the slower old crocks. We could feel the engines, trying so hard, and saw the *Royal Sovereign*, obviously making great effort, with smoke pouring from her black-cowled funnel.

There was a vague feeling of frustration. Later we had news of *Warspite* scoring a hit. But we were not to be entirely left out of the game. Our squadrons were, of course, in action against the Italian fleet, though, on these occasions, not too successfully, although the strikes must have been frightening the life out of the enemy. Other planes spotted for the big guns of our battleships, and later, 813 Squadron successfully attacked Augusta harbour. Our Sea Gladiators too had their splendid wins of the Regia Aeronautica during their attempts to stop our force.[11]

Another eyewitness from the *Eagle* tells his story thus:

At the time of the Battle of Calabria I was a signal boy, just seventeen years of age. During the battle I was closed up at the after action position, at the foot of the mainmast which would have been used for flag signalling should the foremast have been put out of action. At this position we also had spare signalling projector, telescopes and other paraphernalia of the communications of that era, a very far cry from those of today! Thus, not being on or near the bridge, the after action position was one where time hung on one's hands, and so we spent that time having a good look at how things were going through the telescope and the good old Barr and Stroud binoculars. (This position was only normally activated when a surface action was a possibility, not for aircraft or submarine attack).

HMS *Gloucester* was our support, she having suffered a direct bomb hit on the bridge a few days previously. The battle was at extreme range of course so that little could be seen of the Italian fleet, though what we could see of them soon made it obvious that they were retiring at high speed. As I remember it was a lovely day, weatherwise, visibility excellent. A truly grand sight to see one's ships trying their utmost to get within range of the enemy, battle ensigns streaming out, signal flags flying, signal projectors flashing orders. *Warspite* looked a real tower of strength dashing ahead, all on her own, firing at maximum range, our other battleships being too old and slow to get much within range.[12]

Nine more Swordfish were flown off from *Eagle* at 1545 and steered towards the enemy just over the horizon. At 1548 the *Warspite* catapulted off her second Walrus amphibion for scouting duties 'Q' and all these aircraft were soon in touch with Campioni's main force which were now formed up in two groups of line ahead, with the 8-inch cruisers ahead and slightly west of the two battleships.

Unfortunately the *Eagle*'s aircraft again chose the leading ships as their targets, selecting the heavy cruisers rather than the battleships which were some distance astern of them. But in the interim much had happened.

While the two other British battleships were straining to catch up with the flagship their destroyer flotillas had naturally been champing at the bit. At 1525 Cunningham gave them their head and ordered their release from screening in order for them to concentrate on the disengaged bow ready to counter-attack any Italian destroyers' movements or to hold themselves fully ready to launch their own torpedo assault on the enemy. The 14th flotilla was released by *Warspite* at once, the 2nd by *Malaya* at 1545 and the 10th by *Royal Sovereign*, now far astern, at 1552. By 1600 all these flotillas had worked their way north to get themselves into the most favourable position for action. *Janus* and *Juno* joined the 14th Flotilla, *Hero* and *Hereward* the 2nd Flotilla and *Decoy* the 10th

Flotilla for these movements to form three striking forces.

Thus the situation at 1550 was that both fleets were again on parallel courses, slightly diverging, the Italians steering 010 degrees, the *Warspite* 345 degrees. Campioni had his heavy cruisers in line of battle ahead of him, Cunningham likewise had his four light cruisers so deployed. The *Malaya* was gradually coming up in support of *Warspite*, but still out of range, while the *Royal Sovereign* was still too far astern to affect the issue. The *Eagle* had her nine torpedo bombers in the air on their way towards the Italian fleet and the British destroyers were beginning to pass east of the *Warspite* on their way to concentrate in the van, the 14th Flotilla (*Nubian*, *Mohawk*, *Juno* and *Janus*) leading, followed by the 10th Flotilla (*Stuart*, *Dainty*, *Defender* and *Decoy*) and the 2nd Flotilla further astern (*Hyperion*, *Hero*, *Hereward*, *Hostile*, *Hasty* and *Ilex*). The Italian light cruisers had effectively removed themselves from between the two heavyweights and their destroyers, apart from *Alfieri*'s squadron, had not yet shown much of themselves.

At 1551 these forces again came in view of each other.

CHAPTER FIVE

A Single Shell

With the dispositions of the British and Italian fleets both worked out to the mutual satisfaction, as far as it could be achieved, of their respective commanders, the battle now rapidly approached a climax. Tovey took his four ships on a course of 310 degrees to re-establish direct contact with the enemy and the *Warspite* steered 345 degrees to cut the corner and make up some of the ground she had lost in marking time for the *Malaya*.

At 1551 the Italian and British main fleets sighted each other again on slightly converging courses and the battle re-commenced with renewed fury. Both sides' battleships came into action simultaneously two minutes later. The *Warspite*'s gunners, in fine fettle after their earlier limbering up, were soon on target and achieving straddles on the right hand battleship of the Italian line, which was correctly taken for the flagship, the *Giulio Cesare*, at a range of 26,000 yards on a bearing of 287 degrees.

On the Italian side both *Cesare* and *Cavour* opened fire at the same moment on the orders of Admiral Brivonesi, the 5th Division Commander and Chief of Staff to Campioni. Although British accounts state that both Italian battleships immediately concentrated their fire on the *Warspite* herself, the Italian records are clear that this was, initially, not so. *Cesare* commenced firing at 1553 at an estimated range of 26,400 yards on the *Warspite*. The *Cavour,* on the other hand, commenced fire against the second British battleship of the formation – the *Malaya* according to her reports. However as she registered the range as at least 30,000 yards she may have even been trying to reach the *Royal Sovereign* by mistake, which, with several knots speed less than her two companions, was far astern. *Malaya* herself came into action on a bearing of 180 degrees from *Warspite* and fired four salvos at the *Cavour* at the extreme elevation of her 15-inch guns, but as these all fell short it is probable that *Cavour*'s own ranging shots, from her smaller 12.6-inch guns, also fell far short of their target and more in the vicinity of the *Warspite*.

Several of the British destroyers, still moving up on the disengaged side of the *Warspite*, had some very uncomfortable moments as 'overs' from the two Italian battleships fell in among them at 1554, but none were hit.

At the onset of the battleship duel Admiral Campioni ordered his heavy cruisers of the *Pola* group onto a bearing of 040 degrees from his flagship with the objective of closing to within extreme range of their 8-inch guns and adding their considerable weight of fire to enfilade the head of the British line while the *Warspite* was fully occupied with the *Cesare*. This was complied with by Paladini's powerful force. Already well ahead of the British van this course, if held, would have, with the Italian cruiser's superior speed, have soon brought them into the ideal position of crossing the British 'T' in a classical manner and the combined broadsides of these six powerful ships would have inflicted heavy punishment on the thinly protected ships of Tovey's force as well as being of considerable value in diverting the *Warspite* from her main task. It was a well-conceived move by Campioni and one which showed every chance of a successful outcome.

The two main combatants now slugged it out for seven minutes, both sides achieving straddles. The Italian salvos were falling around *Warspite* within 1,000 yards but their spread was large. The closest the British flagship came to be hit was by one closely bunched salvo which crashed into the sea about two cables off *Warspite*'s port bow. On their part the Italians record that the *Warspite*'s shooting was consistently good at this period, with very small dispersion and progressively landing closer and closer to the *Cesare*. Inevitably such excellent marksmanship was rewarded.

At 1559 a 15-inch shell from the *Warspite* hit the Italian flagship amidships. Admiral Cunningham recorded:

> I had been watching the great splashes of our 15-inch salvos straddling the target when, at 4 p.m., I saw the great orange-coloured flash of a heavy explosion at the base of the enemy flagship's funnels. It was followed by an upheaval of smoke, and I knew that she had been heavily hit at the prodigious range of thirteen miles.[1]

Captain Piazza of the *Cesare* recalled how:

> The projectile crashed into our rear funnel on the starboard side and punched through the armoured citadel below through the left bulkhead, perforated the deck below and penetrated through into the casemate underneath, tearing asunder the bulkhead and entered the NCO's mess,

which it destroyed. It left a small hole in the armour deck below and stopped in front of the armoured bulkhead in front.[2]

In addition to decimating the crews and one of the guns of the light AA batteries on the starboard side, and the severe structural damage by the explosion and splinters, a fire broke out in the casemate and the mess itself and the resultant fumes and smoke were sucked in by the turbine ventilators into numbers 4, 5, 6 and 7 boiler rooms. Here their crews were quickly overcome and had to be evacuated. Many of the crews passed out and one died of asphyxia. With the loss of these four boilers' power the speed of the Italian flagship soon began to drop noticeably. Within a short time it had been reduced to eighteen knots.

Admiral Campioni reported that:

The speed of the *Cesare* herself rapidly reduced to twenty, then eighteen knots; and when it was realised on the bridge that *Cesare* was losing ground in relation to the *Cavour* it was reported that four of the boilers were out of action. Because of the seriousness of this *Cesare* pulled out of line leaving the *Cavour* to continue the fight with the heavy cruisers of *Pola*'s group, all of which were pressing ahead and firing on the three enemy battleships.[3]

He decided however, that the odds were now too great against his force, with three battleships against one, and at 1602, *Cavour* also hauled out of line and followed *Cesare* on her new course of 270° away from the British fleet. In the interim Paladini's heavy cruisers continued to duel with Tovey's ships and also engaged the leading ship of the British battle-line.

That single 15-inch shell had decided the battle, for at one moment Campioni had found himself working into a very favourable position and the next he was confronted with the grim prospect of how to extradite his damaged ship and his whole force from a fast closing enemy fleet of superior, in terms of capital ships, power.

At 1605, therefore, he ordered his destroyer flotillas in to make torpedo attacks and lay smoke to cover his withdrawal. The issue was further complicated for him for it was then that *Eagle*'s striking force arrived on the scene and began their attacks on his only intact squadron, the 8-inch cruisers of Paladini.

That the Italians were in serious trouble was soon obvious from the bridge of the *Warspite*. The enemy's gunnery, at first good and fairly accurate, had quickly fallen off even before the *Warspite*'s hit and had become ragged. As Cunningham wrote in his despatch:

> *Warspite*'s hit on one of the enemy battleships at 26,000 yards range might perhaps be described as a lucky one. Its tactical effect was to induce the enemy to turn away and break off the action, which was unfortunate, but strategically it probably has had an important effect on the Italian mentality.[4]

This was apparent from the resultant signals and manoeuverings of the Italian fleet. Again as Cunningham recorded: 'A feature of the action was the value, and in some cases the amusement, derived from intercepted plain language enemy signals.'[5] Indeed the Italians seem to have shown very lax discipline in this respect throughout the action, as Admiral Power recalls:

> Quite soon after I came on the bridge *Warspite* got a hit on the *Cesare*, amidships by the funnels. The Italians immediately turned away and with superior speed soon ran out of range while their light forces made a highly effective smoke screen. We intercepted an Italian signal saying 'I am constrained to retire', which made everybody laugh, and shortly afterwards another complaining that they were being bombed by their own aircraft, which made us laugh even more after our experiences (very unpleasant) of being bombed on the previous two days.[6]

The intervention of the Italian battleships was now almost over, Admiral Campioni recorded that:

> On her new route, *Cesare* continued to fire against the enemy from astern until the target became hidden by the curtain of smoke extending across our vision laid by our light forces to cover our withdrawal. Some groups had missed the turn of the *Cesare*, which had now come onto route 230 degrees and as a result in short time contact was lost with these formations ...[7]

Meanwhile attempts were being made to control the fires and restore power from the boilers, but not until 1645 were six boilers again in full operation. Again requests were sent out for intervention as promised by the Air Force.

Warspite soon lost sight of both Italian battleships after their turn away and firing was checked at 1604 after a total of seventeen salvos had been got away. She had attempted to close the enemy on course 310 degrees, but was still only making seventeen knots, one knot *slower* than the damaged *Cesare* and had no hope of catching them before they vanished into the smoke. The plucky *Malaya* had also made a brave attempt to get into the act, firing another four salvos, but again these all fell short of the target before it disappeared and she also ceased fire at 1608. The Navigating Officer of the *Malaya* remembers the action as being of a well-tried pattern:

> As regards the action, it was a sort of set-piece of many a peacetime exercise. The destroyers went into attack, without much success I feel, while the battlefleets engaged at long range. Hardly another Jutland, considering the number of ships involved! Now *Malaya* (typical of our pre-war preparedness!) had been refitted but her guns had not been given the extra elevation as had the *Warspite*'s, so that, though we fired some rounds at our maximum range the results were innocuous, but very early on the *Warspite* registered a direct hit on the *Cesare*. This was enough for the enemy who turned and ran, and they had the legs of us, having been modernised, unlike the poor old *Malaya*![8]

Far astern *Royal Sovereign* had no opportunity to fire at all, much to the disgust of her seasoned gunners.

Another brief lull in the battle then ensued as far as the surface ships were concerned, but in the interim the cruisers had again got into the act. Led by the *Pola*, the 1st Division, under Admiral Matteucci in *Zara*, and the 3rd Division, under Cattaneo in *Trento*, had responded to the orders of Admiral Campioni to close the head of the British line and they were quickly in action, as Paladini later recorded:

> From 1550 to 1600 all the 10,000-ton cruisers opened fire in sequence, in the order *Trento* at 1555, *Fiume* at 1558, *Bolzano*, *Zara* and *Pola* at 1600 and *Gorizia* at 1601. As our ships opened fire the enemy cruisers replied. Their fire was accurate but, in the main, ineffective. Only the *Bolzano* was hit, by three splinters, at 1605, which penetrated her stern and caused damage to her wing rudders, jamming them to the left. The ship made a complete turn with all her guns still firing and then some further near misses astern freed the jam and she resumed her place in line again.[9]

The British cruisers had opened fire on the Italians, holding a course of 310 degrees at a range of about 23,000 yards and quickly closed in. The *Orion* commenced firing at 1599, *Neptune* and *Sydney* at 1600 and *Liverpool* at 1602. They were, of course, far outranged by the Italian heavy cruisers but Tovey steered towards the enemy to close the gap and it was the *Neptune* which first straddled her target, the *Bolzano*, causing her discomfort.

At 1603 Paladini received news of the *Cesare*'s damage and Campioni signalled to him, 'My course is 270 degrees, my speed is 20 knots' and ordered the cruisers to make smoke. By 1617 the Italian cruisers started to do this, and, as their smoke obscured their targets, began falling silent. *Trento* ceased firing at 1609, *Fiume* at 1605, *Bolzano* at 1620 once she had extricated herself, *Zara* at 1616, *Pola* about 1604 and *Gorizia* at 1612. As the smokescreen thickened and spread the British guns also fell silent again for a time.

During this exchange Paladini's ships had been receiving the unwelcomed attentions of *Eagle*'s striking force which appeared on the scene at 1545 and commenced their attacks. The Fleet Air Arm Swordfish attacked in three waves of three aircraft each, attacking from ahead of the line of Italian cruisers and choosing as their targets the ships at the head of the line which they correctly identified as 8-inch cruisers. Despite being fully occupied with the main action, the Italian cruisers put up a heavy wall of flak to deter the torpedo bombers but all the British aircraft came through this unscathed and made their drops on the leading cruiser's starboard side between her bow and beam bearings at close range. From the splashes and spray and through the hail of flak they were convinced that at least one of their missiles had struck this vessel, which they reported as a hit on a 'Bolzano' class cruiser.

They had in fact attacked the 3rd Division and *Bolzano* was leading the line. The Swordfish were engaged between 1610 and 1615 and almost all of their drops were made against this vessel, as Italian records show. Violently swerving and jinking, *Bolzano*, however, avoided every torpedo aimed at her. She also claimed to have shot down two of her attackers for certain and another she claimed probably destroyed by her AA fire. Some of the other cruisers also claimed to have destroyed one of the attackers, but, like the Fleet Air Arm men, their assessments were wrong and no British plane was lost in this attack, all returning safely to the *Eagle*.

The verdict of one Fleet Air Arm pilot on the attack was self-critical:

Looking back, it does seem that we failed miserably, but it was the first time that we had experienced anything quite like it. A Swordfish is a slow aeroplane and is not an ideal aircraft for daylight attacks on very heavily defended targets, for one is within range of opposition for a very long time up to the point of dropping the torpedoes, and also a very long time is spent getting out of range afterwards. The heavy guns barrage was also most disturbing. Our aim was not good and we failed in our objective. It is interesting to note however that the Italians also suffered from 'First Night Nerves' and also failed to score any hits on us.

On return to the carrier our aircraft were refuelled and rearmed but, by that time the Italians were steaming at 30 knots or more and a Swordfish at its maximum loaded speed of around 90 knots would never have caught up with them so we were stood down.

Most of the squadron had been together for some while, although we had started to get a number of new pilots and observers. The attack was taken very much as a routine affair, though, in the event, I think we were all somewhat surprised at our reception. Things very quickly returned to normal routine.[10]

Back aboard the carrier the Swordfish reports were studied and their claim of a hit on *Bolzano* was signalled to Cunningham, but, fortunately, for it was completely untrue, it did not reach him until 1715. Had he have got it earlier he might have gone after the cripple but as it was he kept clear of the smoke and possible torpedo traps awaiting him on the other side. As Admiral Power concludes: 'It would of course have been folly to pass through the enemy smoke, with a host of destroyers waiting to attack us as we emerged.[11]

Meanwhile the *Warspite* had come into action again as the *Trento* emerged for a brief period beyond the smokescreen and was quickly taken under fire at a range of 24,000 yards on a bearing of 313 degrees. Cunningham appreciated that this ship might well be working her way round to the north and was determined to head off any such move. Six salvos of 15-inch were directed towards this target, three of which, *Trento* later reported, landed very close, before she ducked back behind the screen once more. By this time *Warspite* was well out of range of the Italians' main armaments, although *Zara* fired six last salvos before vanishing again. *Warspite* again ceased fire at this time. Most of the fire from Paladini's ships had been directed at the British destroyer flotillas and in support of his own destroyers' attack, from 1602 onwards, the destroyers of the 10th and 14th Flotillas in the van receiving the attentions of the 8-inch shells of the enemy before they were driven off, but again, no British destroyer was hit.

Three minutes later the Italian destroyer attack started to develop and they were observed from the flagship's bridge to be moving out across to starboard from the van of the enemy's fleet to make torpedo attacks. The British destroyers were therefore, at 1614, given the order to counter-attack in the classical manner after three torpedoes were observed passing close to the 14th Flotilla's ships. With Tovey's four ships of the 7th Cruiser Squadron in support, the British destroyers moved 'joyously' forward to meet their Italian opposite numbers.

Campioni, concerned with his falling speed in relation with the British, whom he expected to be pursuing him at rather more than the seventeen knots *Warspite* was making at this time, decided to send in his destroyer squadrons to buy him time by torpedo attack and smoke-making. In this the Italian destroyers were entirely successful, even though their attacks were described as half-hearted, timid and not pushed home. This to a great extent is true, but the purpose of their orders was achieved perfectly, for beyond the great pall of smoke they laid down the British would not venture.

It is interesting to note that post-war study of the Battle of Jutland had held for many the lesson that it was Jellicoe's turn away from the threat of German torpedo attack that had lost the day, and, although this was disputed and the turn-away accepted as the only alternative for heavy ships in such conditions, many held that by turning *towards* the attack the peril was nearly as much lessened but contact maintained. Cunningham was one of the most aggressive of British C-in-Cs in the Second World War, but even he, under a similar threat as Jellicoe had been, with a smokescreen instead of the darkness of night, was forced to turn away and keep his distance in a like manner.[12]

The Italian destroyer squadrons made their attacks, not in concert as a massed torpedo assault, which might have been dangerous indeed, but in dribs and drabs whenever the opportunity presented itself to them, depending on how they were situated when the flagship was hit. For those that attacked later, their own smoke made things as difficult for them as the British.

Being on the flank closest to the British 7th Cruiser Squadron, it was the 9th Squadron that made the first assault. Although Campioni had the fear of the British battleships uppermost in his mind at this time, and expected his boats to deter these vessels, it was inevitable that the ships of Tovey's squadron, being in advance of the *Warspite* and *Malaya*, would bear the brunt of the attacks initially until the British destroyers moved out in their turn, and so it turned out.

The *Alfieri* (Captain Daretti) led her unit (*Oriani, Carducci* and *Gioberti*), on the leading edges of the Italian fleet, being, at 1545, positioned about one mile NNE of the leading heavy cruiser, *Bolzano*, on a northerly course, and had been trying to place herself in a more useful position to launch a torpedo attack on her own initiative by steering first 040 degrees and then 060 degrees.

Thus steering towards the British van the unit was already under gunfire from the British cruisers and destroyers from 1600 until 1616, and commenced returning that fire from their forward guns at 1601. When they received the general order to make smoke and launch a torpedo attack at 1605 therefore, they were already fully committed to such a course and, at a range of 13,500 yards they launched between them a total of five torpedoes on a bearing of 032 degrees against the enemy cruisers, who they observed were moving on a course WNW. Smoke from the 8th Division had meanwhile obscured them and they could not tell if they made any hits or not, but it was probably their torpedoes which passed through the ranks of the British 14th Flotilla at 1614 near the end of their runs.

Dodging and weaving, the 9th Squadron made its way back into the shelter of the smoke surrounded by shell splashes, but save for minor splinter damage to the *Alfieri* herself, all escaped being hit.

Much further south the two remaining destroyers of the 7th Squadron under Captain Baldo in the *Freccia*, with the *Saetta*, were on station close astern of the Italian battleships and when the heavy ships began their duelling these frail craft found themselves in a precarious state with 15-inch shells pitching all about then, any one of which would have blown them out of the water. Baldo therefore shifted over to the disengaged side of the *Cesare* and *Cavour*, to the left, and when shortly afterwards *Cesare* was hit they commenced laying smoke to cover her withdrawal, sweeping round north-east of the battleship where they found themselves on an ideal bearing to make a torpedo attack. Baldo therefore maintained this course and, at 1618, these two destroyers launched their torpedoes at a range of 8,500 yards, again taking as their targets the cruisers of Tovey's squadron. They also opened fire with their guns as they turned under cover of the 9th Squadron's smoke and escaped most of the retaliation because of this.

The captain of *Saetta*, Commander Unger Di Lowemberg, was convinced that they had scored one torpedo hit on a British cruiser for he observed a tall column of water rise at her side at about the time his torpedoes should have completed their runs. However as no British ships were in fact struck by torpedoes at any time during the action, this was probably a near-miss from the 8-inch shells of the Paladini cruisers. During their subsequent withdrawal both destroyers came under heavy shell fire from a group of four British destroyers, but escaped unscathed.

The four destroyers of the 11th Squadron, (*Artigliere, Camicia Nera, Aviere* and *Geniere*) led by Captain Margottini, were on the disengaged side of the 1st Division when the order to attack was received, and, at 1607, they put their helms over and cut across their heavy cruisers, passing between the *Gorizia* and *Fiume*, on a course of 105 degrees. Once clear of their own cruisers they sighted the British 6-inch cruisers at 1615 and adjusted their own course to 090 degrees, rapidly closing the gap. They started making smoke immediately with the dual aim of protecting their own approach and covering the destroyers which had already attacked and were retreating under heavy fire.

The 11th Squadron itself immediately became the target of the British return fire but again, although surrounded by 6-inch and 4.7-inch shell bursts, it escaped any damage. *Artigliere* herself returned fire with her full outfit of torpedoes at a range of 13,800 yards at what she took to be a battleship. The smokescreen from the *Artigliere* had up to then effectively concealed her compatriots, but as she swung away from her launching position the other three destroyers ran clear of the smoke and also turned to fire at 1620, at a range of 11,000 yards. Seven torpedoes were aimed at the oncoming battleship and three at the British cruisers. In spite of the heavy pall of smoke this squadron remained under heavy fire during their withdrawal until 1630. Two minutes later the *Geniere* was attacked at low level by one of the returning Swordfish. She engaged it with her machine-guns and claimed to have shot it down, but this, we now know, was not so.

The 12th Squadron departed for their attack at 1607 from a position slightly astern of the 11th, and passed across the sterns of the *Pola* group (1st Division). By the time they had come clear of their own cruiser line their course was set towards the enemy, with the *Lanciere* leading, commanded by Captain D'Arienzo, and followed by the *Carabiniere, Corazziere* and *Ascari*. Almost at once they found themselves enveloped in the smoke laid by the 11th Squadron which made their approach and identification of their targets' position most difficult, for the British ships appeared and vanished through the wreaths of man-made fog at irregular intervals. At 1612 D'Arienzo caught a glimpse of a battleship ahead of him at about a range of 19,000 yards and took violent avoiding action while seeking a good attacking point. This was made more complicated by the attentions of a British aircraft which made feint attacks against the squadron, and by the attentions of the British cruisers and destroyers which took them under fire whenever gaps appeared on the smoke.

By 1622 the 12th Squadron found themselves in a position 030 degrees from the enemy battleship at a range of 14,000 yards and D'Arienzo ordered the torpedo launch, but before all his ships could comply they were again taken under fire from both this ship and the cruisers and destroyers ahead of her. In consequence only the *Corrazziere* got off three torpedoes against the second of a group of battleships (presumably the *Malaya*) while *Ascari* fired one against a cruiser target. D'Arienzo meanwhile hauled his squadron around to escape the withering fire and, seeking safety in the smoke again, awaited a better opportunity to complete his attack.

Meanwhile the two ships of the 14th Squadron, without the *Da Noli* which had broken down, arrived on the scene of the battle from Taranto. These were the *Vivaldi* (Captain Galati) and the *Pancaldo* (Commander Merini), and they at once found themselves pitched into a high-speed and highly confused situation. At 1355 they took station with the 4th Division, and were instructed by Admiral Moriondo to place themselves ahead of the light cruisers. This they failed to do, having insufficient margin of speed over the cruisers to make headway. Then at 1515, on contact being made with the enemy, they were placed on the left hand side of the leading ships of the 4th Division, *Barbiano* and *Giussano* (the *Cadorna* and *Diaz* having fallen out earlier as we have seen) in order not to interfere with their gunnery by fouling them with their smoke.

At 1609 Admiral Merini released them to the attack in compliance with Campioni's orders. They were at this time in a position almost abreast of the *Cesare* and immediately steered on a course of about 090 degrees towards the British which they estimated were about 25,000 yards away. Galati's two ships soon came under heavy fire from the secondary armament of both the *Warspite* and *Malaya* which was so accurate that, when within 18,000 yards, the Italians were forced to break off their attack run and seek shelter in the smoke on a course of 240 degrees following the general turn-away by the main force, and were completely unable to fire.

 . Meanwhile D'Arienzo was plunging about between the two lines of warships in the smoke seeking another opportunity to complete his own attack with the 12th Squadron's four destroyers. For a time they steered south-west and soon came under heavy fire again from guns of medium calibre (6-inch from the two battleships or the cruisers of the 7th Squadron, most probably the latter) to which the Italian destroyers found time to reply to with their own 4.7-inch guns.

At 1645 the *Lanciere* launched three torpedoes at two cruisers which were heading northward and then took refuge in the smoke once more and followed the general retirement of the fleet. The British ships soon vanished from view astern. This attack by the *Lanciere* marked the end of the Italian destroyer attack and soon all ships were lost to view from both sides.

On the British side the picture was a confused one also, with Italian destroyers appearing and re-appearing out of the dense cloud of smoke to fire torpedoes at long range and then vanish before they could be properly engaged.

At 1535 Captain Mack, Senior Destroyer Officer in the *Nubian*, was reforming his three flotillas to counter-attack on a course of 350 degrees, north by west, with the 14th Flotilla, *Nubian*, *Mohawk*, *Juno* and *Janus* and the 2nd Flotilla, *Hyperion*, *Hero*, *Hereward*, *Hostile*, *Hasty* and *Ilex* to the south-east and the 10th Flotilla, *Stuart*, *Dainty*, *Defender* and *Decoy* to the south-west of him. The 2nd Flotilla was in single line ahead at 25 knots on bearing 140 degrees from *Nubian*, the 10th similarly disposed at 27 knots, on a bearing 220 degrees. During this forming up period the torpedoes from the 9th Squadron passed through their ranks and two salvos from the same group's guns landed close to the *Stuart*.

The order to attack was received at 1614 and at once the British destroyers, then some four miles east-north-east of *Warspite*, swung round to the west and increased speed to 29 knots to close the enemy.

It was *Stuart*'s moment. With her battle ensign streaming from the foremast and the Australian flag at the main, the oldest destroyer in the action, she was in the van when speed was increased to thirty knots at 1617, and was the first to open fire two minutes later; her opening salvo, at a range of 12,600 yards, appearing to score a hit. The 2nd and 14th Flotilla opened fire shortly afterwards, and the 7th Cruiser Squadron also engaged the enemy destroyers.[13]

The three flotillas were at this time disposed with guides on a line of bearing 220 degrees, destroyers disposed 180 degrees from guides, course 300 degrees. This formation was held, with the flotillas adjusting their positions relative to each other to keep their fields of fire clear. The Italian destroyers, estimated at a strength of two flotillas, worked their way across to starboard of their main fleet to attack, which, in British accounts, lacked vigour.

As soon as they had (presumably) fired torpedoes they turned away westward making smoke. It was observed that the second flotilla to attack retired through the smoke made by the first flotilla. Spasmodic firing was opened by all forces during the short intervals in which the enemy was in range and not obscured by smoke. No hits were observed by *Warspite*'s aircraft.[14]

Two torpedoes passed close astern of the *Nubian* during this phase but there were no hits. Similarly although British gunfire was accurate no hard hits were obtained (although some were claimed) on the Italian ships and the engagement petered out into a long-range firing practice at disappearing targets. The later attacks against the British battleships were, as we have seen, beaten off by their 6-inch secondary armament with little difficulty, the *Warspite* firing five salvos and the *Malaya* one between 1639 and 1641.

Italian signals continued to be intercepted on *Warspite* and once gave a warning that they were approaching the submarine line. This not unexpected trap, coupled with the uncertain hazards behind the smoke, which Cunningham later described as 'very effective in completely covering his high speed retirement', convinced the C-in-C that it would be unwise to play the enemy game and plunge straight into the smokescreen. Instead the British battleships altered course to work their way round north and to the windward of the smokescreen, and at 1635 course was altered to 340 degrees.

The British destroyers came clear of the smoke by 1700 but there was no sight of any enemy vessels beyond it at all to the western horizon. The 2nd Flotilla continued beyond the smoke while the 14th circled to the north-east, but at 1654 all destroyers were ordered to concentrate on the 7th Cruiser Squadron. The main fighting had, finally, finished and the British were left in sole charge of the field of battle.

CHAPTER SIX

Bombs, Bombs and More Bombs

Campioni's decision to break off the engagement was not fully appreciated by the British, who assumed that he merely had no stomach for the fight. While it is certainly true that by British standards the conduct of the Italian Fleet was certainly lacking as far as aggression was concerned, Campioni's initial plan and his subsequent early deployment, surely cannot be faulted.

He was aware that in battleships, which in 1940 were still the crucial factor in a naval battle despite many post-war assertions to the contrary, he was outnumbered three to two. He also knew that he had some margin of speed over the three British heavyweights. His plans were based on these factors on the hope that intervention by the submarines and bombers would help to tip the scales in his favour. In the event he was badly let down by the latter while the former had no chance to play any constructive part due to the British refusal to fall into the prepared trap.

With regard to the actual surface ship fighting in these circumstances, Campioni adopted the only sensible course of action open to him. To have taken his two battleships with their smaller calibre guns straight into an eye-to-eye slugging match with the three British ships which opposed him would, although welcomed with open-arms by Cunningham's men who wanted nothing better, have been pure suicide for the Italians. Campioni was not a fool; he probably realised that the British battleships, ship-for-ship, although old and, save in one case, not modernised as his own veterans, were far better trained and equipped for such a duel than his own. For twenty years the British had been practising the classic line-of-battle combat based on the lessons they had learned at Jutland until they were highly proficient. Although much criticised for this concentration of the 'line-of-battle' concept by post-war historians it was one area of naval warfare in which the British had no peers. Designed with a view of combat against the powerful Japanese battle fleet in mind, it would have been more than a match for the Italians who had no previous experience of this type of warfare and whose concepts of such fighting were, in one British admiral's view, at least two decades out of date compared with the British.

Therefore for Campioni to use his speed to dictate the course of the action, and thus effectively reduce the British three-to-two superiority into his own two-to-one superiority made plain sense, and the British, always eager for battle no matter what the odds, were forced to comply. The fact that he was wise to refrain from a slugging match was rapidly confirmed to him by the speed with which *Warspite*'s gunners hit him in the ribs at extreme range and could have only emphasised his early fears on that score.

Once this hit had been achieved with the resultant loss of power and speed his one trump over Cunningham's slower force had gone and he was clearly in danger of losing one, if not both, his battleships very quickly for even the *Royal Sovereign* had a two knot margin over the crippled *Cesare* and could have finished her off at leisure while *Warspite* and *Malaya* continued to occupy *Cavour*.

Campioni's one aim after that blow was therefore to extradite his main force from an unenviable position and, here again, he accomplished it with some ease. The Italian destroyers were given the specific task of shielding his withdrawal with smoke and deterring the British from following, at what should have been *superior* speed to the *Cesare*, and by making torpedo attacks. Although by British terms again, the delivery of these attacks was lacking dash and conviction, they were completely successful in attaining the objective, and thus the Italians got their crippled battleship home from what should have been her graveyard.

It is ironical from the Italian point of view that the intervention they most sought, from the bombers of the Regia Aeronautica, only took place after the Italian fleet had been so handicapped and not before. Rather than the British fleet being harassed by the superior Italian air power, it was the Italian cruisers and destroyers which during the battle found themselves being molested, albeit ineffectually, by the small British air complement. These, if not very effective in hitting ships, proved to be of great distraction, especially to the heavy cruisers, which, in theory, should have gobbled up the four British light cruisers with the greatest of ease. Part of the blame for the failure of the Italian 8-inch cruisers to play a more effective role, however, must be placed on Campioni, who utilised them as an extension of his own battle line and held them rigidly in place, although here again his enveloping movement to the north-west by these fast, powerful ships, would, had it been completed before *Cesare* was damaged, have put Cunningham in a lot of trouble.

With the ending of the gun duel however, Campioni's sole problem was to get his ships safely back to port and away from an intact and still most determined enemy. He expected much closer pursuit than he actually got, and knew that further torpedo bomber attacks from the *Eagle* would only be a matter of time, and that they might, third time out, have scored another crippling hit on one of his battleships, enabling the British heavy ships to come up with her and finish the job. He was cut off from his Taranto base to the north, had received no fighter cover despite repeated requests and knew that the only aircraft he could rely on, a few torpedo-bomber floatplanes of the Navy Air Arm, lay to the west, as did the only other main bases to which he could withdraw. His course therefore was due west as fast as he could go, but it took some time for all his scattered forces, cruisers and destroyers returning from their attacks, to reform with any degree of cohesion on this new track, and their subsequent, somewhat confused, re-assembly was watched from above by the Walrus from *Warspite*, with considerable amusement. But all the time he was taking his ships nearer to safety while the British hesitantly pushed their way around to the north of his smoke barrier. When last observed by the British scout planes, the Italian fleet was about ten miles off Cape Spartivento (not to be confused with a similar headland in Sardinia), and steering south-west at eighteen knots. The reactions of the British lower deck are recorded for us by one young sailor aboard the *Eagle*:

> And so eventually the chase was called off and we returned to our normal convoy covering routine. A little dispirited at not being able to have really brought the enemy to battle, but morale absolutely sky-high. During the night the leading signalman (one of the real old school) brought out his bottle of Navy rum in celebration – the first I had tasted, being too young of course to draw my tot. (Needless to say one was not supposed to bottle one's tot, and until one was rated Petty Officer it was diluted with water in an attempt to stop this practice – but many used to bottle it nevertheless, putting a handful of raisins in the bottle first, and it used to keep quite tolerably well!)[1]

With the end of the surface ship action came, at long last, the long-awaited intervention of the Italian Air Force. Their main bases in this area lay at Catania and other Sicilian airfields, where the headquarters of the II Squadron Area lay and they had on hand at this time some 14 squadrons of bombers with another five in reserve. There was also the aircraft of IV ZAT (Zone Area Territoriale) based in Puglia with further aircraft on hand. Not until 1505 did Supermarina and Superaero between them get off the urgent requests made by Campioni for intervention which he had expected much earlier; the first squadron got airborne from Gela airbase in south-east Sicily at 1535, and was followed, as they became available, by other units from both the Regia Aeronautica and the Navy Air Arm, from bases in Lecce and Brindisi. They made their attacks thus:[2]

Unit	Number of aircraft	Time of attack
37° Stormo	7	1643
34° Stormo	9	1645-1710
34° Stormo	12	1705
41° Stormo	10	1705
37° Stormo	6	1745
40° Gruppo	3	1745
37° Stormo	13	1750
40° Gruppo	3	1755
35° Stormo	3	1800
30° Stormo	10	1840
41° Stormo	9	1847
35° Stormo	6	1900
36° Stormo	9	1900
40° Gruppo	3	1910
11° Stormo	10	1915
36° Stormo	10	1945
34° Stormo	3	2110

We have already discussed the problems of high-level bombing as employed by the Italian Air Force with regard to warship targets and this was invariably the method used on this day, and subsequently. But we should also consider the type of weapons carried by these big three-engined aircraft, mainly S81s and SM79s as before in attacking heavily armoured ships. In all these 126 bombers, without help of navy bombers, dropped a total of 514 bombs on this day against warship targets, and failed to score a hit with a single one! That was bad enough, but when one analyses the types of bombs used it is clear that even if their percentage of hits had been anything other than zero, they could not have expected to have sunk, or even crippled, any of Cunningham's three battleships, despite his own fears for their safety. Only eight bombs from that total were of 500-kg, and these, though they might have inflicted some damage on exposed upperworks and light gun mounts, or, as in the *Gloucester*'s case, by a lucky hit on the bridge, they could in no way have seriously damaged, and certainly never sunk, even an old battleship. Of the remaining total, 236 bombs were of 250-kg, which might have inflicted damage on the *Eagle*'s flight deck easily enough, or on a light cruiser or destroyer, which were the most difficult targets to hit because of their speed. The remaining 270 were of 100-kg, which had very little value against warships unless they hit with a complete salvo.

So not only were the tactics (high-level as opposed to the far more accurate dive-bombing used by the Germans, Americans and Japanese) wrong, but the weapons, in the main, were wrong too. Their aiming was very good and they were perhaps unlucky not to hit more often, but this only exposed the waste that high-level methods always generated for little or no result.

What was much worse than any of these things, certainly as far as the Italian Navy was concerned, was the Italian bombers' lack of accurate identification of their targets, for they attacked their own ships on this day as much as the British fleet. Again this was a common failing among land-based bombing crews, one that was as common to the German, British and American air forces in the war as to the Italians. Most of these organisations were built solely for altitude attacks against large surface targets, like cities, which remained stationary and covered a wide area. Air chiefs, although always loudly claiming that their heavy bombers would drive ships from any sea within their range pre-war, had not much concern for this type of attack, concentrating more on getting through to Paris, Berlin or London, and in consequence the land-based air forces always showed a lamentable lack of accuracy in both identifying and hitting ship targets, a problem only solved when either the ships were anchored or they had dive-bombers on hand to do the job accurately. In the case of the Italians who had devoted more attention than most to the problem, the air force had been assigned the task of driving the Royal Navy from the Mediterranean as one of its main duties. Thus their accuracy was better than most, but, as was proved this day, still left a great deal to recommend it.

Those Italian bombers that found their correct opponents were sufficient, however, to cause Cunningham's fleet much discomfort as it cruised westward in sight of the Calabrian mountains, in the hope that the Italian fleet might still wish to take up the challenge again. In this they were doomed to disappointment. From 1700 the fleet cruised on a course of 270 degrees with the destroyers ahead of them, in company with the 7th Cruiser Squadron and at 1735 turned onto 200 degrees to within twenty-five miles of the Punto Stilo lighthouse. By this time it was clear that the Italians were not coming back and could not be intercepted before reaching the Messina Straits and at 1830 Cunningham turned away from the coast on 160 degrees and then, at 1930, to 130 degrees, to the south-east. At dusk, 2115, course was set 220 degrees for a position to the south of Malta to resume their original plan of covering their own convoys. All this cruising on the Italians' doorstep was of course accompanied by almost continuous bombing.

> Between 1640 and 1925 a series of heavy bombing attacks were made on our fleet by enemy aircraft operating from short bases. *Warspite* was bombed at 1641, 1715, 1735, 1823 and 1911. *Eagle* was bombed at 1743, 1809, 1826, 1842 and 1900. These two ships received the most attention but the 7th Cruiser Squadron received numerous attacks and many bombs fell near the destroyers. In some cases attacks were made from a considerable height. There were no hits and the fleet suffered no damage but there were numerous near misses and a few minor casualties from splinters. *Malaya* claimed to have damaged two aircraft with AA fire but no enemy machines were definitely seen to crash.[3]

Meanwhile Campioni's units had also been having a taste of the same treatment. His fleet had adopted a course of 230 degrees to pass south of Calabria and make for their bases in Sicily and Basso Tirreno, and the *Cesare* entered the Straits of Messina at about 2100, while the 7th Division proceeded to Palermo.

However while passing through the Straits these ships received orders from Supermarina to go instead to Naples. Also steering for Messina were the damaged ships, *Cardorna*, *Freccia* and *Saetta*, while the 3rd Division accompanied the *Cesare* and the *Cavour*, *Pola* and the 1st, 4th and 8th Divisions headed for Augusta. At 0100 on the 10th, however, these units also received orders from Supermarina, who feared torpedo bomber attacks on the Sicilian ports, to detach *Cavour*, *Pola* and the 1st Division also to Naples. But it was while these units were still south of Calabria that their final ordeal was undergone.

'Unfortunately,' wrote the Italian aviation historian, General Santoro, 'because of difficulties in identifying our ships and the enemy ships on which precise information was lacking', adding, 'fortunately without results.'[4]

He concluded that during the time the aircraft were airborne the relative position of the two fleets, both of which it will be remembered were moving on similar courses and speeds, had changed so that wireless signals sent out by the Commander of II Squadra Aerea were out of date. Moreover the R/T equipment in many groups failed to pick up corrections as they were broadcast. An additional point is that, from the great height from which many of these attacks were delivered there was little or no chance of the airmen being able to precisely recognise any difference between the two squadrons. Certainly the Italian Navy was sometimes forced to defend itself with intense AA fire which would lend support to the bombers thinking that they were in fact attacking hostile ships.

Another factor is that the various units made their attacks piecemeal and were not co-ordinated and controlled in the air except by their local unit leaders. Some units in fact did start to carry out attacks on their own ships but recognised them for what they were and did not complete their bombing runs. And, in the same manner, on several occasions the Italian ships recognised their own aircraft and refrained from firing, despite the bombing. Repeated attempts were made to signal these formations, 'The enemy are astern' or 'The enemy are to the east', but these were not always effective.[5]

Admiral Campioni is understandably bitter when he writes;

> My repeated requests for bombing attacks against the enemy fleet should have identified the location of our ships but by 1330 the local air commander (Commander Marina Messina) of the Fleet Air Arm liaison section had not even acknowledged my calls for assistance; only Marina Taranto. Finally in response to my requests for intervention by bomber aircraft at 1625 I was informed that they were sending 24 aircraft.[6]

Once the surface action commenced Campioni had little chance to sent further signals for help as he was fully preoccupied.

It was clear that there was complete lack of liaison between the Italian Navy and Air Force, which was perhaps understandable at this stage of the war; after all, it took many years for the British services to obtain close control and effective co-operation between their own two services and even in 1943 Allied airmen were bombing British destroyers in the Sicilian Straits during the evacuation of Tunisia and sinking British minesweepers off Normandy in 1944 with rocket attacks, while the Germans had experienced similar trouble in the Heligoland Bight in 1939 when the Luftwaffe sank two of their own destroyers with heavy loss of life and when no

British ships at all were in the area. At the Battle of Midway in 1942, bombers of the USAAF attacked an American submarine and reported the confirmed sinking of a Japanese cruiser! On the airmen's part they were always to complain that trigger-happy gunners aboard warships tended to fire at anything that flew and ask questions later, a feeling confirmed by the treatment of a Hurricane fighter defending Russia Convoy PQ 18, which had been in full sight of all the ships of the convoy for over a week on its catapult, but, upon being launched, was immediately fired on by every merchant ship in the vicinity.

Be that as it may, enough bombs were aimed at the Italian warships by their own pilots to cause a first-class row afterwards when the battle was being analysed. As Count Ciano was to remark in his Diary:

> The real controversy in the matter of the naval engagement is not between us and the British, but between our Air Force and Navy. Admiral Cavagnari [Commander-in-Chief of the Italian Navy] maintains that our air action was completely lacking during the first phase of the encounter, but that when it finally came it was directed against our own ships, which for six hours withstood the bombardment of our aeroplanes. Other information also gives the lie to the glowing reports of our Air Force. I confess that I am incredulous too. Mussolini, on the other hand, is not. Today he said that within three days the Italian Navy has annihilated 50 per cent of the British naval potential in the Mediterranean. Perhaps this is somewhat exaggerated.[7]

Indeed it was. These estimates came not just from the events in the Eastern Basin however, for over in the Western Mediterranean the Italian bombers had also been in action for most of the day against the ships of Force H, and here, although their claims of hits and damage inflicted were equally bizarre, they did have far greater deterrent effect than against Cunningham's fleet.

Admiral Somerville's command was hampered by lack of sufficient destroyers with good endurance at this time, for the older ships of the 13th Flotilla which supplemented his own slender screen for important operations were not up to par in this respect. He decided therefore to limit his diversionary foray merely to the air attack on Cagliari. It was fixed for dawn on 10th July. Force H had duly sailed at 0700 on the 8th and by the mid-afternoon of the 9th were some fifty miles south of Minorca when the first air attacks commenced.

Although Force H was better equipped than Cunningham's fleet to deal with air attack, as it had a radar warning set fitted on the battleship *Valiant* and the dive bombers of the Skua type, which doubled as low performance fighters, embarked in the *Ark Royal*, no form of fighter direction in conjunction with the radar had been installed and this limited its use and effectiveness.

In fact little or no warning was received of the first Italian attack; the bombers were only sighted a few seconds before the bombs arrived. Six bombers carried out this attack in two sub-flights of three, and, as they were not engaged by AA fire until after their withdrawal, their bomb-aimers were able to concentrate on their targets with impunity. The accuracy of the attack caused some splinter damage but no hits were scored. Nonetheless it was an unpleasant indication of how vulnerable the ships were.

At 1750 the second attack developed with far more aircraft, some eighteen SM79s of 32° Stormo being involved. Heavy AA fire engaged these aircraft at long range without scoring any hits on the bombers, but it was sufficient to put them off their stroke and the nearest bombs dropped fell some five miles from the fleet. At 1836 a third heavy raid developed out of the sun, by 22 bombers of 8° Stormo under Generale di Brigata Aerea Stefano Cagna. Their bombs were dropped with considerable accuracy and near misses were scored on the *Hood*, *Ark Royal* and destroyers on the screen. Despite the intervention of the Fleet Air Arm Skuas, who shot down two of the bombers and damaged others, Admiral Somerville decided that the risk to his valuable ships, especially to the only modern carrier in the fleet, was too great on a purely diversionary role and, after consultation with his staff, he decided to abandon his sortie and the course of the force was reversed after nightfall. During their return one of his screening destroyers, *Escort*, was torpedoed by the Italian submarine *Marconi* (Commander Chialamberto) and, after attempts at salvage, was sunk, but this was the only casualty to Force H.

Although Admiral Somerville himself termed the operation '... an unsatisfactory outing' it did have the effect of drawing a little of the fire from Cunningham.

In the night Cunningham took his fleet south of Malta and en route, at 0500, he sent in to that base several of his destroyers which badly needed refuelling, and others to act as escorts for the convoys: *Stuart*, with only fifteen tons of oil fuel left to her when she arrived, *Dainty*, *Defender*, *Hyperion*, *Hostile*, *Hasty*, *Ilex* and *Juno*. The rest of the fleet remained concentrated south of the island and at dawn was in position 35°24′ N, 15°17′ E, steering west. The Italian air force seems to have completely lost them at this time, for although heavy attack was launched at Valletta itself, although again failing to hit any of the ships there, the fleet had an undisturbed day. When their oiling had been completed most of the first group of destroyers sailed from Malta at 1115 and rejoined the fleet at 1525, whereupon the second group were duly detached, *Hero, Hereward, Decoy, Vampire* and *Voyager*, the last three being assigned for the escort of convoy MS1 after fuelling.

Convoy MF1 had, in fact, already sailed, at 2300 on the 9th July, Vice-Admiral Malta reasoned that the Italians would be so busy with Cunningham that they would leave the convoy alone, and in this he received the full backing of the C-in-C. The destroyers *Jervis, Diamond* and *Vendetta*, already at Malta, provided the initial destroyer screen, and they were joined at dawn on the 11th by the damaged *Gloucester* and the *Stuart* from the main fleet. At 2030 the battleship *Royal Sovereign* with the destroyers *Nubian, Mohawk* and *Janus* were also detached to refuel at Malta.

Meanwhile Cunningham had not been idle. Sunderlands had carried out reconnaissance of the Italian base of Augusta in Sicily in the hope of locating some of the reported cripples sheltering there and duly reported back that they had sighted three cruisers and eight destroyers anchored in that port. These were the ships of the 4th and 8th Divisions, as we have seen. Supermarina, however, had suspected something of the sort was in the offing and during the 10th both cruiser squadrons were ordered to sail for Taranto, the 8th at 1705 and the 4th at 1905. Consequently when the *Eagle*'s striking force of Swordfish arrived to carry out a dusk torpedo attack on these units, they found the cupboard was bare. Most flights therefore aborted their attack and returned with their torpedoes, but one flight of four located a Navigatori class destroyer in a small bay to the northward and concentrated their attentions on her.

This was the destroyer *Pancaldo* (Commander Luigi Merini) from the 14th Squadron. She was moored to a buoy undergoing minor repairs after the battle, and consequently had not sailed with the rest of her unit. At 2140 the Swordfish carried out their attack on her by moonlight. One torpedo hit the breakwater, another ran ashore and the third exploded on the coast in the vicinity of a gun battery. However the fourth scored a direct hit on the destroyer and she sank in shallow water with the loss of sixteen lives. (She was subsequently salvaged and put back into service, finally being sunk off Cape Bon during the evacuation of Tunisia on 30th April 1943). The Swordfish themselves, landed at an airfield on Malta after the strike to replenish.

That same evening the 7th Cruiser Squadron had been detached to sweep along in the wake of the Convoy MS1 as additional protection, but there were no other incidents. At dawn on the 11th the fleet re-assembled ready for the homeward run to Alexandria. At 0800 in position 35°10′ N, 15°00′ E the *Royal Sovereign, Hero, Hereward, Nubian, Mohawk* and *Janus* rejoined the fleet and the striking force flew from Malta to re-embark aboard *Eagle*. Cunningham decided to push on to Alexandria in his flagship, leaving Rear Admiral Pridham-Wippell to cover the convoy movements with the rest of the fleet and so, accordingly, at 0900, the *Warspite*, screened by the *Nubian, Mohawk, Juno* and *Janus*, increased speed to nineteen knots leaving the rest to follow at twelve.

> We had decided to try a more southerly route on our return journey to avoid the bombing we had experienced from the Dodecanese on our way west. We very soon found out our mistake. The inevitable shadowers appeared and called up the bombers from the Libyan airfields, and on 11th July we were heartily bombed until sunset. Rear Admiral Pridham-Wippell had the same experience, though rather more of it.[8]

And nor did the convoys themselves escape attention. MS1 sailed on the 10th escorted by *Decoy, Vampire* and *Voyager* and during the forenoon of the 11th they were surprised by high-flying bombers and one stick of bombs straddled the *Vampire*. Her captain, Commander Walsh, wrote:

> The blast effect when straddled blew everybody on the upper deck flat, some ratings finding themselves some yards from where they had been standing. The moral effect of the bombing was negligible until the straddle occurred on 11th July, after which there were signs of irritation at not being able to reply and a slight nervousness when the penetrating power of the splinters was observed.[9]

The old *Vampire* had not even the puny 3-inch HA gun fitted to some destroyers with which to answer these attacks. It would have been useless at the height from which the bombing was carried out but it was found that it gave the crews of destroyers so fitted some moral uplift. The extensive splinter damage sustained by *Vampire* in this attack holed the superstructure, bridge, boats and funnels, as well as punching five holes in her hull, two under water.

As the C-in-C was passing not too far away at the time of this attack, the *Vampire*'s main casualty, Commissioned Gunner (T) J.H. Endicott, RN, hit by splinters, was given a better chance with the more extensive facilities on board the destroyer *Mohawk* and he was transferred. *Janus* replaced *Vampire* on the convoy's screen. Unfortunately Endicott died of his wounds that night.

The bombing continued without pause. The *Warspite* was subjected to five attacks between 1248 and 1815, some 66 bombs being aimed at her without success. Captain A.W. Fitzroy, the Air Direction Officer, later recalled this period as consisting of 'Bombs, bombs and bombs!' Admiral Power recalls:

> This Italian high level pattern bombing was really very unpleasant and accurate. Ships were continually straddled by the patterns, which threw up huge dirty black columns of water twice as high as our masts. It was miraculous that no one was hit, apart from splinters. Often even big ships were totally obscured by splashes and one heaved a sigh of relief as they emerged unscathed. Our AA gunfire, though intense, achieved very little.
>
> After some experience of bombing I got tired of watching the bombs fall without being able to do anything about it. I caused myself to be armed with a rifle so that I could have a crack if anything came low enough, as a morale booster. On our way home this rifle was leaning against the (allegedly armoured) bridge screen beside me when a splinter came in and cut the rifle in half about the lower band. I sent it down to the Gunner with a note to say that I found it unsatisfactory and wanted another. Some days later I was presented by the Gunnery officer with the muzzle end suitably mounted and inscribed 'S.O.O. – his musket'. I still have it.[10]

One young cruiser officer summed up the difference in feelings towards shelling and bombing:

> It's difficult to remember with accuracy but I think that once battle was joined, near miss shells did not worry me, but we were not hit and had no casualties. In practices I used to get tensed up and flinch from the blast of the forward guns but in the real thing I did not even notice our own guns firing. High level bombing appeared to be very accurate and it always seemed likely that we should get hit but our only casualty was a signal rating who got some shrapnel in his neck. Normally it was almost over before one appreciated it had started and the first thing we heard was a loud hissing as the bomb hit the water, but we were straddled quite frequently and it was a relief when we approached Alexandria each time to know the bombing was over for a few days.[11]

Between 1112 and 1804 the 1st Battle Squadron was attacked twelve times, about 120 bombs being dropped and four attacks in all were carried out on convoy MS1, but with only the single fatality of Gunner Endicott, plus two others in the fleet. The night brought peace but the dawning of the 12th saw only the renewal of these attacks with the aircraft from the Aegean now being in range.

Early on the morning of the 12th the 7th Cruiser Squadron rejoined the C-in-C with his four ships, but only the *Liverpool* and *Sydney* stayed with the *Warspite*, the *Orion* and *Neptune* being sent to reinforce the AA strength of the fast convoy. The bombing was even more intense that day than the day before. The *Warspite*'s group was bombed seventeen times between 0850 and 1150; some 300 bombs, it was estimated, fell around her this day. The *Liverpool* had two killed and several wounded by a near-miss this morning but again no ships were hit. Admiral Cunningham was to write:

Particularly do I remember a most virulent attack on 12th July during our return passage to Alexandria when twenty-four heavy bombs fell along the port side of the ship simultaneously, with another dozen on our starboard bow, all within two hundred yards, but slightly out of line. Other ships had much the same sort of experience.[12]

Rear Admiral Pridham-Wippell's main force had the same treatment in rather smaller doses. Some three attacks developed between 1110 and 1804. Twenty-five bombs were dropped on the battleships and the aircraft carrier, with some very near misses, but, once again, no direct hits were registered. The 1st Battle Squadron probably owed much of its immunity to the gallant work of the two obsolete Gladiators embarked which provided a thin screen of fighter cover. As *Eagle* did not usually carry fighters in her complement of seventeen planes the three biplanes had to be ranged on deck to one side during normal flying operations by the Swordfish, nor were there any normal fighter pilots aboard, but two of the Swordfish pilots volunteered to 'have a go' having previously flown the type and they performed wonders.

The Commander (Flying), Charles L. Keighly-Peach took off and made an attack but was beaten off, receiving a bullet wound in his thigh. Nothing daunted he took off again in subsequent attacks and between them the Gladiators claimed to have shot down two or three of their tormentors.

In another effort to avoid the worst effects of this bombing the fleet steered towards the Egyptian coast and some slight relief was afforded by the arrival overhead, in the closing stages of their passage, of a few Blenheim fighters of 252 Wing, RAF, Middle East which arrived late on the 12th. No further bombing attacks developed after that time. It was noted that the aircraft shadowing the fleet directed the attacking squadrons to the target by transmitting 'longs' by W/T at intervals. In future operations this knowledge was put to good use by Alexandria W/T station which signalled the fleet which wave-length was being used for this purpose, enabling the fleet to sometimes jam these long enough to throw the Italian aircraft off course.

For the final stages of the journey to Alexandria further cover for the slow convoy was provided by the 3rd Cruiser Squadron, *Caledon* and *Capetown*, which rendezvoused with it at 1000 on the 13th in position 33°50' N, 23°00' E. And on the arrival of the *Warspite* and her group at Alexandria at 0600 on the same day, the battleship *Ramillies*, screened by the destroyers *Diamond*, *Havock*, *Imperial* and *Vendetta* sailed to give the same cover to the slow convoy. The final bombing attacks of the operation took place against Pridham-Wippell's ships between 1056 and 1623, with no more success than previously. These ships finally entered Alexandria harbour early on the 14th, and the *Ramillies*, 3rd Cruiser Squadron and the slow convoy arrived on the 15th at 0900, thus bringing to a satisfactory conclusion MA5.

CHAPTER SEVEN

Aftermath

We have seen how the claims by the Italian airmen had influenced Mussolini into thinking a smashing blow had been dealt to the Royal Navy over this four day period and the subsequent radio bulletins broadcast reflected that completely false impression in the week which followed.

One post-war Italian historian has summarised the operation as follows:

> An objective analysis of the engagement must reach the conclusion that the results were about equal. No ship was sunk; the four hits suffered by the Italian ships had no serious consequences, and the same was true with regard to the damage suffered by the *Neptune* and the *Warspite* [sic]. Both parties succeeded in the primary purpose for which they had taken to sea; that is, to get their respective convoys through to their destinations. Each failed to prevent the operations of the other because neither understood the other's purposes soon enough. It must be remembered, however, that the British, having departed on the evening of 8th July on a decisive offensive action to destroy the Italian Fleet, failed totally to complete this mission; yet the situation was most favourable to them and the plans had been announced numerous times by Admiral Cunningham.[1]

A less objective statement has seldom been written, although it follows the author's general tone throughout his book. How anyone can state that an Italian fleet, who had already rid itself of the complications of its convoys, was within a few hours' steaming of its main bases and had the whole of the Italian Air Force on hand had not a 'more favourable' position than Cunningham's slower and smaller assembly with the convoy still under its wing and over a thousand miles from its own base is almost beyond comprehension.

As we have seen from Ciano's reflections, Italian claims were doubted even at the time. The Italian leader's need to present his people with news of a great naval victory at this time was great, both to offset the German dominance in military matters and to paper over the inactivity of his army in Libya. Whether or not the Duce really believed the battle had been a victory or not he had no choice but to pretend that it was. Again, as Ciano noted, his German allies were *not* impressed:

> ... he finds solace in instructing the press to play up the naval battle of a
> week ago. But we have received information, even from German sources,
> that the damage inflicted on the British Navy is about nil. The Italian
> Navy is also of this opinion, while the Italian Air Force tends to
> exaggerate. I only hope that the version given by the Air Force is true,
> otherwise it will cost us dignity and prestige even with the Germans.[2]

It was to cost the Italians just that, and, more important, at Calabria they took a knock to their morale from which they were never to recover. As one German naval historian was later to observe:

> The main features of the Punta Stilo action were:
> (1) Unsatisfactory results by Italian aircraft, which only used high-level
>   bombing.
> (2) Lack of practice in co-operation between the Italian Navy and Air
>   Force.
> (3) Italian failure to pursue, or to use their light forces in night attacks.
> (4) Greater confidence in the British Fleet, and less confidence among
>   the Italians.[3]

It was this latter point which was most apparent on the British side.

Already they were far from impressed with the Italians as fighting men, the abrupt retreat by Campioni after just one shell hit, confirmed among the men of Cunningham's fleet, from the C-in-C himself to the lower deck, that they were the masters of the enemy. Cunningham himself was to conclude in his report on the operation that:

> The meagre material results derived from this brief meeting with the
> Italian fleet were naturally very disappointing to me and all under my
> command, but the action was not without value. It must have shown the
> Italians that their air force and submarines cannot stop our fleet
> penetrating into the central Mediterranean and that only their main fleet
> can seriously interfere with our operating there. It established, I think,
> a certain degree of moral ascendency, since although superior in
> battleships, our fleet was heavily outnumbered in cruisers and
> destroyers, and the Italians had strong shore-based air forces within easy
> range, compared to our few carrier-borne aircraft.

On our side the action has shown those without previous war experience how difficult it is to hit with the gun at long range, and therefore the necessity of closing in, when this can be done, in order to get decisive results. [Tovey was never to forget this particular lesson, when, as C-in-C, Home Fleet, the *King George V* and *Rodney* had cornered the *Bismarck* and were pounding her to oblivion, he is reported to have told his captains, 'Get closer – I can't see enough hits!'] It showed that high level bombing, even on the heavy and accurate scale experienced during these operations, yields few hits and that it is more alarming than dangerous.

Finally, these operations and the action off Calabria produced throughout the fleet a determination to overcome the air menace and not to let it interfere with our freedom of manoeuvre and hence our control of the Mediterranean.[4]

This renewed optimism had its counterpart in Whitehall where the progress of the operation had been watched closely and with some anxiety due to the alarming effect the Luftwaffe dive-bombers had had earlier on the Norwegian Campaign and at Dunkirk. The fact that the Regia Aeronautica, so long much more feared by the pre-war politicians than by the sailors, was in fact another example of Mussolini's huff-and-puff, and that his Navy had run away (the true reasons for this not being known at that time of course) gave them renewed confidence that the Eastern Mediterranean might, after all, be held, despite the misgivings of the air marshals. The First Sea Lord, Sir Dudley Pound wrote to the Premier, Winston Churchill, that:

We have gained experience of the air conditions in the Western Mediterranean, and as soon as the present operation on which the Eastern Fleet [*sic*] is employed is completed we shall know pretty well what we are faced with in the Eastern Mediterranean. There is no doubt that both Force H and the Eastern Mediterranean Fleet work under a grave disadvantage, inasmuch as it is not possible to give them fighter protection as we do in the North Sea when ships are in the bombing area.[5]

On the matériel side the British had also absorbed some hard lessons. When Pound re-iterated London's determination to maintain a strong fleet in the Eastern basin he asked Cunningham what he considered his outstanding needs, and ABC had no hesitation in spelling them out to him.

Admiral Power recalls that:

> In our discussions after this trip we felt that it was urgent that we should
> have another battleship whose guns could outrange or at least equal the
> Italians as *Warspite* was the only one we had. We also felt that we had
> found by experience that we could never move without being sighted and
> severely bombed. We had been lucky so far but casualties were inevitable
> if it went on, and we could not afford many.[6]

Cunningham's reply to Pound stressed this point; 'I must have one
more ship that can shoot at good range', he said and with regard to
his heavily outnumbered and outranged light cruisers he considered
they required the stiffening of a couple of 8-inch cruisers, he would,
he said, 'dearly like the *York* and *Exeter*',[7] which were the most
modern of the 8-inch cruisers with speeds of 32 knots. The *Eagle* had
done wonders with what she had, but she was painfully slow and her
aircraft complement was meagre while her deck protection was
pathetic against bombing. An armoured deck carrier with a good
complement of the latest Fleet fighters, the Fulmar, would,
Cunningham felt, make all the difference, along with a couple of AA
cruisers to give the convoys some protection also.

To these requests Pound acted with alacrity, and, considering the
desperate plight we found ourselves in at home with the threat of
invasion imminent, it must be said, generously. Within a short time
Cunningham received all in the way of naval reinforcements he
asked for, or that could be spared. The modernised battleship
Valiant, along with her older sister *Barham*, were sent out to him
replacing the *Royal Sovereign* and *Ramillies* which were intially
assigned to Force H, and the *Malaya* which was in need of a refit.
The modernised *Queen Elizabeth* was to join his flag as soon as
possible. The latter, like the *Valiant*, had been rebuilt to a far greater
degree than *Warspite*, with a powerful battery of the latest AA guns,
increased elevation for her main guns and radar. The *Illustrious* was
also sent out and the anti-aircraft cruisers *Calcutta* and *Coventry*. He
also got the two 8-inch cruisers he had requested: *York*, and, because
the *Exeter* was still repairing action damage from the River Plate
battle, the *Kent*. Unfortunately the latter arrived with chronic
condensor trouble and had to be replaced by the *Berwick* later. A few
modern destroyers of the G and H classes were also transferred to his
command from Gibraltar to help build his slender destroyer
strength.

So reinforcements and renewed confidence were the main result
on the British side as a result of the action off Calabria. For the
Italians their first brush with the Royal Navy seemed to have only

increased their caution. Certainly the Regia Aeronautica was never again to attack in such overwhelming strength and power as they did between 8th and 12th July. Perhaps their complete lack of achievement disheartened them but future encounters with that force were only in dribs and drabs by comparison. The high-level bomber as a ship-buster had obviously failed and henceforth the Italian air force was to concentrate its efforts more and more on the torpedo bomber; conversion of S79s aircraft for this role had already begun and within a short while they were to achieve far more important results with this weapon against Cunningham's fleet than by any other. Their attempts to imitate the Germans' success with dive-bombers turned out to be a fiasco; the one squadron of home-built aircraft of these types failed to even get into the action. The Italians turned to their allies for the remedy and began forming squadrons with purchased Ju 87 Stukas, but it was the arrival of the real thing in the hands of the trained dive bomber pilots of the Luftwaffe that were finally to turn the scales in the air-sea war in the Mediterranean in the following January.

Their large submarine arm was also relatively impotent. Their two early victories with this arm, the sinking of the light cruiser *Calypso* and the destroyer *Escort* within the first month of hostilities, were never subsequently built on and again it required the introduction of German submarines into the Mediterranean to redress the balance.

On the results of their surface ships' performances they could, perhaps, have been said to have been unlucky.

> Moreover their shooting was also pretty accurate. They got early straddles and the spread of their salvos was not excessive, again it was luck that our ships fitted the gaps. My only criticism was the lack of enterprise of their destroyers which could have made dangerous attacks out of their smoke screen and didn't. We were left with a feeling that they were really aghast at their temerity in challenging us at all.[8]

This viewpoint was never to change and the battle (named the Action off Calabria by the British and the Battle of Punto Stilo by the Italians) is important in the history of the Mediterranean warfare story for that reason if no other.

II

The Passage of Force 'Y'
11th September 1940

THE STRANGE SILENCE

CHAPTER EIGHT

A Loss of Confidence

It was soon after the outbreak of World War II that Admiral of the Fleet Sir Dudley Pound, First Sea Lord and Chief of Naval Staff, had approved the appointment of Vice Admiral Sir Dudley North to succeed Rear-Admiral Norman A. Wodehouse CB as Flag Officer Commanding, North Atlantic from 1st November 1939. North sailed from England aboard the steamer *Narkunda* on the 10th of that month and duly took over his new appointment on the 17th. There was nothing remarkable in that appointment, and nor was FOCNA, (or ACNA, Admiral Commanding North Atlantic Station), one of the 'top operational commands in the Royal Navy' as has been claimed.[1] The appointment of senior admirals for such posts was not considered as crucial as those selections for front line duties on the outbreak of the war, and in November 1939 Gibraltar was very much a backwater. Nor was there any reasonable likelihood of its being anything else in a war in which Britain and France were combined against Germany. Even should Italy sooner or later throw in her lot with her Axis partner, the whole of the Western Mediterranean lay between Gibraltar and the enemy, and astride that route lay the bulk of the French Navy with bases at Toulon in southern France and Mers-el-Kebir and Bizerta in its North African colonies to outflank it.[2]

Dudley North's career up to that time had been one of steady, if undistinguished, progress up the ladder rung-by-rung, with no major upsets to mark him as anything other than a career officer. He was well liked generally in the Service but not considered of outstanding ability and, had the war not intervened, would have gone on to the retired list in the normal course of events within a few years; he was fifty-seven. After promotion to captain in 1919 he had served twice as flag-captain, in the Atlantic and Reserve Fleets, as Director of Operations at the Admiralty and as Chief-of-Staff to Admiral Sir John Kelly with the Home Fleet. Although it is true, as one historian has noted, Sir John was not one who suffered 'fools or incompetents gladly',[3] there is nothing to indicate that North was destined to become an outstandingly successful commander, although he did not put a foot wrong in the appointments he held. It was while he was serving as senior equerry to HRH Prince of Wales aboard the battle-cruisers *Renown* and *Repulse* during the world tours of the 1920s that he had first made connections with Royalty that were to give him the (perhaps unfortunate and unjust) reputation of the 'epitome of the courtier sailor'. Further associations in this direction were cemented on his appointment as Rear-Admiral Commanding HM Yachts between 1934 and 1939. Such an appointment was indeed at that period 'a decidedly inactive command',[4] and such a long period away from the centre of active naval affairs would certainly preclude any hopes of a sea-going command in 1939; the suggestion that he was destined for the highest rank in the Service is nonsense.[5]

Sir Dudley Pound knew Sir Dudley North well and the two men were so much opposites in their attitudes and methods that it is little wonder that their relationship was never more than one of friendly formality. Nonetheless it is doubted whether Pound would ever had considered North suitable for any other appointment than the one he received. Indeed a sailor with the charm and popularity of North, which was combined with an average ability to organise routine administration quite satisfactorily, would appear to have been both a fair and most suitable appointment as things stood in the late autumn of 1939. North indeed was quite delighted with his appointment and the suggestion that Pound always harboured some deep grudge against North is surely shown to be quite unfounded by this very selection.

It must have been with some satisfaction therefore that Pound had found a relatively undemanding post for North where his particular qualities could find a most useful purpose and his limitations should not be unduly put to the test. Pound, the 'supreme centraliser',[6] had more pressing matters on his mind as the war got underway, not the least being the return of Winston Spencer Churchill as First Lord of the Admiralty. Indeed relations between Pound and Churchill were initially at far greater strain than those between Pound and North. Churchill was at first not at all taken by the First Sea Lord and he was certainly not Churchill's own choice, as has been alleged. The fact that Pound was appointed as First Sea Lord some three months *before* Churchill's own return to the Admiralty surely invalidates this common assertion.

Fortunately for the future direction of the naval war, after some preliminary skirmishing, the two men developed a working relationship with each other based on mutual respect, and, in Churchill's case it seems, some genuine affection. Another allegation with regard to this working relationship is that Churchill took to Pound because he was able to mould the Admiral to his will. It is certain that Churchill's earlier experience as First Sea Lord during World War I, and in particular his traumatic encounters with Admiral Sir John Fisher, made him wary in his approaches to any First Sea Lord.[7] However Pound was of a temperament that avoided direct clash of wills but, nonetheless, was far more effective in putting a brake on Churchill's more wilder and outrageous schemes.

As First Lord Churchill at once showed a far-from-normal interest in the day-to-day running of events at the Admiralty and, as always, showed an aptitude for introducing all manner of ideas for 'offensively minded' operations, the majority of which were far beyond the bounds of the existing Naval resources to implement at that time. It required no little tact to deflate these often completely unrealistic notions, and it also required much patience to handle such a human dynamo. These qualities Pound possessed in abundance and it is thanks to him that such suicidal measures as Operation Catherine were talked quietly into well-deserved obscurity. Men of action like Chatfield or Cunningham might well have exploded in the face of such notions, in which case they would have been replaced, more likely than not by far lesser men. Pound had the ability to ride out most of the Churchill-originated storms, although from time to time even he was worn down and his better judgement finally overruled, as with the *Prince of Wales* and *Repulse* disaster.

The fact that the Chiefs-of-Staffs, Pound, General Sir John Dill (Chief of the Imperial General Staff) and Air Chief Marshal Sir Cyril Newall (Chief of the Air Staff), tried to make realistic assessments of situations which ran counter to Churchill's desire for action, any action, did not make their running of the existing war easier, since considerable time and effort had to be put into presenting detailed cases against. Because of this Churchill, when he later became Premier and Minister of Defence, dubbed the Joint Planners 'Masters of Negation'. It cannot have helped those with longer memories than the average politician that this same Premier who was urging them to make bricks without straw, had been the minister largely responsible for their glaring deficiencies in matériel when, as Chancellor of the Exchequer in 1924, he introduced the pernicious 'Ten Year Rule'.[8]

One final facet that should be mentioned with regard to the relationship between the First Sea Lord and Churchill, and one that was seen to be of some relevance to the story as it developed, is the contentious issue of the state of Pound's health at this time and later. There is little doubt that Pound was not one hundred per cent physically fit for he suffered from osteo-arthritis of the left hip. Nor did the Premier's unusual hours help matters, resulting as they did in lack of sleep for all his aides and staff. The issue hotly debated is the degree to which any illness affected his judgements and his ability to carry them out in a satisfactory manner. Here there are two very extreme schools of thought. On the one hand, it is said that Pound showed no signs of physical deterioration before his stroke in 1943 and that his habit of nodding off, or at least appearing to slumber during important meetings, was nothing new, although it might appear to be more than it was to those who did not know him well. Thus Captain Litchfield was to write that:

> Pound's momentary catnaps when he was tired and his habit of closing his eyes when in thought were well known more than twenty years before his death, and his enjoyment of a hard day's shooting whenever the opportunity offered during the war, as well as his continued relaxation in driving himself in his fast car, do not support the view that he was a 'sick, worn-out figure'.[9]

On the other hand Captain Roskill's recent revelations would appear to throw strong evidence that he was far from enjoying good health at this period.[10] In fairness to Pound the fact that when he did suffer his stroke he very quickly confided the fact to Churchill and tendered his immediate resignation would seem to indicate to this author that such a man would place his duty to his country and the Navy first and foremost, and would hardly cling to office for the sake of it if he genuinely felt the job was beyond his capacity.

One other figure will loom large in the story, and that is Churchill's successor as First Lord of the Admiralty when he himself became Premier. This was Albert Victor Alexander, one-time First Lord in an earlier administration (1929-31 under Ramsay MacDonald). He had retained his interest in naval matters as chief opposition spokesman in the House but was more generally known for his work with the Co-operative movement. Called 'The Wooden Battleship', he appears to have been very much a middle man, somewhat overawed by Churchill and always deferring in respect of professional advice from his admirals and advisers. He shared

Pound's stamina, which was just as well, as he also shared the First Sea Lord's reputation for fairness and impartiality, that is, until the time of Admiral North's replacement.

Let us now examine North's new command as it existed in the early part of his tenure. The great fortress of the Rock of Gibraltar had been British since its seizure by Admiral Sir George Rooke in 1704, and due to its vital position in guarding and dominating the narrow western gate to the Mediterranean Sea it had been fought for and held against constant diplomatic pressure ever since. Since Victorian times it had not featured to a great extent in actual warfare but its strategic location was always that it was kept up.

During the inter-war years the great harbour was frequently used as the meeting place for both the Home and Mediterranean Fleets, emphasising the fact that it could cover both the eastern Atlantic and the western basin of the Mediterranean and was an important staging post and fuelling depot for the rapid interchange of fleets between both stations.

On the outbreak of war the North Atlantic Station seemed a relatively minor one. The bulk of the Royal Navy was concentrated in Home Waters to meet the German threat, while the main units of the Mediterranean Fleet proper, under Admiral Andrew Cunningham, had forsaken the Fleet's traditional base of Malta and lay at Alexandria awaiting Italy's decision whether to join the war or not. When, after a few weeks, it became apparent that Mussolini was standing on the sidelines despite his pre-war boasting, the bulk of the Mediterranean Fleet was gradually withdrawn to bolster the more important commands, and it was not until the situation in the Mediterranean again became menacing in May 1940 that it was again built up. North's command, however, being smaller, was not so affected and remained fairly constant throughout the 'Phoney War' period. Here it should be noted that ACNAS was subordinate to Admiral Cunningham in the Eastern Basin in the overall scheme of things.

North himself moved into the official residence, 'The Mount' on the western slope of the Rock. He ran his command, which included the post of Admiral Superintendent of the Dockyard, from the office block known as 'The Tower' on the water's edge of the dockyard itself. Here was located his staff with direct lines by phone to all the main defence stations on the Rock itself. It could also be connected to the flagships of seagoing commands while they were in harbour, thus giving North and his Chief of Staff, Captain R.G. Duke, immediate access in times of emergency or crisis with every major commander on the Rock.

North of course worked hand-in-hand with the Rock's Governor, General Sir Clive Liddell. He was directly responsible to the War Office in London and had under his command the fortress batteries, the shore defences and AA defences as well as the routine administration of the colony. General Liddell, a distinguished and highly respected and well-liked officer, worked closely with Dudley North, and both men responded to each other and built up an efficient and amicable partnership which worked without any apparent hitches.

When North first assumed his command, the naval forces at his disposal consisted of the depot ship *Cormorant*, the official 'flagship' of the command, and the nine destroyers of the 13th Destroyer Flotilla. This was the local defence flotilla whose duties included local convoy work out in the Atlantic and patrol work to cover the Straits of Gibraltar. Captain (D) 13th Flotilla was Captain Francis De Winton in the flotilla leader *Keppel*, and his command consisted of the 25th Division, *Velox*, *Vidette*, *Vortigern* and *Watchman*, and the 26th Division, *Active*, *Douglas*, *Wishart* and *Wrestler*. Most of these ships were old vessels of the 'V' and 'W' classes built between 1917 and 1918 and hastily re-commissioned on outbreak of war. Although old they were quite capable of the duties required of them, their main role being anti-submarine patrol and blockade enforcing. The two flotilla leaders *Keppel* and *Douglas* (the latter being used as a 'private' ship), and the *Wishart*, were marginally newer, being completed in the early 1920s, while the one relatively modern ship, *Active*, had been in reserve in the Mediterranean before the war and was activated in the flotilla as she was on hand. One other old destroyer, the *Wryneck*, was present at this time, but she was not part of North's command and was undergoing conversion to an escort destroyer in the Gibraltar dockyard. The *Wrestler* was also in dock, having ASDIC (anti-submarine acoustic detection device) fitted, as were the minesweeper *Gossamer* and the tug *St Omar*.[11]

Limited as the functions of the North Atlantic Station were at this time this force was obviously quite inadequate and plans were in hand to build it up in strength as ships became available.

The shore defences of the Rock on outbreak of war consisted of No 3 Coast Regiment, RA commanded by Lieutenant-Colonel J.R. Laurie, and comprised the 4th Heavy Battery, RA, commanded by Major H.G. Wainwright, the 26th Heavy Battery, RA, commanded by Major G.R. Kimmitt, and the 27th Heavy Battery (Lloyds Company) RA, commanded by Major A.J. Caulfield. Its equipment strength on the outbreak of war totalled seven 9.2-inch guns, six 6-inch guns and six 6-pdr guns, but here again plans were in hand to strengthen and modernise these equipments.[12]

As to air strength there was, in truth, little. So short were the home defences and those units allocated to France with the BEF that nothing could be spared for such a remote spot as Gibraltar in November 1939. For general reconnaissance duties part of No 202 Squadron, with its pre-war headquarters at Malta, was based at Gibraltar from 1938 on and was equipped with eleven Saro London flying boats which operated from their base at Gun Port Wharf under Squadron Leader T.Q. Horner from August 1940. Also on hand for target towing and other diverse duties, such as short-range reconnaissance over the Straits, were three Fairey Swordfish floatplanes of No 3 Anti-Aircraft Co-Operation Unit.

Group Captain T.Q. Horner, the unit's CO, described the RAF position as follows:

No 3 AACU operated three Swordfish floatplanes from Gunport Wharf, where there was a crane big enough to lift the aircraft into and out of the water. The main object of the unit was anti-aircraft co-operation with the Army land-based AA batteries. When the need arose, we used them for short-range patrols.

No 202 Squadron operated London flying-boats – varying in number from six to eleven – from No 20 shed on the destroyer pens at the north end of the harbour. Land was reclaimed in the vicinity, on which a slipway and hangar and camp were built for us. However, at the material time, No 20 shed had just changed its role from coal shed to Squadron Headquarters Offices!!! – conditions were rugged. There was no operational landing strip at Gibraltar at this time – this came later.[13]

This was the modest force under North's immediate jurisdiction and it is little wonder that Admiral Cunningham, writing to welcome North to his wartime command, commented that they were expected to work miracles and of '... making bricks without straw, which out here we are all engaged in'. He added that he was worried lest enemy submarines slipped into the Mediterranean in search of easy pickings while they were still not fully organised. It was one of the main duties of North's nine destroyers to prevent this of course.

Cunningham went on: 'I tried to ease the strain there by making the Admiralty form the east-bound convoys at home and the west-bound at Port Said and not re-form them at Gibraltar ...' He also suggested an early convention to sort naval area command matters out between himself, North and the French Admiral (Sud), Admiral Jean Estéva, at Toulon.[14]

Obviously close co-operation with the powerful French forces was essential, but pre-war planning had not progressed very much in resolving this problem, other than in general terms,[15] whereby the western basin should be primarily a French responsibility Cunningham's fleet would take care of the eastern.[16]

At local level the short endurance of North's old destroyers led to requests that the French might help out during the period of shortages of suitable escorts by taking over some of the convoy work between Gibraltar and the UK. This was agreed during a meeting of Chiefs of Staff at Marceau, but was hardly an unqualified success. Although Admiral Estéva visited North at the Rock and stayed overnight as his guest to work out the details the French ships only participated in one complete operation before withdrawing from the scheme on the grounds their ships needed refitting,[17] so once again North's slender resources had to take over in assisting with this chore. All he could do was to make representations to London asking for more destroyers and more modern ships with greater endurance. But as this was a request which was being repeated by almost every naval C-in-C around the world there was little chance of his demands being met at once.

This brief flirtation probably only confirmed the First Sea Lord's pre-war viewpoint on the worth of the French Navy as an ally,[18] but it did give Dudley North the opportunity of working with, and getting to know, his French comrades-in-arms at close range. Again North's own natural charm and personality seem to have won respect from those Frenchmen he came in contact with, and, although he spoke French indifferently (he was fluent in German), a friendly relationship was the result, perhaps the only result, of this experiment. That is not to say necessarily that North became a fervent admirer of the French and their ways. Because he could work with them, and, to a point, understand their views it was later to be alleged that his objective judgement was warped in their favour. Whereas this seems to have been the case with Captain Holland,[19] it is by no means certain that North was so affected. He was however a kindly and thoughtful person, perhaps more ready to see the other point of view than normal, and this was to add to his undoing.

With regard to the day-to-day workings of the base there seems to be no trace of discord among the officers who served under him at this time and his work in this regard was evidently satisfactory to Their Lordships, who promoted him to full Admiral on 8th May 1940. The slow but steady build up of forces at the Rock had continued up to this time. Around Christmas 1939, Captain De Winton was ordered to establish himself ashore to facilitate liaison, embarking in *Keppel* only for important operations, like Mers-el-Kebir. This helped the control of his widely scattered units and this arrangement worked well.[20] One outsider who visited Gibraltar at this period however, was not altogether impressed with the way the base was run compared with those closer to the front line.

> ... my ship called at Gib in June 1940 and I formed the impression that in general terms the command set up both operational and admin. was a bit sleepy and there was a general air of some discontent, albeit in a mild way. Or to put it another way, I didn't feel that the place was really alert.[21]

Perhaps it was a natural reaction in those who had spent the first nine months far from the main action and who could therefore not really be expected to be as much on their toes as others under direct fire. Nonetheless there were not, at this stage, many hints that the Admiralty was in fact dissatisfied with the manner in which North was running things at Gibraltar.

By May 1940 the improvements were nearing completion. The 13th Flotilla still consisted of the same ships as on outbreak of war, and with losses being sustained off Norway there was still no immediate likelihood of their being replaced by modern ships, but North's strength in lesser vessels had been steadily supplemented and he now had the 7th Anti-Submarine Group, (four trawlers fitted with ASDIC), four minesweeping trawlers, five armed boarding vessels, four Western Patrol trawlers and five tugs to help in local patrols.[22]

Ashore improvements to the Coastal Defence Batteries had continued. The original heavy guns, the Mk X 9.2-inch gun on Mk V mountings had been installed in 1935-36. These weapons had a maximum range of 29,600 yards.[23] Further light weapons were being mounted throughout this period as the battery records show and

most of these were operational by September.[24] 4th Heavy Battery
completed a new work named Levant in May, and another armed
with 4-inch guns, Martin, at the same time. The Upper Battery and
Breackneck batteries were fully manned at all times, Buffadero at
night only. 26th Heavy Battery had full complements at its lighter
weapons mounted at North Mole, Detached Mole and South Mole
with the battery HQ established afloat in the armed yacht *Lorna* in
the harbour. 4th Heavy Battery had its 6-inch guns established at
Genista, Devil's Gap, with 9.2s at Spur, O'Hara and Lord Airey.
Another old 9.2-inch was mounted at the centre top of the Rock
facing north, but could traverse east or west. It dated back to 1901
and was never fired. It was named Rock Gun and could, had it have
been necessary, have engaged targets on the Spanish mainland.
Others were put into place at this time as the commander of 4th
Heavy Battery recalls:

> I emplaced two old World War I 4-inch guns at Mediterranean Road to
> engage the approach from Spain on the east and two World War I 9.2-
> inch howitzers to fire north right over the Rock from Windmill Hill
> Flats.[25]

It was the modernised 9.2s of 4th Heavy Battery that covered the
Straits that are the most relevant to this story however.

> Maximum range was 29,600 yards and could reach Ceuta, North Africa,
> across the Straits at 25,500 yards, the height of these guns varied but
> averaged about 1,200 feet against the height of the Rock, 1,300 feet plus.
> Both AP and HE shell were provided.

Thus fully modernised and fully registered no part of the Strait of
Gibraltar was uncovered by these guns which had a rate of fire of two
to three rounds per minute with a well-trained gun crew handling
and firing a standard 380 lb HE shell. All these mountings were of
the barbette type, with the gun emplaced in a sunken pit so that the
muzzle just cleared the parapet. The revolving working steel
platform around the gun itself formed a protective cover for the pit
with the hydraulic machinery safe below it. As such they were
practically invulnerable to fire from afloat mounted high up as they
were, although they were wide open to sustained bombing attack.[26]
    Although fully designed specifically for defence against
battleships, for which even the modern 35,000 tonners of the 1930s
were considered fair game, very little actual practice against afloat

targets had been undertaken since the outbreak of the war, and none at all against high speed warships.[27] They were, in the main, *defensive* weapons in nature, and not *offensive*, but they most certainly effectively covered the Straits of Gibraltar completely at this point. Furthermore although the 9.2-inch gun, as a mark of naval gun, was ancient, those mounted at the Rock just three or four years before the war were fully modernised versions, with the latest in both fire-control and other equipment, and considered suitable for dealing with the most modern battleships then under construction.[28]

Up to May and the time of his promotion therefore, Admiral North had some reason to feel that his command was steadily improving in strength and that the measures he and the Governor had applied met with the approval of the authorities at home. No serious test had yet been made but the running of the base was proceeding normally. His confidence was reinforced by messages from London of an encouraging nature; thus early in 1940 he received from Admiral Pound the following signal:

> From what I hear, you have undoubtedly made great improvements at Gibraltar and things are running much more smoothly.[29]

Then the roof started to fall in.

If Admiral North was working under considerable pressure at Gibraltar with inadequate resources, the situation back home at the Admiralty was even more complex. Although of course North had only a small staff to help him cope, the general lack of sufficient resources was a world-wide problem for the Navy, and, as the war began to hot up, the unpreparedness of the nation for total war was making itself more and more manifest. It was on the broad shoulders of Admiral Pound that the bulk of these problems fell, more so, because it was in his nature to try and carry more than his share of the workload, frequently unnecessarily so, many people feel, while trying to steer the erratic First Lord away from his quainter ideas of naval strategy.

Captain S.W. Roskill, our most distinguished living naval historian, has, from close personal knowledge, painted a most moving picture of Admiral Pound at this period from which the following extracts are relevant to our story:

> Although troubles and difficulties were pouring in on him, and the Navy suffered not a few unpleasant reverses at that time, his equanimity

remained undisturbed, he never seemed pressed for time, and he never cut short what one had to tell him, even if it was of secondary importance. His questions were always shrewd and very much to the point, and he always had to grasp every detail of the subject under discussion.

Also worthy of note was his absolute impartiality, an important point in view of future wild accusations.

> ... he was incapable of favouritism, and even when things had gone wrong for officers who were very close to him he scorned to intervene on their behalf, insisting (as they themselves would surely in any case have wished), that their actions *should be judged by the due process of service law and custom.**

As Roskill also stated: '... the Navy could not have found a better man to fill the office of First Sea Lord.'[30]

The 'troubles and difficulties' had begun with the pointless loss of the battleship *Royal Oak*, the carrier *Courageous*, the German mining and submarine campaigns and the inability of the Home Fleet to intercept German heavy ships on their various sorties. With the Norwegian Campaign the difficulties multiplied rapidly and the vulnerability of warships to dive bombing began to manifest itself, for pre-war policies had left the Navy with both useless anti-aircraft weapons and insufficient of them. The Admiralty, and in particular Pound, therefore, were at full stretch from early April onwards and it perhaps understandable if the smaller and less urgent needs and requirements put forward by Admiral North should more and more meet with less sympathy and more irritation as the overall situation deteriorated rapidly. In May came the German *Blitzkrieg*, the collapse of the Allied land forces and with them the disintegration of the whole Allied War Plan. With the evacuation of the BEF from Dunkirk and the Continent, the surrender of the Belgium and French armies in the field and the Armistice concluded unilaterally with the Axis powers by France, the British nation found itself in a most perilous situation. We were quite literally fighting for our very lives and the threat of imminent invasion was a most immediate consideration, and one which, once the Royal Navy and RAF had been beaten down, the nation could have done little to prevent.

Such was the ghastly situation the Admiralty found itself in in

---

* My italics

June 1940, a situation almost unthinkable a month before. Losses in warships, and especially in that most needed of vessels, the destroyer, were alarmingly high and growing now that the Channel was the front line, and yet somehow enough had to be found to smash any invasion attempt. The air war over Britian, a softening up as a prelude to invasion, was getting well under way but would not be won until September; even then it would still be touch and go. With the loss of a major Allied fleet came the double blow of the addition of an extra enemy to contend with, as Italy finally took the plunge. What precious few ships that could be spared therefore had to go to Cunningham again, while in the western basin a detached force was hastily assembled and sent out to work from Gibraltar under a retired naval officer, Vice-Admiral Sir James Somerville, Force H. It was originally sent out for a specific purpose, to replace the French Fleet based at Mers-el-Kebir near Oran, in case of failure to reach a satisfactory agreement on their deployment away from German control.

The relationship between Admiral Sir Dudley North and Vice-Admiral Sir James Somerville, both officially and on a personal level, is of vital import to our story.

The original Admiralty Message (A.M.) setting up Force H read as follows:

From Admiralty.
1. A detached squadron known as Force H under the command of Vice-Admiral Sir James Somerville has been constituted as follows:
   HM ships – *Ark Royal, Hood, Resolution, Valiant, Arethusa, Faulknor, Foxhound, Fearless, Escapade, Forester, Foresight, Escort.*
2. The following ships will join Force H when they enter the limits of the North Atlantic:
   HM ships – *Nelson, Enterprise, Delhi, Fame, Fury.*
   HMC ships – *St Laurent, Skeena.*
3. Force H will for the present be based at Gibraltar.
4. Subject to any instructions which may be given by the Admiralty the tasks of Force H will be –
   (a) To prevent units of the Italian Fleet from breaking out of the Mediterranean.
   (b) To carry out offensive operations against the Italian Fleet and Italian coasts.[31]

It will be noted that the wording reads 'detached' squadron and not 'independent'. Admiral North was superior in rank to Vice-Admiral Somerville and many such 'detached' forces had been set up before this time, in particular during the hunt for the pocket battleships in 1939. On the other hand it can reasonably be argued that these directives left a certain ambiguity in the chain of command from which all else followed. It has been suggested that even had Admiral North sought further clarification of this point the Admiralty would have had extreme difficulty in providing him with a clear answer themselves. Indeed when it later came to this and a clearer definition was considered essential, it took Their Lordships three months to issue modifications, and these in themselves would not necessarily have changed North's actions had they been in force at this time. As Captain Roskill stated: 'The truth is that the chain of command was ill-defined and that such vagueness, besides being operationally dangerous, placed the responsible officers in an unfair position.'[32]

Vice-Admiral Somerville had an interview with Pound on the afternoon of 27th June in which his new command was discussed as well as its initial task, which had nothing to do with the Italian Navy at all. Somerville was told that his first job would be to ensure that the French warships at Mers-el-Kebir were put out of reach of the Axis, by one means or another, including force.

As his biographer stated later, the thought of the possibility of having to fire upon his recent allies, should negotiations fail, was as 'abhorrent to Somerville as to everyone else concerned',[33] but the new First Lord of the Admiralty, Alexander, who was also present at this meeting, later recalled that Somerville fully understood his duty and was prepared, then, to carry out his orders if needs be.

> He said to me in my room at the Admiralty: 'I quite recognise that, however repugnant this job may seem, the Government know it has got to be done, in the interests of the safety of the nation'.[34]

Alexander later claimed that this resolution to do his duty changed after he arrived at Gibraltar and conferred with Admiral North. Certainly no British naval officer treated the decision at Mers-el-Kebir and elsewhere with anything other than revulsion, and North was no exception. North and Somerville were old friends and got on together exceptionally well, although, again, their characters could hardly have been more different. One destroyer officer at that time who know both men well has given this description of their respective merits.

> I had served with Admiral North before the war, when he was flag captain to Admiral Commanding the Reserve Fleet in Portsmouth, to whom I

was flag lieutenant and signal officer. So I knew him quite well and liked him. Admiral North had a distinguished career before promotion to Rear-Admiral in 1932 but commanding the Royal Yachts from 1934 to 1939 had deprived him of any recent operational experience. He was, however, a most capable, respected and much liked officer.

Admiral Somerville was a few years junior to North in age and seniority. As a lieutenant commander I had served under Somerville when he was Commodore RN Barracks Portsmouth in 1933. This gave me the opportunity to realise his sterling qualities. From 1936 to 1938 Somerville commanded the 45 Mediterranean destroyers and was C-in-C East Indies from 1938 for about a year. So he had much operational experience behind him when he took command of Force H at Gibraltar. He was an extrovert, his quick brain and lively wit making him somewhat intolerant of those lacking these gifts and he was fearless in speaking his mind to higher authority. In 1940 I took part in a number of operations with Force H under Somerville and considered him to be a great sea commander, in whom I had the utmost confidence.[35]

The fall of France and the entry of Italy naturally made Gibraltar a far more important command than hitherto almost overnight. It now became one of only three vital British links in the Mediterranean, with Malta in the centre untenable to all save small striking forces, and Alexandria, in neutral Egypt, the main fleet base far to the east guarding the Suez Canal. When early doubts about our ability to hold the Mediterranean at all were replaced by a firm resolution to do just that, the vulnerability of Gibraltar itself became a major consideration. Spain was still neutral, but was governed by a dictatorship that owed its position to direct help from Germany and Italy scant years before. It needed little imagination to envisage either Spain joining the Axis in the sure knowledge that with their help again she would regain Gibraltar, or else giving German Panzers the right of access through her territory to do the jobs themselves. Indeed just this very prospect was planned in great detail by Hitler and his staff, and Operation Felix was very much on the cards at that time.[36]

Admiral North was asked to assess the chances of holding out against such an attack in July and his reply was so tinged with pessimism (or realism depending on one's point of view) that the first grave doubts were raised in Whitehall as to whether Admiral North was any longer the right man for the job in the new situation of desperation the nation now found itself in. North's view was that Gibraltar would rapidly become 'untenable', a view shared later by Somerville, and this may well have been perfectly true, but with all at home preparing to defend their homeland in a last ditch resistance something more resolute was obviously hoped for from ACNAS than this. Thus the first expression of displeasure at North's attitude was aired, as a memorandum recalled later, on North's 'rather defeatist attitude of mind he adopted in July 1940 when the question was raised on the feasibility of defence of the Rock against hostile action from Spain. You will recall that the First Lord commented particularly on this aspect.'[37] So already Alexander was doubtful and these doubts were soon fuelled with added materials.

The final catalyst was the attack upon the French Fleet at Mers-el-Kebir which took place on 3rd July 1940 and which had a traumatic effect on French and British alike. In particular the sensitive North reacted as he had done once before, many years ago. He retired to his office, sat down and began to compose a letter. It reflected the feelings of himself and his brother officers at Gibraltar on what he felt to be a grave mistake on the Admiralty's part. It was a brave and noble thing to do but it was also highly rash. North's message of 4th July 1940 read thus:

MOST SECRET AND PERSONAL   OPERATION CATAPULT

1 On the conclusion of Operation Catapult I desire to forward for the information of Their Lordships the following notes which I made regarding the discussions which preceded that operation. I have just read these notes to Admirals Somerville and Wells on their return to Gibraltar, and they state that they are in full agreement with them.

2 Vice-Admiral Somerville arrived at Gibraltar p.m. 30th June, and on arrival disclosed to me the Government's intentions about Oran. I immediately said I was absolutely opposed to the use of force, that the French would probably fight and that Admiral Gensoul had said he would submit to no other power taking control of his ships.

3 At a meeting on board *Hood* that evening, attended by Admirals Somerville, Wells and myself and the captains and staff officers concerned, all the flag officers and captains were opposed to the use of force. Opinion against the use of force was so strong that I felt an unofficial protest must be made, and I told Admiral Somerville next morning that I was considering sending a separate protest. I also made a suggestion that he should be authorized to withdraw his force at the last moment without using force, and he said he would embody this suggestion in his telegram to the Admiralty. I said that if he sent me a copy of his telegram and it appeared emphatic enough, I would not send a separate protest. He later showed me his telegram and said he had not mentioned me specifically because I had already given my opinion to the Admiralty in another telegram (1220/26th June). This telegram (1220/1st July) appeared to fulfil what I wanted, but at the same time I

did resolve that I might still send another message of protest. I completely abandoned this idea on reading Admiralty Message 0103/2nd July addressed to the Vice-Admiral, Force H, in which it was stated that the Government was determined to use force, and that this decision had been come to after the receipt and consideration of the message from Vice-Admiral, Force H.

4 I felt that nothing more could be done. Admiral Somerville shared my apprehensions and said that the carrying out of this operation was entirely repugnant to him.

5 On attending the meeting in *Hood* to discuss the actual carrying out of the operation, I emphasized the importance of making sure that the reason for the arrival of the fleet off Oran should be known to all officers and men of the French Fleet before any action was taken. Admiral Somerville said he quite agreed and was making the most careful arrangements to his end.

6 In spite of the Admiralty's decision, I still hoped that when it came to the point, if it was found that resistance was to be expected, there might be time for the Admiralty to cancel the use of force, but I now understand that instructions were given to the Vice-Admiral, Force H that the use of force was not to be delayed.

7 It is realised of course that the final decision on the necessity for this operation had to be made by the Cabinet, and that this decision was undoubtedly governed by factors of which we are not aware. At the same time it may be of value to place on record the views which prevailed here, in the light of our knowledge of the situation.[38]

From the moment this message arrived at the Admiralty Admiral Sir Dudley North was living on borrowed time as far as his future as ACNAS was concerned.

North had met the French Admiral Gensoul at Mers-el-Kebir before the attack took place. He sailed aboard the destroyer *Douglas* from Gibraltar on 23rd June and the following day was received with full ceremony aboard the *Dunkerque*. North only spoke French poorly but nonetheless established a rapport with the French Admiral. The atmosphere in the French Fleet was funereal but when North had asked Gensoul for the attitude they would take should the Armistice be signed, he was left in no doubt that they would follow whatever orders came from France, without question or hesitation. He was told that Darlan would order the ships to be sunk rather than handed over to the enemy but that there was little chance of their continuing the struggle against the enemy. His determination in this matter had made a deep impression on North who had tried to convey this feeling to Whitehall at the time. But the War Cabinet's resolution was stronger.

For the First Lord, First Sea Lord, the Premier and every one of the Chiefs of Staff the decision taken to use force at Mers-el-Kebir was not a lightly taken one. Post-war analysis is unduly harsh for it is rarely that it is considered in the context of the actual time it was taken: the desperateness of our plight as a nation, our utter dependence of command of the sea for immediate existence at all and for long-term plans to prevail despite the odds and the fact that, no matter how honourable and just and good-intentioned the French admirals were who gave their word that their fleet would not fall into Axis hands, the ships' ultimate fate lay not with them but with Adolf Hitler. He had the strength, all of it, to decide France's fate and his word was hardly one that the British War Cabinet was liable in July 1940 to take at face value, no matter how much store the French set by the Armistice terms. No other solemn and binding treaty that Hitler had signed had lasted long or counted for anything once it had achieved its purpose.

Clearly then resolution was the quality that was required from all senior naval commanders at this time and so North's letter, although well-intentioned, struck a somewhat jarring note in Whitehall. Although the Germans hoped we were down and out as a nation and France believed it, and although Hitler certainly wished to conclude a peace with Britain without further bloodshed at this stage, it was the opinions of the uncommitted major powers that were of the most concern to the War Cabinet. It is known that the American Ambassador in London was sending back gloomy reports at this time, but happily Churchill's rapport with Roosevelt enabled him to convince the latter that we were far from defeated and would fight on regardless.

In the case of the giant Continental nation to the east, the Soviet Union, the Cabinet was eager to give them the same impression. On 28th June the Soviet Ambassador, Maisky, called on Alexander and sounded him out on our chances at sea now that we were alone. He expressed the opinion that we were in some trouble, and went on thus with regard the attitude of the French Navy:

Well, we know that Mr Duff Cooper has been to Casablanca and that his report is not at all encouraging; in fact there is little prospect now of their fighting. The admirals and generals have decided on allegiance to Pétain's Government; the junior officers, many of them may wish to fight, but they lack any lead and there is of course pressure upon them with regard to their families in France. This means that the French Fleet at Oran and other places would not be with us, and might be used against us. Could we possibly manage the situation in such circumstances?

I replied that we should have a good try. Maisky said: 'Try, yes, but will you succeed?', to which I answered, 'You know, Mr Maisky, what the British mean by trying when they are at war.'[39]

Much later Alexander remembered this as one typical incident of how the action at Mers-el-Kebir, hateful though it was, silenced with one blow, all such doubts. And not just neutrals were impressed. The Italian Foreign Minister noted in his diary:

It is too early to judge the consequences of the British action. For the moment it proves that the fighting spirit of His Britannic Majesty's fleet is quite alive, and still has the aggressive ruthlessness of the captains and pirates of the seventeenth century.[40]

It was certainly Alexander, already upset by North's previous apparent attitude, who initiated moves to get rid of ACNAS upon receipt of his letter and he sought both Churchill's[41] and Pound's[42] opinions on the matter. On 17th July he authorised the official reply to North's unfortunate minute and sent a copy of both to Churchill. His covering Memo contained the following note for the Premier:

I would add I suggested to the First Sea Lord that it should be for consideration to supersede FOCNA but he does not think there is a strong enough case for this.[43]

Churchill certainly shared Alexander's opinion of North at this time, as was evidenced by his reply to Alexander on 20th July:

It is evident that Admiral Dudley North has not got the root of the matter in him, and I should be very glad to see you replace him by a more resolute and clear-sighted officer.[44]

It was Admiral Sir Dudley Pound, later to be so vilified in the matter, who, while agreeing that North was not shaping up in this regard, stood up to the pressure from both the Premier and the First Lord and gave Admiral North one final chance. He did it, to be sure, by a technical argument, stating that he did not feel there was a strong enough case for North's replacement, but he often overrode the Premier thus and usually, as in this instance, won his point. As Alexander later recalled: 'Both the Prime Minister and myself took a poor view of Admiral North's attitude on Oran. Sir Dudley Pound said, in effect, that he did not like it either but he understood it ...'[45] which also indicates that Pound himself was not remote from the repugnance felt by most other senior naval officers at the affair, although he recognised its necessity.

Again the impartiality and fairness of Pound here should be stressed and, because of it, North continued his command, but not before receiving a sharp warning from Their Lordships that he was near the limit of their patience. The Admiralty's reply on 17th July as first drafted by the Deputy Secretary, Sir James Sidney Barnes, read as follows:

> I propose a reply on the following lines should be sent:
> 'Opinions of senior officers are always of value before an operation is carried out; but once the operation has taken place Their Lordships deprecate comments on a policy which has been decided by the Admiralty in the light of factors which were unknown to officers on the spot. In this case Their Lordships were never under the delusion that the French Fleet would not fight in the last instance, and this fact was taken fully into consideration in the preliminary deliberations.
>   Their Lordships were under no misapprehensions how repugnant the operation would be to all officers concerned, but they cannot allow such considerations to influence decisions in war.'

This was approved by Pound but Alexander felt it was not strong enough a warning. He added the word 'strongly' before 'deprecate', and after the words 'in war', added 'and are surprised that comments of the kind received should be made.'

He noted that these amendments, and a consideraton to supersede FOCNA should be made because:

> I feel at the critical stage we have reached in our national affairs, it is of the highest importance that I may be able to rely on the Board of Admiralty orders when finally given being very firmly carried out without question.

Pound commented on this saying that in this instance there had been no question that Their Lordships' instructions had not been carried out and that there could, therefore, be no question of superseding North. He did however agree to Alexander's amendments and 'in order to strengthen still further this letter' he made two more of his own: after 'in the light of factors which were' he added 'either known or' and after the second paragraph inserted a new third paragraph which contained the plainest warning to North yet: 'The contents of the first part of Paragraph 6 of your letter show a most dangerous lack of appreciation of the manner in which it is intended to conduct the war'.[46]

As thus the missive was sent off on 17th July 1940 to North. As Alexander recalled of FOCNA:

> His principal fault was in connection with Oran. He would probably have been recalled then but for the plea by Sir Dudley Pound that he should be given a further chance. He was however severely warned ...'[47]

Churchill was certainly not convinced but went along with this decision, although a later, undated, memo from the Premier to Alexander contained his thinking on re-jigging the Naval High Command, in which Admiral North certainly had no future place in his scheme of things.[48] It can be fairly stated therefore that although perhaps at this point Admiral North had lost the confidence of both the Premier and the First Lord, the confidence of Pound, though severely under test, was not shaken enough to sanction his removal. But from this point on North was skating on very thin ice indeed, a fact which his subsequent apology did nothing to nullify. On 6th August North expressed his 'deep regret' that his comments should have earned him such a 'reproof' from the Admiralty.[49] He did not, he stated, intend his notes to be taken as any criticism of the decision to carry out the action against the French at Mers-el-Kebir and nor did his opposition to such actions arise out of 'sentimental attachment to our late allies, but from strong doubts as to its effect on the course of the war'. He also said that he fully realised that there was no room in war for 'false scruples or for sentiment', but this was subsequently to cut no ice with Their Lordships. It was deeds not words that would henceforth decide their opinion of the value of Admiral North at Gibraltar.

CHAPTER NINE

An Ill-Defined Relationship

In the immediate aftermath of Mers-el-Kebir there was naturally some uncertainty among the local commanders as to what the next steps were to be vis-à-vis the surviving French units which could be met at sea at any time. To clarify the position the Admiralty signalled to all commands late on 4th July 1940, as follows:

IMMEDIATE

1 As result of action at Oran, intentions of Bordeaux government are at present uncertain, but it is possible we may be at war with France shortly. HM ships are, for the present, to be guided by the following instructions.

2. Ships are not to approach inside twenty miles of France or French colonial possessions in those areas where French submarines may be operating as French Admiralty have issued warning that British ships will be attacked without warning up to that distance from coast.

3. Ships must be prepared for attack but should not (R) not fire first shot.

4. Contact with equal or superior French forces should be avoided as whilst it is desired to get control of as many French ships as possible, it would not be to our advantage to incur an equivalent loss in so doing.

5. If a definitely inferior French force is met action should be taken as follows:

(a) The French force is to be ordered to stop and if necessary forced to do so.

(b) An officer is then to be sent on board and is to convey in writing HMG's instructions that French force should proceed to a British port in company with HM ship.

(c) The French commanding officer is to be informed that commanding officer of HM ship has orders to use force if necessary and that it is much hoped that this will not be the case.

(d) The French CO should be informed that our object is to ensure that French ships do not fall into enemy hands, as was promised by Admiral Darlan.

(e) The CO is to be informed that the officers and ship's company will be repatriated.[1]

However this order came too late to prevent further French losses. Prior to Mers-el-Kebir North's command had been reinforced by the submarines *Pandora* and *Proteus* and these had been despatched to patrol off Oran and Algiers while Mers-el-Kebir was taking place, with instructions to attack all French warships. This order was only intended to cover the period of the operation but this was not spelled out and the two submarines were still on patrol when the bulk of Force H returned to Gibraltar.

During the afternoon of 4th July the *Proteus* sighted the French seaplane carrier *Commandante Teste*, which, having survived the bombardment earlier, was escaping to Toulon. Fortunately the submarine was unable to get in a suitable firing position and the French ship proceeded unscathed. However the *Pandora* sighted what she took to be a French cruiser heading from Oran to Bizerta and went into her attack. At 1632 on the 4th *Pandora* fired a full spread of four torpedoes at this target, which was in fact the French sloop *Rigault de Genouilly*, and hit her with at least two of them, sinking her at once. Admiral Phillips regretted this mistake and apologised that same night for the incident, which was not repeated.

On the 8th, however, torpedo bombers from the carrier *Hermes* attacked the French battleship *Richelieu* at Dakar and scored one hit which effectively immobilised her for a year, although the bulk of her armament remained effective. Her sister ship, *Jean Bart*, lay at Casablanca and plans were put in hand for Force H to deal with her. However it was ascertained in time that she was in such an incomplete state, minus most of her armament and with little ammunition, and as other more urgent matters interposed themselves, she was spared the fate of her fellow battleships at Mers-el-Kebir until the Allied landings in 1942, when an American battleship dealt with her.

Meanwhile the Admiralty informed North and Somerville, among others, of the latest position with regard French intentions which they gleaned from intercepted signals. On 5th July they sent the following information:

MOST IMMEDIATE

All French surface vessels submarines and aircraft were ordered at 0715 on 5th July not to attack British men of war on the high seas, but to be ready to reply to an attack. Only those British merchant vessels which enter the forbidden zone 20 miles round the French coast are to be captured.[2]

So now they knew that it was a 'Stand-Off' situation between the two fleets, but Admiral North as the officer directly responsible for control of the Straits of Gibraltar through which French naval traffic might be expected requested further clarification of the situation from the Admiralty in a signal of the same date:

IMMEDIATE
My 2356/3 your 1400/5 and War Office 75489 4th July request clarification of action in the event of French warships passing through the Straits.[3]

The Admiralty reply came early next morning.

IMMEDIATE
Your 2014/5 not to SO Force (H) Comply with para 3 of my 2005/4.[4]

This however seemed to contradict a War Office signal of 4th July which instructed the Governor to ensure action was taken by the fortress batteries to prevent French men-of-war passing through the Straits 'pending clarification of the naval situation,'[5] and North therefore requested further amplification on this point in a signal despatched on the afternoon of the 6th thus:

IMMEDIATE
Your 0226/6 War Office 75489/4/9 to Governor Gibraltar approving that action be taken to prevent passage of French warships through Straits pending clarification of Naval situation. This is not in accordance with paragraph 3 Admiralty Message 2005/4. Present instructions to Straits patrol are to permit passage of French warships unless they commit a hostile act.[6]

Their Lordships replied to this early on the 7th and both brought War Office policy in line with their own and re-emphasised that the last sentence in North's 1644/6th above was now to be replaced by the more detailed instructions already specified. He was thus left in no doubts.

IMMEDIATE
Your 2025/6.* French warships passing through Straits should be treated as in paragraphs 3, 4 and 5 of my 2005/4. Forts at Gibraltar

---

* This was the time of receipt in the Admiralty of North's 1644/6th and not time of origin as it should have been quoted.

should assist you to carry out these instructions if possible. War Office will be requested to amend their instructions.[7]

Several points may be noted from the above exchange of signals. Firstly, that the prefix IMMEDIATE was used all the time and, by constant usage it had lost some of its urgency, its over-use had debased its priority. Secondly North had, in his signals, shown himself to be fully aware that *he* was responsible for local events in and around the Straits and thirdly, by omitting Force H from the addresses of their 0226/6th specifically the Admiralty had shown that otherwise their signals duly applied to that unit in other orders regarding control of the Straits.

The Admiralty further modified their instructions with a signal on 8th July thus:

IMPORTANT
French submarines submerged or unescorted on the surface are to be treated as hostile.[8]

Yet further modification followed on 12th July after deliberations at top level on future policy towards France. This amendment read as follows and is of vital importance to our story for it was interpreted by North and Somerville in a different way to that intended by the Admiralty.

IMPORTANT
My 2005/4 not to all addressees, and my 1357/8.
(a) *Richelieu* has now been dealt with and *Jean Bart* could not complete for a considerable period even at her building yard.
(b) The further maintenance of the present state of tension between French Navy and ourselves is very undesirable and might even lead to war with that country.
(c) HM Government have consequently reviewed our policy regarding the French Navy and have decided to take no further action in regard to the French ships in French colonial or North African ports. We shall however reserve the right to take action in regard to French warships proceeding to enemy controlled ports. So far as submarines are concerned we shall follow the rules which were first generally accepted in the Nyon convention and which were subsequently acted upon during the present war in respect of Italian submarines while that country was neutral. These rules are (i) that submarines found submerged outside certain limited areas to be agreed upon will be treated as hostile; (ii) that submarines on the surface outside the same areas will be treated as

hostile unless accompanied by a French surface warship.

(d) It is desired that this policy as given in above para (c) shall be communicated via Naval channels to the French Admiralty, and the Commander-in-Chief, Mediterranean, or in his absence CS 3 is accordingly requested to inform Admiral Godfroy and to ask that the French will propose submarine exercise areas if they wish to make use of them. No action is to be taken by other addressees.

(e) Pending further instructions ships must be prepared for attack when meeting French warships but should not repeat not fire the first shot.[9]

Yet a further modification followed on the 12th thus:

For the present French warships under control of French Government should be treated as neutral war vessels if approaching a defended port.[10]

North's supporters argue, quite reasonably, that the vital phrase in point (c) of the 8th July signal, 'We shall however reserve the right to take action in regard to French warships ...' was not strictly an *instruction* to North to take action, despite the fact that this is the interpretation the Admiralty later placed on it. Again ambiguity was apparent. The War Cabinet obviously meant their message to leave no doubt in French minds that the British would not tolerate any such movement, and that, should it be contemplated there was no doubt it would be opposed by force. As a threat it worked, or at least was never challenged by the French, for they never in fact contemplated such an action. It was the *possibility* of this happening that affected North who had no concrete evidence that it would not, and it was on this that the Admiralty felt their wrath was justified.

North duly passed message to the British consul-general at Tangier to notify the French Admiral Ollive of our new intentions, thus:

IMMEDIATE

Please arrange for the following message to be delivered as soon as possible to Admiral Ollive in whatever manner you consider most suitable for purpose of relieving present tension. At the same time in case it may suit French authorities not to make this assurance public it might be advisable to ensure discreetly that purport of message becomes generally known in Casablanca.

I am authorised by my Government to inform you that it is their intention to take no further action against French warships while they are lying in French Colonial or North African ports.

In communicating this assurance I desire to add that no one regretted more than the Royal Navy the necessary but painful duty they had to perform at Oran and Dakar. We do not forget that France was so recently our ally and our sole purpose is the defeat of Germany, our common enemy.[11]

The Italian entry into the war on 10th June had re-emphasised the importance of the Straits with regard to anti-submarine operations, which was one of the main tasks of the ships under North. The Italians soon started probing at the British defences in this respect and on 5th/6th June two submarines had sailed from their bases at Cagliari to try and reach the Atlantic. The *Finzi* passed through the Straits undetected on 13th June and operated for a time off the Canary Islands, re-passing the Straits on 6th July and reaching her base on the 13th. The other boat was less fortunate. This vessel, the *Cappellini*, was detected and attacked by one of the anti-submarine trawlers of North's command on 14th June. The destroyer *Wrestler* took up the hunt and the damaged submarine was forced to seek refuge in neutral Ceuta where she remained from 15th to 24th June before eluding patrols and returning to Cagliari.

Their actual passage of the Straits, submerged despite the strong currents, had proved to be a practical proposition for the big Italian submarines, with the added incentive of requests from their German ally for help. Germany had very few combat ready submarines in the summer of 1940 although a huge building programme was underway. In contrast Italy started the war with over a hundred submarines. Plans were therefore made to set up an Italian submarine base at Bordeaux so that they could co-ordinate attacks with the Germans and this base, BETASOM, was duly formed on 1st September. The first wave of submarines was despatched between 27th August and 6th October, eight boats sailing and all arriving safely after penetrating the Straits of Gibraltar and these soon began Atlantic operations.[12]

It was clear therefore that North's command as it then stood was not strong enough to prevent this traffic and urgent steps were put in hand by the Admiralty to implement his requests for more modern ships of better range, a far from easy task for Their Lordships with most of the modern ships being required for anti-invasion duties at home (on 6th September the first major invasion warning had been sounded in Britain), while many others were still in dockyard hands repairing damage from action in Norway and off Dunkirk. The arrival of Force H brought with it the welcome reinforcement of the seven modern destroyers of the 8th Flotilla, under Captain De Salis, but of course their main function was to screen Force H on its various operations. In point of fact both commands were short of destroyers and the Admiralty had informed both North and Somerville that those they had were to be interchangeable between the commands as the need arose, thus:

MOST SECRET
1 Reference para. 4 (b) of my 1724/28. You are to inform Admiralty in advance of your intentions regarding operations against the Italian coast.
2 The 13th Destroyer Flotilla is to be placed at your disposal for any operations for which destroyers immediately under your command are not adequate.
3 When Force H is in harbour the destroyers attached to it are to assist in the patrol of the straits of Gibraltar as required by FOCNA.[13]

This worked well in practice, as Captain De Winton recalls:

When Force H arrived at the end of June 1940 and Somerville assumed command, he brought with him (from the Home Fleet) about six or seven destroyers of the E and F classes, led by *Faulknor*. Captain A.F. De Salis and I had been term mates and knew each other very well. It was agreed between Admirals North and Somerville that the latter should take as many of my destroyers that he needed for an operation and that Admiral North could spare. We never, in my time, had the slightest difficulty about this. For the operation at Mers-el-Kebir on 3rd July I embarked in *Keppel* taking with me *Active*, *Wrestler*, *Vortigern* and *Vidette*. De Salis had six of his 8th Flotilla, so the force had a quite adequate screen of eleven destroyers. And so it was for subsequent operations and 'club-runs' as the passing of reinforcements through to Malta were called.[14]

It was a month later that the Admiralty were at last able to replace some of North's destroyers with more modern ships and on 14th July the *Keppel*, *Active*, *Watchman*, *Vortigern* and *Douglas* left Gibraltar for the United Kingdom to form the 12th Flotilla. Their places in the 13th Flotilla were taken by the *Hotspur*, *Gallant*, *Greyhound* and *Encounter* which arrived at the Rock on 30th July and the *Griffin* and *Velox* which arrived from home on 17th August.[15]

Several major operations then took place aimed at reinforcing Malta or creating diversions in the western basin while Admiral Cunningham's main fleet sortied in the east, and during these the

Escort of the 8th Flotilla was torpedoed and sunk by the Italian submarine *Marconi* just east of Gibraltar on 11th July.

North's submarine strength, however, remained scanty. The *Pandora* and *Proteus* were used to transport urgent supplies to Malta in August and remained there for further operations but their places were due to be taken by the more modern vessels *Triad*, *Truant*, *Triton* and *Tetrarch* and steps were taken to set up the 8th Flotilla at Gibraltar.

The parsimonious state of the Rock's air strength continued for, with the Battle of Britain approaching its height, no fighters could be spared. Even the limited range of the old London flying boats had to be endured despite pleas for modern replacements. The squadron was high on the list of reconnaissance units to be re-equipped with the modern American Catalina flying boats when supplies became available under new contracts, but the first of these could not be expected until well into the New Year.

The Rock's only defence against air attacks, be they French Glenn Martin bombers from North Africa or the deadly Stuka dive bombers of the Luftwaffe, which were known to be ready to enforce Felix, or the spasmodic long-range sortie by Italian three-engined bombers, lay with the AA guns, which were also sparse, and not, initially, very well-trained, although they rapidly improved in efficiency. They included some of the first of the new automatic cannon, the Bofors 40-mm gun, a most effective weapon in well-trained hands, and superior to anything mounted in Royal Navy ships at this time. When the Fleet was in harbour their own guns supplemented the Rock's AA batteries of course. It was perhaps fortunate that Italian air raids were the only ones to manifest themselves at this period and these only spasmodically, as on the night of 20th/21st August when *Renown*'s gunners brought down a SM 82.[16]

Radar, which was soon to play such a crucial part in the defence of Britain, was in its early infancy at Gibraltar at this time, *but it did exist*. An early air warning set had been installed by the Navy at the Spyglass position and was under test during August and September. It was a Type 78Z RDF set and initially the reception was poor. On 9th September, however, Somerville visited the installation and reported on it as follows:

> I witnessed further trials of the Type 79Z RDF set on shore and found that a punctured condensor had been the cause of poor operation in

previous trials. The set now gives reasonably good indication of range up to 40 or 50 miles but the prevalence of land echoes makes it very difficult to obtain accurate bearings. As a means of medium distance warning of approach, the set now serves a useful purpose, but does not enable a long distance plot to be obtained. It appears that either a set with short wavelength or else larger aerial arrays will be required to deal with the difficult local conditions for RD/F.[17]

The Type 79Z was a naval radar developed as a long range warning set against enemy aircraft, of 15-20kw with a 7 metre wavelength. This set was first fitted in the light cruiser *Sheffield* in August 1938 and soon afterward in the battleship *Rodney*. With it aircraft could be detected at 10,000 feet at a range of 53 miles. In the middle of 1939 the set's power was increased up to 90kw giving 60 miles range. Trials took place just before the war and forty sets were ordered, delivery of the first commencing in 1940 and Gibraltar received one of the first. Despite the gloomy report of Somerville the set performed well enough to be handed over to the military authorities in September and played a large part in the subsequent Vichy bombing raids, although it is never mentioned in accounts of this period.

Somerville also commented in the same report on the low efficiency of both the Army AA batteries and searchlight positions, putting this down, in part, to the fact that the fleet had been away giving no scope for further training exercises.

I visited General Mason MacFarlane and discussed with him the lamentable exhibition given by the A/A defences during the previous night's exercises. I was assured that immediate action would be taken to correct the many deficiencies which had been noted. The searchlight exercise was repeated at 2100 and was in all respects far more satisfactory than on the previous occasion.[18]

Somerville was of course very much interested in the work of the Fleet Air Arm; he was thus 'air minded' to a degree that few flag officers at this time were, as another section of his report makes clear:

I inspected the Fleet Air Arm section established on the North Front and went up in a Swordfish aircraft in order to obtain a view of the harbour as seen from bombing aircraft. It was clear that, for high level bombing, ships alongside the Moles presented a difficult target. For dive bombing, however, the target presented is favourable.[19]

With regard to the other parts of their duties the escorting of the local HG convoys was another chore for the destroyers based at the Rock. The convoy's normal escorts of sloops and corvettes were thus supplemented by at least one of the local destroyers for part of its outward journey across the Bay of Biscay, and in similar manner, incoming convoys from the UK were met and escorted in. Submarines en route to either Gibraltar or onward to the eastern basin were also met out in the Bay by a destroyer in the same manner, yet another chore for North's limited number of ships, while all the time essential refits and boiler cleaning always ensured a few more were not available at any one time. While Force H was in harbour its own destroyers, as indicated, could help out, but there were always more chores for these little ships than there were ships to do them. Meantime the old Londons kept up their patrols and worked with hunting teams of destroyers both east and west of the Straits themselves but, despite several suspect sightings, no Italian submarines were actually sunk at this time by the Gibraltar forces.

Happily at this time the question of the French did not complicate things for some time after Mers-el-Kebir, much to the delight of both Somerville and North, but when Somerville returned to the UK briefly during the re-organisation of his command (when he changed flagship from *Hood* to *Renown* and visited London in August), he learned of the new moves afoot to establish the Free French movement, under General Charles de Gaulle in the French African colonies. His own feelings on the matter were that the plan would only succeed if it was unopposed, but as he was not directly involved (although the bulk of his command *was*) he had little influence on the matter.

We need not here be over-concerned with the arguments that preceded the Dakar operation, codenamed Menace, save to note that Churchill later freely admitted that he '... undertook in an exceptional degree the initiation and advocacy of the Dakar expedition'.[20] Very fine and detailed accounts of this fiasco already exist,[21] but some background information is essential to understand the subsequent events at Gibraltar and off Casablanca.

Briefly then, de Gaulle had left the ruins of a floundering France on 16th June embarking in the destroyer *Milan* (a ship which, with some grim irony, we shall be meeting again in these pages) at Brest and spending his first night in exile in the Hyde Park Hotel in London.[22] His refusal to accept the Armistice conducted by the French Government made him a focal point for other Frenchmen of a like mind and so the 'Free French' movement was born. This movement was at first tiny, but his fiery and dignified defiance of defeat gradually attracted a larger following, no more so than in the African colonies of France. On 13th August de Gaulle despatched three special aides to Lagos, Nigeria, charged with rallying these colonies to his cause, particularly those in the French Cameroons and French Equatorial Africa (Gabon, Chad, Middle Congo and Ubangi-Shari). He also had hopes of a similar campaign in French West Africa (comprising the colonies of Dahomey, Guinea, Ivory Coast, Niger, Sudan, Senegal and Mauretania). Of these places by far the most important from a prestige point of view was Senegal, placed on the hump of Africa with its fine port of Dakar providing a strategic post which enamoured itself to Britain in particular. There was little support for de Gaulle in North Africa (Tunisia, Algeria and Morocco) but it was firmly felt in London by all parties that the other locations would come over with little prompting, and indeed initial reaction seemed to confirm this view.

There was also a strong feeling in Britain that unless someone acted quickly in this vast area German penetration would be rapid, with very severe consequences for Britain's own enormous responsibilities in the area. In particular, German control of Dakar would be of enormous danger in the fight for the sea routes. Although we now know that the German Navy was advocating such a policy, Hitler was playing for very different stakes and no serious infiltration ever took place, but the apparent threat at the time seemed obvious.

Thus it was that the Menace Expedition was launched. The omens seemed good for already, on 29th August, Chad colony had declared itself for de Gaulle thus:

LIBREVILLE
After conference, at which were present Military Commander, Public Attorney, President Chamber of Commerce and President Ex-servicemen, Gabon territory gives Free France its enthusiastic adhesion and full support.[23]

It seemed in London that the arrival of the Expedition with strong naval support was all that was required to bring the rest into a similar line. To emphasise the point the British cruiser *Delhi* was despatched to Pointe Noire in the neighbouring Middle Congo to lend weight to the Free French infiltration. She was to be the catalyst that finally spurred the Vichy authorities into action and indirectly led to Admiral North's misfortune.

Although a large part of the escorting naval force to cover Operation Menace was to come from Force H based at Gibraltar, although the Flag Officer Force H himself had been told of the general plan by the First Sea Lord and although the route of the Expedition convoy lay in part through that area of the Eastern Atlantic under control of FOCNA, Admiral North was not among those senior officers officially let in on the actual operational plans themselves. This seems almost incredible but it is known to be so. Security on the operation was unbelievably lax in every other direction; the Free French themselves were especially voluble about their probable destination and conditions of secrecy at the port of embarkation were pathetic. Nevertheless it must be emphasised that, in spite of this initial debacle, the Vichy French authorities *had no idea whatsoever* that Dakar was the destination of the Expedition, nor did they know a large Free French force was on the move.

Yet if, as Churchill later confirmed, Admiral North '... was *not* in the Dakar circle',[24] he most certainly knew quite a lot about Menace and that it was directed against the French. For a start Somerville knew from his earlier meetings and from the fact that most of his command was to take part. Did he confide this information to North? It would seem extremely unlikely that he did not do so for their working relationship was very close indeed. For this we have North's own words to Captain Roskill:

> ... your comments seem to indicate that you have a very erroneous idea of the respective relations of Admiral Somerville and myself. We worked together in everything. We were connected by telephone. He did nothing without telling me, and I did nothing without telling him.[25]

Somerville himself later stated in an official report that: 'The possibility of this movement being connected with Operation Menace was considered',[26] which seems a firm enough indication that *he* knew what was happening, and that therefore North surely knew also that something big was afoot against the French.

North later confided to Admiral Sir Herbert Richmond that: 'I knew from various facts but they had not troubled to inform me officially.'[27]

We also have the statement from North's former Chief of Staff, Captain R.G. Duke, that:

> My recollection is that we *did* know *officially* that Admiral Cunningham's

force was passing through the Station, and that it was directed against French Equatorial Africa somewhere; and that later we gathered from intercepted signals more about it, but where our official information stopped and the guesswork started, I cannot remember.[28]

The Menace Expedition sailed from England on 31st August as Convoy MP and headed out into the Atlantic, passing west of the Azores on 5th September on its way to Freetown, Sierra Leone. Meanwhile North and Somerville had been conducting a series of local events which had kept them fully occupied; there had also been another deluge of signals. The first of these was a long message sent by the British Naval Attaché in Madrid to the Director of Naval Intelligence, Admiralty. It was an update on the French Navy and its content certainly profoundly influenced North's subsequent thinking.

French NA returned from Vichy. His attitude improved. Admiral Darlan instructed him to maintain close contact with me, but discreetly because of German observation, and to tell me that French spirit of resistance was increasing and disarmament would not be real. NA stated French ships at Toulon remained in condition to fight. Disarmament condition not there. He had not been there himself, but his wife is there now and returns to Madrid in fifteen days when he will give me details. Attitude of officers and men much less hostile to us.

General Huntziger, Chief of French part of armistice commission, was at Vichy from Wiesbaden to report, where he told NA German demands were stiffening, also that every night about 0100 the AA guns started firing which went on for some time. Germans were very disturbed by persistent character of British raids.

There is now no communication of any kind between Occupied France and the rest except for German officials, and the border is very strongly held by Germans, but a few people straggle through. These report grave food shortage, general requisitioning by Germans, long enforced hours in certain factories, and change of feeling among French from depression to exasperation. Our raids on French aerodromes, etc. are not resented. Paris is a dead city. No cars. Everyone has left who can. Markets almost emptied. People deliberately ignore Germans. Stories of fraternization and pictures of admiring crowds watching German bands are lies. Intense resentment everywhere at German attack on church. Lutheran services have been held in Chapel Ile St Denis. Archbishop of Paris was prisoner in his house for five days recently.

Notre Dame used for Nazi pagan ceremonies which included loaves of bread and a swastika on a table before High Altar.

Some officials and officers corps of disarmament commissions are only

Germans in unoccupied France. Ditto Italians, who are much less arrogant than Germans.

General French feeling is hope in us and intention to join in again when possible.

NA gave me message from Vichy Government for Ambassador. This he is reporting himself.[29]

This highly coloured and slanted viewpoint naturally impressed North, who had received similar indications earlier. He summed up his feelings later in this manner:

Since receiving Admiralty message 0241 of 12th July 1940, I had received no information which led me to think that relations with Vichy Government had changed for the worse. I had reason to believe from my local intelligence that the attitude of the French Navy was becoming less hostile, and this was confirmed when I received Naval Attaché, Madrid's 1842 of 5th September, to the Director of Naval Intelligence. This reported a distinct improvement in the attitude of the French Navy, and indicated that Admiral Darlan himself desired contact to be maintained with the British Naval Attaché at Madrid.[30]

Equally important was the fact that Admiral North was firmly convinced that Admiralty Message 0241/12/7 had cancelled out the instructions contained in the earlier AM 0012/7/7. When this was later queried in 1951 he was adamant on the point:

As regards AM 0012/7/7 you are I think the first person who has ever contended that it was not cancelled by AM 0241/12/7. If only Admiral Somerville was alive, he would soon assure you that all those of us at Gibraltar considered 0012 washed out. I include the Governor again because he controlled the Fortress guns, such as they were![31]

Before summarising the situation at Gibraltar on the eve of the passage of the French squadron let us examine in some detail the current movements taking place.

The most recent major operation conducted by Force H had been the passage through the Mediterranean of reinforcements for Admiral Cunningham's main Mediterranean Fleet. The whole operation was codenamed Hats, and the ships sailed from Gibraltar on the morning of 30th August.

The subsequent foray proceeded smoothly with little opposition, the only casualty being the destroyer *Garland* from Cunningham's command, which was being brought back to England after a refit at Malta, to be handed over to the Polish Navy. Four of the 13th Flotilla, *Gallant, Greyhound, Griffin* and *Hotspur*, had gone through to Malta and they returned later with *Garland*. On their way back, unsupported, they were subjected to heavy bombing and *Garland* was near missed and damaged. She was towed for a while by *Griffin* until she could again get underway under her own power and all five destroyers arrived back at Gibraltar at 2020 on 5th September; the *Garland* went straight into dockyard hands for repairs to her boilers.

Meanwhile the battleship *Barham* and destroyers *Echo, Eclipse, Escapade* and *Inglefield* had also arrived at Gibraltar from the Home Fleet, to refuel and prepare for Menace. The harbour was therefore unusually busy at this period. Local movements went on as before of course. The homeward bound convoy HG43 sailed on 4th September escorted by the sloop *Wellington* and, for part of their journey, the destroyers *Wishart* and *Fortune*, but *Wishart* developed condensor defects and had to return next day and go into dock for repairs. Her place was taken by the destroyer *Vidette*, which sailed on the 5th with *Royal Scotsman* to join the convoy. On the same day the destroyer *Wrestler* sailed to rendezvous with the submarines *Triad* and *Truant* in 36°22′ N, 09°48′ W and escort them back to the Rock to join North's command.

During routine anti-submarine patrols one London flying boat was forced to ditch and was towed back to Gibraltar by the destroyer *Forester*. On the 6th the two submarines and *Wrestler* duly arrived safely and Somerville inspected the submarine crews on the 10th, finding them fully ready for action, he being 'favourably impressed by the general appearance, efficiency and confident spirit of the officers and men'.[32]

Also on the 6th the main units designed to cover the Menace landings sailed from the Rock to rendezvous with the Expedition: *Ark Royal*, battleships *Barham*, and *Resolution* and destroyers *Faulknor, Fortune, Fury, Foresight, Forester, Greyhound, Inglefield, Eclipse, Escapade*, with *Echo* joining them next day after being delayed by defects. The inclusion of one of North's destroyers, *Greyhound*, was necessary to take the place of *Firedrake* of the 8th Flotilla which was in dock for boiler cleaning.

As these ships slipped over the western horizon the harbour seemed very empty and it will be convenient at this point to summarise exactly what ships were left on hand at Gibraltar for

Somerville and North to meet any unexpected emergency. These were as follows:

Force H:
Battle-cruiser. *Renown* (Flag Vice-Admiral J. Somerville, commanded by Captain C.E.B. Simeon ADC).

North Atlantic:
Destroyers:
Hotspur   (Commander   H.F.H. Layman, DSO)
Griffin (Lieutenant Commander J. Lee Barber)
Encounter (Lieutenant Commander E.V.St J. Morgan)
Wrestler (Lieutenant Commander E.N.V. Currey)
Velox (Commander J.C. Colvill)
Vidette (Lieutenant Commander E.N. Walmsley)

Submarines:
Triad (Lieutenant Commander G.S. Stevenson Salt)
Truant   (Lieutenant   Commander H.A.V. Haggard)
Anti-Submarine Trawlers: 4
Minesweeping Trawlers: 4
Armed Boarding Vessels: 5
Western Patrol Trawlers: 4
Tugs: 5

In dockyard hands:
Destroyers:
Garland (Polish)
Firedrake (Lieutenant   Commander S.H. Norris)
Gallant   (Lieutenant   Commander C.P.F. Brown)
Wishart (Commander E.T. Cooper)

The only incident untoward to occur on the 7th was the passage through the Straits of a small French convoy. This comprised the escort sloop *Elan* and the trawler *Pescagel* from Casablanca en route to Oran. They were inspected at close range by destroyers on patrol in the Straits and allowed to proceed without hindrance as they passed the Straits at dusk, and they arrived at Oran on the 9th. This sign of the return of normality was another pointer taken by North that relationships with the French were improving. *No* French convoys had attempted to pass the Straits since Mers-el-Kebir but now things appeared to be reverting to routine.[33] But in fact there was a *special significance* to this pair of ships, for they had in fact been specially despatched by the French to test the climate and degree of interference the British were prepared to make, in readiness for a much more important operation they had planned; of this more later.[34]

Patrol work went on as normal by sea and air. On 9th September the destroyers *Hotspur*, *Griffin* and *Encounter* sailed to carry out an anti-submarine sweep between Gibraltar and Alboran Island to the east under command of Commander H.F.H. Layman, the senior officer of the division.[35] Co-operating with them were two London flying boats of 202 Squadron. Seven of these venerable aircraft were on station at this time. First introduced into the Royal Air Force in 1936, a total of 29 were on strength on outbreak of war, the Mark II outfitting 202 Squadron in 1938. They were general reconnaissance flying boats with a crew of six. They were of all-metal structure and powered by two 1,000 hp Bristol Pegasus engines, which gave them a maximum speed of 155 mph, a cruising speed of 129 mph and a range of 1,740 maximum, or 1,100, normal with 5.2 hours' endurance. They could carry up to 2,000 lbs of bombs and were defensively armed with three Lewis guns, one in the bow and two amidships. Supplementing these were the three Fairey Swordfish floatplanes of 3 AA Co-Operation Unit, powered by a single Pegasus III engine, of which only one was serviceable at this time. They were suitable for short-range patrols only. They had a crew of two.

The *Wishart* completed her repairs and joined the *Velox*, *Vidette* and *Wrestler* on local patrols off the Rock; Commander E.T. Cooper was the senior officer of that division. This, it will be recalled, was at a time when the first Italian submarines were penetrating the Straits to set up their base at Bordeaux, so the expectation of sightings was high. On the 10th, at 1530, one of the Londons, (L7043) sighted a line of air bubbles coming to the surface and moving slowly northwards in 36°02′ N, 03°29′ W. The flying boat at once made an attack releasing her bombs 'dead on target', but there was no apparent result.[36] One of the destroyers hastened to the scene and dropped depth charges, again with no concrete result. The patrols continued eastward, the three destroyers steaming through the darkness in line abreast while the flying boats returned to their base for the night. In the Straits the other division continued their duties. The captain of *Vidette* later wrote:

There was no duty destroyer inside as such. Various, mainly anti-submarine, patrols were instituted to the west of Gib. One usually spent four days on patrol and on relief returned to Gibraltar and immediately topped up with fuel. As you entered harbour, Captain D advised what Notice for Steam was to be kept, usually 1 Hour, 4 Hours of Boiler Clean. *Wrestler* was used often for boarding ships enforcing a contraband control and was usually stationed to the south or south-east of Gib. It must be remembered that apart from patrolling the Straits and providing additional escorts for Force H when required, the 13th DF were also called upon to provide Convoy Escorts.[37]

Thus it was on the 10th when *Vidette* was relieved by *Wishart* and returned to her normal berth at the destroyer pens at the north end of the harbour. Apart from the great bulk of *Renown* dominating the South Mole, berthed bows-on to the entrance and the two submarines lying side by side further along, the harbour was empty of major warships. In the dockyard lay the destroyers *Garland*, *Gallant* and *Firedrake*, all quite inoperational. It was a calm and peaceful Tuesday evening and everything appeared normal on the surface. But already the ether had been alive with messages again as events began to gather momentum.

A spate of signals, ever since the unfortunate business at Mers-el-Kebir, had been received at Gibraltar giving the Admiralty's instructions, mostly contradictory, as to what action to take if French warships were met at sea. These were often received about 0200 or 0300. They were known to us as 'Pyjama Signals'. Many were couched in language unusual to naval signals, and in general left the recipients, Flag Officer Gibraltar and Flag Officer Force H, wondering what they meant. By early September the latest signal seemed to mean that French warships met at sea should be reported but not molested. At the same time the Admiralty would not wish any French ships to return to German occupied ports in France; it was difficult to think that any ships would wish to do so.[38]

Another officer recalled that 'masses of intelligence came into Gib much of which never came to pass! So I don't think anyone really believed the telegrams ...'[39]

After the Naval Attaché, Madrid's long signal had been received the Admiralty issued their own appreciation of the position in an intelligence report of moderate reliability to several commanders, including North and Somerville. This revealed that a source in Lisbon had predicted that the Germans intended to occupy the whole of France and particularly Marseille on the pretext that Pétain was losing control. There was a great deal of truth in this report as we shall see. It went on: 'Axis agents had already been sent to Tunis and Algeria and possibly Morocco, to incite populations against de Gaulle and present French Government as having collapsed.'[40] This signal would probably reinforce North's feelings that the French would be trying to escape from threatened Vichy at this time.

On the evening of the 9th Admiral North received a signal directly to him, and repeated to the Foreign Office which read:

IMMEDIATE
Following from Jacques.
French squadron in Mediterranean may try to pass Straits of Gibraltar proceeding westwards for unknown destination. This attempt may be timed to take place within the next seventy-two hours.[41]

This signal from the British Consul-General at Tangier had been despatched at 1824 on the 9th and was received by North at 2045 that same evening while he was dining with Somerville at The Mount. The information came from a highly regarded informant, (graded 'A' in reliability). 'Jacques' was in fact Captain Charles Jean Luizet, a French Army Intelligence Officer on the staff at Tangier. He had secretly joined the Free French cause earlier and was well-placed to give accurate data. Admiral North did nothing on receipt of this signal other than ensure that it had, as requested, been duly repeated to the Foreign Office in London for transmission to the Admiralty.

The signal went its leisurely way through the process of passing from department to department. It was repeated on to Whitehall at 1850 and arrived in the Foreign Office at 0750 on the 10th. Here it went into the strange limbo particular to Government departments. Being prefixed 'Immediate' held no guarantee that it would receive instant de-coding treatment, for, as we have seen, everyone prefixed their messages in the same way. Thus Tangier's signal had to take its turn with several hundred other messages from Ambassadors and the like the world over. It did not finally emerge again in de-coded form until *several days* later. For this departmental sloth, in the finest traditions of the Civil Service, Churchill offered up the following excuse post-war:

At this time we were under almost continuous bombardment in London. Owing to the recurrent stoppages of work through air raids, arrears had accumulated in the cipher branch. The message was not marked 'Important' and was deciphered only in its turn.[42]

The same excuse is offered up in the War Cabinet Office in 1942 in their monograph on Dakar, thus: 'It was not marked important, and, owing to arrears and to stopping work in air raids, it did not reach the Admiralty till the 14th.'[43]

Too much is made of the fact that there were only small daytime air raids on 9th, 10th and 11th September. The point is surely that when the Air Raid warnings went, the staff took to the shelters, which in the Foreign Office Communications Department were some considerable distance from the working office itself, which meant inevitable prolonged delays until the 'All Clear' sounded. It is immaterial whether the cause of the warning each time consisted of a large raid by many bombers or by a single aircraft, the delay was caused in either instance.[44] Even if there had been no raids at all there would have still have been been considerable delay due to the enormous backlog of messages and the arrival of others bearing a higher priority than Immediate. In all events there is no record of any departmental head or officer receiving reprimand.

When Professor Marder writes that North had no reason to suppose that the Admiralty would fail to receive this message he is paraphrasing North's own report which stated that, 'I had no reason to suppose that the Admiralty would fail to receive this message since the procedure followed was normal in all respects.' Their Lordships' opinion was that the passage of so large a squadron at the time Menace was being prepared was not a 'normal' situation and called for more vigorous reaction.

As it was, North assumed that the Admiralty had received the message, and, that had they required any action they would have told him so. Hearing nothing further that day he assumed all was well. After dining with Somerville at the Official Residence on the evening of the 10th therefore, North turned in for the night, confident that all was in order. However soon after midnight North received an urgent telephone call from his Chief of Staff. A message had been received from Captain Alan Hillgarth, the British Naval Attaché, Madrid. Timed at 1809 on the 10th it arrived at Gibraltar at 0008 on the 11th and was de-coded within twenty minutes. It read as follows:

IMMEDIATE
French Admiralty to me begins: please advise naval authorities Gibraltar

departure from Toulon 9th September three cruisers type *Georges Leygues* and three French cruisers *Le Fantasque* class which will pass Straits a.m. 11th. National (?)Indicatives painted Ends. Destination not known.[45]

Clearly then the French were on the move, and in some strength.

What had brought about this large deployment of naval units after such a long period of apparent quiescence?

CHAPTER TEN

The Mission of Force Y

That the French Navy in 1939 was one of the most modern in the world was due to the work between the wars of Georges Leygues who was Minister of Marine for seven years from 1926. Under his guidance the French Navy was planned after the Treaty of Washington, to match that of Italy. In the years leading up to the First World War France had fallen badly behind in naval matters, falling from second place to a poor fifth and having a fleet full of experimental types of little fighting value. It had not shone during the war and took part in no major actions, even in the Mediterranean theatre, save at the Dardanelles. But under Leygues the foundation was laid for a highly effective fleet. Limited in size to fourth place with Italy, behind Britain, USA and Japan, and with limited funds, France nonetheless began a reconstruction programme which produced a series of warship designs the equals of any navy of the 1930s.

This work was taken over by François Darlan, and he guided each programme through with tenacity and loving care until the fleet of 1939 was widely regarded as his creation; certainly he was highly respected by the whole of the navy, while his achievement was acknowleged abroad by the other major powers, as a great one. It is important to stress just how much influence Darlan wielded over the French Navy and the respect his word commanded, for it was far greater than the equivalent Commander-in-Chief in Britain for example.[1] Having created a superb fighting weapon it was natural that Darlan would cherish it and he remained fiercely opposed to any interference in Navy matters by outside parties. On the collapse of France it was the French Navy's internal organisation that held firm as a rock and efficient while those of the Army and Government crumbled. Thus the Navy's signalling organisation was the only reliable means of communication during those traumatic days and they had far greater awareness and grip on events than anyone else.

Darlan did not like the British at all,[2] resenting both the freezing of France's fleet to that of the size of Italy's, instead of both Italy *and*

Germany, and the British agreement with Nazi Germany of 1935, taken without consultation. He saw Dunkirk and Mers-el-Kebir as betrayals. Nonetheless he saw to it that his fleet performed its duty well, within its limitations, up to the Armistice in 1940. Although it was still behind the Royal Navy in many ways, such as in night fighting, anti-submarine methods, radar and the like, and was less efficient in sea keeping, in some ways the French Navy was ahead, as in the development of efficient anti-aircraft weapons and the submarine. France's re-armament started earlier than Britain's, and in the battle-cruisers *Dunkerque* and *Strasbourg* it was led by fine modern ships. The even larger battleships *Jean Bart* and *Richelieu* then completing in June 1940, were superb ships, on paper far more powerful than Britain's newest battleships,[3] and ready far earlier, and it was expected therefore that France would play a far greater role in the war at sea in 1939 than in 1914.

The Armistice completely changed the picture of course. Darlan was determined to maintain the powerful fleet in its state of high efficiency and readiness, but was not prepared either to allow the Axis to lay their hands on it, or to keep fighting on the side of Britain. He wished to keep strictly neutral, thinking that Britain was finished anyway and not wishing to squander France's last major asset in needless sacrifice. Of course in Britain, fighting for her very life, the existence of such a powerful force, if allied to the two Axis fleets, represented a latent threat, for only Hitler's word stood between Darlan's sincere intentions and more realistic possibilities. So Mers-el-Kebir, and almost total rift between the former allies.

Darlan's immediate reaction after Mers-el-Kebir was one of fury; indeed he wished to order the French fleet to sea to give battle with Force H there and then, but wiser counsels prevailed and between July and September a gradual thaw had set in as we have seen, with both sides wishing to avoid further provocation though reserving their attitude on various issues.

The French dilemma was a very real and complex one. On the one hand were the demands of the Axis powers under the terms of the Armistice that the French disarm almost totally under supervision.[4] On the other was Darlan's desire to evade this by every means possible until such time as an opportunity arose to renew the conflict with his fleet intact. Thus all negotiations were delicate and the constant abrasion of British policy against the French colonies at this time threatened to wreck the fine balance Darlan was trying to achieve.

The eruption of the Free French movement and its subversion of the African colonies pushed this balance to the limits. Already the French were under renewed pressure from the Axis to comply with the Armistice terms. A temporary relaxation of the harsher dictates with regard to disarming had taken place in the aftermath of Mers-el-Kebir, but by mid-July the Axis were again leaning heavily on France.

On 15th July the German Armistice Commission, led by General Karl Stülpnagel, presented fresh demands to the President of the French Delegation, General Charles Huntziger, at Wiesbaden. These called for the Axis use of the French Mediterranean ports in France and North Africa along with its airfields, use of the Casablanca railway and other items which would result in little less than a German occupation of Morocco, Algeria and Tunisia. The Pétain Government resisted these demands furiously, but it was in a weak position and although Germany did not press them for the moment (Hitler hoped to negotiate an agreement) they were obviously looking for any excuse to elbow their way into Africa and thus forestall the British. The infiltration of the Free French into the colonies south of this area would obviously give them just cause to claim that France was going back on the Armistice terms by allowing Britain, through her Free French 'puppets', to raise these vast domains and re-arm and re-equip them against the Axis.

Thus although the incidents at Mers-el-Kebir and Casablanca did not much concern the Germans,[5] the rallying of Chad to de Gaulle and the obtaining by the British thereby of the strategically important air base of Fort Lamy roused them to fresh resolve. The Reich representatives on the Armistice Commission demanded that France honour her obligations by making a determined attempt to re-capture such places and, further, to ensure that no further defections took place in a similar manner. In order to forestall any Axis moves therefore the French decided that they must make some show of force.

Again this was difficult, as Paul Baudouin, Minister for Foreign Affairs, discovered when he questioned the French Navy about their ability to defend the African colonies against a British attack. There was no possible way an all-out assault could be resisted, he was told. But it had not come to this stage yet and it might be possible, with a limited display of strength, to prevent any further bloodless conquests by the Free French. For this purpose a powerful naval squadron off the coast would ensure that no further infiltration took place by clearing away all British merchant ships and warships from within twenty miles of the coast. Small detachments of troops would be moved into the suspect areas to back up internally this quarantine, and these could be transported in from the more reliable colonies to the north.[6] In enforcing this blockade the French would be doing no more than carrying out their declared intentions, which the British had hitherto accepted, but on the other hand they would show the Axis that they were capable of controlling their own territories.

The French attitude had been broadcast to all units on 4th and 5th July, immediately after Mers-el-Kebir, thus:

> Because of the hostile attitude of the British navy attack all British warships met, seize and conduct to a French port all merchant ships.[7]

Which was modified the next day thus:

> Do not attack any British warships on the high seas but be on guard to reply against force.
> It is forbidden to all British ships and aircraft to penetrate within twenty miles of the French or French colonial coastlines without being attacked without warning.[8]

This latter order was, as we have seen, embodied in the British Admiralty's own instructions, with reservations and both sides had kept to them to the letter after the incidents of summer. To implement their proposals it was not therefore necessary for the French to modify these instructions in any way as they saw it.

Moreover events in Equatorial Africa had already caused local naval units to be placed in a similar situation with the stepping up of British activity in the Middle Congo and Gabon. French anxiety that the lid was about to blow off this area came to a head with reports of the establishment of regular British naval patrols from the South Atlantic Station cruisers and events early in September at Pointe Noire.

Before examining the ticklish situation that arose here two further points on the French position should be made regarding the vulnerability to outside pressure. Firstly Germany's Axis partner, Italy was far more intransigent with regard to the fate of the French Navy, understandably so for with the French warships concentrated in the Mediterranean Italy had the most to fear, should it revive. They were adamant that it be disarmed, but, as always, Germany had the last word. Italy of course was hoping to gain from any sign of French weakness in the same way as Germany, but her ambitions were the old ones of gaining Tunisia, Corsica and Nice. These pre-war parrot cries of Mussolini's followers were the main reason they had gone to war and Germany's insistence that Italy only occupy what she had gained by force of arms left the Italians both empty-handed and resentful after the Armistice. No opportunity would be overlooked by the Italians to get control of these places should a fresh opportunity arise.[9]

Secondly, yet a third power stood to gain should France visibly indicate that she was impotent in Africa: Fascist Spain. Although she was exhausted by her own Civil War, and by no means certain that Britain was finished, Hitler made attempts to woo her into action, and his plans for Gibraltar were dependent on her co-operation. The restoration of Gibraltar to her was only part of the bait however, for she had long had her eye on French Morocco.

According to the terms of the 1912 Algerian Treaty Morocco was divided into two protectorates, the small northern enclave being administered by Spain, the bulk of the country by France. But there was an important proviso in that treaty in that should at any time France be unable to maintain that protectorate through her own weakness or will, Spain could, by legal right, assume that mantle, and in mid-1940 Spain was obviously in a nice position, had she chosen, to make that claim good.[10]

So, in every respect, the Government at Vichy had to make *some* show of force, and the news received by them on 29th August of Chad Colony's defection brought matters to a head, and immediate reinforcements were ordered into the neighbouring colonies.

The presence of the British cruiser *Delhi* at Pointe Noire further raised French fears: 'From a simple police action the intervention at Pointe Noire threatened to turn into an open conflict with the British Navy', wrote Hervé Cras. On the other hand, 'Gaullist infiltrations into Gabon were accentuated. The tone of the appeals from Larminat left no doubt of their intentions ...'[11]

Meanwhile back in France events were now in train to put a stop to this. On 27 August Rear Admiral Jean Bourragué, commanding the 4th Cruiser Squadron at Toulon, and flying his flag in the light cruiser *George Leygues*, was given his initial orders to prepare a special squadron from the 4th Cruiser Squadron and the 10th Destroyer Flotilla for a secret mission. Under the terms of the Armistice of course all these ships were de-activated and considerable work had to be got underway to get the ships ready for sea again quickly in fighting trim. Fuel, ammunition and provisions had to be topped up and crews brought up to full strength from peace-time complements, in some cases with drafts from other warships. While these preparations duly got underway the French formally applied to the German Armistice Commission for permission to mount the operation. This application was made on 30th August and at first met with a negative response.

Nonetheless preparations at Toulon continued, and the squadron was officially designated Force Y on the 30th. Considerable re-shuffling of ships and men ensued. One of the super-destroyers originally earmarked for the operation, *L'Indomptable*,[12] had to be replaced and commands assigned. The captain of the cruiser *Montcalm* was replaced by the captain of the *Jean de Vienne*, Captain Maurice Ferrière, Captain Budu Lemonnier took command of the cruiser *Georges Leygues*. Captain Jean Broussignac assumed command of the cruiser *Gloire*, while the 10th DCT[13] was commanded by the Divisional senior officer, Captain Paul Auguste Still, with his flag in *Le Fantasque*; *L'Audacieux* was commanded by Commander Ernest Derrien and *Le Malin* by Commander Edouard Desprez.

What with the haste of the preparations and their unusual nature there was as little secrecy about the activities of Force Y at Toulon as there had been with the sailing organisation of Force M at Liverpool. In both cases the mission was the common talk of the dockyards and the local bars. Strangely enough in *both* cases not a single word of it leaked out to the enemy!

Meantime the Germans were deliberating on events and finally gave the mission their sanction, subject to Italian approval. Admiral Raeder later detailed the reasoning behind it in his report for the afternoon of 6th September.

6. *Treatment of the French Colonies:*

In the French possessions in Equatorial Africa there is an open break with Pétain's government and a swing over to General de Gaulle. There is danger that unrest and revolt might spread to the French West African colonies. The economic situation in the colonies, particularly as regards foodstuffs, is used by Britain as a means of exerting pressure. An agreement between the colonies and Britain, and revolt against France would jeopardize our own chances of controlling the African area; the danger exists that strategically important West African ports might be used for British convoy activities and that we might lose a valuable source of supplies for Europe. The danger of an attack on the part of the

USA is not entirely out of the question, in view of the possibilities for such action.

Far-sighted German measures are necessary to counteract any development of this kind. Therefore the Naval Staff agrees in principle to sending French naval forces to the areas threatened; to the resumption of merchant traffic between the colonies and neutral countries by means of French and neutral vessels, in order to alleviate economic difficulties; and to the attempt to re-establish merchant shipping between France and her colonies.

A condition is that ships must be scuttled in the event of capture by British forces. Germany and Italy must have the opportunity to control the vessels. There must be economic advantages to Germany and German right of recall.[14]

On 30th August the French Naval Command issued detailed instructions to cover eventualities in the threatened area of Chad, Cameroon and the French Congo. These were to be a general guide for Force Y's operations as well as to local forces.

For the correct attitude to observe against the British here are directives which annul all other previous directives given.

1 Abstain from all attacks on British warships at least if they are not approaching within less than twenty miles of the shore or if they are not directly menacing.

2 Ensure a good level of preventive security and be ready to react promptly against all attacks, wherever they happen. Take steps for air reprisals to be rapidly launched.

3 These directives are independent of those which I have especially given or those I have given for particular operations.

4 This answers Telegram 2323 of 30th August, Admiral Sud.

5 Confirm receipt to me.[15]

The Italians were more suspicious than the Germans of the motives for sending such a large French force out of the Mediterranean and out of their immediate supervision, but finally Turin gave their approval on 1st September. However, they made additional conditions. It was insisted that the French agree to resist any British attacks on their squadron and that, should the worst come to the worst, they would scuttle their ships rather than allow the Royal Navy to capture them. To these conditions the French were obliged to agree, on the surface anyway, though an all-out fight was the very last thing that they sought for Force Y, as their subsequent orders and actions were to show. However they had to appear to go along with these Axis demands while all the time working behind the scenes to see that nothing of this nature happened.[16]

The Axis commentary on these events seemed to indicate that they were taken in well enough; a note at the time recorded:

> On 1st September 1940, however, after the Italian High Command had studied the situation, the French were granted permission to send three cruisers to the West African coast. A guarantee had to be given that the ships would resist any British attack. In the event of a deterioration of the situation in West Africa, the Italian High Command promised to consider the possibility of releasing more of the warships in Toulon.[17]

In the interim however the Italians wanted the screw tightened up on the French whom they suspected, with much justification, of stalling on disarmament. In their formal reply of 3rd September they stated that although the sailing of Force Y was agreed to they wanted the immediate re-introduction of the naval clause in the Armistice agreement, it had been suspended since 4th July due to Mers-el-Kebir. They demanded the complete disarming of the remaining French warships at Toulon to be completed by 30th September.

The French, through General Huntziger, protested at this and their delegation at Wiesbaden delivered a strong protest to General von Stülpnagel, president of the German Armistice Commission, adding a memorandum to the effect that the state of the fleet, coupled with a further run-down, exposed the French Empire to grave risks at the moment of the first unrest.[18]

Stülpnagel countered by reminding them that authorisation for the use of certain formations had already been given, and this was not affected, but that this did not change the obligations of France to fulfil her duties to disarm strictly according to the time-table laid down in the Armistice Conditions. He concluded with a threat, which the French recognised only too well, that, should the French Government be unable to re-establish order in her endangered territories, the German and Italian Governments reserved their attitudes!

Meanwhile Darlan was busy organising the sortie and laying the groundwork to ensure as far as possible that it went without a hitch. The greatest danger to Force Y lay in its passage through the Straits of Gibraltar, both unavoidable and impossible to pass without detection by day or night. As it could not evade detection Darlan did everything he could to both gauge the mood of the British and ensure that there was not the slightest provocation to goad them into action.

Firstly Admiral D'Harcourt at Casablanca was instructed to test the water by sending through the Straits an experimental convoy to see what action the Royal Navy took, as nothing of this nature had been tried since July. Basic details of Force Y's mission were also sent to him and this was the information 'Jacques' obtained at Casablanca and duly passed on. The convoy consisted of the armed trawler *Pescagel* escorted by the sloop *Elan*. The convoy sailed on 7th September and, as we have seen, passed through the Straits without hindrance, arriving at Oran on the 9th. D'Harcourt noted with satisfaction that: '*Pescagel* and *Elan* both passed Gibraltar yesterday evening, safely in the mist'.[19] A later diary entry noted that: '*Elan* and *Pescagel* arrived at Oran without difficulties. The English had a good look at *Pescagel* and demanded nothing.'[20] The experiment was a complete success and the omens seemed good for Force Y; this information was duly passed on to Vichy.

Darlan's general orders to Force Y were the subject of a message sent on 3rd September:

SECRET

The 4th Cruiser Division and *Fantasque, Malin* and *Audacieux* will sail from Toulon on a date to be subsequently fixed and strike a direct route for Dakar, stopping at Casablanca, under the command of the Admiral Commanding the 4th Cruiser Division, to place themselves at the disposal of the Governor General of AOF for a policing mission and any other liaison duty that is necessary. In carrying out this mission you are to avoid any hostile actions and gesture of provocation towards British forces, other than when you are menaced by hostile action directly from shore or ships. The route is direct from Toulon to Gibraltar; the passage through the Straits of Gibraltar to be taken at daybreak and at high speed. The force you are to command will be designated as Force Y.[21]

A further secret and personal message dated 5th September followed which contained up to the minute information on the set-up in the threatened area for Bourragué to be put in the picture. The plan, as envisaged by the French at that time, was that an attack on Pointe Noire was to be organised for 15th September, but the main object of the exercise was to keep all these colonies firmly under French control at Vichy. They relied almost completely on the active presence of this large naval force off the coast to sway events and trusted also in the resumption of normal commercial traffic with the homeland, once the British blockade had been made ineffectual by their presence, to restore confidence.

To ensure that the British at Gibraltar did not have cause to suspect, it was intended that they should be informed of the passage of Force Y through the Straits, but this was to be done at the last possible moment to ensure that they did not have time to organise any force to oppose them. The British would not have the time to make malevolent dispositions. The sailing date was fixed for 1600 on 9th September (French time) and a speed was calculated which would bring the French squadron to the most dangerous part of the journey, the Straits themselves, at sunrise on the 11th. There would thus be no cause for misunderstanding which an attempted night passage might have provoked.

These operational plans were known to few outside the Admiral's immediate staff aboard the *George Leygues* and essential commanders at Toulon and Casablanca. For example, although their destination was widely talked about around the harbour area, officially little of the actual operations themselves was communicated to the ship's officers. The captain of the *Gloire*, Captain Jean Broussignac, later recalled that:

> I never at any time had direct knowledge of the orders, instructions etc received by Admiral Bourragué. He only told us on departure; 'I know the aim of our mission is to re-establish our control over the colony of Gabon which is in a state of dissidence. We are to transport there a contingent of black troops to help us in our action.' We certainly knew that there would be an enormous chance that we would run foul of English opposition; firstly on the voyage past Gibraltar and later in the Atlantic. Had precise instructions been given to our Admiral for this eventuality or had the decision been left to his own initiative? I only knew I was simply ready to do whatever he ordered. I had the impression that we would leave such things a little at random and that we would hope that surprise and rapid execution would be able to give us some slight chance of success.[22]

At 1100 on the morning of the 4th September, Admiral Charles Platon, Vichy Secretary for the Colonies, visited Admiral Bourragué aboard his flagship in Toulon harbour and the situation was discussed. That afternoon, at 1630, Bourragué himself flew to Vichy for an interview with Admiral Darlan and a final briefing, returning by air at 1900 on the 5th. Next morning the CO's of the six warships were summoned to a meeting aboard the *Georges Leygues* at 1000. All was now ready for the sortie.

What manner of man had Darlan entrusted with this most difficult and delicate of missions? From his record it would seem that Darlan had picked wisely, for Bourragué was a very experienced

(*Right*) The Prime Minister, Winston Spencer Churchill, in May 1940.

(*Below*) Admiral of the Fleet Sir Dudley Pound, First Sea Lord.

HM battleship *Warspite*. Rebuilt pre-war, she was the only British heavy ship with the speed and range to get into action at Calabria.

HM battleship *Malaya*. Not modernised like her former sister, her guns lacked sufficient elevation to match the range of the Italian ships.

(*Right*) Admiral Sir Andrew B. Cunningham, C-in-C, Mediterranean. A fearless fighter with a fine contempt for the enemy and pressure from Whitehall alike.

(*Right*) The Italian Fleet Commander, Inigo Campioni, on the bridge of his flagship during the battle of Calabria. Badly let down by the Air Force, he was faced with an unenviable choice.

The total British air continge
was contained in HM aircr
carrier *Eagle*. Old, slow ar
with no proper fighter aircr
great hopes were pinned
her young pilots to slow do
the flying enemy.

British Air Power. The Fai
Swordfish, Torpedo Bomb
Reconnaissance and
maid-of-all-work, these ol
bi-planes were obsolete
before war broke out, yet w
on to carve a legend. A
striking force takes off fro
HMS *Eagle* during the bat

Italian Air Power. The Sm
'Sparrow', long-range
bomber and mainstay of th
Regia Aeronautica in 1940.
the standards of the day t
tri-motor monoplane was
formidable adversary and
squadrons were highly skill
in mass attacks on warshi

Photographed from the Italian flagship, the battleship *Conte di Cavour* opens fire with a full salvo against the British fleet.

The Italian heavy cruiser *Fiume* looses off an 8-inch salvo, her guns trained on an extreme after bearing.

Climax of the battle. The Italian flagship *Giulio Cesare* is hit by a 15-inch shell at extreme range from the *Warspite*; two other shells from the same salvo land close ahead of her.

The damage caused aboard the *Cesare* after her first direct hit. Several light AA guns have been wiped out and her after funnel pierced as well as her main deck.

The Italian heavy cruiser *Fiume*. One of several 8-inch cruisers available to the Italians at the battle, she attempted to work round ahead of the British fleet, but was driven back by the *Warspite's* accurate shooting.

The Italian destroyer *Bersagliere,* of the 13th Squadron, was typical of the Italian destroyers of this period; faster than their British opposite numbers and equal in armament, their tactics and training fell far short of expectations.

The British destroyer HMS *Janus* was one of the most modern of that type in the Fleet at the battle of Calabria. She was part of the 14th Flotilla whose counter-attack was called off before they could close the enemy.

Bombs, bombs and more bombs. The battleship *Malaya* is surrounded by great columns of spray from near misses the day after the battle of Calabria.

The *Eagle* (*centre*) and *Royal Sovereign* (*extreme left*) framed by bursting bombs during the battle, as seen from HM cruiser *Neptune*.

A. V. Alexander, First Lord of the Admiralty in 1940.

Admiral Sir Dudley North with General Sir Clive Liddell, the Governor of Gibraltar, and the latter's Chief of Staff, at Gibraltar in 1940.

(*Left*) The Tower, by Gibraltar's dockside, Admi North's Office HQ at the Ro

(*Left*) A 9.2-inch gun positi atop the Rock. These weapons were the largest guns of the Fortress Command's Coastal Defer Batteries and had the range cover the whole Straits.

(*Right*) Gibraltar from the Straits. A destroyer of the 13th Flotilla approaches t harbour at Gibraltar, early 1940. The harbour moles just be made out with the upperworks of the ships projecting above them.

(*Left*) Vice-Admiral Sir James Somerville, Senior Officer, Force H, a 1942 photograph, on the bridge of his flagship. (*Below*) HM battle-cruiser *Renown*, flagship of Force H in 1940.

(*Left*) Captain F. S. De Winton, Captain (D) 13th Destroyer Flotilla, in the gardens of North's official residence, The Mount, in 1940.

(*Below*) Ships of the 13th Destroyer Flotilla. HM destroyer *Velox*, one of the oldest destroyers in the Royal Navy. A 1939 photograph showing her appearance as she was in 1940 with one bank of triple torpedo tubes and one bank of double torpedo tubes.

Ships of the 13th Destroyer Flotilla. HM destroyer *Wishart*, one of the divisional leaders of the flotilla. This is a 1931 photo but she was little changed in 1940.

(*Left*) Admiral of the Fleet Jean Louis Darlan, Commander-in-Chief of the French Navy in 1940. His main aim in 1940 was to preserve his fleet as a fighting unit intact for future eventualities. (*Right*) Rear Admiral Celestin Jean Bourragué, Commander of Force Y in 1940. He was chosen by Darlan for his tact and sensitivity for what was known to be a delicate and hazardous mission.

The light cruiser *Georges Leygues*, flagship of Force Y; a pre-war photograph. All these French cruisers were fitted to carry spotting aircraft on a catapult aft, but none actually had their floatplanes embarked for this particular mission. (*Insert*) Captain Budú Lemonnier, captain of the *Georges Leygues*. A 1943 photograph. (*Below*) The light cruiser *Montcalm* of Force Y, a pre-war photograph.

(*Left*) Captain Jean Paul Broussignac, captain of the *Gloire*. He kept his crew ready for action during the passage of the Straits.

The light cruiser *Gloire*, A pre-war photograph. After the dash from Toulon and the escape from Casablanca her turbines broke down in a sortie from Dakar and she was escorted away by the British before the abortive operation took place.

The *contre-torpilleur* (super-destroyer) *Le Fantasque*, leader of the 10th DCT, commanded by Captain Paul Auguste Still. A 1940 photo at Toulon.

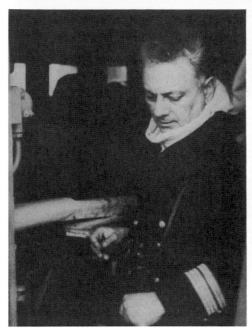

(*Left*) Captain Edouard Desprez, captain of *Le Malin*. A 1944 photograph taken off the Normandy beachhead. (*Right*) Captain Ernest Derrien, captain of *L'Audacieux*, a later wartime photograph after his promotion.

The super-destroyer *Le Malin* of the 10th DCT, a pre-war photo.

The super-destroyer *L'Audacieux*. A 1936 photograph. After she reached Dakar she was badly damaged in action there. Later, under repair, she was again heavily damaged during the Allied landings of 1942.

Ships of the 13th Flotilla HM destroyer *Hotspur*, divisional leader of the flotilla and the first to sight the French force. A veteran of Narvik, she is seen in this early 1940 photograph before her after bank of torpedo tubes had been replaced by a 3-inch AA gun.

Ships of the 13th Flotilla HM destroyer *Griffin*. This photograph was taken in 1941 off Crete and shows the wartime modifications which applied to *Hotspur* and *Encounter* also at this time.

Captain H. F. H. Layman on the bridge of *Hotspur*. As Senior Divisional Officer of the force which sighted the French squadron he gave clear reports to Gibraltar and decided to shadow them, but was later called off.

Admiral Domenico Cavagnari, Chief of the Italian Naval Staff in September 1940. He was the Chief Naval Representative on the Italian Armistice Commission. The Italians were less eager to grant the Vichy authorities permission to sail reinforcements from Toulon to Libreville than the Germans, and imposed much sterner conditions on the passage of Force Y.

The British submarine *Truant*, one of two fully-operational submarines in harbour at Gibraltar when Force Y passed through the Straits. She was a modern vessel and she and her sister *Triad* had seen much war experience off Norway a few weeks before joining North's command. The *Truant* went on to become one of the most famous British submarines and had a long period of service in the Royal Navy. This is a post-war photograph.

The harbour at Casablanca, first stop for Force Y, and blockaded in vain by Force H after the French had slipped away. This is a 1936 photograph.

Ships of the 13th Flotilla. HM destroyer *Vidette*. Her 4-inch guns drove off the French super-destroyer *Milan* in a brief encounter in the early hours of the morning. This is a later wartime photograph, taken about 1941, when her after bank of tubes had been replaced by an AA gun. (*Inset*) Lieutenant Eric Walmsley, captain of the destroyer *Vidette*. The youngest destroyer captain in the force at this time, it fell to him to make the vital decision to open fire off Casablanca. A later wartime photo after his promotion.

Ships of the 13th Flotilla. HM destroyer *Encounter*. This is a 1938 photograph showing her before her after tubes had been landed and replaced by a 3-inch gun, as they had by September 1940.

The super-destroyer *Milan*. Returning to Casablanca from a convoy duty she ran into Force H and was fired upon before establishing her identity.

(*Left*) Captain Louis Plumejeaud, captain of the *Milan*. Due to deciphering difficulties he was unaware that Force H was at sea. He withdrew his command and did not fire despite his warm reception and brought his vessel safely into Casablanca. (*Right*) Captain Hubert Monraisse, a later wartime photograph. After being fired on and his Hawk fighter damaged by the London flying boat over Casablanca, he shot it into the sea. He was later killed in action over Germany flying Spitfires in 1944.

(Left) Harold Macmillan. *(Right)* Admiral of the Fleet Earl Mountbatten of Burma was First Sea Lord in 1955. An old friend of North's he did all he could to help him and finally brought him some comfort. This is a 1955 photograph taken on his assumption of office.

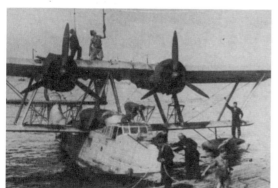

(Above, left) A Saro London flying boat of No 202 Squadron. These old aircraft were North's only long-range reconnaissance aircraft and were very slow and vulnerable.

Vichy Air Power:
(Above right) A Curtiss Hawk 75 fighter of the French Air Force and *(Bottom)* Glenn Martin 167F light bomber of the kind used to shadow Force H off Casablanca.

The Battle of Spartivento. Seen from the escorting cruiser *Sheffield*, the *Ark Royal* launches her striking force to attack the Italian fleet.

The Swordfish attack. Splashes from their torpedoes can be seen as one torpedo bomber pushes on inside the Italian destroyer screen. Despite their bravery the young Fleet Air Arm pilots again achieved no hits.

The opposing cruisers were soon in action. Here the Italian heavy cruiser *Trieste*, making smoke and steaming hard, is close-missed by a salvo from her British opposite number.

HM battle-cruiser *Renown* in action at Spartivento. Admiral Somerville's flagship fires salvos at extreme range as the Italian fleet retreats across her bows.

Renown's 15-inch shells had a similar effect on the Italians as *Warspite's* had at Calabria. Here a wide-spread salvo falls just short astern an Italian light cruiser.

Under heavy fire from *Renown*, the Italians broke off the battle as fast as they could. An Italian destroyer lays down a heavy smokescreen for protection.

Mission accomplished!
In line ahead *Renown, Ramillies* and *Berwick* after the battle had been called off.

officer, highly regarded by his men and with a good background of leadership in most areas of the Navy. A contemporary described him thus:

> Admiral Bourragué was a native of Bearn, a man of great intelligence and pleasant temperament. I had never met him before I assumed command of the *Gloire* but very quickly I had friendly and trustful relations with him.[23]

He was never to need his tact and knowledge of the sea more than on this particular mission which was fraught with danger and difficulties.

While the ships thus prepared to get under way Darlan had been laying his plans to tip off the British without alerting the Axis he had done so. Despite the anger at events earlier in the year tentative diplomatic relations had been re-established by several back doors in the intervening period. For example Admiral Gabriel Auphan had resumed discreet contact with Admiral Tom Phillips in London through the offices of Monsieur Dupuis, the Canadian Minister. From such contacts and the passage of the trial convoy the French Admiralty was almost certain that the passage of their ships would not be opposed, but precautions were still essential for trust was far from absolute.

A key link in the next move was the special relationship maintained by the British and French Naval Attachés in neutral Madrid, Captain Alan Hillgarth and Captain Rambert Delaye. Hillgarth later described how this came about:

> At the time of the collapse of France I had done my best to persuade him to throw in his lot with us and had offered to provide for his wife and children till France was free again. After a lot of thought Captain Delaye refused, but he was grateful. After Mers-el-Kebir he kept away from me, but a little later he came around to see me – always we met in his house or mine ...
>
> The Admiralty got into the habit of passing messages – about ships and crews and so forth – to the French Ministry of Marine at Vichy through me, and the French Minister of Marine replied and instituted inquiries – and protests – by the same channel. I was able, also, to pick up a certain amount of quite useful information, and on several occasions Delaye told me things or hinted at them, obviously hoping they would be passed on. Once or twice he gave them to me in the form of messages for me from the French Ministry of Marine – always verbal, of course. He would say, 'I have been told to give you the following message.'[24]

For the execution of his plan Darlan, certainly in this instance, determined to make the fullest use of Hillgarth and on 6th September he signalled Delaye as follows:

1. Three cruisers type *Georges Leygues* and three destroyers will leave Toulon around 9th September for Casablanca and Dakar. To avoid misunderstanding the ships will pass the Straits of Gibraltar at dawn but in daylight and with national markings painted up on their upperworks.
    2. So that no misunderstanding can be claimed by the British they should be advised of the day of the passage, I repeat the day only, telling them however that this passage would be made in the morning only. So that they would have insufficient time to take counter-action it is essential that the British authorities are held in ignorance of the passage for as long as possible.
    3. The advice of the passage during J Day is to reach the British authorities at Gibraltar at Zero hour Greenwich Mean Time on Day J.
    4. As soon as the firm date is known for the departure from Toulon of our naval force anticipated in Part 1, I will send, in personal code, a conventional telegram as follows, 'J-such day'. This will mean that the information of the passage on the morning of J Day should be sent to the British authorities at Gibraltar at Zero hour GMT of this J Day.
5. As from now study the conditions and expedient times which you require to ensure that this information reaches the British Naval Attaché as per (3).
6. You should also advise the Spanish Naval Authorities on the same day.
7. Confirm receipt.[25]

As Delaye later recalled; 'I had received orders from the French Admiralty to warn the British Naval Attaché of the immediate passage through the Straits of a cruiser division, which I did.'[26] How he did this Hillgarth later described:

On the afternoon of 10th September he came to see me – having telephoned half an hour earlier. We talked for several minutes about nothing in particular, and then he said, 'Oh yes, I've been told to give you a message this afternoon. From the Ministry of Marine. Please tell your naval authorities at Gibraltar that three cruisers of *Georges Leygues* class and three of the *Fantasque* class left Toulon on the 9th and will pass through the Straits am on the 11th. The national flag is painted on the sides.'
    I said, 'That was yesterday. You might have let me know before.'
    He made a face and shrugged his shoulders. I then asked where they were going, to which he replied that he didn't know any more than what he had been told to tell me. He then finished his whisky and soda and

went, and I went to the Embassy as fast as I could and sent the ciphered signal you got – my 1809.

I knew – from previous examples – that both Delaye and someone in Vichy, who was probably Auphan, were telling me things now and then that they weren't supposed to tell, I believe in order to have a stake in both camps; a form of insurance. I was almost certain in this instance from what he said and the way he said it that he'd been told not to tell me sooner. Perhaps he had even told me several hours before he should have done so.

I didn't know about Dakar, though I had guessed something was going on. The Ambassador knew but wasn't available till dinner time, when I told him of Delaye's message and he approved what I had done, but still he didn't mention Dakar. All the same I felt I must get the news through at once and so sent the brief 'Immediate' signal addressed to Admiralty (DNI) and repeated to you.[27]

This was not the only warning the French gave. At 1000 (French time) on the same day Delaye had duped Hillgarth and passed the message, the Spanish Foreign Minister, Colonel Juan Beigbeder, sent for the British Ambassador in Spain, Sir Samuel Hoare, and relayed the same titbit, which Delaye had prompted him on earlier, knowing that, due to the pro-British attitude of Beigbeder, it would also reach the right ears.[28] And so it did.

We know that North duly received Hillgarth's signal; what action then did our Ambassador take on receipt of this news, knowing, as he did, all about Dakar? It is difficult to say, even after this passage of time, but it seems that he did little or nothing. What he claimed to have done he described later thus: 'As there was not a moment to be lost, I thanked him for the news and at once went to the Embassy where I telegraphed it to Gibraltar.'[29] He later amplified this statement still further: 'I stayed with the Minister for only two or three minutes and hurried off to my naval attaché's flat, where, together, we drafted two most urgent telegrams to the Admiralty and the admiral at Gibraltar.'[30]

These versions and Hillgarth's do not match of course; one or the other got the truth mixed up in later years, or the story grew in the telling. Certainly Hillgarth later denied that Hoare ever visited him at his flat to draft the telegram, and there is apparently absolutely no record of any such urgent messages originating from Hoare at that time on record.[31] If he did indeed send these telegrams as he claims they seemed to have ended up in some limbo en route. Be that as it may, nothing was *received* from Hoare which just left Hillgarth's message to be acted upon, as Gascoigne's warning had already vanished into the maw of the Foreign Office as we have seen.

Completely unaware of how their well-laid plans were coming unstuck through muddle on the British side, the French were satisfied that they had done all they could to ensure a satisfactory passage for Force Y. It must be stressed again here that they knew nothing of the forthcoming Menace operation; had they done so, they would not have been so confident of an easy passage. The French authorities at Vichy and Toulon, however, *were* aware by 8th September that the Free French leader had left England, destination unknown. This information came from the Spanish Ambassador in London, the Duke of Alba, who communicated the fact to Madrid where it reached Vichy from their Madrid envoy.[32] This source gave de Gaulle's most likely destination as Morocco. All French naval authorities were advised of this fact in a signal that same day:

> From a reliable source of information, de Gaulle has left by unspecified transport towards French Africa. Governor-General Algeria, Resident French Morocco, High Commissioner Equatorial Africa advised by their Secretaries of State.
> 2. It is strictly essential to secure him if the possibility occurs.
> 3. Confirm receipt.[33]

His possible mode of transport was suspected to be by submarine to effect a secret landing, a suspicion added to by the fact that Free French agents were so put ashore near Agadir on 21st September with a wireless transmitter. They had no inkling at this date that a full invasion force was on its way. It had no effect on their dispositions with regard to Force Y however. Local defence commanders were, nominally, on the alert after this date of course, but it was Admiral D'Harcourt at Casablanca who was most immediately concerned for this was the first port of call for the squadron. His forces comprised air and military units and a large naval force, the bulk of which was ready to render assistance to Force Y if called upon, 3 destroyers, 10 sloops and 4 submarines were fully operational and the battleship *Jean Bart*, 5 destroyers, 11 sloops and 9 submarines refitting.[34]

The French air strength in the region was large, but declining, it too being subjected to the Armistice conditions of disbandment, and most units were in the process of running down in numbers at this time. A total of 25 bombers and 26 fighters were on hand, Air Maroc being subordinated to the Navy under D'Harcourt on this station.

Commander of Air Maroc was Général Bouscat. His main strength consisted of modern aircraft purchased from the USA before the Armistice.

The fighters were Curtiss Hawk 75As, the first of which was delivered to France in February 1939 and were the equivalent of the American Mohawk fighter, the export version of the USAC P36A. It was a single-seater, monoplane fighter of all-metal stressed construction. 500 had been ordered by France and all but 91 were delivered before the Armistice. They were powered by a single 1,200 hp Wright Cyclone GR1820 engine which gave them a maximum speed of 302 mph and a ceiling of 32,700 feet. They were armed with six .303 machine-guns in the wings and could be adapted to carry up to a total weight of 400 pounds of bombs. Completely outclassed in European warfare they were still by any stretch of the imagination more than a match for anything else in West Africa at this time. These were the equipment of I/4 and II/5 units, while III/4 was equipped with French-built Dwoitine 510s. These took no part in our story, however, and the main unit with which we are concerned was I/5 which had an establishment of 12 Hawks.

The bomber unit I/22 was also equipped with American aircraft, in this case the Glenn Martin 167, known to the British, who also used it, as the Maryland. First designed in 1938 it was a twin-engined mid-wing monoplane, powered by two 1,200 Pratt & Whitney Twin Wasps giving it a maximum speed of 278 mph at 11,800 feet, with a ceiling of 26,000 feet. A contract for 115 of these (167Fs) was placed in January 1939 for France, the first of which flew in August of that year. It had a range of 750 miles and was armed with six machine guns and could carry 1,800 pounds of bombs. Again, although fighter-bait in Europe, it was more than adequate for African duties.

Despite this armoury there was never any contemplation on the French side about actually *fighting* their way through the Straits unless they were forced into situations in which they were left with no other alternative. For one thing it would have been suicide, in their opinion, to try and force the Straits with three light cruisers and three destroyers. Remember that at the time the operation was being planned Force H at Gibraltar was at formidable strength, with *Renown*, *Barham* and *Resolution*, *Ark Royal* and a host of destroyers on hand. It would have been unthinkable for Force Y to have taken on such a force in combat. It was merely lucky coincidence, as they saw it, that when Force Y did finally sail Force H and the Gibraltar-based warships had been reduced to an all-time low. There is no record however of whether anyone in the Ministry of Marine put two and two together and linked de Gaulle's vanishing act from Britain and the departure of the bulk of Force H out into the Atlantic.[35]

But certainly the defences of Gibraltar were placed under close scrutiny in the days before Force Y sailed by both Axis and Vichy patrols and France knew exactly the strength of North's forces at the Rock on a day-to-day basis as reports show. Thus the German War Diary stated on the 10th '... reports from the Navy at Oran state that billeting at Gibraltar are one battleship and one destroyer, east of the Straits are patrolling three destroyers and off Cap Tres Forca are three destroyers heading eastward.'[36] Which is the exact disposition of the major ships available to North and Somerville that day as we have seen.

By late afternoon all was ready in Toulon harbour. The ships were fully oiled, ammunitioned and stored, although anxiety was felt for the condition of some of them whose engines were none too reliable. They had also embarked their cargo for the operation which consisted of 150 tons of food (4,000 rations) and some specialist personnel and AA materials, all for the garrison at Dakar. At Casablanca they were to embark detachments of coloured troops for Chad Colony, but when they left Toulon this was their sum total of cargo and passengers. Despite this both British and French accounts of the incident attribute Force Y with all manner of warlike goods. Thus we have Churchill's wildly inaccurate assertions at the time:

> The whole scheme of a bloodless landing and occupation by General de Gaulle seemed to me ruined by the arrival of the French squadron, probably carrying reinforcements, good gunners and bitter-minded Vichy officers, to decide the Governor, to pervert the garrison and man the batteries.[37]

And again:

> It soon proved however that the Vichy partisans were masters, and there can be no doubt that the arrival of the Vichy cruisers with their troops had blotted out any hope of Dakar joining the Free French movement.[38]

And further:

> ... the French cruiser squadron, with its reinforcements of Vichy partisans, carrying with it in physical as well as moral form the authority

of the French Republic slipped through the Straits of Gibraltar. I had no doubt from that moment that the situation had been transformed ...[39]

Churchill wrote much the same at the time of Dakar when explaining the debacle away to Australian Premier Menzies:

> The situation at Dakar was revolutionised by arrival of French ships from Toulon with Vichy personnel and the manning of the batteries by the hostile French Navy.[40]

All of which was the purest imagination on his part. Other historians followed suit each claim being wilder than the one before it. Thus Robert Aron:

> A squadron of ships which had remained faithful to Vichy and which was composed of three cruisers of the *Georges Leygues* class and three destroyers, passed through the Straits of Gibraltar on 11th September without being intercepted and went to reinforce the defence of Dakar.[41]

Robert Mengin is in no doubt:

> Joined by the *Primauguet* from Casablanca, the vessels put into Dakar, where they landed marine gunners of undoubted loyalty to the Marshal to man the batteries ...[42]

To Geoffrey Warner the French knew all about Dakar beforehand:

> The French government had got wind of a possible Gaullist attack on Dakar and had obtained authorization from the Germans and Italians to send naval reinforcements.[43]

Admiral William James comments that:

> It was later learnt that Force Y had brought ammunition and spare parts for the *Richelieu* and replacement propellers for those damaged in the British attack on 7th and 8th July.[44]

It would appear that he gleaned this information from the book by Vice-Admiral Emile Muselier, which was equally wrong in this respect.[45] In fact there were *no* 'Vichy partisans', *no* manning of the Dakar batteries by the French Navy, *no* marine gunners landed *who affected the issue*, *no* spare propellers for the *Richelieu* and the French had *no* idea of Dakar being the subject of a major assault.

On 7th September Bourragué signalled Darlan that all was ready thus: 'Getting under way 9/9 at 16.00 hrs.'[46]

Darlan also laid on further precautions: 'Order given for air reconnaissance over Gibraltar at 0900 and 1000.'[47]

These aircraft duly reported back on 10th September as follows:

At 0909 on 9th reconnaissance over Gibraltar reports 1: Only one heavy warship in harbour. 2: 20 transports in the roads 3: 4 destroyers patrolling east of the Straits.[48]

And later they amplified this:

At 1600 on 10th. 1 battleship and 1 destroyer in harbour. Three destroyers to the east of the Straits. At 1640 in 15°N. off Cape Fourches, three destroyers close together moving east.[49]

At 1600 on 9th September, the six warships of Force Y sailed from Toulon harbour and set course south-west at a steady 25 knots, passing north and west of the Balearic Islands that night and steaming steadily on a straight course the next day and evening. By midnight they were passing Cape Palos near Cartagena on the south-east hump of Spain and a few hours later, still undetected, they reached the vicinity of Cape de Gata. In the inky darkness the squadron, steaming in line ahead, changed course directly to the west and, at high speed, Force Y slid silently towards Gibraltar.

CHAPTER ELEVEN

'Bon Voyage'

When Hillgarth's signal reached Admiral North at The Mount half an hour after midnight on the morning of 11th September it was the second such signal he had received from reliable sources of information on the matter. True, it was 'only' marked 'Immediate' and that it was only *repeated* to him, the main recipient being the Admiralty, but nonetheless it should have conveyed some sort of urgency, for the mere size of the squadron alone indicated that something unusual was afoot. Hillgarth is not to be blamed for the priority of that signal; as he later stated, had he known of Menace he would have upgraded it to 'Most Immediate' and added 'Personal for First Sea Lord'.[1]

But Hillgarth did not know. However Admiral North did know about Menace, if not 'officially', from the Admiralty, whom Professor Marder criticises for not having given North official notification. But North knew indirectly through Somerville and intercepted signals. If Hillgarth's reaction would have been to mark up the urgency of the signal why did not the same thought strike Admiral North when he received it?

He gave his reasons many times in the years that followed. Firstly, he assumed with some justification that both Gascoigne's signal of the day before, and Hillgarth's signal, only repeated to himself, had reached their destinations, and that they had not only reached the Admiralty but reached them in good time for them to react. The former should have been in their hands since the morning of the 10th, the latter since just before midnight on the same day. Had the Admiralty felt that the movement of the French squadron was dangerous to our cause in any way, North reasoned, they would have sent him instructions to do something about it. He heard nothing and so he assumed that the French movements excited no response from London, and that therefore they wished them to be left alone.

The fact that no instructions of any sort with regard to the interception of these ships had been received by me from the Admiralty after the Consul General's Tangier message, confirmed this conclusion, and I decided that no action should be taken to interfere with their passage through the Straits unless of course the Admiralty ordered me to intercept them.[2]

Secondly he convinced himself from Hillgarth's earlier signals and local information that the French were no longer hostile to Britain and would not pose any threat to British forces. In fact from these sources he assumed that, far from being a threat to British interests, the French warships may have sailed from Toulon to escape from Axis influence and the rumoured German take-over of Vichy itself. Such a move, if true, was surely one to be encouraged, for placing the French fleet out of Axis reach had been the driving force and whole point of the bloody business of Mers-el-Kebir and its aftermath. If the French were doing this themselves without coercion so much the better.North even expressed the opinion that perhaps a secret deal had been done with the French for just such a movement, of which he had no knowledge.

In view of what had so recently transpired it appeared clear to me that this force was taking advantage of an opportunity to leave Toulon for Casablanca in order to escape from the German and Italian control liable to occur at the former port.[3]

Thirdly, according to his interpretation of the none-too-clear orders and counter-orders he had received since July, he was under the firm impression that Vichy French naval units were to be left alone unless the Admiralty ordered otherwise. Only *inferior* French units were to be stopped, anyway, and North felt that this squadron was superior to the units under his command and that they could not enforce such an option even if he felt it was desired, which he did not.

If attacked the French would have inevitably received powerful air support from Casablanca, whereas I had no aircraft except for a few old London flying boats. Gibraltar moreover would have been heavily bombed.
    Had the French adopted the daring tactics which might have been expected even Vice-Admiral Somerville, brave and efficient Flag Officer as I esteem him to be, might not have come out of the conflict unscathed. The engagement might easily have resulted in the crippling, or even possible sinking of *Renown*, involving the loss of the services of a capital ship, which it was important we should avoid at that time. All this as a result of my own action and *directly* contrary to para 4 of Admiralty Message 2005/9th July ...

To all this must be added the almost inevitable violation of Spanish territorial waters by our forces during the action. This bug-bear was always with me and it was well known at this time it would not need very much to push General Franco from his position of non-belligerency, into joining force with the Axis powers ...[4]

Fourthly, even if he had felt that the action was necessary, he was not responsible for ordering Force H to sea; that responsibility lay with Admiral Somerville as force commander, or with the Admiralty, which had hitherto always signalled Force H's instructions for missions directly from London. Moreover Admiral Somerville and General Liddell were both of the same opinion as himself on the matter. 'The Governor said to me on the telephone, "It looks as if the French are really coming to their senses at last".'[5]

And so beyond ascertaining that Hillgarth's message had been passed on to the Admiralty North did no more than before. He later claimed that Hillgarth's signal was sent over to Somerville in the *Renown*, but if it was the latter did not subsequently mention receipt of it before 0800/11th. He also later arranged for the French ships to be shadowed by aircraft the next day to confirm their destination was south to Casablanca. Somebody, either North or his Staff Officer, Intelligence, signalled to the two groups of destroyers out on their patrols to the effect that the French squadron was expected and for them to report them if they were sighted.

It would have been a very natural action by the FOCNA's Staff Officer Intelligence, to whom the Naval Attaché's signal was addressed, to relay the information to ships at sea who might encounter the French force. There is no evidence available to Admiralty to support the picture of Admiral North awake and thinking at 0215 but even if there were, any thought that emerged was misdirected, since he did nothing to put himself in a position to execute Admiralty orders should they arrive.[6]

Whoever originated it, the signal went out to the 13th Flotilla's ships at 0215 thus:

IMPORTANT
Report reliability unassessed states three cruisers 'Georges Leygues' Class and three destroyers 'La Fantasque' class all from Toulon destination unknown will pass Straits today 11th. Report immediately if sighted.[7]

It is not known what time the RAF were alerted, probably very much later, for the records of No 3 AACU carry the following entry of 11th September: 'Enemy units may attempt to penetrate the Straits. From 0630 A/S patrol between Spartel and Europa.'[8] This entry is more obviously relating to the passage of Italian submarines and was a common one at this time. Orders for No 202 Squadron also record only details of renewing the anti-submarine sweep with the destroyers interrupted by nightfall the day before. None of the war diaries of the artillery batteries at the fortress show any special alert details at all for 11th September. For two hours silence descended upon the Rock.

Some 120 miles to the east the three destroyers, *Hotspur*, *Griffin* and *Encounter*, were carrying out a routine anti-submarine sweep in line abreast at twelve knots, with the senior officer's ship, *Hotspur*, in the centre, to cover as wide a swathe with their asdics as possible.[10] Commander H.F.H. Layman took in the 0215 signal and, having received the Tangier and Madrid signals earlier, decided that he would shadow the French squadron if indeed it did appear, although he had no orders to do so.

> Coming from Toulon, in Metropolitan France, it seemed to me most improbable that a Vichy French squadron could be in any way helping the British cause. I knew there was some British operation going on in the Atlantic but had no idea of its object. But I did feel quite certain that the patrolling ships with me would be needed for some purpose in Gibraltar. I had, of course, copies of the policy signals about the French warships ... but thought these would be over-ridden by the sudden appearance of such a large Vichy force, whose destination was not known. In any case, it is a cardinal principle that it is essential to keep in touch with any 'enemy' ship sighted, so long as this is feasible or unless orders to the contrary are received.[11]

It was at 0445 on the 11th that the *Hotspur* sighted the French squadron, which were blacked out save for their navigational lights. They were moving at 25 knots or more and the British destroyers had to light up an extra boiler to move from their sub-hunting speed to match that of Force Y. Commander Layman at once ordered his ships, all of which were completely darkened and invisible to the French,[12] to shadow. He also got off a sighting report:

IMMEDIATE
Six unknown ships in position 036°00′ N; 004°01′ W steering 270°. Am shadowing.[13]

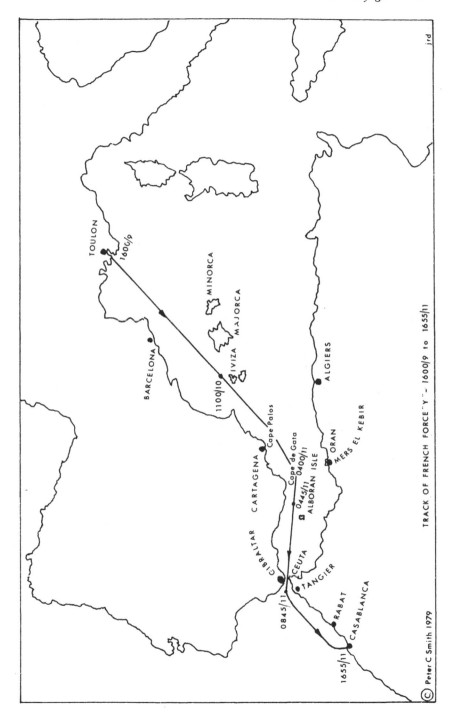

TOULON

1600/9

MINORCA

BARCELONA

IVIZA MAJORCA

1100/10

ALGIERS

Cape Palos

MERS EL KEBIR

Cape de Gata

0445/11 0400/11

CARTAGENA

ORAN

ALBORAN ISLE

GIBRALTAR

CEUTA

TANGIER

0845/11

RABAT

CASABLANCA

1655/11

TRACK OF FRENCH FORCE "Y" – 1600/9 to 1655/11

© Peter C Smith 1979

jrd

This signal was received by ACNAS at 0512. As all operational signals in the Gibraltar command were immediately relayed by Gibraltar W/T to Whitehall W/T this and subsequent signals sent to North were all relayed to the Admiralty.[14]

The Vichy squadron, when sighted, was in single line ahead and the British destroyers followed in the same formation, the *Hotspur* leading followed by *Griffin* and *Encounter*, about one mile astern of the rear Vichy ship.[15]

> Our destroyers shadowed well astern of the French. We were completely darkened and at such a distance the bow waves would not be visible. With the French doing 25 knots and burning navigation lights any lookout astern would be very difficult and rather improbable.[16]

At 0525 Commander Layman made an amplifying report:

> IMMEDIATE
> Probably warships. Proceeding at high speed.[17]

The commander of the *Griffin* recalled the ease with which they picked up the French squadron: 'We met up with them steaming with normal lights in the middle watch and shadowed them back towards Gibraltar, reporting their position and speed.'[18] Of course the French were making no great attempt at concealment, quite the reverse.

The skipper of the third British destroyer, *Encounter*, relates:

> First sighting was made I believe by the *Hotspur*, and *Griffin* and *Encounter* took up shadowing positions. The operation proceeded without incident until we were approaching Gibraltar when we were ordered to cease shadowing and return on patrol. We were, of course, unaware of what was passing between Gibraltar and Whitehall as those messages were transmitted on a wavelength and in a code to which we were not privy.[19]

It was at 0555 that North signalled direct to Commander Layman: Cease shadowing resume your patrol.'[20] Commander Layman was astonished at this signal:

> Thinking I must have made a bad blunder, I made one more signal to North saying that I had disengaged from the shadowing without being sighted by the French. [This last signal is not given in North's account but was definitely made].[21]

He later amplified his feelings:

I regarded the Vichy Squadron, coming from Toulon, destination unknown, with the utmost suspicion and felt quite certain that I should be needed at Gib, especially as there was an acute shortage of ships immediately available to screen *Renown*. I knew we had some very large operation going on out in the Atlantic, but I did not know that its destination was Dakar. ACNA *did* know this. I most strongly felt I should take the initiative at once by shadowing, in sure anticipation of receiving orders re French from ACNA and/or Admiralty. Any delay would have resulted in a waste of valuable time and, more important, losing touch with the Vichy French Squadron. On being told to cease shadowing and resume my patrol I could only conclude that the Admiralty had given orders to ACNA to let the French through the Straits unhindered. It did not seem to be case for using the Nelsonic blind eye![22]

Despite his misgivings, therefore, Commander Layman complied with North's order and the three destroyers came about once more, slowed down, and resumed their anti-submarine sweep eastward. The French ships soon vanished to the west into the low mist that covered the Straits at this time.

This sea mist was very thick for a time, just before dawn; the French reported that they were forced to reduce speed because of it and there were fears that their strict time-table might suffer, but, after three-quarters of an hour, around 0745, it began to disperse and they quickly made up the distance lost. This same mist also prevented the first air patrols from Gibraltar making contact at all, thus giving support to Commander Layman's fears.

London Flying Boat K6930 had taken off from Gun Port Wharf at 0530 that morning to continue co-operation with Layman's destroyers in their anti-submarine sweep. She reported that the *Hotspur* had contacted six French warships steering west at high speed, but she herself could not find them due to the mist. She was relieved at 1000 by London K5908 but she too failed to sight the French squadron at first.[23]

Captain Layman's ships had turned back at 0605 and not for almost an hour and a half did another British unit sight the French squadron, which by that time was approaching the Rock. What had prompted North's signal and what action was being taken at Gibraltar as the French ships neared the most perilous part of their journey? To find the answers we must return to 0512 and the receipt at North's HQ of Layman's initial sighting report.

Admiral North was awakened for the second night running when Captain Duke rang him at 0515 that morning to report the *Hotspur*'s first sighting signal, according to Monks.[24] Aboard his flagship *Renown* in the harbour Admiral Somerville was woken by his own officers, who had also taken in this signal, some five minutes *earlier*, at 0510. North and Somerville consulted and Somerville then took instant action.

Somerville later recorded:

> This confirmed the intimation given in Consul General, Tangier's message 1824 of 9th September, that French Naval Forces might proceed out of the Mediterranean, possibly within 72 hours following his message. *It should be noted that the source of this information had hitherto proved somewhat unreliable.*[*]
>
> I ordered *Renown* to be at one hour's notice for full speed, together with *Vidette*, the only available destroyer of the 13th Flotilla.
>
> I considered putting to sea to the westward in *Renown* but decided that, owing to lack of destroyer escort, this was inadvisable; further, it seemed unlikely that *Renown* could make sufficient ground to the west to avoid being sighted by the French force. It seemed to me most improbable that the force would proceed to a Bay Port and that Casablanca was the probable destination. So far as I was aware, it was not the policy of HM Government to interfere with the movements of French warships to French controlled ports. The possibility of this movement being connected with Operation Menace was considered but in view of the report from the Naval Attaché at Madrid, 1842 dated 5th September, 1940, it appeared to me that quite possibly the French wished to remove these ships in order to prevent their seizure by the Germans in retaliation for any action taken by us at Dakar. The prolonged absence from Gibraltar of *Ark Royal* and other ships attached to Force H, together with the departure of *Barham* must by this time have given rise to some conjecture that operations to the south were contemplated.
>
> In view of the Consul-General, Tangier's message 1842 of 9th September and the Naval Attaché, Madrid's 1809/10th September (*received by me at 0800, 11th September*)[*] I assumed that the Admiralty were fully aware of this movement of French ships and that had any action been required by me to intercept I should have received instructions to this effect. I assumed that, as no instructions had been given, it was the policy to avoid any incidents with the French at this juncture and that this movement was regarded as being favourable rather than unfavourable to our cause.[25]

The following points should be noted from the above. Firstly, that Somerville had not received information from North regarding the

---

* *My* italics.

Hillgarth signal 1809/10th and was not to receive it until 0800 that morning. Secondly, that he had placed no great store on the accuracy of Hillgarth's information up to that date, but nonetheless cited Hillgarth's message, which he got two-and-a-half hours later, as one reason why he did not put to sea. Thirdly, he considered both Menace and Dakar as potential targets for the French squadron, although later rejecting them as the less likely options.

Half an hour after the first sighting report came in, *Hotspur's* second signal arrived and North was again informed by Duke. This was at 0535. Another ten minutes elapsed. Somerville had brought the *Renown* and *Vidette* to an hour's notice to steam at 0545. Ten more minutes passed before North signalled his decision, he signalled to *Hotspur*: 'Cease shadowing, resume your patrol.'[26]

Twenty minutes later, after a telephone consultation with Somerville, North informed the Admiralty of his decision thus:

IMMEDIATE
NA Madrid's 1805/10. *Hotspur* sighted lights of six ships probably warships steering west at high speed 36°03' N; 004°14' W. I have directed *Hotspur* to take no action.[27]

An hour later he amplified this signal to the Admiralty in this manner:

IMMEDIATE
My 0617 intend to keep in touch with this force by air and will report probable destination.[28]

Further significant points to be noted here are that, firstly, by ordering *Hotspur* to cease shadowing, Admiral North showed that he was aware that responsibility for local events and commands to the 13th Flotilla were *his*, not Somerville's. *Renown* was the only active unit of Force H at Gibraltar it should be remembered; all the destroyers were of the 13th Flotilla and under North's *direct* command, not Somerville's. Secondly, that Somerville's decision to bring *Renown* to one hour's notice to steam was made *before* North's decision to call off the shadowing destroyers, although later Somerville fully approved of such action, fearing, it has been stated, that the 'aggressive' destroyers might become embroiled with the French squadron.[29] Thirdly, that one of the reasons Somerville gave for not ordering *Renown* to sea was lack of screening destroyers, only *Vidette* being in harbour as we have seen. But this overlooks two factors. Firstly that there were three other destroyers of the 13th Flotilla on local patrols in the Straits who could have joined *Renown* and *Vidette* as they steamed westward, and secondly that by ordering *Hotspur*'s group to break off shadowing and resume their patrol a further three destroyers, and these the most modern ships available, were removed from the scene. As their senior officer has since recalled: 'With the shortage of ships at Gibraltar, why not allow *Hotspur*'s party to continue a harmless shadowing (which could be called off at any minute) instead of sending them back some 120 miles away?'[30]

Finally North's intention to shadow the French force by *air* and report their destination by that method rather than interpose a surface force, no matter what composition, between them and the route north to German-held Biscay ports, was in itself a gamble, and it was this that settled his fate as Flag Officer, North Atlantic Station, had he but known it. Why was this so? Because no matter how vague and contradictory his previous orders might have been, one thing was completely clear and beyond dispute: the Admiralty and the Cabinet on no account wished to see Vichy warships at German-controlled ports, particularly so at this time when the threat of imminent invasion lay over the nation, and Germany needed every warship she could get her hands on to replace her own losses off Norway. It was spelled out, but even if he had no specific orders to that effect, it must have been obviously a thing to prevent. Sending a single London flying boat to follow the squadron was fine, if he was *absolutely certain* that they were to proceed to the south, but how could Admiral North, or Admiral Somerville, be so certain? True, their discussions brought agreement that they *felt* the French would do so, and they did in fact do so, but what, the Admiralty subsequently asked, would have happened had they turned north? Nothing the old London could have done would have stopped them, and the only ships that might have prevented it were sitting in Gibraltar or steaming back away from the French. The whole Admiralty case really came down to the fact that North, in effect, made no effective dispositions to prevent such an eventuality. After all, his only firm information stated blankly, 'Destination not known.'

Captain Roskill on the other hand argues that, in the light of his instructions, Admiral North took the only course open to him that did not run counter to the instruction, which he believed still was in force, that he must 'avoid contact with equal or superior [French] forces', although he does raise the point that:

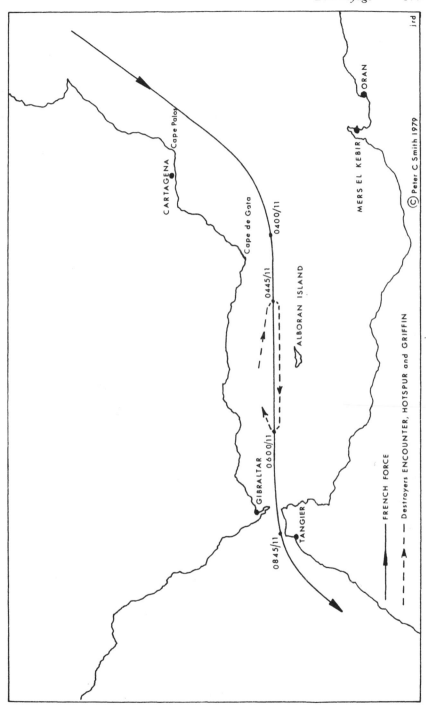

It is, perhaps, possible to take the view that, as soon as he knew about the approach of the French squadron, Admiral North should have pressed the Admiralty for an immediate decision regarding any action which he might be required to take against it. But his assumption that the Admiralty had received the Madrid report was certainly justified.[31]

Finally on Admiral North's side it is of course impossible to argue, as Their Lordships appeared to do, that *reserving* a right is the same as *exercising* a right, and the impression given is that North was the victim of a verbal trap in this respect.

The second signal North sent to the Admiralty stating that he intended to keep in touch by air was probably followed by orders to the RAF units to do just that, hitherto, as we have seen, they were still conducting routine A/S patrols, and not until No 202's third sortie, which took off at 1045, were the operational orders changed to 'Fleet Recce'.

According to Group Captain Horner, the Londons had a brief sighting earlier of their quarry:

> The incident, as I remember it, started with the sighting of the three French cruisers just after they had entered a large area of fog well to the west of Gibraltar. The crew of the London on patrol had spotted the three wakes disappearing into the fog and managed to identify the vessels creating them. As we were not equipped with radar at this time it was a considerable achievement by the crew. The Swordfish was subsequently put up to report on the actual passage through the Straits, which were free of fog.[32]

Meanwhile the French squadron was clearing the mist patches ready for its final run past the Rock. As can be imagined, tension was high aboard the French ships as they came out into the watery sunlight. The first contact with the British came at 0730. As the mist dropped away the leading French vessel, the destroyer *Le Fantasque* sighted one of the British destroyers, on local patrol to the east of the Straits, on a bearing 250°. She was closing the French ships when first sighted and Captain Paul Still signalled back along the line to Admiral Bourragué aboard the *Georges Leygues*: 'Ennemi en Vue'.[33]

Bourragué replied immediately by signal to his whole force: 'Battle Stations for Force Y'.[34]

Aboard the French ships there was sudden activity, this was the moment they knew would be decisive. Although they had no intentions of fighting their way through unless unavoidable, every precaution was taken. As Hervé Cras was to recall:

Admiral Bourragué knew that the British Navy would be informed that Force Y was being sent to Africa. He could therefore reasonably hope that nothing would oppose the free passage of his force. Having said that, there is no doubt that the ships of Force Y were at their action stations during the crossing of the Straits. But this was of course done in a discreet and inconspicuous way. I know the method well enough having taken part, on board another destroyer, in a great many escort missions between Casablanca and Oran in 1941.[35]

This is confirmed by the captain of the *Gloire*:

For the passage were the personnel at combat stations? Mine certainly were, because I am sure that if I had not received a direct order to that effect, I would have ordered it myself, or at least, 'Alert Stations'.[36]

Soon after, a second British destroyer was sighted, further off. Neither approached too close to the French ships but kept near for a while on a parallel course; neither British destroyer made any signals and both kept their guns trained fore-and-aft, as did the French ships. They just looked at each other. One of these British destroyers was the *Wrestler*, which, as her CO recalled:

On the day in question we spent some time within a few cables of the French squadron as it made its way in broad daylight and at a moderate speed ...[37]

After an interval of about half-an-hour the British destroyers dropped away to resume their normal patrols and their signals brought to the scene Swordfish floatplane K8354, which paced the squadron as it proceeded towards the Straits. It reported:

Six French cruisers sighted 160°, Europa 10 miles at 0800 – three of 'La Galissionière' and 'Fantasque' types respectively. Proceeded west, reaching 270° Cape Spartel 5 miles at 0935.[38]

With the little floatplane riding hard on them, Force Y pushed on, having, at 0836, increased speed for the final run, as previously instructed, to 27 knots. The British destroyers had vanished astern into the mist.[39] Some six minutes earlier, at 0830, the French ships had been sighted by the Port War Signal Station at Gibraltar, who informed Admiral North.

It was now broad daylight and the six French warships, at high speed, made a brave sight as they sped along in line astern, their nationality markings clearly seen and large French tricolour flags flying. They were close-in and eyewitnesses aboard the *Renown* watched them pass. One young midshipman at that time recalled:

> I was at my action station, the Air Defence Position immediately abaft the 15-inch Main Director when the French ships passed through. It was a bright, clear day with maximum visibility and they could be seen against the African coast. We were not at action stations as such, but we were ready and may well have been at Quarters Clear Guns (from which a full action state would have been reached very quickly). The admiral may have well been on the bridge. I can only remember that I wasn't the only one there and that there was an air of anticipation.[40]

The *Renown*'s Duty Staff Officer also got a good view:

> I watched them through glasses at a range of about five miles. My recollection is that they were painted a lightish grey and flew the tricolour. I don't remember any feeling of tension, only surprise, and some amusement. Also a feeling of wondering what the hell we ought to do about them, in the absence of any instructions from the Admiralty.[41]

A young gunnery officer from the same ship remembered the incident thus:

> I can remember that day very well. There was an alert in the early hours of the morning and *Renown* was brought to short notice for steam – it was said that a French squadron was on passage westwards through the Straits of Gibraltar. We all waited for something to happen, and sure enough the French force appeared round Europa Point at about 0800 (you can't see much to the eastward from the dockyard). As far as I remember they were in line ahead and I had a good view of them through binoculars – they were steaming fast and flying large French national flags. I cannot recall seeing pendant numbers but they were certainly close enough to have been seen.

He continued:

> ... although *Renown* was at full action stations, we were ordered to do nothing that might be thought to be a hostile act – guns were firmly trained fore and aft. As part of the 'clearing for action' drill the 15-inch armament were testing firing circuits ... this is done by firing electrically a tiny tube of gunpowder in the breech of the gun and it makes a 'plop' like a rifle shot. I remember the captain being angry that they were doing this because the French might have mistaken this for gunfire! This proves the point that the French were very close at that time (about 3

miles?), but I remember thinking that the sound would hardly carry that far![42]

As to the *Renown*'s state of readiness this was confirmed by brief entries in the ship's log thus:

0630. Hands employed preparing for sea. Ship at 1 hour's notice.

And later:

0800. Hands employed as required.[43]

As the French ships swept past the signal station flashed out a polite enquiry: '*Qui êtes vous?*', to which they replied, 'French cruisers and French destroyers.'

'What names?' – '*Gloire, Georges Leygues, Montcalm, Fantasque, Audacieux, Malin.*'

'Thank you'.[44]

North and his staff officers knew some of these ships, which had for a brief time served under his command at the Rock at the time of the convoy experiment. Pleased that nothing untoward had happened North turned to his Chief of Staff and ordered him to send another signal and a few minutes later it flickered out across the Straits: '*Bon Voyage.*'

Immediately after sending this signal North again telephoned Somerville aboard the *Renown* and told him of his action, to which Somerville again expressed complete agreement. Aboard the French warships, now leaving the Rock astern as they headed out into the Atlantic, the feeling was one of immense relief, the worst was over!

Many years later Bourragué's Chief of Staff, Capitaine Gabriel Rebuffel, recalled that they were all: '... very relieved to get past the Straits without interference.'[45]

The Swordfish floatplane kept them company until they reached the vicinity of Cape Spartel, then, around 1000, turned back at the limit of her endurance. Her place was taken by London flying boat K6909 and she sighted the French force heading on a course for Casablanca.[46]

In fact it was at 0940 that Bourragué had changed course onto 235°, and reduced speed to 25 knots for the final leg of his journey. At 1002 he ordered his ships to stand down from battle stations and later that afternoon he signalled Darlan the good news: 'Crossing without incident.'[47]

At 1400 London L7043 took off at Gibraltar to take up the shadowing of the French. She flew down the African coast was able to report that Force Y had entered harbour. She also sighted a French submarine off the port.[48]

The relief in Force Y was shared both at Casablanca, and in Vichy. At the former port Admiral D'Harcourt noted at 0900:

Force Y passed Gibraltar at high speed, sailing westward en route to Casablanca. Advised General Bouscat to keep his aircraft alert and ready. Reconnaissance and fighter escort will be provided tomorrow morning.

This was for the resumption of Force Y's journey south of course. At 1600 he noted: 'The 4th D.C. and three *Malins* are in sight.'[49]

Back at Gibraltar in the interim, much had happened, although all still seemed calm on the surface. The Germans apparently suspected nothing of the French scheme to get their squadron safely through the Straits; their comments on the matter reflect no surprise that there were no incidents: 'The three French cruisers and three flotilla leaders have, early on the 11th, passed the Straits of Gibraltar without incident.'[50]

However, in order to allay any suspicion at their easy passage, the French deputation to the German Armistice Commission refrained from any mention of their behind the scenes activities; indeed they stated blandly on the 18th that *no* prior warning had been given to the British. This indicated that the Gibraltar forces had been caught unawares by Force Y and had got through by luck and sheer bravado. Again it appears that the Germans were satisfied by this story, more so in the light of subsequent events at the Rock that afternoon.

At the Rock itself North and Somerville were quite convinced that they had done the right thing in allowing the French squadron to pass through because still no word had come from London for them to take any other action.

'On the morning of the 11th North and Somerville (who had been acquainted by North) were waiting almost in agony for the orders that did not come', wrote Captain Hillgarth many years later.[51] This would seem to be something of an exaggeration, their feelings as claimed for themselves were of tranquillity and relief rather than any agony of spirit, but nonetheless both felt that in the absence of any instruction nothing more was required of them.

At 1020 therefore Somerville phoned through to North from *Renown* and stated that as no further immediate action seemed forthcoming he was proposing to revert to the normal two hours' notice for steam, and this action North duly approved. 'At noon, therefore, I ordered *Renown* and the destroyers concerned to revert to two hours notice for steam.'[52]

Again it should be noted that North's approval of Somerville's suggestion indicates seniority responsibility. Also that, by this time, the other destroyers on patrol had been put on the alert as Somerville is talking about destroyers and not just the *Vidette*.

Gibraltar reverted to the calmness of a routine day for an hour, but this peace was rudely shattered at 1307 when AM 1239/11th suddenly arrived from the Admiralty instructing the *Renown* and all available destroyers to raise steam for full speed. The ships under Layman were immediately recalled, but at best could not hope to return to Gibraltar until 1800 and then they needed to be refuelled. The *Griffin* was already refuelling and to provide more immediate support all the remaining destroyers on Straits patrol were also recalled and ordered to refuel with all despatch.

Somerville and North were conferring at The Tower when the Admiralty message arrived, and were just about to leave for The Mount. They had been expressing their mutual relief at not becoming entangled with the French again when Pound's message was handed to them:

IMMEDIATE
HMS *Renown* and all available destroyers raise steam for full speed.[53]

It was a bombshell and Somerville at once returned to *Renown* to comply. This signal was an hour later followed by a second, of even more startling nature:

MOST IMMEDIATE
My 1239/11. Proceed to sea and endeavour obtain contact French force. Further instruction follows.[54]

Despite every endeavour there was no way in which Somerville could immediately comply with this order for he still had insufficient destroyers to form even a token screen. And even if they had been ready the French force had a five hour start and there was obviously no chance at all of the *Renown* overhauling them. The best that could be done was the ordering into the air of the London flying boat, as we have seen, at 1400, to try and gain contact, and this was done. After another hour there was still only a token force ready to sail, the *Renown*, *Griffin* and *Vidette*; the *Velox* was still fuelling and could not be ready until 1640.

At 1500 tugs secured alongside the *Renown* to shift her from her berth and the two destroyers slipped in readiness. While they were still making ready for sailing yet a third urgent message came winging hotly over the wires from Whitehall, being received at Gibraltar at 1546.

MOST IMMEDIATE
My 1347/11. (A) If French Force is proceeding southward inform them there is no objection to their going to Casablanca but that they cannot be permitted to go to Dakar which is under German influence.
(B) If force appears proceeding Bay Ports inform them this cannot be permitted as these ports are in German hands.
(C) In A and B minimum force to be used to enforce compliance.[55]

To Admiral Somerville these messages, especially the last two, were exasperating in the extreme and the volatile commander is reported to have exploded, 'They must be mad!'[56]

At 1600 *Renown* piped 'Hands secure ship for sea' and at 1619 the great battle-cruiser slipped and proceeded, passing the Mole entrance at 1635 with *Griffin* and *Vidette* in attendance; they were joined by *Velox*, which had cut short her fuelling, before they left the Bay. Even before they left Gibraltar harbour, Pilot Officer Foot's aerial sighting report had been received stating that the French squadron was sighted steaming hard for Casablanca. It did nothing to improve Somerville's temper. He later wrote to his wife:

Off we went with the usual vague and general, that they mustn't come here, or there, and if necessary force must be used to stop it. Well, how the hell I was expected to stop all six, I don't quite know. Anyway, they had got such a start that I had no hope of catching them before they got to the place around the corner, so I had to go on to see that they did not get any farther south.[57]

At 1700 the British squadron increased speed to twenty knots and at 1745 came onto course 245° to the south-west and increased speed to 24 knots, keeping thirty miles outside French waters to avoid detection and further incident.[58] The *London*'s report of Force Y's arrival at 1610 came in.

My appreciation of the situation at this stage [Somerville wrote in his Official Report] was as follows. The French force might complete with oil that evening and continue to the southward. To counter this high speed was necessary in order to reach an intercepting position. On the other hand, the Force might remain at Casablanca for some days; in this case economy of fuel was essential in order to enable the patrol to be maintained. I therefore decided to continue to the southward at high speed with *Renown* and the three screening destroyers and to order the three additional destroyers [*Hotspur, Encounter* and *Wishart*], who would shortly be available, to join me at a more economical speed, so that they could screen *Renown* in the event of the operation being prolonged.[59]

The four British ships headed southwest zigzagging into the dusk and, at 2104, the *Renown* took in yet another signal from the Admiralty, timed at 2006, instructing Somerville to set up a patrol south of Casablanca in order to prevent the French squadron sailing south from that port. It was a clear night with a bright moon giving maximum visibility. Such conditions made it impossible for Somerville to set up a close blockade of Casablanca and also made ideal conditions for Vichy submarines operating from that port.

Somerville therefore decided to push on as far south as he could to get between Casablanca and Dakar, which he obviously sensed was the sensitive spot, in the hope that further aerial reconnaissance at dawn would clarify the position. He accordingly signalled North back at Gibraltar, stating that it was essential that a dawn reconnaissance should be carried out over Casablanca and that maximum air surveillance must be maintained over that port throughout the daylight hours of the 12th. There was little else he could do then than press on at his best speed. Meanwhile Layman's three destroyers had hastily topped up and left Gibraltar later that evening to effect a rendezvous with Somerville. *Hotspur*'s night order book records:

Gib to off Casablanca.
Course 230°, 22 knots. *Hotspur, Encounter* and *Wishart* in line abreast to starboard 5 cables apart. Zig Zag 15 commenced midnight. We may see Laroche Light. We shall RV with FOH in *Renown* at 0800 (12th).[60]

But it was all too late.

CHAPTER TWELVE

The Strange Silence

If one puts oneself in the place of Admirals Somerville and North during the afternoon of 11th September it is impossible not to sympathise with them in both their feelings of mystification and anger at being ordered to stop the French squadron some five hours *after* it had passed beneath the muzzles of their guns. It obviously made no sense at all to them in the light of events as they had interpreted them and it is easy to understand why they felt at this time that the Admiralty staff must have been asleep. Post-war historians have no similar excuses however. But what had really happened back in London during that fateful night of 10th/11th September that had provoked such an, apparently, tardy response? To try and find some of the answers we must turn the clock back to just before midnight on 10th September, some sixteen hours before the *Renown* set forth on her hopeless quest.

Hillgarth's signal had arrived at the Admiralty at 2350 hours. Remember that it was marked 'Immediate', like so many other signals. In normal circumstances this should have sufficed to bring it to the attention of those officers responsible, but because there were so many 'Immediates' before it may not have aroused the attention it deserved. Later Hillgarth was to bemoan this fact and state that, had he known he would have given it far higher priority, 'Most Immediate' and 'Personal for First Sea Lord'.[1] The reason he did not do so is, as we have seen, was that he was *not* told, either by the Admiralty or the British Ambassador in Madrid, anything about the impending operation at Dakar. Even *after* receiving Delaye's message and confiding it to Hoare, he was not let into the secret, it appears, at least not right away. Hillgarth is therefore completely blameless in this respect. He later saw this secrecy as misplaced and the real root of all the subsequent trouble, but as both Hoare (officially) and North (unofficially) knew of Dakar and Menace Hillgarth is needlessly reproaching himself as both were far senior to him. Nonetheless the marking given to the message was the first of a series of misfortunes concerned with his telegram.

The debasement of the prefix 'Immediate' had already been commented upon. But here again we should reiterate that it was quite common at this stage of the war for relatively unimportant messages and signals to be given higher prefixes than they warranted. The natural concern of any originator of such a message is that his information is read and acted upon as quickly as possible and there is a normal human failing involved in that everyone considered *his* information as the more important and wished to place as great an emphasis upon it as possible. But allocating an unduly high priority to a signal can be as bad an error as giving it too low a prefix as it defeats the whole system. A firm grip is necessary to prevent such practices, and later an improved system was introduced which partly eliminated such risk, although the problem, being a human one, could never be entirely eradicated. Discrimination is therefore vital in the transmission of such signals, and in this case that discrimination seems not to have been utilised resulting in both the Tangier signal, and perhaps the Madrid signal, getting off to a bad start. In the case of the former the juggling with words, '... it was not marked Important ...', when in fact it was graded higher than that,[2] used by both Churchill and the War Cabinet version certainly added weight to those who felt North was made a scapegoat in this matter and gave them valuable ammunition, justifiably so.

However Hillgarth's signal does not seem to have been delayed quite so long through this reason, nor was its decoding tardily carried out. Once deciphered the signal was passed to the duty captain on watch at the Admiralty, who in turn quickly took it to the Director of Operations (Foreign), Captain R.H. Bevan. Bevan it was who received it at about 0600 that morning (some sources differ),[3] 11th September, in its de-coded form with the minimum of delay.

Captain Bevan was asleep in bed when the signal was brought to him. He, of course, was completely in the picture with regard to Dakar and Menace but, surprisingly, failed completely to take any immediate action to bring the signal's content to the attention of Admiral Pound, who was sleeping at the Admiralty as he often did. Pound was in the same building but Bevan decided not to disturb him and merely added Hillgarth's signal, despite its 'Immediate' prefix, to the pile awaiting distribution to the various departments heads at 0800. Why?

The generally accepted theory by the supporters of Admiral North in putting forward their case is that Bevan saw nothing untoward in the passage of the French cruiser squadron past Gibraltar in the light of current Admiralty policy. In other words, he thought exactly as Admiral North did that they presented no threat, even to Menace itself, and that it was not the Admiralty's wish to stop them anyway. If he did then it was with far less justification than the old Admiral at the Rock, for Bevan was *fully* informed. Thus Captain Roskill wrote:

> Bevan must surely have been aware of the latest, if ambiguous, developments in the Government's policy with regard to French warships, and also with the plans and progress of the Operation Menace; but he may not have appreciated the possible significance of the French ships' movements in relation to the latter.[4]

And Professor Marder writes:

> To be fair to Bevan (I can find no record of any case he may have made for himself), he may not have regarded the message as especially significant when read in the light of current Admiralty policy. This could be interpreted to mean, as it was by Admirals North and Somerville, that the avoidance of incidents was the governing factor.[5]

Churchill's viewpoint was this:

> It should have been obvious to this officer, who was himself fully informed of the Dakar expedition, that the message was of decisive importance. He took no instant action on it, but let it go forward in the ordinary way with the First Sea Lord's telegrams.[6]

This is far harsher and his subsequent reactions were equally so, but it must be recorded that according to Pound Bevan *himself* fully admitted later that he had acted incorrectly and had made a mistake. Thus he wrote that Captain Bevan '... failed to take immediate action which he acknowledged he should have done by reporting the signal at once to his senior officers.'[7]

If this is indeed the case it invalidates the arguments that he read the current Admiralty policy in the same manner as Admiral North had done.

Another viewpoint is that the reason Bevan made no outcry afterwards in the same manner as Admiral North, was not because he knew he had acted incorrectly but that he was of a different temperament to North. Captain Bevan in fact left the Admiralty soon after this incident to take command of the light cruiser HMNZ *Leander*, then operating in the Red Sea and Indian Ocean, far from the main centre of the war at sea. Captain Roskill himself served under him in the same ship, and later took over command of the *Leander* from him. He therefore knew Bevan very well indeed and gives this portrait of him and the possible reason for his silence:

> About Bob Bevan, I knew him very well and liked him very much as a rather simple but absolutely honest man. I went out as his commander in *Leander* and only took command after he was invalided home because X-rays had revealed a patch on one lung. I have always thought that he was made a victim for an error which was by no means only his. Of course Bevan was deeply hurt by the whole affair; but with the war in a very difficult state he could hardly have defended himself without being very disloyal to his superiors – which was wholly foreign to his character.[8]

Whatever the real reason Bevan was adjudged to be guilty and was relieved, on 20th September, from his post; he received a strong rebuke at the same time in the form of a letter telling him that his conduct had earned for himself, '... Their Lordships' displeasure'.[9]

Bob Bevan took his caning quietly and with dignity and was soon moved to his new position as *Leander*'s CO. The lightness of his punishment however infuriated the vindictive Premier. It was Bevan, *not* North, who was the subject of Churchill's venomous remarks during his subsequent speech to the Commons to explain the Dakar fiasco to an angry House on 8th October. Thus:

> By a series of accidents, and some errors which have been made the subject of disciplinary action or are now subject to formal inquiry, neither the First Sea Lord nor the Cabinet was informed of the approach of these ships to the Straits of Gibraltar until it was too late to stop them passing through.[10]

Even North himself got it right in that, if there was a scapegoat, it was Bevan and not himself, for after listening to Churchill's speech later he was to write home to his wife:

> From what I could gather from the reports of the speech, it looks more as if some unfortunate devil in the Admiralty is going to suffer, not as if they are going to tell me, in the old naval parlance, 'to haul down my flag and come ashore'. I think, that it will be hard luck on the scapegoat ...[11]

The Premier wanted Bevan's blood. On 19th October he minuted Alexander demanding that Bevan should be placed on half-pay unless that officer claimed the right of a court martial. Bevan, stormed Churchill, was guilty of '... a most serious and disastrous failure in responsibility ... contributing to a far worse misfortune ...'[12]

Alexander duly took legal advice and had to inform the Premier that such action would not be desirable. Although Bevan *could* be tried by court martial, '... the prisoner's right of a plea of mitigation of sentence would put the Board of Admiralty in an extremely awkward position as he would certainly say he had already been punished', [by his dismissal]. The same applied to the question of placing Bevan on half-pay; furthermore such persecution would, in Alexander's viewpoint, create, 'a sense of injustice in the fleet'.[13]

Churchill was far from satisfied with this reply and replied that he did not consider the expression of Their Lordships' displeasure as an adequate sentence for Bevan's error. He pushed for further action. 'I consider the officer should be placed on half-pay and trust you will be able to meet my wishes.'[14] Alexander was not one to stand up to the Premier in such a scalp-hunting mood and he duly passed this on to Admiral Pound for his opinion. As so often before Pound would have none of Winston's witch-hunting in his service. He advised Alexander that it was for the Board of Admiralty to decide on such matters, *not* the Premier and, further, that the type of action Churchill was seeking in this matter was '... not only contrary to naval justice but also to civil practice'.[15]

Alexander duly passed this firm rebuke on to the irate Premier with the note that although he wished to 'meet your wishes', his advice had been that it was not wise to inflict what would have amounted to a second punishment of Bevan.[16] With this Churchill had to be satisfied but he refused to concede the point and terminated this far from magnanimous exchange with a disgruntled growl:

> The premature infliction of a minor and altogether inadequate punishment is now held to bar proper disciplinary treatment of a gross case of neglect of duty in a Staff Officer. I greatly regret the result.[17]

A further point has been raised about Bevan's punishment. Churchill was not the only person outside the Admiralty who found it inadequate. Post-war historians have commented on it in this form also; thus the Plimmers found it 'remarkably light'.[18] Was it because the Admiralty felt that, in his case, but not North's, there was room for some leniency as to the interpretation of Admiralty policy, or was there something more sinister involved? Here we come to the point that Bevan was not perhaps solely guilty of failure to recognise the Madrid signal's importance. This argument was first raised by Captain Roskill in a letter to his chief at the Cabinet Office, A.B. Acheson of the Historical Section, thus:

> I went into this matter very carefully and although it is difficult to be absolutely certain what happened, my investigations seem to make it quite clear that the message was not regarded by anyone in the Admiralty as being of exceptional significance, *when read in the light of current policy regarding movement of French warships.* As soon as it was received the signal was distributed to all the various members of the Naval Staff, and it was, without doubt 'on the file' at the daily meeting of the Naval Staff held at 9.30 next morning. Yet neither the Vice nor the Assistant Chiefs of Naval Staff nor the Director of any Staff Division at any time chose to call particular attention to it.[19]

Captain Roskill concluded later from this that:

> As to Captain Bevan, though the initial error was certainly his it seems true to say that it was compounded by more highly placed officers on the staff; and therein may lie the reason why Pound considered a fairly mild reprimand adequate and stood out against any more severe punishment.[20]

Was then Bevan the real scapegoat for the errors of his seniors? Why, if the Madrid signal was so vital, did not the ACNS or VCNS or even Pound himself draw attention to it? And what of the subsequent signals from the Rock, which followed it in? As to the latter point it can only once more be tardy deciphering that held them up until after 0800. As to the former we shall probably never knew for certain either way.

The officers concerned were VCNS, Admiral Tom Phillips, ACNS, Vice-Admiral Sir Geoffrey Blake (Foreign), Rear Admirals Henry Moore (Trade) and A.J. Power (Home), and they assembled at the Chiefs of Staff meeting later that morning. It was here that the first news of the French squadron's passage was apparently to reach them through the offices of Pound's secretary, Acting Captain Ronald Brockman.

Before leaving the unfortunate Captain Bevan one final point of interest should be touched upon. Although Professor Marder states that he can find no record of any defence Bevan might have made for himself, and it has been mooted that the VCNS might have one of the prime movers behind the Admiralty's intransigence in the matter, there is some indication that Bevan and Phillips both thought somewhat differently on North's culpability, although the evidence to that effect is slender and at third or fourth hand. Nonetheless it is deserving of inclusion for it is relevant. It is to be found in an exchange of letters North had in the early 1950s with the distinguished naval historian Captain Russell Grenfell, who at one time was seriously studying North's case with a view to writing a book about it. In the autumn of 1951 Grenfell wrote to North that:

> I do assure you it will make all the difference to the book if I can be the first to 'spring the mine', so to speak. I am meeting Bevan tomorrow. He has already given me information showing that Tom Phillips thought at the time you were quite correct and I expect to get more.[21]

This meeting took place on Thursday 27th September and later Grenfell reported to North: 'I've just seen Bevan who was DOD and it is clear *that neither the VNCS nor ACNS thought he had failed.*'[22]*

Thus it appears that it was during the COS meeting that Brockman hurried to Pound and laid before him the *Hotspur*'s sighting report of Force Y which had been passed on by North at 0617 and was received in the Admiralty at 0740. The subsequent signals relayed at 0711 and 0917 arrived at the Admiralty at 0742 and 1043, while the Madrid signal did not reach Pound until later. It should be emphasised that the arrival of the *Hotspur* sighting report was the *first* Pound knew about the French ships. He acted immediately and telephoned the Admiralty to order *Renown* and destroyers to raise steam at once, and this signal went out, as we have seen, at 1239, being received by Somerville half an hour later. Pound meantime had to attend the War Cabinet meeting which commenced at 1230 and at once raised the issue for a decision to be made. The minutes of the meeting make interesting reading.

> The First Sea Lord said that the Naval Attaché at Madrid had been informed by the French Naval authorities that six French cruisers had left Toulon on 9th September and intended to pass through the Straits on the 11th. The FONA had been informed. The question was, what instructions should be given to him.[23]

* *My* italics

The alternative destinations of the French warships were tabulated:

(1) The French ships after passing through the Straits might turn north to German-controlled ports in France.
(2) They might turn south for Casablanca, in which case their object might be to leave Toulon in anticipation of a German occupation of southern France.
(3) Or, again, they might be instructed to go to Dakar, with a view to putting a stop to Operation 'Menace'.

As regards (1) First Sea Lord said that we had always told the French that if their ships attempted to go to German occupied ports we reserved the right of action. Clearly, therefore, we could not agree to the French ships turning north after leaving Gibraltar.

As between alternatives (2) and (3), the view of the War Cabinet was that in many ways it would be desirable that these French ships should go to Casablanca. The question arose, however, whether if we said that we would let them go to Casablanca but not to Dakar, this would show that we had some interest in Dakar. But this would not be material if the object of the French in sending the ships to Dakar was to forestall our operation of which they had obtained knowledge.

It was agreed that it would be most undesirable to allow these French ships to go to Dakar, where their arrival might make all the difference between a favourable and an unfavourable attitude when the Menace expedition arrived. Further we could argue that we had information that Dakar was German controlled but Casablanca was not.

Summing up the discussion, the Prime Minister proposed, and the War Cabinet agreed, to authorise the First Lord to send instructions to the FONA, on the following basis:

1: *Renown* should get in touch with the French ships and ask their destinations, making it clear we could not allow them to proceed to German controlled ports.
2: If the reply was that they were going south, we should ask whether they were going to Casablanca. If so, they should be informed that we were prepared to agree to them proceeding to that port. The French ships should be shadowed if they went to Casablanca.
3: If the French ships should try to proceed beyond Casablanca to Dakar, we should say that we were unable to agree to that course. The First Lord of the Admiralty was also invited to give directions that two of the cruisers forming part of Force M should be stationed so as to make sure that the French ships did not make their way into Dakar.[24]

Pound hurried back to the Admiralty from Richmond Terrace across The Mall and these instructions became Admiralty Messages 1347 and 1429 respectively. In North's favour several points emerge from the above.

As Heckstall-Smith later wrote: 'Pound and his staff must have known that it was impossible for Somerville to contact the French. Therefore it must be assumed that the Admiralty was not free to act without the Cabinet's permission.' He also added the opinion that: 'On the evidence, it seems obvious that Pound's staff were not worried about the passage of these ships through the Straits, and that it was only after the War Cabinet had been told that, as Somerville put it, the Admiralty "burst into song".'[25]

The same impression is gleaned from Marder's statement that 'Pound would do no more without War Cabinet approval.'[26]

However, as we have seen, Pound was already enroute to the War Cabinet anyway, and he did *not* wait until they had been told before he 'burst into song'; he got off an Immediate signal as soon as *he* knew what was afoot and *then* carried on to the meeting. Also, as the War Cabinet minute stresses, it was already the Government's stated policy that they would take action against any attempt by French warships to go north, and that they had already informed the French of this. They therefore expected that this would be done anyway, as a matter of course. *This* is the relevant part as far as Admiral North's future was concerned.

It can be argued that Pound's hurried signal was not decisive enough, but it was the best that he could do, at the moment in time the news reached him, to re-emphasise the fact. Perhaps North could hardly be blamed for rushing in where Pound feared to tread if Marder and Heckstall-Smith's assumptions are correct that Pound *would not* act further, but it seems he had no immediate opportunity of doing so before the already scheduled meeting started.

As to the practicability of the orders issued so late in the day, there was obviously, as Heckstall-Smith pointed out, no chance that *Renown* could catch the Frenchmen *before* they reached Casablanca now, but they might be stopped from going further south, provided that Somerville could place himself south of that port before they re-sailed, and these were the instructions sent to him later that day. However the chances of interception, even then, were not that good, given the limited number of British ships involved and the largeness of the region to be patrolled. As Pound later duly informed Churchill:

It must be realised, however, that even if everything had gone right there could have been no certainty whatever that these French ships would not have been able to evade the patrol which *Renown* and other ships were

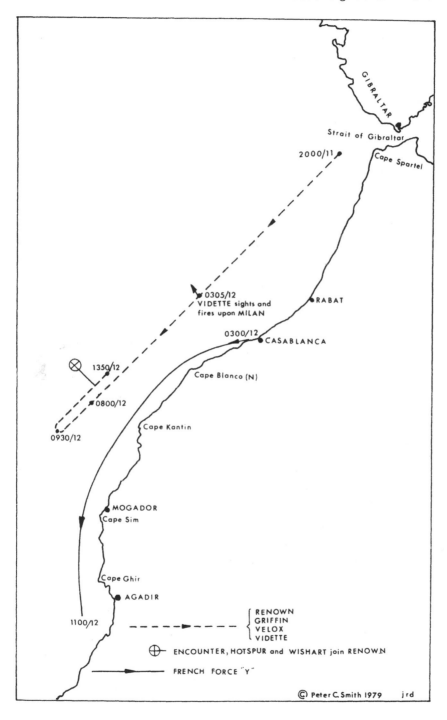

GIBRALTAR

Strait of Gibraltar

Cape Spartel

2000/11

0305/12
VIDETTE sights and
fires upon MILAN

RABAT

0300/12

CASABLANCA

Cape Blanco (N)

1350/12

0800/12

Cape Kantin

0930/12

MOGADOR
Cape Sim

Cape Ghir

AGADIR

1100/12

RENOWN
GRIFFIN
VELOX
VIDETTE

ENCOUNTER, HOTSPUR and WISHART join RENOWN

FRENCH FORCE "Y"

© Peter C. Smith 1979   jrd

maintaining south of Casablanca. The interception of ships of the high speed of the French ships is a very difficult thing unless a very large number of ships are available to do this.[27]

No, it remains the fact that the only practical place in which the French ships could have been intercepted with any chance at all was the Straits of Gibraltar, and this had not been done. At the time of the War Cabinet meeting they were still unsure whether the French squadron had gone north to Channel or Biscay ports, with all that that implied, and nothing physical had been done to prevent that either. Admiral Pound also stated that:

> In order that the *Renown* might have been in a position to get ahead of the French ships as they passed through the Straits of Gibraltar, it would have been necessary to take action previous to the information that *Hotspur* gave, that six ships burning lights and apparently men-of-war, had been sighted about fifty miles to the east of Gibraltar at 0515/11.
>
> This advance information might have been obtained either from Foreign Office telegram No 340 from HM Consul General, Tangier, or from Naval Attaché Madrid's signal 1809/10. As you are aware, the Foreign Office telegram was not circulated until the forenoon of 14th September. Naval Attaché, Madrid's telegram was received in the Admiralty at 2350/10 and as soon as deciphered was reported to the Duty Captain, who in turn called DOD (F) and showed him the signal, but the latter unfortunately took no action. Captain Bevan, the DOD (F) concerned, has since left the Admiralty but he has now been informed that he has incurred Their Lordships' displeasure on account of this incident. Consequently neither of these telegrams, giving advance information of the passage of the French ships, having reached either VCNS or myself, the first intimation we had was the receipt of the information contained in *Hotspur*'s signal, which was passed to the Admiralty by FOCNA. This signal was not received in the Admiralty until after the French ships had actually passed through the Straits.
>
> Immediately it came to my knowledge I ordered *Renown* to raise steam, and she was subsequently ordered to sea. Admiral North, the FOCNA, has been asked for his reasons in writing why *Renown* was not ordered to raise steam immediately *Hotspur*'s signal was received.[28]

Professor Marder states that the rationale for the first paragraph of this statement is not clear.[29] Certainly the *Renown* could have intercepted the French ships in the Straits, if pushed to it, after *Hotspur*'s first sighting. We shall examine this in detail later, but Admiral North himself stated that it could have been done. He later wrote that with *Renown* at one hour's notice to steam she could have

'... proceeded to sea at 0700 which allowed ample time to intercept the French ships which did not pass the Straits until 1¾ hours later.'[30]

Thus, due to what Churchill later termed 'a chapter of accidents', Force Y, at 1610 on the 11th entered the safety of Casablanca harbour. The intentions of the Admiral were to rest, replenish, embark his small detachments of Sengalese infantry and some fresh food, the latter for the Dakar garrison *en route*, the former from there for his true and final destination, Libreville. But his plans soon had to be re-cast with the utmost urgency. Let us therefore retrace our steps to the evening of the 11th at Casablanca itself and see what led to this.

Admiral D'Harcourt recorded the arrival safely of Force Y at Casablanca, at 1615 and shortly after berthing Admiral Bourragué called on him, as requested, at his HQ. They dined together with Captain Chatelet of *Georges Leygues* and over their meal they discussed events in Vichy since the Armistice. D'Harcourt learned that the morale of the populace was low, but not in the Navy, 'Morale is good in the cruisers', he recorded later.[31] It was while they were still dining that D'Harcourt received two important signals from the north which immediately affected the situation.

The first signal was timed at 1730 GMT and came from a lookout position near Cape Spartel, the headland on the north-west tip of Africa, which stated that 'one battleship and four destroyers', had been sighted offshore steering south-west. At 1845 GMT came a more inaccurate, but more alarming, second signal: 'two cruisers and four destroyers or an aircraft carrier and four destroyers', had been spotted further along the same route as the previous sighting.[31]

D'Harcourt took immediate steps. It was obvious that the British at Gibraltar were on the move, and in considerable force if all these reports were accurate. (As we know, the first sighting was of *Renown* and her three destroyers, the second of Layman's three additional destroyers.) Two things were feared: the first was that a heavy squadron might be on their way to bombard Force Y while it lay at anchor at Casablanca, in the style of Mers-el-Kebir, which was still very fresh in every French Naval officer's mind. D'Harcourt feared that such a bombardment would cause enormous casualties not only to the warships of his command but to the great concentration of merchant shipping that lay in the bay and among the civilian population ashore as well. He had no wish to be on the receiving end of such an eventuality. Secondly, if no bombardment in fact took place,

Bourragué and his squadron would be trapped, to use his own expression, '...like rats in a hole'.[32]

At 1832 therefore he advised Bourragué of the situation (the latter had returned to his ship *Georges Leygues*) and he also alerted his own forces. At 1830 he signalled to the three submarines on patrol off Casablanca, the *Amazone*, *Amphitrite* and *Sybille*: 'One battleship and four destroyers Cape Spartel 1730 hours, course 245.'[33]

At 1841 the shore defence were placed on full alert from midnight and five minutes later D'Harcourt was in touch with General Bouscat of the Air Force, at Rabat. He was requested to have his fighter force and bomber force ready for immediate action at daybreak on the 12th.[34]

Further sightings continued to come in from the north. At 1945 he received:

Four destroyers and one ship looking like a cruiser or an aircraft carrier passed by Spartel. Estimated speed 18 knots, seems superior to that of first group.

(The original in fact signalled two aircraft carriers and was corrected at 2000). Again D'Harcourt passed this on to the submarines, Rabat air base and Bourragué. At 2200 GMT Bourragué decided to get underway as soon as possible and hasty recall signals were despatched ashore. A feverish preparation now began in the darkness to get the squadron to sea before the net could close on them. The submarines were notified that Force Y hoped to sail from Casablanca at 0300 GMT (0200 British local time) and Rabat and other commands were also notified, the Air Force at 2330 being asked to conduct aerial reconnaissance on the morning of the 12th between the parallels of Mehedhya and Safi. The destroyer *Milan* at sea in the danger zone was also signalled to be on the alert. She was due into Casablanca on the morning of the 12th on her way back from Cape Ortegal where she had been escorting *Lipari* on a convoy mission. Her signal went out at fifteen minutes past midnight.[35] Unfortunately for the *Milan* the cypher key had been changed from the previous day and she had not been informed of this fact; it therefore took a long while for her to decipher the flood of messages from Casablanca. She was soon to receive far stronger confirmation that the British were stirring.[36]

All was hustle and bustle at the dockyard as Force Y readied itself. The captain of the *Gloire* recalled that their visit was 'feverishly curtailed';[37] indeed several of their passengers were left adrift when the time came and much of the provisions of fresh food they had hoped to carry was never loaded.[38]

D'Harcourt and his staff were still equally busy throughout the night. At 0036 Air Rabat was requested to ready a fighter patrol to take off from Casablanca at daybreak 'to catch up with the cruisers who will be following the coast towards the south to protect them for as long as their radius of action permits'. Obviously the fear that the *Ark Royal* might launch attacks was in their mind as well as the need to fend off shadowers. The submarine *Antilope* was ordered to get under way as soon as Force Y sailed in order to take up a patrol position west of the sectors occupied by the other three submarines already at sea.

At 0130 hours (0030) the ships of Force Y began to leave harbour; *Malin* sailed at 0200 GMT with *Montcalm* to carry out a sweep ahead, *Gloire* at 0220, *Georges Leygues* at 0250, *Audacieux* at 0310 and *Fantasque*, the last, at 0330 (0230 British time). *Antilope* duly sailed at 0430 GMT. At 0540 Air Maroc informed D'Harcourt that they could not lay on fighter cover, which was bad news, for already, before the ships of Bourragué's squadron had all left, word was coming in of sightings of British forces up and down the coast, which indicated that they may had already left it too late to escape

Forming up around 0400 Force Y set course south at high speed in the darkness, hugging the shoreline as far in as they could evade detection, in two groups. At 0500 (British time) three Glenn Martin bombers of Air Maroc took off to search ahead and astern of the French squadron and at 0605 they sighted Bourragué's two groups some thirty kilometres off Dar El Hachmi ben Toumi, on a south-west course. Behind them, in the darkness off Casablanca, the British trap snapped shut.

It did not, however, completely snap on empty ocean, as previous post-war accounts would leave one to think. Indeed, had Force H ventured closer inshore, inside the French twenty mile limit, it would have been very close indeed to Force Y; it is even just possible that interception would have been made. But not a hint of this is contained in most of the accounts so far published.[39] Let us first then, ignore these and then see what *really* took place off Casablanca that night and the following days.

CHAPTER THIRTEEN

Clash by Night

We left Admiral Somerville last with the *Renown*, *Griffin*, *Velox* and *Vidette* steering south-west off Casablanca in order to get into position south of that port before morning to await aerial reconnaissance reports of the situation. They were steering a mean course 220° at a speed of 24 knots, when in the approximate position 34°01′ N, 08°33′ W, the destroyer *Vidette* suddenly sighted a ship, darkened save for a faint white light about her bridge, bearing 160° approximately six miles off.[1]

By 0238 the mysterious vessel was bearing 170° and had altered her course to about 230°. Lieutenant Walmsley of the *Vidette* at once altered course to 190° and increased speed to 28 knots to close and investigate, at the same time signalling to the *Renown* astern of her: 'Suspicious ship on port bow, investigating'.[2]

Only the first word of this signal was acknowledged from the flagship. Lieutenant (later Commander) Walmsley later recalled those moments vividly:

> I remember I had not long put my head down in my sea cabin (a settee out of the conning position below the bridge), when the bridge buzzer went. A darkened ship on the port bow; you go through the drill practised many times in the gunnery school and exercises, wait for the reports, Director – On, Searchlight – On, Starshell – Ready, Order – "Make the Challenge". The Yeoman sings out 'No reply' and you order 'Open Fire'. It seems I didn't illuminate with star shell. At a mile range the searchlight would provide all the illumination necessary. I am not too sure but I think I identified her by the French ensign she was wearing.[3]

In fact the *Vidette*, with hands closed up at Action Stations, made the challenge slowly, four times but no reply or any notice was taken of these signals according to her report. By 0251 the range had come down to about 3,000 yards and the challenge was again made four times, again with no response and shortly afterwards the *Vidette*'s

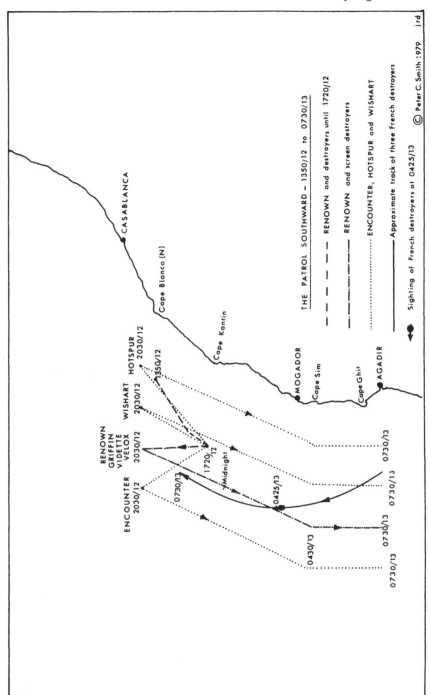

searchlight snapped on as the shutters were lifted revealing in its merciless glow a four-funnelled destroyer.

The visibility at this time was good and the unknown ship had altered to a course which placed herself in a favourable position to make a torpedo attack on the *Renown*. Because of this, and because still no answer had been received to the challenges made Walmsley gave the order to open fire, and, at 0300, both A and B 4-inch guns roared out at a range of 2,000 yards.[4]

It was of course the unhappy *Milan* who was her victim. In his report Captain Plumejeaud described the event thus:

> At 3 a.m. local time, heading towards the Cape of Casablanca on course 113, at a speed of ten knots, showing navigation lights, a British ship tried to stop the *Milan* in the following manner. The ship, which seemed to be following us off the stern, broke out of column to starboard, came around to bearing 150 and made a few signals by Aldis. Almost immediately she lit a searchlight and then fired into our bow three or four shots. It was exactly 3.05 a.m. Before the shooting started the *Milan* tried to signal 'What Ship' with a searchlight.[5]

Walmsley's report goes on:

> Two salvos were fired which were observed to fall short of the destroyer's quarter. After the second salvo had been fired, pendants on her bow were sighted and she flashed 'What ship' by light. I judged her to be French and 'friendly' so ordered 'Cease fire'. Whereupon she retired at high speed under a smoke screen on a course of about 340°.[6]

Vidette signalled *Renown*: '1FR DR 140'[7] and followed this up two minutes later with the amplification:

> My 0305. French destroyer making smoke and holding fire. Present course 340°. Speed 25 knots bearing 330°. My position ZTCS 5529.[8]

The *Vidette*'s vigorous action unsettled poor Plumejeaud:

> At that moment it seemed that we were probably dealing with a cruiser of the 'Arethusa' class which was 4,000 or 5,000 metres away. The *Milan* freed herself by setting the helm 25 to the left, ordering engines to 20 knots and making the four boilers produce smoke. All these manoeuvres were executed without delay. In the meantime all hands were called to action stations. To hide behind her smokescreen, the *Milan* went first to 310, then moved north. As we came out of the smoke we were able to

read the signal 'Stop' from the searchlight. Continuing to produce smoke for a while, the *Milan* was making 25, 30 and then 34 knots as she progressively returned to 130, heading towards Casablanca.[9]

Despite Plumejeaud's time operating with the British fleet in happier days his ship recognition was not too hot, which is not surprising in the circumstances. The ancient little *Vidette* with her 4-inch popguns would probably have been flattered to hear herself described as an 'Arethusa' class cruiser, and Commander Walmsley was amused when he later learnt of this description. But humour came later. It could have been a worse incident than it was, for had the *Milan* have wished to torpedo the *Renown* she might well have been able to do so had not *Vidette* been so alert. Equally so the French were showing considerable restraint under pressure of being fired upon, for they did not fire back in this, or subsequent, incidents. The affair also emphasised several other more important points. It showed how the danger of a clash with the French was always on the cards in such circumstances and how the advantage might not always go to the stronger force in night encounters in pre-radar days. It also showed how difficult it was for Somerville to carry out his orders to use minimum force, but still stop and interrogate French forces, not knowing what their reaction might be.

Before the chase led one of his only three escorts too far away and left him vulnerable to submarine attack on that clear and moonlit night, Somerville issued a recall to the *Vidette* at 0318 but she did not again make contact until 0500, when she was told to take station astern of *Renown* and submit her report by shaded light.[10] Her pursuit of *Milan* took her small distance from the British squadron, as Plumejeaud's report makes clear:

It seems that the cruiser did not chase for more than a quarter of an hour. I reduced my speed on reaching the 100 metre depth line, then to 15 knots at the 50 metre depth lines and cruised in front of Casablanca awaiting daylight.[11]

While here she sent off her own sighting report to Morocco Navy HQ which was received by them at 0545.[12]

As Commander Walmsley later recalled, the situation vis-à-vis the French at this time was 'uncomfortable', to say the least, 'as our instructions were not to fire the first shot.' Admiral Somerville later commented on the incident thus:

Vidette acted properly, as a unit of the screen, in taking immediate steps to ensure that the suspicious vessel sighted was prevented from taking up a position from which an attack on *Renown* could be delivered.

The occurrence as witnessed from *Renown* indicated that, at the time fire was opened, the French destroyer was in such a position that she no longer constituted a direct danger to the Fleet. This would not necessarily have been apparent to *Vidette* whose attention was fully occupied in dealing with the suspected enemy.

Since the illumination by searchlight disclosed the identity of the destroyer beyond reasonable doubt and since as has subsequently been ascertained, from the Commanding Officer, HMS *Vidette*, the guns and tubes of the French ship were trained fore and aft, *Vidette* would have been justified in withholding fire in accordance with paragraph 4 of Admiral Commanding, North Atlantic's Memo 465/2438 of 10th July which directs that 'Ships must be prepared for attack but should not fire first shot.'

On the other hand the failure of the French destroyer to switch on navigation lights and establish her identity immediately when challenged and subsequent failure to immediately withdraw from the vicinity of belligerent vessels, of necessity lay her open to attack, and I consider therefore that the responsibility for any damage or casualties that might have occurred, must rest with the French ship.[13]

Happily, this time, there was none on either side.

It was perhaps also fortunate for the *Vidette* that another French vessel showed restraint that night for, at 0500 GMT the submarine *Amphitrite* caught sight of a destroyer some thirty miles west of Casablanca and duly reported her without making an attack.[14] This incident showed how wise Somerville was in not pushing in closer than the thirty mile limit as he forbade his force to do, for the four Vichy submarines could hardly have failed to spot the *Renown* and would have had every justification in attacking her. Had they done so, the *Renown*, with her slender screen, might well have been disabled close inshore and subsequently sunk or captured by the French. He was in an impossible position in this case, and it is no reflection on him that the Force Y ships, which were well inshore and to the south of him by now, evaded him completely. Of course Somerville at this time had no idea the birds had flown.

Somerville kept pushing on southward to interpose himself between Force Y and Dakar but it was soon obvious that the force was under constant watch by the French. At 0822 a Glenn Martin aircraft was sighted on the Port quarter, patiently shadowing the British force.[15] This aircraft duly reported back to base at Rabat: '1 battleship and three destroyers on a south west course 100 km off Cape Cantin'. The force diverted to the north as the plane passed overhead, and this was also duly noted.[16]

Why had Somerville decided to turn back north at this time? The answer is that, in contrast to the highly accurate and precise sighting report made by the French aircraft that morning, Somerville's own reports coming in from the London flying boats over Casablanca were completely inaccurate. This is yet another point not made in subsequent accounts, for example: 'It was not until late afternoon of the 13th that aircraft were able to search the harbour conclusively.'[17] And again: 'Reconnaissance planes from Gibraltar made repeated flights over Casablanca during daylight on 11th and 12th September without success owing to the persistent mist.'[18] And finally: 'Because a heavy haze overhung Casablanca, he was unable to ascertain from the spotter planes which North had deployed from Gibraltar whether or not the cruisers were still in harbour.'[19]

There *was* a heavy haze over the harbour but far from being uncertain of whether the French units were there or not, the report received by Somerville was unequivocal, as Somerville himself later recorded:

At 0923 when *Renown* was in position 32°20′ N, 10°30′ W, reconnaissance aircraft reported that three cruisers and three destroyers had been identified in Casablanca, and possibly more. I consequently altered course to the north-eastward to effect a rendezvous with the three additional destroyers (*Hotspur*, *Encounter* and *Wishart*), whom I had previously instructed to steer 220° at 16 knots.

I reported to the Admiralty in message 1109/12 that it was my intention to carry out a line of bearing patrol between Cape Blanco and Agadir, steaming south by night and north by day, with the inshore destroyer 20 miles from the coast. I also reported that the weather was unsuitable for oiling at sea and consequently, unless it improved, two of my destroyers would have to leave patrol at dusk the following day and a third 24 hours later.[20]

The first two were the *Velox* and *Vidette*, the third, *Griffin*.

So it was because of what he took to be *precise* information of the continued presence of the Force Y that he had received from North that Somerville instituted his subsequent patrol. We know this information was completely wrong. What had gone wrong and why was it not vetted, for accuracy, before being sent on to him?

We can find the following confirmation in the diary of No 202

Squadron. At 0640 London K6930 took off from Gibraltar to comply with Admiral Somerville's requests to search Casablanca harbour, and 'to ascertain whether French units contacted on 11th were still in harbour'. This aircraft returned at 1125 and her sighting report, received by Somerville at 0923, was that the presence of Force Y was 'confirmed'.[21]

At 1300 that same day a second London was sent off on the same mission, K5908. She returned at 2000 that night and her sighting report on the French squadron was 'confirmed'.[22]

Thus both Somerville, and through him, Pound, Churchill and the Menace commanders, were all under the illusion, throughout most of the 12th September and later, that Force Y was *still* in harbour at Casablanca when in fact it was far to the south heading for Dakar. Pound and the Admiralty have been taken to task for not ordering the *Ark Royal* and the various cruisers attached to Force M, the ships covering the Dakar expedition, to intercept Force Y as they were south of them at this time and in a good position to do so; *Ark* could have flown off air searches, but they were told the French ships were still in Casablanca by Gibraltar. As Somerville later commented some days later:

> It will be recalled that the air recce from Gibraltar reported these ships lay in harbour during the forenoon and afternoon of Thursday 12th September. Subsequent interrogation of pilots and observers showed this report was not based on positive identification. Had this been known on forenoon of 12th September it is possible that by continuing her southerly course *Renown* might have intercepted the French force.[23]

This we now know would not have happened (Force Y had too large a lead) but, had the Admiralty have been told, Force M might have been able to do so. Lack of precise information or detail between Admiral North and the Admiralty may have been very poor, but not *all* the lack of communication was on the Admiralty's side. We also know that the location of Force M was known to the French at Casablanca, and was relayed to Admiral Bourragué, and further, that it worried him so much that it initiated yet another change of his plans.[24]

Unaware, then, that each mile was doubling the distance between him and his quarry, Admiral Somerville steamed steadily northward throughout the forenoon of 12th September and, at 1330, in position 33°5′ N, 9°40′ W, he effected his rendezvous with Layman's destroyer division coming down from Gibraltar, whereupon the combined force once more turned southwest. Somerville's general instructions to his force had been issued on the evening of the 11th; they read as follows:

For your information:
French Squadron which passed Gibraltar this morning has arrived Casablanca. We have instructions to keep touch with them and if making for Dakar or Bay Ports to inform them that such movements cannot be allowed. Use of force may become necessary.[25]

Somerville, now that he had sufficient ships on hand, could now organise a more widespread search pattern to cover his patrol beat. It was designed so that if the French squadron sailed from Casablanca that night at dusk, (around 2000), and headed south at a speed of 25 knots, Somerville's grid of ships would be south of their estimated furthest south position at dawn on the 13th. He was only too acutely aware, as was the Admiralty, that with the small number of ships available such a search could not be fully effective and that French air patrols, fully pressed home, would give Force Y good warning of his ambush, but it was the best that could be done. Accordingly he signalled his plan to the destroyers in company:

(a) *The Search*. When ordered ships are to spread to be in position by 2030, 30 miles apart on a line 270° from Eastern Unit in position 360° Cape Cantin. Sequence of units from west to east; One, *Encounter*. Two, *Renown*, *Velox*, *Vidette*, *Griffin*. Three, *Wishart*. Four, *Hotspur*. Initial course 205° turning to 180° at 0430 and to 360° at 0730 thence returning along tracks. Speed made good going south 17 knots, going north 14½ knots, zig zag independently. *Hotspur* not to approach within twenty miles of the French coast.
(b) *Policy*. On sighting report and shadow. Do not communicate substance of my 2015/11 (above) unless ordered. Attention is drawn to paragraph 4 of Admiral Commanding, North Atlantic's Memorandum No 455/2458 of 10th July.[26] [This latter reiterated that ships must be prepared for attack but should not fire the first shot, Somerville's reference to it herein, shows that FOCNA had, in this instance at least, binding authority over Force H's policy]

While the destroyers spread to their search and patrol positions Somerville received, at 1634, the second air reconnaissance report stating 'Disposition confirmed', relayed to him by North. As he noted: 'Although by no means clear, this report implied that the cruisers and destroyers were still in Casablanca.'[27]

Meanwhile many, many miles to the south of him Bourragué was harbouring grave fears following his own aircraft's frequent reports of groups of hostile ships all about him. The Glenn Martins of Air Maroc had been airborne throughout the day and had been sending back a steady stream of sightings. *Renown*'s group was first located by them at 0730 GMT and at 0845 she was again picked up, as we have seen. At 0900 another aircraft located Force Y, then some forty kilometres (twenty-five miles) north of Cape Cantin, and, an hour later, D'Harcourt asked Bouscat to lay on further air patrols that same afternoon between 29°30′ and 32°30′ to provide further information. Two more bombers took off from Casablanca at 1330 GMT to comply with this request, both being forbidden to radio back their reports but to hold them until they landed for fear they might be intercepted and Force Y's location deduced. One of these aircraft again made contact with the French force some twenty-five miles north-west of Agadir at 1400. The second aircraft located Layman's three destroyers while they were steering to rendezvous with *Renown*, but, sticking to her orders, she did not report this until she landed at her base once more: 'At 1515 GMT, 3 ships, probably light ships of foreign nationality, 8 miles west of Mogador, on south course, average speed.'[28]

Plotting these fixes as they came in on his operations map on the bridge of the *Georges Leygues*, the French Admiral began to get the firm impression that he was being boxed in on all sides and that he would soon be surrounded and cut off. 'The scene was becoming a little too crowded for his taste ...', recorded Cras.[29]

Bourragué decided that his only hope was to crack on speed in order to reach the haven of Dakar before these groups closed in on him. But there was a snag to this, for his super-fast super-destroyers just did not have the fuel bunkerage to sustain them over the 1,000 mile-plus distance he had to cover if they ran at the high speed of 27 knots he planned. Although it is often stressed, in assessing their merits, that they were good for over 40 knots speed in service they could only achieve this in short bursts and dashes; their endurance was just one of their faults. This lack of staying power, even at 27 knots, was a handicap which would hold Force Y back and so Bourragué decided on a calculated risk, not for the last time, and determined to send them back to Casablanca, while he pushed on with just the light cruisers. In order to evade the searching British forces, who, from the reports he had, seemed to be not too far offshore on his track, he ordered them to make a wide swing out into the Atlantic during their run back north, which, he calculated, would take them well clear of *Renown* and company. Accordingly Bourragué signalled to Captain Still at 2050,[30] and five minutes later they complied.[31]

While the three super-destroyers turned their little hulls back north towards the *Renown*'s search party and headed north-west at 20 knots, the three light cruisers increased their speed at 2115[32] to 27 knots and sped on south. By 1000 GMT on the 14th they were sweeping past Cape Vert well in the clear. Alas for Still, his sweep out into the Atlantic, far from taking him away from Somerville, was taking him straight into his arms and he would have been safer had he stuck to the twenty mile limit as before where he would have only had the *Hotspur* barring his path.

It was at 0405 (0305 GMT in the French reports) that the inevitable contact was made between the ships of Force H and Force Y. The *Griffin*, leading *Renown*'s screen, was stationed on the flagship's starboard bow in position 31°25′ N, 11°30′ W when she suddenly sighted three dark shapes steering 020° at an estimated speed of 20-25 knots. The forces rapidly closed each other and soon they were spotted by watchers on the *Renown*'s bridge and were positively identified as destroyers of the 'Fantasque' class.[33] The CO of the *Vidette* remembers this contact very well:

> The next night, again in the middle watch after I had put my head down, the buzzer went. This time two French destroyers were sighted by us. They were in line abreast and one passed to starboard of us, the other to port. *Renown* could clearly see them so no particular action was taken by me but I remember thinking they were waiting until they were abreast me, before blowing me out of the water. I thought they were the *Mogador* class which carried eight 5.5-inch guns.[34]

But no, they were Still's ships who must have been as alarmed as Walmsley at running into a British battle-cruiser in the middle of what they had fondly hoped was an empty area of ocean. Both sides held their course, and their fire, and within brief moments, with only a swish of bow waves in the darkness, the two squadrons swept close by each other almost within touching distance. One wrong decision and guns and torpedoes would have been threshing the water, but the moment passed and very soon the two squadrons had left each other behind. Still later reported: 'In position 31°24′ N, 11°30′ W, a destroyer and a battleship. No reaction.'[35]

One can almost sense the feeling of surprised relief in Still's signal and he could hardly have believed his luck at coming out scot-free after such an encounter. On his part Admiral Somerville was left with little choice but to let the French ships go their way. He contented himself with merely informing the Admiralty of the encounter, which he did in his signal at 0425/13. Why were these ships, which were after all his quarry, even though they were not the main units of Force Y, allowed to sail past him when his instructions were to stop and parley with them?

In the first place it was quite impracticable for him to do so, even had he had wished to. The fleeting encounter was over in much less then five minutes, the ships were on opposite courses and by the time the *Renown* could have hauled round in pursuit the French destroyers would have been miles away in any direction in the early half-light. It is true, as the French captain later reported to Admiral D'Harcourt, that 'the sea was not rough and the moon was bright',[36] but Somerville would have had little chance of overhauling Still's ships once they had passed him and vanished. Even in the remote possibility that he could have done so they could have outpaced him, unencumbered as they were by the slower cruisers.

Secondly they were heading *away* from Dakar, not towards it. Somerville's instructions were to stop any warships reaching that port, but if they were going in the opposite direction, towards Casablanca or out into the Atlantic, away from the Menace convoy and its destination, he had no real reason to stop them. As Professor Marder stated: '... if not toward Dakar, Somerville's instructions were to leave any such ships alone.'[37]

Finally there is the clincher in the form of the two signals he had already received which confirmed that Force Y was still in harbour at Casablanca. If this was so then obviously these must be other ships coming up from the south about which he had no knowledge. As they were positively identified as being of the 'Fantasque' class however, (the whereabouts of all should have been pretty common knowledge in the Royal Navy) it must have given rise in Somerville's mind to serious doubts about the accuracy of those reports he had received from Gibraltar. As shrewd a person as Somerville probably started putting two and two together and began to realise that Force Y had in fact left Casablanca long before, despite Gibraltar's affirmations that they had not.

Nonetheless, despite any such doubts, Somerville held to his plan and Force H continued south until 0730 on the 13th, when, according to schedule, they reversed course and began to backtrack northward. The only change of policy was brought about by Somerville's fear that the French destroyers would have reported him and that Vichy submarines from Casablanca might therefore be lying in wait for *Renown*. To counter this *Renown*'s group exchanged places on the search grid with the *Wishart*. The whole formation then began to sweep back towards Casablanca at sixteen knots. *Velox* and *Vidette* were beginning to get very low on oil fuel and the sea was still too high to permit alongside fuelling of these destroyers from the *Renown* herself.

If Somerville did start to have doubts on the position of Force Y at this time, they were amplified by a new sighting report which he received that morning. London flying boat K6930 was airborne from Gun Port Wharf at 0640 on the morning of the 13th to carry out a further reconnaissance of Casablanca. When she arrived she found the French fully alert and was heavily fired on by the AA batteries there. This kept her up at 10,000 feet and from this height she stooged around for three hours. She reported that 'No movement observed and warships were in belt of thick haze.'[38] Gibraltar forwarded this on to Somerville and he received the following message at 0905 that morning: 'Warships in harbour, unable to identify type, thick haze, no movement.'[39]

This was followed by another signal timed at 1110 which simply stated: 'Nothing to report; am returning to base.'[40]

This was, to say the least, unhelpful to Somerville and did nothing to improve his spirits, or his temper. As he later recorded: 'I consequently requested Admiral Commanding, North Atlantic, to insist on more definite and detailed reports giving types and numbers of ships in harbour.'[41]

At 1001 he notified the Admiralty of his fuel situation, pointing out that two of his destroyers would have to be detached by 2030 that night and that this would further reduce his chances of sighting the French ships if they actually sailed that night. He suggested an interception patrol should be set up off Dakar itself, but the Admiralty had already put this in hand. In the afternoon a second London was despatched from Gibraltar, K5908. Although her orders were to push home her search it was by no means an easy task. Firstly, the harbour was still mist enshrouded, although later it cleared. But this only gave the Vichy AA gunners a better chance to vent their wrath at the slow lumbering old seaplane. It was sticking their heads into the lions' den for the French had long ago warned that any aircraft violating their airspace would be shot down. Again they showed restraint, merely trying to warn the London off with AA fire, but after some time their patience ran out. At least K5908 was finally able to get a good look at the harbour. The pilot reported back first that he could see no cruisers at all in the harbour. Two fighters were observed scrambling from the aerodrome to intercept him so he had to sheer off for a time. Just after 1600 he resumed his observations once more and spotted one destroyer entering Casablanca. At 1730 he was over the harbour at 14,000 feet and reported sighting one cruiser. He took a photo and then came under flak fire once more without damage. Fighters were again seen taking off and K5908, after a good try, had no choice but to return to base.[42]

These reports were relayed once more via Gibraltar to the *Renown*, as Somerville recorded:

> At 1408 I received a signal from Admiral Commanding, North Atlantic Station, that air reports and photographs were still inconclusive. Two hours later at 1620, I received an aircraft report that no cruisers at Casablanca. I informed the Admiralty accordingly at 1643 and reported that I could either:
> (a) Arrive Gibraltar with three destroyers, refuel and be ready for sea by 1500/14.
> (b) Arrive Freetown with two destroyers at 1200/19.
> (c) Arrive Freetown unescorted at 1000/16 unescorted.
> and intended to proceed as at (a) after 2000, since the maintenance of the patrol appeared to be no longer required.[43]

The only thing to occupy Somerville during these patrols was the diversions provided by the BBC on the whole affair which he found ludicrous, knowing their statements to be quite untrue. As he wrote home to his wife on a later occasion: 'BBC bulletins today said that the Government never had any intentions of stopping the French cruisers from going south to Dakar, which is a pretty good bender.'[44]

His amusement was shared by the French at Casablanca, Admiral D'Harcourt and his Chief-of-Staff, Captain Costet, tuned in to the same broadcasts: 'Costet and I heard the latest tall story about the Bourragué cruisers' aid to de Gaulle. The Allies *allowed* them to pass!!'[45]

And later he recalled that: 'The British Press affects the hope that the cruisers of the 4th DC and the CTs of the 10th DCT passed into the Atlantic with the aid of the British !!!'[46]

Being in the picture put the admirals on both sides at an advantage, but of course the people being duped by all this rubbish were the British public themselves, including MPs. One of them, later to become one of Admiral North's champions in the House, was Richard Stokes, Labour Member for Ipswich. He got off on the wrong foot right away, stating in the subsequent debate that one only had to read the daily press to see that the ships were coming through Gibraltar and that everyone wondered why and thought that there was a deep plot and that presently all the ships would surrender when they were safely down the west coast of Africa.[47] Quite where he got hold of this story is hard to say; suffice to say that it was completely inaccurate and that no trace can be found in any British newspaper, prior to the passage of the Force Y, to indicate that they were on their way. It was, no doubt, 'Parliamentary latitude'.[48]

Of the two admirals, D'Harcourt at Casablanca had more to celebrate than Somerville pounding his futile beat out at sea. The destroyer that Hatfield had seen entering harbour on the afternoon of the 13th was one of Still's ships which had survived their journey intact, although they had become somewhat separated due to varying fuel stocks. As each made port they reported to D'Harcourt on their night's experiences and the reasons for their return, of which only Still knew precisely. *Le Malin* was the first back, at 1355 GMT, being followed a quarter of an hour later by *L'Audacieux*; Captain Desprez reported that they had been sent back, probably so that the cruisers could proceed at higher speed. He also told D'Harcourt that he had sighted a destroyer, and a large ship, possibly the *Hood*. Captain Still arrived aboard *Le Fantasque* at 1545[49] and he put D'Harcourt more in the picture. He was told to make a large diversion to the west he said and that he had sighted the *Renown* and three destroyers which passed him very close.[50]

Meanwhile the cruisers had been making good, uninterrupted, progress, and quick time. Log entries for this day record only positions as the miles slid by: at 1000 they were in 25°04′ N, 16°20′ W, at 1400 in 23°30′ N, 17°05′ W, and by 1800 on the 13th in 21°50′ N, 17°45′ W.[51] All was going well for the French. For the British however, 13th September was yet another day of confusion and frustration. Back in Madrid Hillgarth had meanwhile received another visit from Delaye during which the further information was given him that the French ships' destination was Dakar or other French colonial ports; this news had formed the basis on which the Admiralty advised Somerville to set up his patrol south of Casablanca, still under the impression at this time, early on the 13th, that the French vessels had been pinpointed by North's aircraft at Casablanca harbour. They estimated that they still had time to stop them, and were also stating that Bourragué's ships would most likely 'embark troops to tackle situation in Duala'.[52]

Heckstall-Smith is quite correct when he states that most of the signals passing between Somerville, North and the Admiralty concerning the French squadron were repeated to Admiral John Cunningham, commander of Force M.

> Cunningham knew, for instance, that the French ships had reached Casablanca and were being watched by the *Renown*. He knew also that Somerville destroyers were running short of oil. And he had also received that Admiralty's signal concerning the possible destination of the French ships, as well as Somerville's Most Immediate Signal, made at 1643 on 13th September, that there were no cruisers in Casablanca. But it was not until 1216 on 14th September that the Admiralty signalled Cunningham telling him that Bourragué's cruisers had left at a time unknown, and ordering him to prevent them entering Dakar.[53]

This is being less than accurate and far less than fair to the Admiralty. Somerville's signal of 1643 did indeed state that he had received an aircraft report that no cruisers were in Casablanca, but, as we have seen, this signal was followed some time later by another, *from the same aircraft*, stating that at 1730 one cruiser *had* been sighted at Casablanca. This, we now know, was false, but it *could* have been true as far as the Admiralty (or North, Somerville and Cunningham for that matter) knew. This was the only firm report they had to go on, there were no others to positively locate Force Y's light cruisers 1,000 miles further south. Which is probably why, at 1947 that same evening, the Admiralty signalled to Somerville again, instructing him to steer towards Dakar at 18 knots and to keep his destroyers with him.[54]

Owing to the acute fuel situation in the *Velox* and *Vidette* there was no question of adopting the same spread formation for the night of the 13th/14th as he had the night before. The *Hotspur*, *Encounter* and *Wishart* were concentrated to replace these two, which were detached to Gibraltar at 2000 that evening. *Renown* retained *Griffin* on the screen and these five ships turned back south at this time.

In London that evening a Chiefs of Staff meeting was held and from the flimsy evidence of the Gibraltar aircraft sightings and *Renown*'s sightings of the night before it was concluded then that the French squadron *had* probably left Casablanca en route for Dakar. It

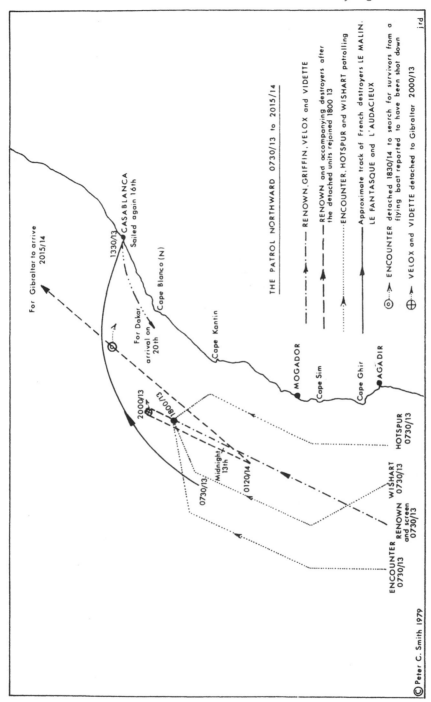

THE PATROL NORTHWARD 0730/13 to 2015/14

—·—·—·→ RENOWN, GRIFFIN, VELOX and VIDETTE

— — — —→ RENOWN and accompanying destroyers after
the detached units rejoined 1800 13

· · · · · · · → ENCOUNTER, HOTSPUR and WISHART patrolling

————→ Approximate track of French destroyers LE MALIN,
LE FANTASQUE and L'AUDACIEUX

⊙—→ ENCOUNTER detached 1830/14 to search for survivors from a
flying boat reported to have been shot down

⊕—→ VELOX and VIDETTE detached to Gibraltar 2000/13

© Peter C. Smith 1979

jrd

was decided to use every possible ship from Force M to try and head them off before they reached that port. Clearly Force H was now no longer in any position to do so but she might be needed back at Gibraltar or off Casablanca in order to prevent any repetition of these reinforcements once Dakar had blown up and accordingly Somerville was given his recall.

> At 0100, when in position 31°50′ N, 10°40′ W, I received Admiralty signal 2335/13 directing me to proceed to Gibraltar and complete with fuel. The Force then proceeded at the maximum speed that the weather permitted to Gibraltar.[55]

This did not mean that the aerial watch on Casablanca was to be relaxed however and plans were made to resume the attempts next morning in order to get a more precise situation report on exactly what ships *were* there. Hitherto the passage of Force Y, although bedevilled by mix-ups and lack of a clear picture, had, thanks to the excellent restraint shown by the French, at least not resulted in loss of life to either side. But now that picture was to change.

An especially early air patrol was laid on by 202 Squadron for the morning of 14th September; London flying boat K5958 took off from Gibraltar at 0430 in the hope of catching the French defences unawares. She managed to get a photograph of the harbour but when she returned at 1130 it was found again to be inconclusive. At 1300 London K9682 took off to try yet again. It was commanded by Flight Lieutenant Bruce MacCallum, with co-pilot Flying Officer Edwin Minchinton and crew of three. His orders were to make a reconnaissance flight over Casablanca and photograph the Tarifa area.[56] Nothing more was heard from K5958 until an SOS call was picked up by Gibraltar at 1532 and then all signals abruptly ceased. The destroyer *Hotspur* with *Renown's* force also reported hearing an SOS signal from an aircraft. No position was given and the signal was not read by any other ship in company, but Somerville passed it on to North.[57]

It was K5958 and, from the French reports, her subsequent fate can be traced.[58] At 1530 the London flying boat was intercepted at a height of over 6,000 feet some two miles offshore by two Curtiss Hawk fighters of 2/5 squadron attached to Casablanca airfield. They had been scrambled at 1516 (1416 GMT) when the London was first sighted, being instructed to intercept the London, ask her business and escort her back outside French air space. The leading

Curtiss was piloted by Captain Hubert Monraisse and both fighters quickly closed the British flying boat which they identified as a Saro-London type. As they drew close the London opened fire on them, but failed to make a fatal hit, although, when Monraisse later landed, holes were found through both his propeller and reserve fuel tank, which was fortunately empty at the time.

Both French aircraft had been flying with guns set to safe when fired upon but, upon receipt of this attack, Monraisse dropped back and armed his machine-guns. Meanwhile the pilot of the London had put his clumsy machine into a dive to try and escape, a futile gesture for the lithe fighter quickly closed the gap again and fired back, scoring at least twenty hits in five passes. The London was well riddled and at once plunged into the sea, exploding as it hit the water and quickly sinking, just a few miles off El Hank.

The submarine *Amazone* (Captain Richard), was returning from her patrol on the surface in the area and witnessed the whole incident. She was quickly on the scene and she found and picked up two survivors who were swimming and then hauled aboard a third who was affected with cramp. These were all crew members, Simpson, Hardy and Graham. Simpson was wounded by a machine-gun bullet, but the other two were unhurt. No trace was found of the pilot and the co-pilot who presumably went down with the wreckage of their aircraft.

Under interrogation aboard the submarine the two fit men stated that they had been told to open fire, but Simpson denied this completely. However a subsequent enquiry upheld Captain Monraisse's action under the circumstances. D'Harcourt authorised a signal to North at Gibraltar informing him that the London had been shot down while violating French air space and giving the names of the three survivors, but this was not done until the 15th.

Meanwhile, back at Gibraltar the worst was feared and London K5261 took off at 1722 to search for K9682 but without result. This hunt was resumed by K5909 next morning at 0630 and again at 1315 by L7043. This latter aircraft, piloted by Pilot Officer Farrar, nearly shared the same fate for while over the area she was also intercepted by three fighters (two Moraines and one Curtiss she reported later). These fighters made shadow attacks on her but did not open fire and she withdrew at her best speed. On her return she learnt that the crew of the missing London were safe but that there was no trace of the pilots.

Force H had also tried to help; Somerville detached the destroyer

Encounter at 1830 on the 14th to assist in the search. She steered towards the area but on receipt of North's signal on the fate of the London, followed *Renown* back to Gibraltar. *Renown, Hotspur, Griffin* and *Wishart* arrived back at the Rock at 2014 on the evening of the 14th, *Encounter* the next morning. It was the end of a futile sortie.[59]

MacCallum was 'a good looking blond Canadian – an excellent flying boat pilot and captain, like so many Canadians, but tended to be belligerent. I suspect he lost his life through pushing his luck beyond the bounds of prudence. He was married, with a wife at Malta.' Pilot Officer Minchington was 'a large, quiet young officer. A good flying boat pilot, and a very capable crew member. He had flown with me on quite a number of patrols.'[60]

Somerville was understandably upset by the whole affair:

> I simply loathe this French stuff as you don't know where you are and a wrong step might bring about all sorts of reactions. The people at home never seem to put themselves in *my* shoes and give me their ideas of what the situation is or what may be expected.[61]

And what of Bourragué? He had pressed on throughout the night and the forenoon of the 14th without further incident. While Cunningham and de Gaulle halted their ships in mid-ocean and talked about what steps to take to halt him, he sped past and by midday the three light cruisers had dropped anchor in Dakar harbour. When, finally, a Skua aircraft from the *Ark Royal* made the first positive sighting of these ships since they passed Gibraltar three days before, they had their awnings rigged as if on a pre-war regatta, and so indeed, for the French, that was all their potentially hazardous voyage had been.

What of the three super-destroyers? They refuelled at Casablanca and embarked the stores and personnel left behind before. On the 16th they sailed again for Dakar. They found the seas empty; the British had withdrawn. By the 19th they had joined their Admiral in Dakar harbour. But all their high-speed steaming was not quite without price for one of them, *Le Fantasque*, developed acute condensor trouble and was immediately put under repair,[62] and these repairs were to keep her out of the first day's fighting when Menace finally became a real live shooting war. The *Gloire* too, had strained her engines, a fact which showed up later, when the three light cruisers subsequently sailed to complete their mission to Libreville. She humiliated herself by breaking down while being pursued by a British cruiser and was escorted away from Dakar, and out of history.

The fear that these units might be joined by others from Toulon was a real one. Back at the Rock Somerville and North had a meeting on the 15th to discuss what they should do if it came to pass. They were gloomy of their prospects and signalled as much to London at 1645 that afternoon. They stated that sufficient warning could not be received in time to ensure such a force was intercepted before the French forces reached the Straits. Should the French force proceed south of Casablanca how close a watch could be maintained, for incidents had to be avoided, the twenty mile limit respected? A closer watch was made impossible by the French submarines and light forces. They requested guidance from the Admiralty.[63]

They received their reply early next morning to the effect that:

(a) French forces were to be shadowed if they left the Mediterranean and instructions regarding further action would then be given.

(b) A limit of twenty miles from French territory need not be adhered to but it was desirable to avoid incidents at this juncture.[64]

It was not until later on the same day, 2054/16th, that North and Somerville received firm information to the effect that the three cruisers of Force Y had been positively identified at Dakar.

During this period of Admiral Somerville's fruitless patrol Admiral North had little to occupy him at Gibraltar other than organising the air searches. Only routine movements disturbed him and the few ships left there. The two submarines, *Triad* and *Truant*, sailed on their patrols in accordance with secret operation MAS 2 on the night of 11th/12th September, and on the same date the only remaining destroyer, *Wrestler*, left the harbour to rendezvous with two more submarines coming across the Bay of Biscay to join North's command, *Triton* and *Tetrarch*; these arrived under her escort on the 14th. On 16th September the French tried another experimental convoy through the Straits, the destroyer *Frondeur* escorting the trawler *Alina* eastward. On completion of their passage the destroyer turned back west through the Straits. Once more they were not molested in any way.[65]

Also on the 16th the Chiefs of Staffs held a midday meeting to discuss the latest developments. Churchill was in full cry at this meeting; he had made his mind up that Force Y's mission was to stop Menace and nothing would shake him of that fixation. Having failed to get Bevan's blood he was lashing about verbally in search of somebody to blame. He came up with our Polish allies:

> The Prime Minister said, at the time the original Scorpio expedition had been conceived it had been necessary to take the Poles into our confidence as they were taking part in it, and gradually word got back to France, with the results that the Vichy Government had shown surprising resource and sent a force of warships, which, after refuelling at Casablanca and eluding our forces sent to intercept them, had arrived at Dakar. This event had altered the whole situation. To continue the operation Menace in these circumstances was, in his opinion, out of the question, and in view of the fact that the French warships might have troops on board, if attempted, end in bloodshed.[66]

Churchill was convinced that the arrival of this squadron would so stiffen the defences of Dakar that Menace should be called off, and this the Chiefs of Staffs agreed to do, unless General de Gaulle had any strong objections. Instead the force should be used to consolidate the position in Equatorial Africa starting from Duala.

However the men on the spot were much dismayed by this attitude. On Force Y they expressed the opinion that its arrival changed little and they were still convinced that the Free French would be met with, at worst, but a token resistance. In this they were far too sanguine. Force Y's warships might not have made a great deal of material difference to Dakar's defenders, who were determined to resist anyway, but their morale-boosting effect should not be overlooked. So although Churchill was wrong in attributing to Force Y greater influence than it had and of bringing 'bitter minded Vichy officers' to take control, he was correct in part in his estimation of the situation overall. Hitherto local commanders on the spot in all theatres had not been fired with enthusiasm for any offensive ideas and the fact that the Menace commanders *were* so enthusiastic and confident won Churchill over to giving them their head. Unfortunately they were soon proven completely wrong and Churchill took much of the blame for the subsequent fiasco.

On the French side at this period they still had no idea that a landing was to be made at Dakar, although, from the orders given to Force Y when they were intercepted by British warships on their way south to Libreville on 19th September, they were now far more alert for some sort of Allied move against their territories and were fully prepared. The interception of Bourragué's ships, plus the cruiser *Primauguet*, and his own submission to force rather than engage in combat with the British cruisers, was too much for Darlan, who again exploded in a fit of rage. The kindly and thoughtful Bourragué, who had so skilfully kept his squadron out of trouble, and had been chosen for his qualities of care and diplomacy, was abruptly dismissed from his command on 20th September and his replacement, Vice-Admiral Emile Lacroix, Commander of the 3rd Squadron at Toulon, was rushed out to Dakar by air to instil a stronger line afloat. That this dismissal was unfair hardly needs stressing; no man could have carried out his orders more to the letter than Bourragué and most difficult orders they were. However he accepted his fall from grace with dignity and raised no fuss. (He was later forgiven by the mercurial Commander-in-Chief and given a staff job.)

Darlan's rage encompassed more than the mere dismissal of the unfortunate commander of the 4th Cruiser Squadron. A reversion was at once ordered to the old hard line against British forces which had come into force in the aftermath of Mers-el-Kebir, but had since been softened down. As we have seen, for the passage of Force Y from Toulon to Casablanca and Dakar the orders had been stressed, over and over again, for the French captains to *avoid* at all costs the use of force or to become involved in any confrontation with the Royal Navy. Now, *after* their arrival at Dakar, but *before* the guns boomed out for Menace, a different note was struck:

> My telegrams 5676-78 cancelled. Attitude to observe henceforth against British in Mediterranean and Atlantic will be as follows.
> 1. Attack all British warships approaching within 20 miles of our coasts and all threatening British warships in whatever channel they may be. These attacks will only naturally be undertaken if the forces at your disposal to carry them out are not manifestly inferior.
> 2. Great vigilance must be exercised to assure your protection and you must be prepared to react against any attack wherever it may be directed.
> 3. Take all necessary action to launch reprisal air attacks at a minutes notice.
> 4. Confirm receipt.[67]

It is worth again noting, in regard to our story, that these new hard-line orders only came into force after the incidents of 19th/20th September and were *not* in force at the time Force Y penetrated the Straits.

So already the passage of Force Y had cost two naval officers their jobs, Bourragué and Bevan. But what of Admiral North? It would seem that in his case judgement had already been passed but there was some delay in executing his punishment. Why was this? Admiral Pound explained:

> It was perfectly obvious on the day that the French cruisers passed through the Straits that Admiral North had not carried out his instructions but while Operation Menace was in progress the Naval Staff were too fully occupied to deal with a question which was in no way urgent.[68]

How had he failed? Simply by failing to take sufficient precautions to prevent the French squadron proceeding north to the Biscay Ports, which, as senior officer on the spot, the Admiralty felt he should have considered as his prime responsibility. As has been recorded his attitude had already come under some searching study and this latest incident was, for Admiral Pound, the last straw. It only now required time to hear his side of the story and pass judgement accordingly, but time was at a premium in September 1940 and far more pressing matters were concerning Pound and his staff at this time than Admiral North's most recent gaffe. An Admiralty memorandum later spelled just some of the priorities thus:

> The conditions prevailing in London obviously affected the urgency with which the post-mortem was pursued. The Battle of Britain was at its height; daily meetings on anti-invasion preparations, at the highest levels; the preoccupation of the Naval Staff with Operation Menace and current operations in the Mediterranean, not to mention the preliminaries in the exchange of Lease-Lend destroyers from the United States, and the day to day business of the war – all took precedence.[69]

This was the most desperate period of the war for Britain and yet it is sometimes argued that all these urgent matters should have been dropped while Admiral North's case was debated. This is absurd of course, but in the light of subsequent history much needless argument might have been saved had the Admiralty indeed found time to deal with North and leave Hitler and Mussolini to wait their turn, along with their bombers and U-boats; then Menace would not then have come into the controversy at all, for it had yet to take place. As it was, the only correspondence that took place between Pound and North prior to Menace was a belated reply by the former to a letter from the latter written in July. This was dashed off on 22nd September and consisted merely of standard courtesy replies to various points North had raised in his own missive. With Menace imminent Pound had no time to open fresh issues. It was again unfortunate that it was sent *when* it was, for it provided yet another red-herring for future historians. The letter read as follows:

My dear North,
... I hope that by now Gibraltar has been put into a thorough state of defence. I remember seeing a telegram from the Governor some time ago saying that if he had another six weeks all would be well.

I am very glad you have got a General [MacFarlane] who is getting a move on, and I only hope that he is improving the AA defences. You may require the latter if the French react to some of the things we are doing and start taking reprisals against you.

I am glad you are now clear of the refugee business, as it must have been very difficult getting them back from Morocco and having to ship them off again. A great many of them are still in London but are being gradually shipped away to warmer climes.

We are all wondering here when or if the invasion is going to start. There is an enormous concentration of small craft in all the Channel ports, but they are being so heavily bombed each night that I think the Germans will either have to start the invasion before they lose their craft, or take them away again. I do not think they can leave the craft there to be bombed indefinitely. They have bombed us out of Dover so I do not see why we should not bomb them out of the Channel ports.

Spain seems very unsettled at the present time, and from all accounts Franco has lost his grip of things and is being run by that horrible brother-in-law of his who is no doubt thoroughly in the pocket of the Germans.

Sam Hoare seems to think that if we can get through the next month or five weeks Spain will come our way.

I do not feel altogether happy about what we are doing in Africa during the next few days as it may well give the Hun the excuse to endeavour to get down to Morocco. However, the situation will clarify in the next day or so. I certainly do not want the Fleet to be driven out of Gibraltar.

With all good luck,
Yours ever,
Dudley Pound.[70]

Having got this off to the Admiral at Gibraltar, and in the text given him a hint to stand by for French air reprisals once Dakar got going, Pound had to devote his attention to more important matters, not least of which was the launching of Menace itself. The operation commenced on the 23rd and things went wrong there from the word go. For a start the Free French were not greeted with open arms but with shells. The show of force put on by Force M flopped miserably due to the prevailing offshore mist and haze which made the battleships' shooting poor. After a series of farcical exchanges during the next two days the whole shambles was broken off. The British had the battleship *Resolution* badly damaged by a Vichy submarine torpedo which kept her out of the war for a year, the battleship *Barham*, cruisers *Australia* and *Delhi* and destroyers *Foresight* and *Inglefield* were slightly damaged by shells and splinters but were soon fully operational again. The French Navy had two submarines sunk, *Ajax* and *Persée*, while one unit of Force Y, the super-destroyer *L'Audacieux*, was severely damaged and beached after an exchange with the *Australia* at close range. It would have been better for her had she stayed in Toulon, for her repairs took a year to complete and then she was again badly bombed by the Americans in 1942. The battleship *Richelieu* and three merchant ships were slightly damaged and the Allies withdrew in humiliation, the laughing stock of the world.

However as a spin-off from this operational failure opportunity was taken to force the issue in Equatorial Africa, and this *was* successful; de Gaulle raised the Cross of Lorraine over a large and useful chunk of Africa giving his cause some credibility and an independent power-base. In this sense the mission of Force Y most certainly failed. Despite threats the Axis did not move into Morocco as a result. The resistance of Vichy at Dakar convinced Germany and Italy that she could be left to defend her own territory and they anyway had other fish to fry closer at home and could not spare their forces. They did, however, refuse to sanction any further movements of the Vichy fleet from Toulon, and when Darlan sought permission to send out the battle-cruiser *Strasbourg*, two 8-inch and one 6-inch cruisers and two divisions of super-destroyers it was turned down flat by General Stülpnagel on 22nd September. So North and Somerville did not have to face the threat of another forcing of the Straits, although Somerville in *Renown* was sent off for a further patrol off Casablanca between 16th and 20th September.

With the abandonment of Menace and the pressure off, the Admiralty found time to commence the preliminary movements in the case of Admiral North and, on September 27th, the following signal was despatched from the Admiralty to FOCNAS:

IMMEDIATE
At what time was NA Madrid's 1809 September 10 received and what action if any was taken on it.[71]

Sir Dudley North's long ordeal was beginning. After hearing his account of events, on 15th October the Admiralty informed him that they could not, '... retain full confidence in an officer who fails in an emergency to take all prudent precautions without waiting for Admiralty instructions. They have accordingly decided that you should be relieved of your present command at the first convenient opportunity.'[72]

Admiral North indignantly tried to get an impartial survey of his case made with several lengthy letters and even, later, an interview with Pound. To no avail. On 31st December 1940 he hauled down his flag and sailed for home.

CHAPTER FOURTEEN

Squaring the Circle

Although North stayed his hand during the war he tried repeatedly to get a hearing but without success until 1954. He gained renewed hope when Britain's most distinguished sailor at that time, Admiral of the Fleet Lord Chatfield, took up his case. He too thought that the Lords might prove a good platform for North but, after consulting with Andrew Cunningham, who had already done much behind the scenes with little success, decided against this line of action. Instead a new and unprecedented plan was formulated. Cunningham had already sounded out the views of Admiral Sir Bruce Fraser, the only surviving Member of the Board from 1940, and both had agreed that the 'Scapegoat' theory would not stand up, although Cunningham pointed out that: 'You know probably better than I that DP was at times rather hasty in finding scapegoats – maybe prodded thereto by Winston.'[1]

Fraser replied that: 'The thing that really upset the First Sea Lord was that North waited for instructions without putting himself in a position in which he could carry out his instructions.' He added that Pound had said to him: ' "How can I continue to place reliance on a flag officer who does not act because he is waiting for instructions?" '[2]

Should Admiral North's case have come to the Lords it was feared that Fraser and Alexander, among others, would speak out strongly against him, and that such public debate on an old-issue would do the reputation of the Royal Navy great harm. Instead it was proposed that a deputation should go to the Admiralty to present their views. But this was no ordinary deputation, for it consisted of no less than five of the most distinguished officers in the service, and the most high-ranking assembly that could be brought to bear, all of them Admirals of the Fleet, and three of them former First Sea Lords themselves. Headed by Chatfield, they were Lord Cork and Orrery (who had led the Somerville Court of Inquiry at Gibraltar in 1940), Lord Cunningham of Hyndhope (C-in-C Mediterranean in 1940),

Sir John Cunningham (Commander of Force M during the Dakar operations) and Sir Algernon Willis (a former C-in-C Mediterranean).

They sought an interview with the First Lord of the Admiralty, J.P.L. Thomas, and addressed to him a memorandum stating their aims, a copy of which they also sent to North:

Sir,

I We, the undersigned, wish respectfully to lay before you the following Memorandum on a subject which we consider to be of the greatest importance to the Service. You will be well aware of the case of Admiral Sir Dudley North, who in December 1940 was dismissed from his command as ACNA by the then Board of Admiralty. Admiral North has continually, we understand, endeavoured to have his very severe sentence without trial re-investigated by a Court Martial, or other Service inquiry. Having so far failed, he is driven to take other means to justify himself. Through his lawyers he has approached Earl Jowitt ... Lord Jowitt having studied the papers, informed him 'he greatly sympathizes with him and would certainly speak on his behalf in the House of Lords on a Motion; but that he considered it should be moved by a Naval Peer'.

II Admiral North has in consequence asked such of us as are Peers, to move a Motion in Parliament on his case. For reasons of loyalty to the Admiralty, we are loath to do this. There is, we have no doubt, an Admiralty side of the case, and a controversy in the House, perhaps between Naval Peers on a matter of past Admiralty action in wartime, might arouse very undesirable public reaction.

III We have therefore decided that our right and proper course is to ask you for an interview at a early date. The object of our deputation would not be to plead Admiral North's case, but respectfully to ask you to set up a confidential inquiry to examine the case; to hear evidence and to report to the Board in the light of all the information available today. Our suggestion will be that such an inquiry should be composed of a few senior Naval Officers with unprejudiced minds, and that for the reasons given by us it should not be delayed. We consider that Admiral North should be heard, with others, by such an inquiry, and be informed of the result. If his character is wholly, or partly, cleared, it should, we shall suggest to you, be publicly announced in a suitable manner.

IV To support our request, we would like to point out certain important considerations:

(i) That there has long been and still exists, a considerable opinion in the Service that Admiral North was unjustly punished; or, if he deserved censure, that his punishment was harsh and excessive. This view indeed has been publicly expressed in writing by Senior Naval Officers and remains unanswered, which we feel is very harmful to the Service.

(ii) The refusal despite his many applications, official and private, to grant him a Court Martial in accordance with Service custom, or another form of inquiry, is not understood in the Service. If it is said the Admiralty have an unanswerable case, an inquiry would endorse it. From this arises, we believe, a suspicion that the Admiralty case is not unanswerable. This also is harmful to the Service.

(iii) From the papers we have carefully studied, it appears that Admiral North, as ACNA, was given in July 1940 some indefinite instructions, which were bound to place him in a difficult position should the eventuality for which the instructions were meant to provide come to pass; he was also definitely told that French ships were not to be interfered with unless proceeding to enemy ports, and that they were in inferior strength.

(iv) Although the political situation changed in the next two months Admiral North's instructions remained unchanged. He was not officially informed of the changes in the Anglo-French political atmosphere; nor was he informed of the Dakar plans, though he probably had some knowledge of them from unofficial sources. As a result, he and his command had a different political mentality from the Admiralty when the crisis arose.

(v) There was some serious negligence in Whitehall which affected the developments on September 10th and 11th. This fact was not publicly made known until many years later when it was stated by Mr Churchill in his book, Volume II.

V On the other side of the case it may be held:

(i) That if Admiral North had sent the *Renown* to sea very early on September 11th in order to watch that the French ships did not turn north to Biscay Ports, she would, although not a superior force, have been in a position to act on any Admiralty orders issued.

(ii) That on receipt of the Naval Attaché Madrid's message at 0008 on September 11th, he might have pressed the Admiralty to break their silence about the French ships, and thus cause the Admiralty to act.

These two possible courses for him, if sustained by evidence, might have amounted either to 'an error of judgement' or to 'neglect of duty'.

VI But it seems clear that both the Admirals concerned, North and Somerville, had individually most carefully considered their duty and had made an agreed and convinced decision that in taking no action they were acting in accordance with Admiralty instructions and intentions. If therefore Admiral North did err in either of the above respects (V (i) and (ii)) it may be maintained, we feel, that the fault was 'error of judgement, a misinterpretation of Admiralty Orders' but was *not* 'negligence of duty'.

VII The sentence summarily carried out was the most severe that could be given in war to a Flag Officer of distinction and high standing.

VIII Those, First Lord, are the facts as many see them today and as they have been publicly stated, and which in the interests of the Service we feel it right to bring to your notice. We therefore most respectfully suggest that it is highly desirable that they should be inquired into by the present Board of Admiralty.

IX Should you, after hearing us at the interview, accept our recommendation of an inquiry, constituted as we have submitted, then we consider that those recommendations should be final. Should the inquiry disclose that Admiral North had been unjustly dealt with, or more severely so than the facts merited, such public statement as you might decide should be made to clear his character. Meanwhile, we have requested Admiral Sir Dudley North to stay his hand.[3]

This was followed by a debate in the Lords on June 15th and then meetings between Macmillan and the Admirals. The second meeting at No 10 was attended by the First Lord, Selkirk, the First Sea Lord, Mountbatten and Admirals of the Fleet Cork and Orrery, Cunningham of Hyndhope, John Cunningham and Willis. Chatfield was sick and could not attend in person, but he did send a remarkably sensible letter in which he set out his views on the North affair. The Premier, Macmillan, first read out this document, which was so complete that they agreed that it form the basis for their discussion.

Chatfield's main arguments were as follows:

1 That the Admiralty could have relieved Admiral North from his position as FOCNA *at any time they had wished to do so*, quite apart from the Force Y incident. That was their undisputed right.
2 But in exercising that right the Admiralty should not make a *charge* of a specific and serious nature against that Admiral. By doing so they laid themselves open, for *any* British sailor (admiral or rating) had the historic right to defend himself against such a charge.
3 Chatfield alleged that the Admiralty's share of the blame for the whole mess was 75 per cent. Knowing this, as the First Sea Lord did, he should have made doubly or trebly careful to ensure that no injustice was done to North. Not only that but the Admiralty should have shouldered their fair share of the blame and not tried to put it all off onto North.
4 As the Secretary of the day saw it in 1940, they were too rash in the form of North's relief. It would have been wiser merely to have told him that he was to be relieved by another admiral at a certain date and moved him on to a position of lesser importance without making any charge as such.

5 He concluded that North's case for vindication rested not so much on the removal of himself from his command in 1940 but the wording of the charge and the charge itself which he resented, and, in Chatfield's view, had every right to resent.

The Premier then expounded the difficulties as he saw them to rectify these faults in 1957. The leading participants on the Admiralty side were dead, as was Somerville on North's; they would have to rely on the uncertain memories of an event of minor proportions which took place in the midst of a busy war, seventeen years before. More important today was the fact that this debate would only weaken the morale of the Royal Navy of 1957, already severely shaken by its sharply declining role in modern warfare and cut back to the bone from its former position.

It was absolutely essential in a fighting service that the men at the sharp end should have faith and confidence in the decisions of its leaders and this confidence would not be improved by a further airing of the events of 1940. Moreover, as they all agreed, a fresh inquiry would produce no facts that had not already been debated at length many times before in print and in the House.

Macmillan had therefore prepared a draft of a statement he was proposing to make in the House on the 23rd, which, he felt, would settle the matter quickly and finally to the satisfaction of both parties. Briefly he proposed to state that North could not be accused of any specific misconduct, but that the Board of Admiralty at that time were completely justified in their decision to remove him from his post.

When asked for their opinions on his proposed statement three of the four Admirals of the Fleet were in accord that it would suffice in removing North's sense of grievance, but Cork and Orrery were not so disposed. He regarded the statement as not going far enough to chastise the Admiralty for their part in the matter. He wanted a firm statement in the House blaming them for their 'disgraceful' behaviour. Macmillan could not agree to this.

After some discussion they reached a compromise solution. Macmillan would add a line indicating that the Admiralty's intentions were not made as clear as they might have been, thereby implying that Admiral North had reasonable room for misinterpretation. The Admirals of the Fleet in return gave the Premier authorisation to state publicly that they agreed with his statement, and they undertook to assure Admiral North that this statement completely vindicated his public honour, as he had all along wished to have done.

On the question of Churchill's involvement, Macmillan was surprised to find opinion that this was considerable so strong in the service. He solved this difficulty by skimming over it with a clever use of words without even mentioning the wartime leader at all. As he wrote to Alexander, the day before he made his speech:

> This is a difficult matter in which there is a lot of feeling and I hope that, when you have read my statement, you will think that I have dealt with it with justice to all concerned and with due regard to the morale of the Royal Navy.[4]

Considering the extremely complex problems and the mountain of material which he, as a layman in Naval matters, had to digest quickly, the Premier's speech was indeed a masterpiece of political wire-walking:

> After careful study of all the papers, questions and debates concerning this affair, I am bound to say that there does not seem to be any difference about the facts of the case. The orders that were given, and the signals that passed backwards and forwards, are on record. It has been suggested that there should be a new inquiry into the facts. But the facts are not really in dispute. The question at issue is the interpretation that should be put on these facts, and the wisdom and justice of the decisions reached by the authorities at the time. I must recall to the House that the period was one of perhaps the most acute danger that has ever beset this country. The Battle of Britain was at its height; the French fighting power had collapsed, and grave uncertainty existed as to whether the powerful French fleet might pass into enemy hands, which, had it happened, would have turned the whole balance of naval power against us.
>
> It is only fair to recall the memories of those anxious days to put ourselves in the position of those who had to make the great decisions. In the circumstances of that period the authorities concerned formed the view that they needed a different naval commander at Gibraltar. I must insist upon the constitutional rights of the Admiralty, and indeed of all those in positions of supreme responsibility, to choose officers in whom they have confidence at moments of supreme crisis. Any other system would be dangerous in peace and fatal in war.
>
> A careful examination of the records has led me to the conclusion that, so far as concerned the passing of the French ships through the Straits of Gibraltar, Admiral North cannot be accused of any dereliction of duty. He obeyed his orders as he interpreted them and some blame must rest on the fact that they were not drawn with complete clarity. Nevertheless,

in those dangerous days the Admiralty felt that they required at Gibraltar an officer who would not content himself with strict adherence to his orders but who would be likely to show a greater degree of resource and initiative in an emergency.

I am convinced that, while we all have a deep understanding for Admiral Sir Dudley North in what must have been a great disappointment to him at the height of his career, it is essential in the Services to maintain the principle that the authorities of the day should have unrestricted discretion in deciding to whom they will entrust high command. I very much deprecate the use of the word 'dismiss' or 'remove' or, still worse, 'sack'. These are phrases which are quite inappropriate to these difficult decisions in conditions of war. Many officers of high rank in all three services were superseded in those harsh days by others who were regarded as more likely to be able to cope with the problems and burdens which confronted them.

In my view a general distinction must be drawn between two things. On the one hand are definite charges of negligence and the like, reflecting on an officer's honour. Any charge of this kind against Admiral Sir Dudley North could not, in my view, be sustained, and I believe that this is generally recognized. On the other hand, the Board of Admiralty have the right, and the duty, to decide on broad grounds whether an officer possessed the qualities necessary for a particular command. These qualities are not easy to define. One of them is the confidence reposed in an officer by his superior. The degree to which an officer possesses these qualities can never be a subject of an inquiry. It can only be a matter for the judgement of his superiors. And I must add that the country owes a great debt to the whole Board of Admiralty, political and professional, and it was constituted in that dark period which led to ultimate victory.

I am satisfied that Admiral North was not the victim of Service or political prejudice. He has nothing with which to reproach himself. He had forty-four years of long, distinguished, and devoted service in the Royal Navy and there is no question of his professional integrity being impugned.

In these circumstances I do not see that anything is to be gained by an inquiry about facts that are well documented and undisputed.[5]

This statement by the Prime Minister was received with mixed feelings. In the Royal Navy as a whole the feeling was one of justice done at last and, as the Admirals of the Fleet wrote to North later, assured him that 'his professional honour was now completely vindicated'. Lord Chatfield, although he still held his reservations about how much the Admiralty was at fault, was generous in his accolades. In a letter to *The Times* he wrote:

All will hope that the last word has now been said about the case of

Admiral Sir Dudley North; but I feel the Royal Navy would wish its gratitude to be expressed to the Prime Minister for the remarkable action he took in solving it.[6]

The press too, in the main, was pleased, although with reservations towards the Churchill connection:

> Qualifications introduced by Mr Macmillan into his balanced judgement were, no doubt, inevitable. Face has to be saved wherever Very Important Persons are concerned and this consideration also explains why an inquiry was deemed imprudent. But, as the Admirals who are best qualified to pilot a course through the tricky waters of Service opinion have expressed themselves as well satisfied, it is reasonable to agree the matter has now been taken as far as it can be.[7]'

The Earl of Cork and Orrery, while also harbouring doubts, wrote to North that: 'I hope the PM's statement gave you satisfaction as I think it will to all your numerous friends and colleagues ...'[8]

Cunningham of Hyndhope wrote in similar tone: 'I thought his statement excellent, very fair, well balanced and I hope you were very happy with what he said.'[9] He also wrote to Captain Roskill that: 'There is no question but that the clearing of Dudley North's reputation has also put you all right as a historian', although he added the rider that, '... mind you I still hold that DN wasn't all that right ...'[10]

Others, then and later, were not so sure that Macmillan had finished the affair satisfactorily. Predictably the *Daily Mirror* was loudest in its criticism: 'The *Mirror* is NOT satisfied', it raged, 'There is nothing here to cheer about.'[11]

More sober voices also held a note of dissatisfaction; the *Daily Mail* asked the question: 'If North lacked the necessary attributes, why was he ever appointed to Gibraltar?'[12], which ignored the change in the circumstances of the base between 1939 and the summer of 1940 completely.

Churchill's comments are not on records yet released to the public but predictably Alexander was not too happy either, though of course for totally different reasons. Macmillan had foreseen this and had written to him with further explanations for his motives.

> I felt convinced from the first that, for the reasons which you put so well in the House of Lords this afternoon, an inquiry would not only be unprofitable but would be undesirable. I wanted to do nothing which

would impair the morale of the Royal Navy which could and, I think, would, not fail to be weakened by further propositions and speculations and recriminations in this affair.[13]

Alexander replied in uncompromising mood:

I am glad you remained firm against the demand for an inquiry, but I do not, however, agree, as the statement goes on to say, that he had 'nothing with which to reproach himself'. If that had been so he would not have been superseded ...

He went on:

His principal fault was in connection with Oran; he would probably have been recalled then but for the pleas by Sir Dudley Pound that he should be given a further chance ...

In regard to the escape of the French cruisers, there were faults elsewhere, particularly in the FO, but it was our view that on his instructions he should have made arrangements to have the French ships followed to ascertain their probable destination and if he had done so, they could have been dealt with on further instructions from the Admiralty. Sir Dudley Pound therefore had no hesitation in making his recommendation for recall which was fully concurred in by myself as First Lord and by Sir Winston Churchill as Minister of Defence.

He concluded:

However, I do not wish to prolong the controversy in view of what you say, but I must reserve the right to put my point of view in any reminiscences, *if I should decide to produce any!!*[14]

This followed the tone of his remarks in the House of Lords, which Macmillan mentioned in his letter, on 23rd May in response to Lord Selkirk's similar statement to the Premier's. He thought the decision taken at the time in regard to Admiral North was completely justified, and thought Macmillan and Selkirk's statements were weaker than those presented in 1954, but, he added: 'I gather that it is felt that some little concession had to be made to Admiral North to set his mind at rest on things, and therefore these words have been included in the statement ...'[15]

But what of Admiral Sir Dudley North himself? How did he feel about these 'little concessions' and the statement as a whole? With a deluge of congratulations pouring in on him from old shipmates, friends and well-wishers and the bulk of the press stating he had been cleared, he should have felt on top of the world surely?

Initially this was so, though not for long. Within a few days he was publicly stating to the media that it had not gone far enough, that he was disappointed, that an inquiry was still necessary and that the wrongs done him had still not been put right. He admitted that the Prime Minister had vindicated him as far as he could, but he remained bitter and unhappy about the outcome. But he seemed to realise that he had had a good innings and that there was little more he could do at his age, or expect to be done in his lifetime.

> I am a very tired man. There is nothing that I can do. There is some satisfaction in hearing that I was not guilty of any dereliction of duty. But the fact remains that someone in the Admiralty said, 'North must go. North must go.' That person was not prepared to give a reason. He left it to the Prime Minister many years later to try to explain it.[16]

Whether this was a final jab at Alexander or Churchill is not clear, but the message was plain enough; for Admiral North justice had *still* not been done. As he later wrote to his old friend Mountbatten, he was undecided just what to do next. In truth there was little that could be done. Admiral North's case had been discussed continually in the press, in the Admiralty, in the service clubs, in the wardrooms of the Navy and in both Houses of Parliament. The whole business of running the country had been set aside in the Mother of Parliaments to try and mete out justice to just one man. It was a great thing for this country that such a thing was possible, but, like Admiral North enquiring for elucidation from the Admiralty in 1940, as Lord Elibank said, it 'could not go on and on'. Although there *was* a second debate in the Lords on July 26th.

Admiral Sir Dudley North lived out the remaining four years of life, as he had the seventeen since 1940, convinced he had been ill-used and made a scapegoat, and at a loss to understand how such a thing could happen to him in the Service to which he had devoted his life and served to the best of his ability. When he died the Royal Navy took him back once more and, off Portland Bill, he was buried at sea from the frigate *Teazer* with full honours. It was, perhaps, a gesture that he would have appreciated even more than his long-cherished inquiry. It showed that the Service still honoured him if the politicians had not.

If Admiral North died still feeling a sense of wrong, how did the verdict of history treat him? He once expressed the opinion that he would have to be content with the epitaph, 'What a damned shame!'

In general, this was so. Certainly the historians who have tackled his story so far, have been, in general, no more satisfied with the final outcome than he was. Long after North, Churchill, Alexander and Pound had passed on, the legend of the 'Scapegoat Admiral' has lingered on. If anything, it has gained in strength rather than died its natural death. 'But, then,' as Professor Marder has written, 'legends never do!'[17]

On the more *material* aspects of the case I have endeavoured to obtain satisfactory answers to the various questions which arose on the actual operational side at that time, as follows.

It is often stated that even had Admiral North appreciated the Admiralty's wishes correctly in this instance, Admiral Somerville, and the ships at his disposal, would have been unable to stop the French squadron and parleyed with them as Churchill had wished, firstly because they would have fought rather than complied with our wishes, and, secondly, that because of this the *Renown* and her old destroyers would not have been able to enforce their will on the powerful French ships. Again nobody can be certain at the possible outcome of a naval battle, for there are too many imponderables, but we can at least set forth some facts and figures on which to make a reasonable assumption before taking this for granted.

What chance would Force H have had should it have come to a fight?
References to the ships at Somerville's disposal are usually sprinkled with the terms 'old' destroyers, or the 'ancient' *Renown*, implying that they were a set of crocks. Old certainly many of them were, including *Renown* herself who first joined the fleet in 1916 in the aftermath of the Battle of Jutland. But were they so helpless as made out?

In the first place *Renown* herself had been completely rebuilt above the waterline in the years prior to the war and only emerged from this modernisation on the day before war broke out. Her engines, guns and fittings therefore, were as modern, indeed more modern, than any of the French ships she might have to engage in combat. Added to this is the fact that the *Renown* was fully combat-worthy and blooded in action and was manned by a crew with a year's war experience in the front line who considered themselves, with some justification, as an élite team. In the Norwegian campaign, only a few months before, the *Renown* had taken on the two most powerful warships in the German Navy, the battle-cruisers *Scharnhorst* and *Gneisenau*, and driven them off in flight. Too much should not be read into this because the encounter took place in atrocious weather conditions and her accompanying destroyers were mistaken for larger units by the Germans in the murk. Moreover their instructions were always to *avoid* combat with British battleships. Nonetheless *Renown* had given more than she got and the effect on the morale of her crew was considerable. In the tranquil weather conditions of the Straits of Gibraltar also, her superior fire-control equipment and modern weaponry would have played a great part, while her main armament of six 15-inch guns, each firing a projectile of a ton, would have far outweighted the broadsides of the French cruisers. On the other hand three cruisers against the German pocket battleship *Graf Spee* had made a mess of her, though what would have been the outcome had she have stood and fought them instead of running is a different matter. One of *Renown*'s gunnery officers sums up the pros and cons.

> From a technical viewpoint, *Renown*'s 15-inch armament was highly efficient and the re-loading time for each gun was about 45 seconds (sometimes less). Guns were normally fired in salvos (one in each turret at a time) when ranging which would give a rate of fire of about 20 seconds.
>
> However, *Renown*'s 15-inch fire control, though modern in itself, had only one main control mechanism so that the turrets could not be split onto more than one target at a time. There was a very antiquated secondary control for Y turret (I know because I was in charge of it!), which would only be used if all else failed. This limitation might have been a serious defect in engaging a number of targets.
>
> A good point for *Renown* was her secondary 4.5-inch armament which was extremely modern and very efficient in both AA and surface action roles. The five twin mountings on each side had two complete control systems each side and it was a matter of seconds to switch the three forward mountings, or two after mountings, either to the fore or the after control, ie you could engage two surface targets on each side if you wished. These guns had a range of 18,000 yards and a rate of fire of about 8 rounds per minute. I think they might have played a big part in any surface action – each side was equivalent gun-power to two destroyers, but better because the guns were very modern (power-loaded).[18]

What of the *Renown*'s engines? After all the great point made about the French ships' attributes was their speed. Nobody can speak with more authority on this than Captain A.W. Gray, who was not only commander in charge of the engineering department of *Renown* but also the technical officer on the staff of Force H. He had stood by *Renown* for two years during her reconstruction and knew her engines and their capabilities inside out.

> We steamed during September and October 1940 10,660 miles and spent thirty days at sea. I think this steaming record speaks sufficiently for the efficiency of *Renown*'s boilers and main engines.[19]

At the Battle of Spartivento, two months later, *Renown* in fact, worked up to a recorded speed of 27½ knots, but, in September Captain Gray estimates she was good for 28 at least.

What then of the destroyers at Somerville's disposal? It can be said that half were indeed old, but the other three were modern ships, completed between 1934 and 1937 and more modern than the French super-destroyers. *Velox*, *Vidette* and *Wishart* of course, *were* ancient, and had not been modernised in any way between the wars at that time. In a straight fight they would have stood very little chance with regard to gun ranges, speed or torpedo equipment, but at this period they still retained their full outfits of the latter weapon, which were not removed until some time later when they converted to escort destroyers. In this respect they carried a heavier punch than their modern sisters, *Encounter*, *Griffin* and *Hotspur*, who had had their own after-bank of torpedo tubes landed ashore and replaced by a single 3-inch HA gun for limited defence against air attacks. In all the British destroyers the small guns, 4-inch and 4.7-inch, were in open, hand-loaded mountings, and were far outranged by the French, but they probably had a far higher rate of fire. The three modern British ships also had *Renown*'s other quality, experience. *Hotspur* indeed had just survived the First Battle of Narvik against odds far greater than expected off Gibraltar and in far more confining waters. There was no lack of aggression among the destroyer skippers moreover, as Somerville was well aware, and in later encounters with German destroyers as large as the French super-destroyers, the smaller British vessels more than held their own.

In the event of intervention by the French bombers the British were, as North later pointed out, quite exposed, with absolutely no fighter defences at all. The *Renown*'s secondary batteries were well equipped to deal with high-level and torpedo bombing and the French had no dive-bombers, but the British destroyers were almost defenceless. The value of the 3-inch AA gun varied from skipper to skipper, but the majority opinion was that it was good for its morale value only.

As to range and endurance, again the British destroyers were low on both, but no more so than the French destroyers, as we have seen. As for their speeds, the accredited figures of 35-36 knots were not always attained after hard service in all weathers, as the engineering officer of the *Hotspur* points out:

> Your figure of around 35 knots is a bit high ... Some 30 knots should have been comfortable for the G and H destroyers but might have been a bit much for the V & Ws.[20]

What of the French ships then? While it cannot be disputed that they were fine modern ships their capabilities have been much played up and their defects never mentioned in the many accounts of the events of 11th September. Let us start with the light cruisers *Georges Leygues*, *Gloire* and *Montcalm*. For light cruisers they were and nothing more! They were *not* 'heavy' cruisers as has been stated,[21] not 'ten-thousand ton vessels' as Robert Mengin writes,[22] and by no stretch of the imagination were they 'battle-cruisers' as Cosgrave insists,[23] but purely and simply light cruisers of some 7,760 tons standard displacement and mounting nine 6-inch guns. Even by light cruiser ratings they were not exceptional, the latest such vessels in the Royal Navy displacing 10,000 tons and carrying twelve 6-inch guns, while those of the American and Japanese navies carried fifteen of these weapons.

Their best speed of 32 knots, was not far in excess of the *Renown*'s and this would have only been achieved at the grave risk of mechanical breakdown after a period of idleness at Toulon, as was shown up subsequently with the fate of the *Gloire*. Their main armament was far outranged by *Renown* of course and, had they have closed her, her armour protection, questionable against an enemy battleship certainly, should have more than sufficed to keep out their puny shells. For their own defence in this respect the French ships were mere tin-cans, their *maximum* armour was 105 mm (4.137 inches) sides and 40 mm (1.576 inches) on the bridge. The *Renown*'s projectiles would have gone through these like a knife through butter. On the morale side we have already quoted D'Harcourt's opinion that this was good. However they had not seen a great deal of real action, although they had been involved in the shooting war for a short period off Norway before they tied up in Toulon harbour.

But there is no doubt at all about their ability and willingness to fight, *should they have been left with no choice*, with the memories of Mersel-Kebir to spur them on and against the very same admiral who had fired on their comrades.

With regard to the super-destroyers, we have discussed their classification earlier. Their gun armament was powerful in size, but not so handy as the British ships' smaller weapons. Their AA guns were far superior to the British of course, but in this case it would not have been a relevant factor. Their speed was most impressive, but could only be obtained in short bursts; still it would have played a significant part in any action in the Straits, and might have been important, although, had they survived such an encounter, they would have had to put into the nearest port to refuel and could not have reached Casablanca. But it is the French ships' torpedo armaments that would have been the decisive factor here. Both cruisers and destroyers mounted powerful batteries of these, against which *Renown* had little defence, again, as Admiral Walwyn confirms:

> If a fight had developed, the French objective would have been to break through to the Atlantic undamaged (they had no repair facilities available). I presume the British aim would have been to stop them – by force if necessary. In a daylight action, which would have to have been fought at fairly close range, the French 6-inch guns would have damaged *Renown* – possibly enough to upset her fire control – but would not have sunk her. The real danger to *Renown* would have been from torpedoes – she was much the same as *Repulse* below the water-line and the latter didn't last long under Japanese air torpedo attack. I say this unashamedly as a Gunnery man – the gun was the crippling agent but seldom sank the enemy except where an explosion did the job eg *Hood*, and the British battle-cruisers at Jutland, *the torpedo was the sinker*.[24]

All in all then it would appear that such an engagement would have had but wasteful results for the British, even had the ships' guns been supported by the powerful guns of the Rock itself, which, it must be remembered, covered the whole width of the Straits. As Admiral Walwyn concludes: 'On the whole I guess that a battle would have been a 'close run thing' but *Renown* would have been badly damaged and possibly sunk by torpedo attack.'[25]

Were there any set plans at that time to block the Straits?
The duty of Force H and FOCNAS were both defined as preventing the Italian Navy from penetrating the Straits. We have seen this was

almost impossible to achieve with regard to enemy submarines once they found they could navigate the Straits submerged. Further waves of Italian submarines followed in October 1940, of which only one or two were actually caught and sunk by the Straits destroyers. The differing density levels of water in the Mediterranean, the change of water temperature and the fast currents in the Straits, all helped render the standard anti-submarine detection device, ASDIC, relatively impotent in this part of the ocean, although there were a few successes. It is stressed that this was in no way the fault of the men on the spot, including North when he was in command, or the destroyer skippers. Later on in the war German submarines penetrated the Straits in equally as large numbers despite the fact that there were far more anti-submarine vessels on hand at Gibraltar than North had in the autumn of 1940. But what of surface ship penetrations? When Force H was in harbour at full strength any such attempt would have been suicidal and the Germans and Italians never attempted it. The French, as we have seen, thought it equally so, hence the need to achieve a *peaceful* passage and tipping off the British they were coming. Had they been challenged in the Straits it is extremely doubtful that they would have wished to fight, though they may have felt they had no option.

When Force H was absent, the defence of the Straits was largely a matter of bluff. The Fortress guns covered the Straits it is true, but fast warships would not give them very much time to engage them at, say, 30 knots. There seems to be no knowledge of any real plan at this stage of the war to utilise North's few ships in such an attempt, although improvisation would be the answer in a real emergency.

Admiral Currey says that the average destroyer skipper was not privy to such plans even if they did exist:

> No doubt there were plans. That's what Staff officers are for. But certainly nobody would have dreamt of discussing them with destroyer COs. 'Ours not to reason why!', though we often wondered![26]

Captain Layman is quite certain that there were *no* such plans: 'No set plan had been promulgated to deal with any hostile force of surface ships breaking into or out of the Mediterranean.'[27]

Captain De Winton recalls that:

> The plan you mention to dispute the passage of an enemy force was discussed between the naval and army staff, but I am sure that no draft

of such plan was settled in my time (up to December 1940). There was certainly no battle plan to block the Straits and I doubt if such was feasible; the gunfire from the Rock must have been considered but I don't think anyone took it at all seriously. So you can say that, in 1940, there was no battle plan to bar the Straits to heavy ships, but the Navy would have had to improvise with what material they had at the time.

Soon after Italy entered the war in June, 1940, Admiralty Intelligence 'lost' the German battle-cruisers *Scharnhorst* and *Gneisenau*. I was ordered to take all available ships of my flotilla to the westward of the Straits to prevent them entering the Med, there being some idea that they would be headed our way to join the Italians. I seemed to have a fairly free hand, and as there was no heavy ship to back us up, I must obviously spread my ships to lookout, but to be able to concentrate quickly if any contact was made. I could only hope to achieve something by a concentrated torpedo attack.[28]

Was there no need for 'Renown' to sail at all to intercept the French?
This seems an odd question to ask but it will be recalled that this was one of the theories put forward in North's defence, that *Renown* did not have to sail from Gibraltar for she could cover the Straits from where she was! In a strictly limited sense this was true, although it was hardly satisfactory and reduced her to merely another fort. The only advantage was that she was safe herself from damage, which was hardly the point. Nor would a later change of berth make her any more ready for sea, as Lieutenant Commander Stuart explains:

There would have been no great advantage in shifting berth for a quicker departure. Bows south at the South Mole was obviously best, as, for a start 'A' and 'B' turrets covered the Straits. There were other points, such as telephone lines, access for road transport such as staff cars. With the ship secured for sea, leaving the berth only meant singling up the berthing wires, getting the gangway out, and away. Also, to have shifted berth would have, to all intents and purposes, put the ship out of action from starting to move until finally secured at a new berth.[29]

Admiral Walwyn is equally adamant on these points:

I think you have got to get the perspective right here. As far as I recall, there was plenty of time for *Renown* to put to sea and get in the path of the French squadron before they arrived – had she been ordered to do so. *Renown*'s berth was always on the South Mole – bows outward. She had steam for full speed and had she been ordered to engage I feel sure that she would have put to sea to do so. I doubt whether any Captain would wish to fight his ship secured to the dockyard Mole! *Renown*'s 15-inch armament could certainly cover the Straits; all targets could be fired on from that berth except when in the process of unberthing and she could have had the French within range for about fifteen minutes; chance of success would have been good – *but* it would have been asking for trouble to do such a thing.[30]

And De Winton adds:

> I think Somerville has been largely misquoted when the impression is given that he took a gloomy view of his chances with a rather limited destroyer screen. The situation of a possible confrontation in the Straits of Gibraltar had been much considered by Admirals North and Somerville and it was rightly felt that any such scramble in such a confined space was neither seamanlike or desirable. Knowing Admiral Somerville quite well I am quite sure he would never have refused an engagement; we always agreed that someone might get hurt and if a fight was needed better it took place well out to sea.[28]

An engagement in the enclosed waters of the Straits of Gibraltar would indeed have been a scramble. The only small point in favour of the British ships is that their destroyers would probably have been able to take better advantage of it than their larger, but more clumsy, French counterparts. A pre-war British study of these big French destroyers had made some scathing criticisms of them as flotilla craft. Admiral Sir Dudley Pound had been C-in-C Mediterranean Fleet at that time and his report read, in part, that he was not convinced that the 'Super-Destroyer' as a type was particularly of merit and he stated that the French liaison officer with his fleet had told him that they were ceasing construction of these vessels after the 'Mogadors', as they had been found too unwieldy to handle in flotilla attacks.[31]

One of the many 'strange silences' of this affair is that no historian has ever mentioned that North had two fully operational submarines at his disposal at Gibraltar. Would they have been any use, either in a possible confrontation or in extending the patrol line north to stop any movement toward Brest? It seems not; they were so slow that they would have needed far more time to dispose themselves to the north-west in time to be an effective deterrent, although there were two others on the way towards Gibraltar from the UK which could, no doubt, have been alerted to intercept Force Y, *had* it have gone north. Nor would they have been of much help in the Straits it seems, though their presence might have helped a little. Commander Walmsley's opinion is: 'I don't think the two submarines were of much use until the French squadron had been located in some port, when they could have been used to patrol unseen off the port and report any movements to sea.[32]

At all events no move was made to utilise the two submarines at all and they continued to lay alongside during the whole passage of Force Y through the Straits. No use seems to have been contemplated for them at all prior to the French reaching Casablanca, as one of the submarine skippers confirms:

> Had I known that *Triad* and *Truant* were being thought of as submarines to keep an eye on the French I would have remembered it. *Triad* and *Truant* were supposed to be urgently required in the Eastern Mediterranean to reinforce the disastrous loss of eight large submarines, all manned by officers and men with years of peacetime training. I would have remembered things concerning Admiral Dudley North because I knew him having served under him when he was captain of *Revenge* in 1926.[33]

This, as we have seen, Somerville and North considered doing later off Casablanca, although this was not proceeded with in the event.

Was Force Y a superior force?

This is a difficult question to answer for so much depended on the will to fight and other imponderables. For the men of Force H, at all but the highest levels, confidence in themselves was universal, as a midshipman of the time remarked:

> There was no discernible feeling that we were up against a superior force or that a major action was likely. We would have taken them on without a second thought.[34]

On the whole this is linked to the next question, which is a more vital one.

Would, in fact, the French force have fought at all?

All indications, both before the passage, and actions during and after the passage of the Straits, would seem to indicate, without much doubt, that the one overriding desire of the French was to *avoid* action, not to seek it. It is perfectly true that, on sighting the patrolling British destroyers, the French ships went to 'Action Stations', and the captain of the *Gloire* had his crew ready for action the whole time. But against this must be set everything else the French did to avoid such a conflict. Admiral Darlan's original orders for example, the ones actually in force until *after* the French ships reached Dakar, were framed to avoid conflict. As Captain Huan records: 'As you can see, the orders were to *avoid* any provocation or any hostile action.'[35]

The distinguished French Naval historian Hervé Cras summed up the alternatives this way:

> Had the British wanted to intervene, two things may have occurred:
> (a) *Renown* and the destroyers would have blocked the way.
>
> In this case we only need to consider what happened in the case of *Primauguet* which Bourragué ordered to turn back. Likewise, he would have withdrawn towards Algiers, maybe even Toulon rather than Mers-el-Kebir.
> (b) *Renown* would have chased after him.
>
> He would have increased his speed and sailed to Casablanca.
>
> I have often met Admiral Bourragué and other officers from Force Y. We then of course conjured up a great many possibilities for the Dakar affair, but we *never* ever considered the eventuality of a battle when crossing the Straits on 11th September. Admiral Bourragué did not want, at any price, a battle against the British. And if Admiral Darlan subsequently demoted him from his command for this when in a bad temper, he soon resented it so little that he made him vice-admiral soon after and called him to an important post.
>
> Therefore I think, with total objectivity, that Admiral Bourragué would have done anything to avoid a battle until that moment when the British might have fired at him.[36]

This statement is given further confirmation, if any were needed, by the actual actions of *Milan*, which, although fired upon, made no retaliation. Even the action of Captain Monraisse in shooting down the London flying boat was after severe provocation, and a hard inquest was held by the French themselves on this matter afterwards.

Commandant Costet, on the Staff of the Naval C-in-C at Casablanca, echoes these thoughts, and those of Admiral Rebuffel, in their relief that it did not come to a fight, which showed how the French viewed it. 'During the whole day following Force Y's departure, we were very anxious, and then very relieved that it did not happen.'[37]

Did Somerville know of the approach of Force Y earlier?

It will be recalled that the first information Somerville had of the approach of the French ships, according to his Report of

Proceedings, was *Hotspur*'s sighting report around 0512, and that he asserts that he did not see the Madrid signal until around 0800 that morning. Admiral North claimed that this Madrid message was sent over to the *Renown* much earlier than this, although he never claimed that he personally was responsible for this. He told Captain Roskill that he and Somerville were in constant touch by telephone, and he also asserted in another place that Somerville would have known of the *contents* of the Madrid signal by the instructions he sent to the destroyers on patrol earlier.[38] Be that as it may Somerville is quite clear that he did not get that Madrid signal until it was too late to act upon it.

There appears to be no log kept of the incoming telephone calls in *Renown* which has survived in the Public Record Office and so this point may never be fully resolved. However Captain M.J. Evans was the Duty Staff Officer aboard *Renown* that night and he is quite clear in his mind of the facts of the matter:

> I have *no* recollection of *any* information about the French ships being at sea until the receipt of *Hotspur*'s signal. Being the Duty Staff Officer I have no doubt that I then went and discussed this with James Somerville and I have *no* recollection of his saying anything about knowing that they were coming. Signals from The Tower would unquestionably be passed direct by telephone to *Renown*, but an encyphered signal, after decoding, would probably be passed by hand.[39]

He confirmed this in a statement to Captain C.P.F. Brown, who also wrote: '... his memory is quite clear that neither Admiral Somerville nor anyone in *Renown* knew that the French ships were at sea until *Hotspur*'s signal arrived when it was too late ...'[40]

This of course omits mention of the signal from Gascoigne earlier which the two Admirals *had* discussed.

What of the subsequent signals sent by 'Hotspur'?

One very puzzling feature of the mix-up at the Admiralty over passing on the deciphered signals from Gibraltar concerns the fate of the signals sent by *Hotspur* subsequent to her original sighting report, which did not reach the First Lord until late that morning. We must assume that they arrived in quick succession and went through the same process. As Captain Layman explains:

> My original signal 0445 reporting ships burning navigation lights and my subsequent signals to North, would all have been relayed to the

Admiralty. All these signals and the further one from North to Admiralty 0617, would have been shown on receipt to the duty officer, Captain Bevan. Duty officers at night time always have the difficulty in deciding whether to awake the boss on receipt of signals and risk a reprimand for waking him unnecessarily. For some reason Bevan must have thought the signals from Gibraltar did not require any immediate action by Pound, especially as there were senior admirals at Gibraltar who ought to be trusted to take some action.[41]

Was Admiralty control of Force H hitherto too tight?

North, and his supporters, always stressed the fact that Force H was a detached command (many said Independent but this was not so), and that as the Admiralty had hitherto controlled its major movements direct Admiral North was justified in waiting for orders in this case. It is certainly true that Force H had been subjected to tight control from Whitehall up to this time. Is this another case of over-centralisation? Captain Roskill has brought to light the fact that, during the Norwegian Campaign, direct intervention was a common occurrence, mainly due to Churchill's own personal interference when First Lord, and that this often led to very dangerous situations which forced Admiral Forbes to protest. There can be no disputing this fact from the evidence Captain Roskill presents but at the time of Force Y's passage Churchill was Premier not First Lord, and, although he certainly did not cease his interventions, he usually did it by bringing pressure to bear on Alexander and Pound. We have seen that Alexander usually complied, but Pound was more resilient in resisting this type of pressure. On the other hand even Pound's most fervent supporters admit that he was prone to over-centralise himself.

In Force H's case however there was more justification than normal in some form of direct Admiralty intervention because of its special position. This squadron was used for specialised operations in the Mediterranean *and* the Atlantic and to organise the knitting together of the movements of both these areas and tie them in with operations in the Eastern Mediterranean required a great deal of organisation, impossible on a local basis at Gibraltar.

All this, on the other hand, did not, in Admiral Pound's view, release Admiral North from the obligations of his rank as man on the spot. As Lord Fraser repeated to me:

Sir Dudley North was not dismissed but relieved of his command and the reason for this was that when he was asked why he didn't send the Fleet to sea he said he was awaiting orders. First Sea Lord said, 'I can't put up with people who say they are awaiting orders because I might have been bombed for all they knew', and so he was relieved.[42]

Another point is that, as Admiral North stated the Admiralty always gave orders to Force H he surely must have expected *some* instructions to come from the Admiralty at any time and ought to have been in a position to act on them with all his forces *if* those orders *were* to intercept. Instead he called off his shadowing destroyers and sent them back east. Admiral Somerville at least brought his one ship to readiness for steam while waiting. Thus:

It is perhaps reasonable to say that North should have made a top priority signal of his intentions to interfere or not with the French passage – when after much delay no reply was received from the Admiralty to his earlier signals; and certainly on receipt of *Hotspur's* sighting report when the cruisers were two hours or more east of Gibraltar. *Renown* was then at one hour's notice, which seems quite adequate. A priority Emergency signal, in plain language (and why not?), would be in the Admiralty within a quarter of an hour. *Renown* could, and probably should, have left harbour and waited off Tarifa (say) or even further to the west if it was necessary to gain time.[43]

The personalities of Admirals North and Pound.

In the respective arguments much has been made of the differing personalities of Admirals North and Pound, and it is suggested that the fact that they were opposites might have led to an inevitable clash. I doubt that this had anything to do with it, but how did their subordinates at that time see the two men?

Captain Brown remembers North as '... a very pleasant, sunny man, a competent captain of a ship, liked by his officers and men, but that – as General Montgomery would say – was his ceiling.'[44]

Captain Layman's memories are the same:

I had to visit Rear-Admiral North at Great Yarmouth where he was Flag Officer in Command later in the war as I had some intercept listening stations for which I was responsible there. I then told North that the Admiralty would have had *Hotspur's* original sighting reports. I thought it might help him by showing how long Admiralty had these signals without taking action. I had served with North (and liked him) when he was junior captain in the Reserve Fleet. We messed together with the admiral to whom North was flag captain, and I was flag lieutenant. I still liked North at Gibraltar but thought he made an error of judgement over the Vichy Squadron![45]

Captain Evans also knew Admiral North earlier:

> North had previously been my captain for a short while. He was a very nice, very sensible, man, but not I would have thought, particularly brilliant or enterprising. He was very short in sea experience during the war.[46]

What of Admiral Pound? One who knew him very well was Captain Litchfield and he gives this portrait of the First Sea Lord:

> There is so much to be said of Pound that it is difficult to give you a portrait in a few words, but in conclusion I would say that he was a master of his profession though not without limitations in a larger context, perhaps more of a driver than a leader of men but universally respected and trusted for his integrity and professional ability. He was a man of very strong decision and personality, not an easy man to know intimately but very good company off duty. He had a stern presence on duty and some people found his abrupt manner and formidable silences unnerving![47]

Even so, I don't think personalities had anything to do with decision to relieve Admiral North at that time, for Pound had too much on his plate, and was far too objective in his decisions to allow personal feelings to enter into this in either direction. Even his most bitter critics admit he was an extremely fair man.

And so we come back to the inevitable final question once more.

Was Admiral North made a scapegoat?
As we have seen despite much evidence, and categorical denials by Pound, Alexander and Churchill themselves, the theory of the 'Scapegoat' persists to this day and will probably always do so. If the Churchill papers, when opened, fail to reveal a *positive* connection and implication the *possibility* will still remain open to speculation. Any documents other than this will be no more able to prove otherwise than Churchill's own personal denial to North did, so it is a 'heads you win, tails I lose' situation as far as Winston is concerned.

An Admiralty investigation in 1957 came up with the statement that: 'There is no evidence that there was pressure from outside the Admiralty at this time to have Admiral North removed'. While admitting that the evidence showed that Churchill was very angry about the whole affair, and especially North's part in it, it concluded; '... there is no evidence whether the Prime Minister discussed the matter at all with the First Lord and/or the First Sea Lord or if he did so what object he may have had in mind.'[48]

Despite this, the consensus, both in and out of the Service, seems to favour some sort of connection between Churchill and Pound's dismissal of North. Lord Altrincham, writing to North in 1953, put one reason for this as Churchill's covering for his dead wartime friend. Stating that Churchill would never allow any inquiry while he was still premier, Altrincham wrote:

> He is, as I have reason to know better than most, blind and fanatical in his devotion to certain old friends, and Dudley Pound was one of these, for he died in harness, as you know, practically under Winston's own eyes. That being the 'nature of the beast', I have always feared Winston in one way or another would block all the avenues to redress which should be open to you.[49]

Captain Roskill concluded from a deep study of the whole affair over a period of thirty years that: '... it is hard to avoid the conclusion that there *was* "Service prejudice" against him on the part of Alexander and Pound.' He also stated that;

> Taken together the foregoing facts do suggest either that Pound's early opinion of North was badly at fault ... or that he was subjected to pressure from above – which can only mean Alexander or Churchill – to have him sacked, and yielded to it.[50]

How did the men on the spot view it, both at the time and since? Commander Juniper wrote:

> Seething with discontent is, in my opinion too strong. No one approved of him being made a political scapegoat, but on this question it should be appreciated that Force H ships knew, greatly admired and were completely loyal to James Somerville, whilst North was inevitably more remote.[51]

Captain Osborne recalls the impression made at the time: 'My other, fairly clear, memory is that of the surprise expressed in *Hotspur*'s wardroom at Dudley North's apparent inactivity.'[52]

On the other hand most recognised, either at the time or since, that his actions had mitigating circumstances, Captain Evans for example:

> I think the Admiralty – possibly the PM – were totally remiss in not

giving instructions as to what they wanted done if a French squadron came through. We could have dealt with them with the greatest of ease. However to open fire on them without knowing clearly British policy, would have been madness.[53]

For the viewpoint of the sister service at the Rock at the time, Group Captain Horner says:

From the RAF point of view, the handling of events left more than a little rancour. The original sighting by the London provided at least four hours warning of the cruisers' approach. There was an appreciable naval presence at Gibraltar at the time. There were land gun batteries at the Rock. However, no effort was made to detain the French ships, and it was understood in fact that a 'bon voyage' signal was sent to them as they went through the Straits. Then panic ensued, and we were called upon to provide coverage far beyond the capability of one squadron (already fully engaged on anti-submarine incidents). The replacement of the C-in-C was considered fully warranted, and caused no surprise to us.[54]

Commander Walmsley of *Vidette* gives the viewpoint of the 13th Flotilla men, North's own command:

All I can say is that my own view and I believe the view of the majority of the other destroyer commanders was complete loyalty and respect for Admiral North, with the feeling that someone had to be the scapegoat in this matter and Admiral North had the role thrust upon him. I thought this unfair. Reflecting on the matter now, I doubt whether one was in possession of all the facts to enable one to pass judgement.[55]

This last line is reflected in my own opinion of the matter, the nagging feeling that, despite the cascade of words on the subject, *all* the facts are somehow still not known. I have tried to find as many as I can, but I do not claim to have finished the story even now, as have my predecessors.

Captain Layman's considered opinion on the case to date was: 'I realise there are very many people who *think* North suffered a great injustice, and I may well be wrong in thinking otherwise.'[56]

Captain Gairdner was serving aboard the destroyer leader *Faulknor* of the 8th Flotilla with the Menace expedition; how did they feel when they heard the news of the French ships passing unchecked and threatening their convoy?

We at Dakar were horrified to find that the ships has passed through unmolested and were on their way to augment an already sizeable enemy force. At a stroke the whole balance of power shifted against us and we thought pretty poorly of DN who had not laid a finger on the ships from his commanding position. We could hardly believe it, coming so soon after Oran.

When we got back to Gib the hue and cry were, I think, in full swing and DN had either disappeared or was packing his bags. It was then that people started asking what the hell the Admiralty had been up to leaving him to make *ad hoc* decisions that carried the most gruesome political overtones. We all felt pretty sorry for him and to this day, and without any real knowledge of what passed between DN and Admiralty, I have felt that he was most shabbily treated. After all, even despite the Oran adventure he stood to burn his fingers badly by doing the wrong thing and it was surely up to his political masters to give him the most precise instructions or at least to say that they would stand by and support his decision whatever that might be.

I believe Admiralty felt that he should of course done some persuasive thing and got them to turn back, but after Oran they were not in any mood to make things easy for us and indeed our force at Dakar suffered considerable damage at their hands. None of this will, I fear, help you at all except to record that we were amazed, perplexed, horrified and incredulous that 'they' had allowed the opposition to the Dakar operation to be so significantly augmented without a shot being fired.[57]

This makes a lot of sense. Captain Ryder wrote:

... in time of war you've got to get the right people in the key positions if you are going to win and this often leads to injustices. I don't think you could call North a live-wire – he hadn't done anything really wrong – he simply failed to use his initiative in what was a tricky situation fraught with serious political consequences and failed to rise to the occasion – most of us would have done a lot worse ...[58]

Finally Captain Litchfield puts the whole sorry affair into very wise and objective perspective thus:

I do not believe that the 'escape' of the French cruisers was, in the event, all that important in the general context of the war, and it might even be argued that if they had been stopped by force the outcome might have been as bad as that of Oran. The French Navy was a very proud service with a high tradition of French 'honour', and had anybody started firing shots across their bows it is quite conceivable that a real sea battle might have ensued – with results that are by no means predictable. But the affair was certainly very badly handled – by North for his astonishing lack of initiative and for doing nothing, and by the

Admiralty for their lack of clear and unambiguous instructions. It was one of many examples during the war when the Admiralty signally failed to give the men-on-the-spot all available information of what was going on – and information is as important as orders to those at the receiving end.[59]

In other words Lord Chatfield had it exactly right in his letter to Macmillan, and his subsequent statement in the House was as fair an *amende honorable* as Sir Dudley North could expect to have at the time. Perhaps, with hindsight, Admiral North might have done better to remember the stricture of his one time Commander-in-Chief, Admiral Sir David Beatty:

Whenever captains find themselves without special directions during an action, either from inability to make out the Admiral's signals, or from unforeseen circumstances rendering previous orders inapplicable, they are to act as their judgement shall direct in making every effort to damage the enemy in all possible ways.[60]

Admiral North's cruel dilemma was in deciding whether or not Force Y *was* an 'enemy' force. It was not a decision any of us would have cared to make at that time. So, although I do not go along with the 'Scapegoat' theory, I *can* agree with absolute conviction that Admiral North should not have had to wait until Macmillan's speech in the House to receive his due. That statement could not have been made by the Admiralty, with so many witnesses dead, but it *could* have been made by Winston Churchill at any time prior to this, especially on receipt of North's first post-war plea. That it was not made at that time is both unjust and sad, and is the reason I subscribe to Admiral North's own words on his place in history:
  'What a damned shame!'

III

The Battle of Spartivento
27 November 1940

'RUN, RABBIT, RUN'

CHAPTER FIFTEEN

A Calculated Risk?

By the autumn of 1940 the complex situation in the Mediterranean had partly resolved itself. After the uncertainties of June and July and of the colossal uncertainties caused by the defection of France and the sundering of all military co-operation with our most powerful ally in that theatre, light was beginning to appear at the end of what was to prove a long long tunnel.

On the credit side Cunningham's drubbing of the Italian Fleet at Calabria had almost at once given the British fleet a momentum of superiority it had already felt but now had proven and this momentum was maintained by a series of smaller engagements with the same result, the flight or humiliation of the enemy. The crescendo of this momentum came with the daring and surprisingly successful Fleet Air Arm attack on the main Italian naval base of Taranto in October which resulted in the crippling of three out of Mussolini's six combat-ready battleships, thus more than making up for any failure to bring them to battle on the high seas and altering the ratio of odds more in Britain's favour than at any time since the fall of France.

In the light of this newly acquired superiority in heavy ships Cunningham was willing to consider in more favourable light some of the hair-raising schemes still welling out of Whitehall in an unending flood, and, though still having to call on his considerable tact and patience with some of these, was now in a position to comply with the more reasonable of such requests. One of these was the proposition that a convoy of fast ships carrying vital personnel and supplies (two for the island of Malta and one for Alexandria) could now be safely fought through the length of the Mediterranean. The codename allocated for this convoy was Operation Collar and it was to provide the catalyst for the final confirmation of the superiority the Royal Navy had established over its larger Italian counterpart in the Mediterranean Sea after only a few months of war. It also showed, yet again, how the temperament of the Prime Minister was often harshly attuned to conditions at sea and that split judgements still continued to dominate political thinking to the detriment of the war effort.

The buoyant Admiral Cunningham had already received another confirmation of apparent lack of reality shown by London with the proposals that the island of Pantellaria, located in the strategic Narrows between Sicily and Tunisia, should be seized by amphibious assault right away, and this plan, Operation Workshop with the driving force of Admiral Lord Keyes behind it, found great favour at home. It was left to Cunningham to point out that although it could be taken and perhaps held, it would merely add another supply task to the already considerable commitment of keeping Malta going and for no great short-term or long-term advantage and it was dropped after much discussion. But the convoy operation held out far greater prospects of usefulness and success. Cunningham embraced it eagerly and expressed the view that any probability of the Italians being able to concentrate a superior force to oppose the passage of such a convoy in the Western Mediterranean was more remote than at any time since the end of August. But Admiral Somerville, whose principal responsibility the protection of the convoy would be until it reached the Narrows, was not so certain, and, in the event, his evaluation proved to be the more realistic.

Somerville, it must be remembered, was not in the happy position that Cunningham was. The latter had a whole string of victories under his belt and could therefore express his views to Whitehall freely with this firm background behind him. In contrast Admiral Somerville had been involved in a whole series of far from happy operations and as a result of this, and, from the anger his defence of Admiral North had aroused at home, knew that he had no such fund of goodwill in the Cabinet. Nonetheless, true to his tradition of fearlessness and truth he evaluated the situation and made his views firmly known. His main strength, Force H, was still inferior in every way to that of Cunningham's main fleet, and, moreover, the shift of the Italian heavy units to the west coast of Italy made it more likely than ever that it was against him that any reaction would be made. He still had only the *Renown* for heavy metal, for although the *Royal Sovereign* had been transferred to his command she was still undergoing necessary repairs to her aged engines and boilers in Gibraltar dockyard. Although Somerville asked that she be added to his force and the Admiralty finally agreed, in the event she could not be made ready in time. So even before the operation commenced Somerville knew he had but one big ship to oppose the three theoretically available enemy big ships.

He had *Ark Royal* for air to be sure, but doubts, as the strikes against the French battle-cruiser *Strasbourg* in July had shown, about the ability of the torpedo bombers to actually hit and slow down fast-moving enemy heavy ships were still being felt due to the proportion of inexperienced crews carried. Again, in the event, these doubts were justified and torpedo bomber strikes were no more successful in their main objective at Spartivento than they had been at Calabria.

In cruiser strength the situation was little better. Force H could only call upon the *Sheffield* and the much older *Despatch*, both 6-inch gun ships. Two more modern ships of the same class as *Sheffield*, the *Southampton* and *Manchester*, would be taking part in the operation but they would be encumbered by the fact that taking passage to Malta aboard them would be no less than 700 RAF and military personnel, which would gravely hamper their fighting efficiency in the event of a surface battle. Indeed this proved a strong bone of contention between Vice-Admiral L.E. Holland, CB, the Vice-Admiral Commanding 18th Cruiser Squadron to which these two ships belonged, and Vice-Admiral Somerville. He submitted a strong doubt about the cruisers being tied down in this way and submitted the following reasons:

> (1) Extreme importance was attached to the safe and timely arrival of the RAF personnel at Alexandria. The best way to ensure this was for the cruisers to proceed independently and rely on their high speed and mobility for the achievement of their object.
> (2) With so many additional (*sic*) on board, the ships were not in a fit condition to fight. If obliged to engage, casualties amongst the RAF personnel might be heavy and the object of this part of the operation compromised.[1]

While Somerville to some degree could only agree to these points he pointed out firmly that the achievement of the *complete* objective, the safe passage of the whole convoy, was more likely to be accomplished by means of a show of force since this might have a deterrent effect on the Italians. To clarify the position Cunningham was consulted on this point and he replied that the personnel should receive priority over the rest of the convoy. However he was overruled by Whitehall again who decreed that this must be subject to the *overriding* consideration that if Italian forces were in sight action taken by the cruisers must be the same as if personnel were not embarked. No compromises from Winston on this score. Engage the enemy was his dictum; everything else was secondary. A spirit to be admired, surely.

As to Admiral Somerville's estimation of the possible enemy strength which could oppose his force, which he put at three battleships, five to seven 8-inch cruisers and many 6-inch cruisers the Admiralty was inclined to scoff but events were to show that this was not far from the truth.

As usual Somerville's somewhat scanty destroyer strength was made up from both the 8th (*Faulknor, Firedrake, Forester* and *Fury*) and the 13th (*Duncan, Wishart*) with the two new additions, the modern *Jaguar* and *Kelvin*, which enabled them to make up one whole flotilla whose eight ships had to screen both convoy and fleet between them. One other destroyer of the 13th Flotilla was present, the *Hotspur*, but she was of limited value in a fleet action or in an anti-submarine role, having earlier rammed and sunk the Italian submarine *Lafole* east of Gibraltar. She was on her way to Malta Dockyard to effect repairs and was minus her asdic and with her speed limited.

Four corvettes were part of the force, the *Gloxinia, Hyacinth, Peony* and *Salvia*, having been sent out from Home to join Cunningham's fleet. They were fitted with LL (anti-magnetic mine) sweeps which restricted their speed to only sixteen knots at best and in practice this was found to be only fourteen![2] Their suitability for screening duties was therefore almost negligible.

Such was Somerville's total strength. Its glaring weakness in the face of what the Italians could, in theory, place against it, is obvious, but in addition to the factors described above there were others not so obvious which lengthened the odds still further. While Collar was still in the planning stage Somerville received instructions to carry out further harassing operations against a Vichy convoy which was expected to enter the Mediterranean on 20th November, and this at a time when his ships needed a respite before the dangerous convoy operation. Not surprisingly his reaction was somewhat peeved, as he wrote to their Lordships at the time:

It appeared to us both that a period for rest and repairs was important for these ships, both from the point of view of the efficiency of the personnel and of the fighting efficiency of the ships. I was anxious that the vigilance and fighting efficiency of the Force should be at its highest since I considered it more than probable that the Italian Fleet might attempt to compensate themselves for the heavy losses sustained at Taranto by the interception of Force H by superior forces during Operation Collar.[3]

Nor was this all. One of the best-kept secrets of the war concerned his main unit, his flagship the battle-cruiser *Renown*. Re-built just before the outbreak of war she presented a brave appearance to the world and was crewed with a team at the highest peak of professionalism. But she was only rebuilt above the waterline, and, although given powerful new engines, her hull remained much as it had been in 1916 when she first took to the water, and this old hull contained grave defects which were never made public. One of her Chief Engineering Officers from a later period wrote:

I remember one reserve feed tank in the double bottom, which always leaked salt water, had active corrosion pits in the bottom plating at least half the thickness of the plate. Caulking was useless to stop these leaks and so we took the somewhat unorthodox step of welding along the riveted seams as well as filling the deep pits.

For much of the war, in Force H and subsequently, *Renown* had a broken back. There was a split right across the top strength deck on the port side and the beginning of a crack on the starboard side. When I joined the ship the port side crack had been repaired by a traverse butt strap double riveted, but this of course was just toying with the trouble for the repaired job was much weaker than the original. As a result we had no reserve margin of hull strength at all. The cause of the failure was similar to that in the *Comets*, namely fatigue caused by stress raisers in the form of relatively sharp corners and unnecessary openings for various purposes in the top strength deck amidships at a position of maximum tensile stress when the ship was hogging. Not only did the funnel and uptake openings have comparatively sharp corners but there were holes for waste, steam and other pipes on the port side and on both sides a large rectangular hatch giving access to the deck below. I could get no constructor to take the matter seriously but when we were told we were to go to the Med for later operations the captain said to me, 'What can we do about the split in the deck, Chief?', and I replied: 'There's nothing we can do, sir, but pray for good weather and that no one puts a fish into us!'[4]

It is perhaps just as well that such defects remained hidden to the majority although they must have been known to the C-in-C who carried this additional burden, along with the many others, lightly in front of his men and his command. Indeed it may be fairly said that Force H's greatest strength lay in the Commander in Chief of Force

H himself and his very able team. Unfortunately it was a strength much put to the test by those who understood not the problems that beset him and looked only for material victories to flaunt in public and knowing little what had to be overcome to achieve them. It was fortunate that Vice-Admiral Somerville enjoyed the absolute confidence of his men at this time of delicate balance. A serving officer aboard the *Renown* at this time describes this very well.

My father had been a contemporary of James Somerville and I myself had known him from boyhood days. He was an outstanding person with a great sense of humour and had previously been Rear Admiral Destroyers in the Med before the war and had flown his flag in the cruiser *Galatea*. By the nepotism that was current in the Navy of those days he had been able to take his former operational staff team with him when he went to Force H.

This meant his small staff were completely in tune with him and were also highly efficient. There were very few of them – Secretary, Flag Lieutenant/Signal Officer, Staff Operations and one or two others. They relied on *Renown* for staff support in other areas, which I think helped to integrate the staff and the ship (never an easy problem). As far as I am aware (I may be wrong) there wasn't an aviator on the staff in spite of the emphasis on air operations, and the air advice came from *Ark Royal*.

The two other key people on the staff were thus also ship's officers of *Renown*. They were Martin Evans, the Navigation Officer, and John Holmes, the Gunnery Officer. Both of these were outstanding people, very highly professional. Strangely enough I was the personal assistant to both – at the same time!

So at Spartivento you had on *Renown*'s bridge a team of really able people, who knew exactly what was expected of them and who knew what their Admiral wanted. This seems to be the right ingredient for success.

They were backed by a highly efficient and high morale ship in *Renown*, commanded by Captain Simeon who had previously been Director of Naval Ordnance. He was much admired and liked by all. He had an endearing stutter which seemed to enhance his personality – (I remember once at Gibraltar I had to 'prosecute' a young cook who had returned on board drunk the night before and who then appeared at the Captain's defaulters' table. I said the cook's action station was in the 4.5-inch ammunition supply. In a very sombre voice Captain Simeon said, 'The enemy aircraft attack – the order is to pass the ammunition – and where is Cook Smith? – ddown bbelow – *ddrunk.*' I doubt if the cook ever drank again!)[5]

However the smooth running of the convoy and reinforcements for the Eastern Basin was but one facet of this operation. As before opportunity was to be taken to knit with other complicated movements from the other end of the Mediterranean and the planning involved to ensure that all the forces involved met according to plan brought further headaches. The successful outcome of Taranto as far as Cunningham was concerned was that it meant he could now reduce his capital ships still further and that some of his other ships which were suffering defects could be brought home via the central route and not face the delays the long-sea voyage round the Cape would involve. Accordingly the battleship *Ramillies*, the 8-inch heavy cruiser *Berwick* and the 6-inch light cruiser *Newcastle* were to sail under cover of the main Mediterranean Fleet from Alexandria, pass through the Straits and rendezvous with Somerville's squadron west of that area on the 27th November. This would achieve two things.

Firstly, for the most dangerous period of the operation, between noon and dusk on the 27th, Somerville would have a welcome addition to his strength for although the three ships from the East were not in top condition they might well deter by their very appearance and make the Italians think twice. Secondly, the destroyers assigned to their escort westward, the *Defender, Greyhound, Griffin* and *Hereward*, along with the anti-aircraft cruiser *Coventry*, would then be in a position to take over the close escort of the merchant ships for the next lap of their journey. (Incidentally the latter three destroyers had recently been serving under Somerville in the 13th Flotilla at Gibraltar and so would be able to fit in with any operations easily. Another point of interest to the C-in-C Force H was that his son was serving in the *Defender* at this time.)

These ships from the East were assigned the codename Force D. The *Ramillies* was of the same class as the *Royal Sovereign* in dock at Gibraltar and shared the general misfortune of that class in that they had not been completely re-built between the wars as had the ships of the *Queen Elizabeth* class. Therefore their best speed was only around 21 knots while the main armament of eight 15-inch guns, had not been modified to increase their elevation to bring their ranges into line with modern battle practice, and they could, in fact, be outranged by the modern Italian ships and even the smaller main guns of the older enemy vessels. As for the cruisers, the *Berwick* had only joined Cunningham recently in order to bolster his 8-inch cruiser strength, when the *Kent* docked, being damaged in the month before, but her stay was a brief one for she was suffering from engine defects. She had had some rows of turbine blades removed and the higher water temperature in the Mediterranean was affecting her vacuum, thus reducing her effective best speed to 27 knots, which was five or six knots slower than her Italian opposite numbers. The *Newcastle* had come from the Far East to join Cunningham, but she too was unreliable now as defects had developed in her boilers.

As a preliminary to the main movements part of Force H was at sea between the 15th and 20th November carrying out Operation White. This was the flying to Malta from the *Argus* of twelve Hurricane fighters of the RAF, led by two Fleet Air Arm Skua dive-bombers. Escort for the carrier was provided by the *Ark Royal*, *Renown*, *Despatch* and *Sheffield* with *Faulknor*, *Fortune*, *Firedrake*, *Forester*, *Foxhound*, *Fury* and *Duncan* and the actual flying-off operations took place to the south-west of Sardinia. The passage of the short-range fighters had been carefully worked out but it ended in complete disaster owing to stronger than expected head winds during their flight. As a result most of the aircraft ran out of fuel far from the airfields and only four Hurricanes and one Skua survived.

This tragedy was compounded in a number of ways. The planned attack on Alghero airfield in Sardinia by *Ark Royal*'s aircraft had to be abandoned on 17th November because of the same weather conditions. The smaller ships were subjected to a further mauling by the weather which further reduced their time to prepare for the main operation and also the time to plan for the staff. But, in addition, it sounded alarms at Rome and in fact gave the Italians a full-scale dress rehearsal for the major action.

Although Supermarina was not aware of the purpose of Operation White, they had been informed of the arrival of the *Argus* at Gibraltar on 14th November, and at 1000 on the morning of the 15th they received notification of the sailing from that harbour of the main units of Force H. On the assumption that a convoy might be underway to Malta they made their preparations. A further sighting by reconnaissance aircraft at noon on the same day gave the course of the British warships as 90°, some fifty miles to the north of Alhucemas, which was enough to set in train their established plan.

The First Division, battleships *Vittorio Veneto* and *Giulio Cesare* and the Third Division, the heavy cruisers *Bolzano*, *Trento* and *Trieste*, each with their accompanying destroyer squadrons, sailed from Naples and Messina respectively and rendezvoused with each other at 1030 on the 16th November. This powerful combined force was by 1630 that evening in an excellent intercepting position some 45 miles

NNE of Ustica. But when it was clear that the British were not coming further east they returned to their bases. The arrival of Force H back at the Rock was also duly reported to them on the evening of the 19th.[6]

This brief sortie showed two things which were to be repeated in the Spartivento action. Firstly, that the estimation by Vice-Admiral Somerville that the Italians were more than ready to utilise their remaining battleships aggressively against Malta convoys and that their determination had not been shaken or affected by Taranto, was the correct one and that the Admiralty feeling that this was not so was completely false. It also showed that the Italians could quickly learn of any British movements but that, in return, their own powerful concentration had gone undetected. Secondly it showed the overriding advantage their central position gave the Italians. They were within a day's steaming of the convoy route and would themselves always have two or three days' notice of British intentions.

Nonetheless the planning for Operation Collar proceeded as planned.

It was on the night of 24th/25th November that the three merchant ships *Clan Forbes*, *Clan Fraser* and *New Zealand Star* with their vital munitions and armoured vehicles for the Eighth Army in Egypt, passed through the Straits of Gibraltar and they were duly joined by the four corvettes *Gloxinia*, *Hyacinth*, *Peony* and *Salvia* to the east of the Straits early on the morning of the 25th. Forces B and F sailed together from the Rock at 0800 on the 25th and their composition was as follows:

Force B had the battle-cruiser *Renown* (Captain C.E.B. Simeon) as flagship of Vice-Admiral Somerville, the aircraft-carrier *Ark Royal* (Captain C.S. Holland), the 6-inch light cruisers *Sheffield* (Captain C.A.A. Larcom) and *Despatch* (Captain D.E. Douglas-Pennant DSC), and the destroyers *Faulknor* (Captain A.F. De Salis), *Firedrake* (Lieutenant-Commander S.H. Norris DSC), *Forester* (Lieutenant-Commander E.B. Tancock DSC), *Fury* (Lieutenant-Commander T.C. Robinson), *Duncan* (Captain A.D.B. James), *Wishart* (Commander E.T. Cooper), *Encounter* (Lieutenant-Commander E.V.St.J. Morgan), *Kelvin* (Commander J.H. Allison DSO) and *Jaguar* (Lieutenant-Commander J.F.W. Hine).

Force F comprised the 6-inch light cruisers *Manchester* (Captain H.A. Packer), flying the flag of VA 18th CS, Vice-Admiral L.E. Holland), and *Southampton* (Captain B.C.B. Brooke), the damaged destroyer *Hotspur* (Captain H.F.H. Layman DSO) and the corvettes came under this designation also as did the merchantmen.

Table 3: British Forces at Sea.				
	Battle-Cruiser	Aircraft Carrier	6-inch cruisers	Destroyers
Force B	1	1	2	9
Force F	–	–	2	1
Total	1	1	4	10

Meanwhile, at the other end of the Mediterranean the ships coming west designated Force D had already sailed on the 24th November. These were the battleship *Ramillies* (Captain H.T. Baille-Groham), the 8-inch cruiser *Berwick* (Captain G.L. Warren), the 6-inch cruiser *Newcastle* (Captain E.A. Aylmer), the anti-aircraft cruiser *Coventry* (Captain W.P. Carne), and destroyers *Defender* (Lieutenant-Commander St J.R.J. Tyrwhitt), *Greyhound* (Commander W.R. Marshall-Adeane), *Griffin* (Lieutenant-Commander J. Lee Barber) and *Hereward* (Lieutenant-Commander C.W. Greening).[7]

Table 4: Force D.					
	Battleship	8-inch cruiser	6-inch cruiser	AA cruiser	Destroyers
Force D	1	1	1	1	4

These ships were accompanied for part of their journey through the eastern Mediterranean by units of the main fleet designated Force C, which consisted of the battleship *Barham* and *Malaya*, the aircraft carrier *Eagle*, and the cruisers *York*, *Glasgow* and *Gloucester* with destroyers, and the carrier's aircraft made a diversionary attack on Tripoli on 26th November. Also at sea covering this movement, and the passage of convoys from Port Said to Piraeus and other operations, was Cunningham himself with his main strength, the battleships *Warspite* and *Valiant*, the aircraft carrier *Illustrious*, cruisers *Orion*, *Ajax* and *Sydney* and destroyers; *Illustrious* again sent her planes to attack Rhodes. In short, on 25th and 26th November the whole Mediterranean sea from end to end was a mass of British shipping movements, an exercise in the use of maritime control hardly equalled in the annals of sea warfare.[8]

For the ships heading east from Gibraltar the first two days were without major incident.

The weather was boisterous again without any mist. The glass was rising, the sea following in strict consonance with it. We tramped the now familiar route, swiftly and without fuss, and by the morrow's dawn the weather was radiant again. It was for this passage that Admiral Somerville made the signal, 'The Chaplains of the Fleet will pray for fog'. Perhaps the chaplains had not yet got into their stride, but the weather this day gave us a clear view for a hundred miles – a hundred miles back to the snow-white cresting of the Sierra Nevada.

In the morning *Ark Royal* exercised her planes. There are some days when luck seems to run badly with the aircraft carriers. This morning she lost one plane on a practice flight – the crew were saved. In the afternoon she had another damaged, crashing in landing on the deck. These things she took in her stride. They did not delay the ordered beauty of our progress. We still steamed on, a straight, inexorable line towards the east.[9]

Behind the smooth phrases of a war correspondent's words, however, these accidents revealed another facet of the weakness of Force H; the inexperience of a large number of the *Ark Royal*'s aircrew.

Other things were not going that smoothly either. The slow speed of the corvettes had been revealed and it was decided that all the complicated planning could not be thrown out of gear because of this unfortunate defect. Accordingly, on the evening of the 26th, these little ships were detached from the main convoy and told to proceed independently.[10] In a surface action their presence would count for little or nothing, but the value of their anti-submarine and minesweeping potential would be greatly missed for the merchantmen.

The paucity of information on the movements, or otherwise, of the enemy, was also causing grave concern on the *Renown*'s bridge. As Somerville himself was to relate:

With the exception of a Sunderland flying boat operating from Malta to cover the area in which our forces would be operating on 27th November, air reconnaissance was limited to that furnished by *Ark Royal* aircraft.

Ark Royal has a high proportion of young and inexperienced pilots and observers. Some of these had to be employed on the initial dawn reconnaissance, since it was necessary to hold the first air striking force in readiness to attack any enemy force attempting to interfere with the concentration of Forces B and F with Force D.

Not only had many of these young observers little or no experience of reporting enemy formations, but the need for maintaining wireless silence, except in the immediate neighbourhood of Gibraltar, provides little opportunity to exercise communications in the air.[11]

Perhaps the men of Force H would not have worried themselves unduly about such matters; all were in no doubts about the outcome should they chance upon any Italian ships during the operation. But Somerville had the responsibility of getting those vital and desperately needed personnel and machines through no matter what, and naturally as he had the whole weight upon his shoulders, his viewpoint was somewhat different. Still, as his biographer correctly emphasises, he did not flinch at the consequences.

> Somerville was too well-known as a fighting leader, not only to the Navy but to the general public to whom Force H had become a familiar name, for him to be summarily sent into obscurity like Dudley North. He correctly sensed that should a satisfactory pretext arise, his head might well fall into the basket. But this did not affect the clear thought he brought to preparations for the coming operation or his readiness to point out, at the risk of being thought over-anxious, the danger which might result from sending an inadequate force to meet an Italian concentration against him.[12]

Had Somerville, and his critics, been privy to events in Supermarina headquarters that day in Rome, they might have been even less confident.

CHAPTER SIXTEEN

Divide and Conquer

It has been seen how, during the preliminary operation, White, the Italian naval high command, Supermarina, at their headquarters in Rome, had received almost instant notification of the sailings and arrivals at Gibraltar. This was a fact of life that the British had become accustomed to, and they realised that no matter how often they rung the changes, it was unavoidable that they could evade detection for long. All they could hope to do was keep from the enemy the nature of their missions and their strength. Alas for Somerville and his men on this occasion, no sooner had Force H sailed than once more the word was flashed to Italy. But at this stage, the Italians still did not know of the presence of the three merchant ships and the value of their human and inert cargo.

It was in fact, as early as 0825, twenty-five minutes after their sailing from the Rock, that the Italians took a coded message notifying them that Force H was out![1] The composition of the British fleet was given correctly also, being said to comprise the *Renown*, *Ark Royal* three cruisers of the *Birmingham*-type and one of the *Delhi*-type and eight destroyers (two of which, *Jaguar* and *Kelvin*, were of a new class and not familiar to the reporting agent, a fact he passed on).

Nor were the Italians in ignorance of the passage of Force D to the East either, for at 1130 on the 25th an Italian civil airliner reported flying over a large concentration of British warships, some ten units being counted, among which was an aircraft carrier and a battleship. She reported them to be about 150 miles on a course of 110° from Malta, steering 330°.

What did they make of these movements?

Although Bragadin states that the earlier concentration of Italian units to intercept Operation White had '... served to inform the British that the Italian battle forces were still operative and had two operative battleships,' and, further that 'This realization forced the enemy to make certain changes in his plans for the protection of the convoy which was to cross the Mediterranean, by bringing in some units of the Alexandria fleet to reinforce the Gibraltar one ...',[2] we know that this is not true, and that only Somerville felt any unease and that the earlier concentration had gone unrecorded. Nonetheless the Italian reaction to the early sightings was positive and without hesitation. Again the available units on hand were given orders to sail to take up their intercepting positions and to offer battle if conditions proved ideal.

They concluded, following further sightings of Force H at 1010 on the 26th, that this group would, if it held its speed and course as it had done, reach the vicinity of Cape Bougaroni at midnight on the 26th, from which position it would be able to launch air attacks against their bases from the carrier (Taranto was still very much in their minds and they expected a repetition against their surviving battleships at anchor on the west coast). Alternatively, they concluded, the operation might be a passing of naval reinforcements eastward to Cunningham through the Straits, and this would explain the British movements in that half of the Mediterranean. They had still *not* sighted the convoy, a major achievement for Somerville's dispositions. Had they done so their reactions might have been different, but throughout the opening stages of the battle the three merchant ships remained unplotted on the chart tables in Rome and on board the Italian flagship. In this it will be seen that, yet again, the Italians were badly served by their aerial reconnaissance units and were left much in the dark subsequently. Despite the example of Calabria earlier in the year, close liaison between the Air Force and Navy still remained lamentable.

On the evening of the 25th November Supermarina had already given their initial instructions to the local defence units, Marilibia, telling them at 1955 that day to place on instant alert all units, including the 14th destroyer squadron at Tripoli, and warning them to be ready for air attacks. All the major units were under direct control of Supermarina itself and these were told at the same time to raise steam for sea within three hours. The commanders of all the naval departments concerned at La Spezia, Naples, Messina and Taranto were instructed to place their bases on full alert and, in addition all commands concerned with convoys to and from Libya were instructed to suspend all further sailings for the time being.

At 0815 the next day, the 26th, Supermarina again set in motion the concentration of their main surface forces at Naples and Messina. They were instructed to sail as quickly as possible at midday. The exception was the 4th Division and they were unable to get underway until the 27th due to refits. They were told to speed things up and eventually got underway at 1340 that day.

To patrol the Straits between Cape Bon and Pantellaria the 10th Torpedo Boat (small escort destroyers) Division was ordered to sail from Trapani that evening and maintain their watch until dawn and these four units, *Alcione, Sagittario, Siro* and *Vega* duly complied. On the night of the 26th/27th, in fact, the *Sirio* actually sighted the ships of Force D penetrating the straits and fired a salvo of torpedoes at large ships, none of which hit. She reported she was undetected and not fired upon in return but took no further part in the preliminary skirmishes.

All was now set, and, at 1010 on the morning of the 26th, the Naval High Command issued their final battle instructions in an operational directive to all units.

The First and Second Squadrons were to sail from Naples and Messina at high speed and effect a junction of their forces around 1800 on the 26th in the position Lat 39°20′, Long 14°20′, some seventy miles south of Capri. From this rendezvous the whole combined force was to steam at a speed of sixteen knots on a course of 260° until the morning of the 27th when aerial reconnaissance was expected to reveal the enemy's full strength, speed and course for them. Upon this their further movements would depend; they were to engage the enemy units if the conditions were considered right.

Four submarines were sent to positions of ambush and the enemy could be drawn towards their patrol lines. These submarines were the *Alagi, Aradam, Axum* and *Diaspro* which were placed to the south of Sardinia. Their actual patrol positions were allocated as follows:

37°40′, 10°00 (Twenty miles north of Cape Blanc di Bizerta).
38°20′, 8°40′ (Forty miles SSW of Cape Spartivento, Sardinia).
38°00′, 9°20′ (30 miles northwest of Galita island).
37°40′, 8°00 (Forty-five miles NNW of Galita island).

They were to patrol initially to the south, then track back north for ninety miles then to turn west. A further two submarines, the *Dessié* and *Tembien* were sent to waiting positions off Malta itself.

The Commander-in-Chief of the main forces at sea was confirmed as Admiral Campioni again, with a long-awaited chance to rectify his unfortunate results at Calabria the previous July. He was already flying his flag aboard the *Vittorio Veneto*. All was now ready for him to make up for that failure.

Between 1150 and 1230 the battleship force sailed from Naples. This consisted of the following units: the battleships *Vittorio Veneto* (Captain Giuseppe Sparzani), flagship, and *Giulio Cesare* (Captain Angelo Varoli Piazza), escorted by the 7th Destroyer Squadron, *Freccia* (Commander Amleto Baldo), *Dardo* (Lieutenant Commander Bruno Salvatori) and *Saetta* (Lieutenant Commander Carlo Unger di Lowemberg), and the 13th Destroyer Squadron, *Granatiere* (Captain Vittorio De Pace), *Alpino* (Commander Giuseppe Marini), *Bersagliere* (Commander Candido Bigliardi) and *Fuciliere* (Commander Alfredo Viglieri).

Also from Naples sailed the heavy cruisers of Admiral Angelo Iachino, second-in-command with his flag in the *Pola* (Captain Manlio De Pisa), with *Fiume* (Captain Giorgio Giorgis) of the 1st Cruiser Division, flying the flag of the Divisional Admiral, Admiral Pellegrino Matteucci, and *Gorizia* (Captain Giuseppe Manfredi), escorted by the 9th Destroyer Squadron, *Alfieri* (Captain Lorenzo Daretti), *Carducci* (Commander Alberto Ginocchio), *Gioberti* (Commander M. Aurelio Raggio) and *Oriani* (Commander Mario Panzani).

The 3rd Division sailed from Messina at 1230 and consisted of the *Trieste* (Captain Umberto Rouselle), flying the flag of Divisional Admiral Luigi Sansonetti, with the *Bolzano* (Captain Franco Maugeri) and *Trento* (Captain Alberto Parmigiano), and escorted by the 12th destroyer squadron, the *Lanciere* (Captain Carmine D'Arienzo), *Ascari* (Commander Sabato Bottiglieri) and *Corazziere* (Lieutenant Commander Carlo Avegno).[3]

Table 5: Italian forces as sea.			
	Battleships	8-inch cruisers	Destroyers
From Naples	2	3	11
From Messina	–	3	3
In total	2	6	14

The aerial forces available to co-ordinate its movements with the fleet based in Sardinia consisted at this time of one squadron (3° *Gruppo*) of land-based fighters for defence of the ships, one maritime bomber group (93° *Gruppo*) equipped with Cant Z506s, and one normal bomber squadron (32°*Stormo*) which was flying the standard Italian tri-motor bomber, the Savoia Marchetti Sm79. They were expected to provide long-range reconnaissance, fighter protection against torpedo bomber attacks on the Italian ships and also to harry and attack the British fleet. This hope was, for the most part, illusory.

As can be seen, based on the information they had at the time, the Italians sailed in considerable strength ready to do battle with Force H alone. They were not aware that Force H was handicapped by the convoy under its wing, of which they knew nothing at all, but Campioni had a fair estimation of his opponents' strength and could be justified in his self-confidence in facing them. No consideration at all seems to have been given that other forces might be linking up with Force H from the eastern basin; only a west-east movement seems to have been envisaged as a possibility. So this feeling of euphoria among the Italians was to last throughout the night of the 26th/27th and well on into the day. But the events of that night in the Sicilian Channel should have given them pause for thought.

It will be recalled how the torpedo boat *Sirio*, one of four on patrol in the Straits that night, had made an abortive attack on Force D. This attack took place at 0033 on the morning of 27th November, and, on its conclusion, and her 'undetected' evasion, the *Sirio* made a sighting report to her base. But in that initial report she merely stated that the target of her attack had been an enemy force, 'unidentified units' was how she phrased it, and this report, made at 0055/27th, conveyed no special significance to Trapani. Seven units sounded a fair-size squadron but nothing more alarming than that.

Campioni therefore effected his rendezvous and pressed on to the westward with his two cruiser squadrons strung out ahead of him, the 1st Division to the north, the 3rd Division on a parallel course to the south with the two battleships following up astern. By 0800 on the 27th the Italians were south of Sardinia, the cruiser squadrons steering slightly south-west, the battleships due west, past Cape Spartivento and heading towards Cape Teulada.

It was not until 0840 that the *Sirio*, on her way back to Trapani after her night exploits, amplified her sighting reports further. She signalled more information at 1000 and this time her message included the vital information that one of the 'unidentified' units that she had attacked the previous night may well have been a battleship (*piuttosto grandi*). This raised a whole new issue in the Italian calculations, and one that was not pleasant for them to contemplate.

The early sightings had been amplified by Trapani by signals to the squadron commander of the torpedo boats, and was duly passed on to Campioni, but it was not until this final amplification that he realised that his supposed superiority might be gravely affected should the two British squadrons join forces before he could make contact. It was obviously essential for him to deal with them one at a time, the question remained uppermost in his mind, did he still have time to do so? The catapult aircraft carried aboard the battleships were launched before dawn to try and locate the British forces urgently. Until they did so there was little he could do but hold his present course and see how things developed.

Although he was still in the dark as to the exact whereabouts and composition of his enemy he still held most of the aces and could still decide whether to engage in battle or to withdraw. He had still enjoyed complete immunity from detection by the British reconnaissance aircraft and Somerville still had not the slightest inkling that the Italian battle fleet was not only out, but fast closing on his own squadron from the north-east at a speed of sixteen knots.[4]

At 0800 on the British side the situation was as follows: the *Renown*, *Ark Royal*, *Sheffield* and their escorting destroyers *Faulknor*, *Firedrake*, *Forester*, *Fury* and *Encounter* were in position 37°48' N, 07°24' E, steering a course at 083° at sixteen knots, ten miles in front of, and to the north-east of, the convoy. In this position they were between the convoy and the Italian bases.

The three merchant ships were proceeding east, north of Cape de Fer in position 37°37' N, 06°54' E. The *Despatch*, *Manchester* and *Southampton* were acting as close cover for this convoy which was screened by the remaining destroyers. The four corvettes, due to their slow speed, had fallen steadily behind the convoy during the night and were now ten miles astern of them.

Force D was bang on time heading west to the north-east of Galitia island but no communication between the two British groups had been established and neither was exactly certain of the whereabouts of the other. In order to gain such contact, and to carry out fighter patrols against expected air attack and anti-submarine patrols, the *Ark Royal* was, at 0800, ordered to send off her aircraft. One section of fighters, one A/S patrol, one meteorological flight and seven reconnaissance Swordfish were duly flown off to comply with these instructions. The Swordfish spread out to cover wide sectors to cover all the areas between Sardinia and the North African coast, their range being such that it was expected that they would be able to make visual contact with Force D off the Skerki Bank.

Evidence that the Italians were also early astir came when the fighter patrol sighted a Cant Z506 approaching the convoy from

Sardinia. After a long chase they caught and shot down this floatplane some ten miles north of Bone before she could make any sighting of the convoy. Subsequently no aerial reports reached Admiral Campioni for some hours. Somerville had already received a signal from Alexandria at 0330 that morning which reported the attack on Force D in the Sicilian Channel, so that subsequent claims in post-war histories that the *Sirio* had gone undetected were plainly untrue.[4] Her attack *had* been noticed and the fear that Force D was now fully plotted in Rome ensured that Somerville was right on his toes at this juncture. He accordingly held on the eastward course ahead of the convoy for some time.

The decision always had to be made at this part of any Malta convoy, whether to station the main units north of the convoy in case of enemy surface ship intervention, or to concentrate all forces to stand off the normal heavy air attacks. Always a balance had to be struck on this issue. In this case Somerville held on until 0900, when, not having heard any sighting reports from his reconnaissance to the contrary, and having absolutely no other indications, other than Force D's sighting, which was not unusual in itself, that the Italian main fleet was out, he duly pulled his heavy units back to the south-west in accordance with established practice to set up a strong anti-aircraft defence for the merchant ships.

Both sides were still in the dark then for the early morning reconnaissance flown by the Cant Z506 from Cagliari at 0755 had already come to grief at the hands of *Ark*'s fighters. But this was not the only Italian aircraft searching for Force H. Both the *Bolzano* and the *Fiume* had catapulted their own scouting planes in accordance with Campioni's earlier instructions; their line of search was Galitia Island-Cape de Fer-Cagliari, in which area it was hoped to make sightings of both British forces. Also with the dawn, the two battleships, now some 30 miles astern of the cruiser squadrons, increased speed to first 17 and then 18 knots to reduce this gap.

However, unknown to Somerville, one of his search planes *had* made contact with the Italian ships. At 0852 one of the Swordfish sighted a group of strange warships and immediately closed to investigate. She quickly identified them as hostile and, at 0906, made an Alarm Report of four cruisers and six destroyers. Unfortunately this first sighting report was never received by any British unit and much time was lost, with Somerville still steering away from the oncoming enemy to rejoin the convoy.

This he sighted at 0920 and adjusted his course to pass astern of the merchant ships and bring his ships on a line south of the convoy to afford the best AA protection in the event of a bomber attack from up-sun and facilitate *Ark*'s flying operations, but while still carrying out this manoeuvre, at 0956, the first confirmation of the Swordfish sighting was received by visual signal from the *Ark Royal*. The time of origin of this message was 0920 and gave the enemy force as consisting of five cruisers and five destroyers.

The report was otherwise vague and no specific mention was made that these vessels were definitely hostile. The composition as reported was very similar to that of Force D and it was held conceivable that the Swordfish might have been reporting contacting with them rather than the enemy. The *Ark Royal* was therefore asked to elaborate on the first brief message, though Somerville was pretty sure that these were the enemy after all. He immediately ordered all units to raise steam for full speed and Captain De Salis, Captain (D) 8th Destroyer Flotilla, was instructed to sort his ships out in readiness. Two were to be assigned to escort and protect *Ark Royal* in her flying operations when she would have to act independently, and two more were left to protect the convoy. It sounded sparse, as it was, for even with the damaged *Hotspur* and the *Despatch* in company their cover was pitiful should the expected air attack develop. But this was all his meagre forces allowed for.

Accordingly De Salis assigned the two new destroyers, *Jaguar* and *Kelvin*, to look after the carrier and the two oldest destroyers, *Duncan* and *Wishart*, to assist *Despatch* and *Hotspur* with the convoy. This left the hardcore veterans of the 8th Flotilla to form up with the battle line ready for surface action, *Faulknor*, *Firedrake*, *Forester*, *Fury* and *Encounter*. *Ark Royal* was told to prepare a torpedo-bomber striking force and the *Despatch* was ordered to take the convoy out of harm's way at full speed on a course of 120°. The anti-aircraft cruiser *Coventry* of Force D was ordered to join the convoy's escort as soon as she could, but the rest of that force was to rendezvous with the *Renown* as quickly as possible; *Ramillies* was signalled Somerville's intended course and speed to comply with this.[5]

All this took a little time but before long some semblance of fighting order came out of the chaos and the Italians had lost their chance to take Force H by surprise. An eyewitness aboard one of the destroyers described the scene:

We turned instantly, and even as we turned we felt the swift upward swing of the vibrations. Immediately the Captain put on another twenty turns. We saw up the line our flotilla leader turning also. We looked south and saw that the first of the Town class cruisers had turned. We looked to the westward and *Renown* was turning too.

And, as she turned, the signal flags crept up to form a line with the cruisers in the van, heading north-east. I shall never forget one fragment of that scene and the splendid excitement, never forget the instant leaping of those ships towards the north. They were like well-trained hounds, swinging immediate and eager to the far calling of the horn. We wanted no signal in that morning. There was no need for the whipping flags upon the yard-arm of the flagship.

'Only', said the Captain, his voice dubious, 'I don't suppose they'll stay'.[6]

At that moment Campioni was having the first grave doubts about whether it was, in fact, wise to stay. As at Calabria he was beginning to feel that events were rapidly getting beyond his control and, as before, his first flush of enthusiasm was wilting under the dictates of harsh reality and his orders. The first firm sighting report that the Italian Admiral had received that morning did not reach him until 1005. Admiral Iachino aboard the *Pola* got a signal from the scout plane of the *Bolzano*, timed at 0945, that she had made contact with the enemy force. This she reported as consisting of one battleship, two cruisers and four destroyers, some 26 miles, 20° from Cape de Fer on a course of 90° and maintaining a speed of sixteen knots. Campioni aboard the *Vittorio Veneto* picked up a similar signal at 1015, and the aircraft kept up a stream of sightings until 1040 without elaborating on the numbers involved.

If her reports were accurate then Campioni was presented with the chance he had been hoping for. A vastly inferior British force lay just below the horizon and he could deal it a heavy blow before the ships from the west could join up with them. It seemed too good an opportunity to miss. As the Italian Admiral himself later recorded, it seemed as though Force D lay in his grasp. 'The numbers of the units (reported by *Bolzano*) coincided exactly with the group of ships reported the previous night off Cape Bon; their position indicated that they had come from the direction of Cape Bon ...'[7]

If he could get in his attack outnumbering the enemy at least two to one, he could annihilate this force and still be left with the choice of whether to withdraw to his bases with a victory under his belt (a tempting option) or stand and await the second British force, also inferior to his own. He decided to do just this and at 1100 he ordered his two battleships to turn south towards the sighting report with the cruisers leading the way. At this stage he was committed to action and the two fleets were on direct contact courses. The Italian battleships increased speed and the *Gorizia* was instructed to fly off her own scout plane to relieve the *Bolzano* plane which had ceased transmission.

It was now a race against time. Could the junction of the two British forces be effected before the Italian fleet hove into sight. Due to his lack of precise or correct information, it was a race that Campioni, had he known it, was doomed to lose.

Meanwhile Somerville was a little better served by his own reconnaissance planes, but, despite some confusion brought about by their conflicting reports, was able to gauge the situation more accurately.

By 1030 the three 6-inch cruisers, *Manchester*, *Sheffield* and *Southampton*, were effecting their concentration in the traditional manner in the van, and these, along with the 8th Flotilla, were stationed 050°, five miles ahead of the flagship on the estimated plot bearing of the Italians. Somerville signalled to Malta at 1032 giving the reported positions of the two Italian battleships as more news came in from the Swordfish of the various Italian formations to the north-east of him. All three Italian formations had now been located by these aircraft, both cruiser divisions and the battleship division astern of them. There remained however some doubt about the actual composition of these various forces, as Somerville himself recorded:

> There were, however, a number of discrepancies between the reports both as to position and composition so that it was not possible to get a clear picture of the situation. It seemed certain that five or six enemy cruisers were present but it was doubtful whether the number of battleships was one, two or three. But, whatever the composition of the enemy force, it was clear to me that in order to achieve my object – the safe and timely arrival of the convoy at its destination – it was essential to show a bold front and attack the enemy as soon as possible.[8]

Accepting the possible odds of three heavy ships against his battle-cruiser Somerville held on north-eastward. At 1058 came the welcome news that Force D was only some 34 miles away from him, 070°. This came from one of the Malta-based Sunderland flying-boats who closed the *Renown* and flashed the news by lamp. Somerville now knew that the required junction of his two groups was certain to be achieved before meeting the enemy and the speed of his force was therefore reduced to 24 knots to effect this and keep his ships between the enemy and the convoy.

Meanwhile he instructed the Sunderland to locate and shadow those enemy units, last reported to be some fifty miles away, and report their numbers more precisely than the Swordfish had so far been able to do.

The abrupt change of course ordered by Campioni, from due west to due east in order to intercept what he took to be Force D, was soon noted and reported by the shadowing Swordfish. At 1115 they duly signalled this to Somerville. It gave the appearance that the Italians were now in full flight for their home bases but Somerville knew that, after his concentration, he might yet be in a position to cut them off. In fact, at this point, Campioni, as we have seen, was still hoping to give battle and was unaware just how close Force H was to the south of him. He was soon to be disillusioned.

CHAPTER SEVENTEEN

Rendezvous Effected

We have seen that Admiral Campioni had reversed the direction of his fleet at 1100 on receipt of the sighting of what he took to be the British force from the eastern basin. Let us examine further the signals and events that led to this decision and the immediate results, remembering always that the prevention of the two British forces meeting was critical to his plans.

He had already sent signals to Supermarina at 1030, letting them know that the enemy had aircraft tracking his every move, and at 1045 and 1100 let them know his intentions of turning east, and the possibility of an engagement with an inferior British force, the one sighted at 0945. Ahead of the C-in-C Admiral Iachino had then to comply with two orders, one to launch further scouting aircraft, (*Gorizia* catapulted a third floatplane off at this time), and secondly to reverse course with all his units. He ordered the 3rd Division astern of his own (on a course of 270°) at a distance of some three miles in readiness for this abrupt change of course. At 1115, having advised Campioni of his intentions, Iachino's big cruisers came about on their new course. Admiral Somerville recorded what happened next:

> The enemy who had originally been reported as steering to the westward, were now reported as altering course to the eastward at 1115.
>
> An observer who witnessed this alteration of course reported that the eastern group of cruisers appeared to be thrown into a state of confusion. The leading ship turned 180° whilst the two following ships turned only 90°. Collision appeared to have been narrowly averted and at one time all three ships appeared to be stopped with their bows nearly touching each other.[1]

Meanwhile Campioni had received a signal from Supermarina, time of origin 1010 and no doubt influenced by the further amplifications of the torpedo boat patrols at Trapani, which gave him further precise instructions; these were to continue cruising to the south of Sardinia probing with his two cruiser divisions until noon, pending results from his aerial reconnaissance. Should nothing positive materialise he was to return to base.[2] As this instruction had obviously been outdated by events, Campioni decided at first to ignore it and hold to his planned intentions.

At the conclusion of their turn eastward and pending their run south-east to make contact with the reported British squadron the positions of the Italian forces were as follows:

The *Pola* group, with Iachino, was some thirty miles 206° from Cape Teulada on Sardinia's south-western tip, on a course of 135° at eighteen knots.

The *Trieste* group was still sorting itself out to take station on the *Pola* group according to Iachino's instructions.

The main force with the two battleships was some twelve miles north of these cruisers at 75°.

Meanwhile the continued, and largely untroubled, presence overhead of the Swordfish from the *Ark Royal*, was causing the Italian admirals much justified concern. While they were groping for their opponents and having to rely solely on their few ship-borne seaplanes for information, the British had a constant watch over their every turn and alteration, and this within a stone's-throw of their own airfields at Sardinia. Admiral Campioni must have reflected bitterly on his experience at Calabria and the knowledge that the Air Force was being no more helpful now than then, must have influenced a great deal his subsequent decisions. In all events at 1120 he was stung into sending a signal to Marina Cagliari asking for the intervention of the promised fighter cover to drive these snoopers away. The response was instant, but by then too late. A flight of three CR42 biplane fighters was sent off at 1138. The channel of communications between the Italian Admiral and his escorting fighters was a tortuous one, the chain of communications for each request and order going from *Vittorio Veneto*'s bridge to Marina Cagliari ashore. They then passed it on to the Air Force authorities, Comando Aeronautica Sardegna, who re-transmitted it to the aircraft themselves. There was no direct link for controlling his fighter cover and consequently it was absolutely ineffective.

It will be noted that the chain of communications from Somerville's Swordfish to *Renown*'s bridge was far more direct, although it went by way of the *Ark Royal*. Even this caused confusion and doubt, as we have already seen, but at least the British admiral was far better served in this respect than his Italian opposite number, and, moreover, he could call on aircraft trained at sea and

F R A N C E

S P A I N

Gibraltar

Convoy and
Force 'H'

FRENCH NORTH AFRICA
(VICHY GOVERNMENT)

The WESTERN
MEDITERRANEAN

⊕ Axis Naval Bases
⚓ " Air Bases

SPEZIA

ITALY

ADRIATIC SEA

YUGOSLAVIA

CORSICA

Grosseto

SARDINIA

TYRRHENIAN SEA

Naples

Taranto

Villacidro
Elmas
Decimomannu
Monseratto

Battle Zone

Force 'H'

Convoy

C. Blanc

Palermo
Trapani
Castelvetrano

Messina

SICILY
Catania
Gerbini

Comiso

Bizerta

C. Bon

Pantelleria

Malta

TUNISIA

Units from Med Fleet

Em

manned by naval personnel, thus much more aware of the needs and problems of the situation than the Italian airman. Although both sides had much to learn about aircraft control in a naval battle, the British were far in advance in this respect.

Despite these handicaps Campioni held on for battle. At 1135 he ordered the cruiser squadrons on to a bearing 195° from *Vittorio Veneto* and aimed to keep his whole fleet in close contact for the final lead-in towards the expected enemy units. He was still under the impression that no junction of the two British forces had taken place, or was likely to take place for some time, and he still felt confident. His thoughts at this time were as follows;

> I had in mind that the English Forces were inferior to the Italian. Furthermore, encounter would be brought about in waters closer to Sicily than Sardinia, that is, in conditions favourable to us.[3]

For these optimistic plans Campioni was relying on totally misleading information, and nor did his sources of contact rectify this lamentable state of affairs for some time. On *Renown*'s bridge, however, things were coming together much more satisfactorily for the British.

Some ten minutes before Campioni had begun his final concentration for battle against an isolated British squadron the welcome sight of *Ramillies* and her consorts greeted British observers with Force H. When they first hove in sight they were bearing 073° some 24 miles off and cutting the corner. It was now a case of slowing down what many thought to be a fleeing enemy fleet, and, as always, this depended upon the effectiveness of the *Ark Royal*'s torpedo bombers. The first striking force of eleven Swordfish were duly flown off at this time.

The shadowing British aircraft continued to send in a stream of reports but their plotting remained vague in some cases and on the *Renown*'s bridge it appeared at this time as if they were facing two enemy battleships at least six cruisers and a host of destroyers. Somerville therefore ordered the *Ramillies* to steer 045° ahead of the oncoming Force H so as not to be left astern in the stern-chase all were sure was now developing. The *Berwick* and *Newcastle* were instructed to join the other cruiser in the line ahead of the fleet and duly complied, extending the line formed by the 18th Cruiser Squadron and *Sheffield*. The escorting destroyers similarly placed themselves at the disposal of the Captain De Salis, an especially poignant sight for Somerville. 'The sight of *Defender* nipping across our stern and round our bows, and the old Bo [his son John] and I waving to one another like mad ...'[4]

The old *Ramillies*, also, made a stirring and heartening sight as she drew closer.

She was magnificent, her great-beamed hull thrusting along, throwing on either side of her enormous bows a fair half of the middle-sea – *Ramillies* driving her 25-year-old engines to unheard-of pressures. Even twenty-five years ago she had a speed of twenty-two knots only. We went past her as a swallow past an eagle. Her guns were trained already, elevated as if they were trying to reach over the barren sea towards the enemy. All the way down her sides the spray leapt high in a succession of angry flourishes. Her wake was broad and as tumbled as the well-trodden pathway of the F's. From her mainmast she flew already her battle flag, a vast white ensign, stiff as a metal banneret upon the wind.[5]

At 1134 therefore the situation on the British side can be summarised thus.

Manchester, *Southampton* and *Sheffield* were steering in single line ahead about five miles fine of *Renown*'s port bow, and *Berwick* and *Newcastle* were hastening to join them from the east. About two miles behind the cruisers Captain De Salis in *Faulknor* was organising the destroyers and planning to station them at three miles, 270°, from his own ships. Ten miles fine on *Renown*'s starboard bow *Ramillies* had started to swing into line on a parallel course making her best speed ever. So far all the defective ships of Force D, had, despite their engineering difficulties, given of their best and the battle line was formed exactly as Somerville had planned.

At 1134, on the last known sighting reports of the enemy's speed and distance, Somerville had ordered an increase in speed to 28 knots and, at 1140, course of the whole British squadron was altered to 050° to close the enemy.

Several British accounts of this action state, quite incorrectly, that at this juncture, *Renown* 'ran a bearing' which forced her drop out of the chase. In view of historical accuracy this matter should be set right, and Captain A.W. Gray, *Renown*'s engineering officer, provides us with the correct information on this as follows:

To my knowledge *no* extra attention was paid to the running of the main machinery other than was always carried out when steaming, and everything had been efficient until information was received at 1140 on the control platform of the main machinery that the temperature of the H.P. Pinion Bearing in the gearing compartment of the starboard inner shaft had increased to 170°. I would remark that since 1015 we had worked up to 28 knots.[6]

His own official report of the incident gives the sequence of events that followed:

> After two days at sea, on 27 November, the temperature of the Aft HP pinion bearing on the starboard inner shaft was reported at 1140 to have increased to 170, the average temperature of the other pinion bearings being 114, which is normal for high speeds. Five minutes later the temperature had dropped to 165 and the bearing oil pressure was increased from the usual 12 lbs to 18 lbs. The ship had worked up to 270 revs from 198 revs in 52 minutes and at 1117 commenced easing down to 216 revs.
>
> At 1135 orders were received to work up to 260 revs, the engines at that time were running at 220 revs, and then increased to 240 revs, with the intention of working up to 260 revs as ordered. *On receipt of the information* concerning the temperature of the Aft HP bearing (ie at 1140) and observing that the ship was about to go into action against the enemy, it was considered essential to keep the starboard inner engine in use if practicable. With this end in view this shaft was run at 240 revs, and the starboard outer increased to 276 revs, the port shafts being run at 260 revs. The temperature of the bearing continued to fluctuate between 153 and 160 at this speed. At 1245 revs ordered were 278 but the starboard inner shaft was kept at 240, observing it was essential to keep the ship in action at the highest possible speed.[7]

At 1154 the Sunderland flying boat that Somerville had sent off to investigate further, returned to the fleet and made a report of six cruisers and eight destroyers bearing 330° at thirty miles from *Renown*, but that no enemy battleships had been seen. The Sunderland then veered off omitting to signal the course and speed of the Italians. This report gave rise to fears that the Italian cruisers might in fact have been trying to work round astern of the British fleet with a view of engaging and destroying the *Ark Royal*, now alone save for her two destroyer escorts, and at some distance from the fleet. This illustrates the comparative helplessness of aircraft carriers away from their escorting battleships in battle, a weakness and vulnerability all too readily ignored by the exponents of air power at sea at the time and since the war. It was sufficient enough a worry to Somerville for him to comment that:

No further report of this group was received during the action and I was consequently in doubts as to its whereabouts and intentions. *Ark Royal* was however between my main forces and the convoy and I considered that returning aircraft would sight and report this group should they attempt to work around to a position from which to attack the convoy. Course was however altered to the north so as not to get too far to the eastward.[8]

It can thus be seen how even the small things, like an incomplete sighting report and concern for the vulnerable aircraft carrier, caused a change in course which gave the Italians many more precious minutes in which to evade destruction. Of such matters are battles decided.

Somerville's slight alteration north took place even as Campioni was changing his course also, away from the oncoming British and towards the safety of the Italian coast. Both movements came about as a result of air sightings and had the effect of opening the gap between the fleets which hitherto had been on converging routes that would have brought them into contact much earlier. For at this time the scales were somewhat lifted from the Italian admiral's eyes, although even so not fully. His aircraft reports were no more accurate than Somerville's.

It was at 1152 that the *Gorizia*'s seaplane signalled the first results of her own sortie. She detailed that one battleship and four destroyers were to the south on a course 090°. Another aerial sighting, much delayed because of the above mentioned chain of communications, was received on the bridge of the *Vittorio Veneto* at 1155. This sighting came from a Regia Aeronautica bomber on a routine mission and she had, at 1110, sighted a British convoy escorted by one battleship, one aircraft carrier and six destroyers. The convoy consisted of three 7,000-ton merchant ships, '... in quadrant K/3653, on a course of 180° some twenty miles from the Italian flagship, bearing 90°, at a speed of 16 knots.'[9]

This was the *very first* intimation that Campioni had received that a British convoy was out, and on receipt of this all the other British movements fell into place. The possibilities presented thus were enormous, could he but take advantage of the situation. It was obvious however to the plotters on the bridge of the Italian battleship that the enemy was much closer than had been previously reported, and if this were so his own cruisers would surely sight them themselves before much longer, they being some 12 miles ahead of the flagship to the WSW. It appeared to him that the two British forces must have combined and be almost upon him (such indeed was the case) and this put a much different complexion on the issue. 'A state of affairs was thus created which, taking into consideration all the information at my disposal, was unfavourable to us numerically and qualitatively.'[10]

Bragadin summarises the situation as it appeared to the Italians at this time in this fashion:

> In view of the critical situation in which the Italian fleet found itself after the Taranto attack, the combat group had received orders to seek battle only when it was in decisively superior force. Consequently, toward noon, when the information was convincing that the British forces were superior to the Italian, Admiral Campioni manoeuvered to avoid contact and to return to base.

He adds: 'Again the inadequacy of Italian air reconnaissance had led to an erroneous command decision.'[11]

Campioni concluded that: 'Under these conditions, in conformity with the spirit and letter of the orders received and with what at the moment I deemed to be my duty, I decided not to become involved in a battle.'[12]

The question now was, had he in fact left it too late to do so? It is interesting to notice that just at the precise moment that Campioni had come to the conclusion that the British groups had joined forces, Somerville was of the opinion that the Italians were still unaware of this fact. In his subsequent report the British admiral expressed the following opinions:

> At this time the prospects of bringing the enemy to action appeared favourable.
> (i) We had effected our concentration of which the enemy appeared to be unaware, since no shadowers had been sighted or reported by RD/F, and his speed had been reported as between 14 and 18 knots, which suggested he was still awaiting the reports of reconnaissance.
> (ii) The sun was immediately astern and if remaining unclouded would give us the advantage of light.
> (iii) There seemed every possibility of a synchronised surface and T/B attack if the nearest position of the enemy was correct, and provided that he did not retire at once at high speed.[13]

But the latter course of action was just what Campioni was deciding to adopt. Nonetheless Somerville was not privy to this decision and made his plans according to his best knowledge of the situation.

Somerville listed his intentions accordingly, as to drive off the enemy from any position from which he could attack the convoy. That was, and remained throughout, as he had said all along it would, his main consideration. Secondly he would accept *some risk* to the convoy, but only if there was a reasonable prospect of sinking one or more of the Italian battleships. The conditions that had to be achieved before he would contemplate the latter course of action he specified as either a hit by the Swordfish torpedoes on one of the enemy capital ships which would reduce her speed to less than twenty knots, or the engagement of the enemy battleships by the *Renown* and *Ramillies together*. Up against one of the most modern battleships in the world neither of the two British veterans could hope to reduce her on their own.

Renown's hot bearing combined with a dirty bottom and paravanes, Somerville later stated in his report, were limiting her best speed to 27½ knots, while of course the *Ramillies* was at least five knots slower than this. As both Italian heavy units were known to have speeds in excess of thirty knots the choice really came down to the simple one of whether or not the Fleet Air Arm crews could score at least one damaging torpedo hit on the enemy battleships. In pre-war exercises this had seemed simple, but as Calabria and the *Strasbourg* incident had already shown, this was far from the case in actual combat conditions.

Whatever the fears being expressed on *Renown*'s bridge the men of the British ships engaged went into the battle fully confident of the outcome. One officer aboard the destroyer leader *Faulknor* wrote: 'I can still recall the excitement when the buzz reached the engine room that we were now between the Italian heavies and their bases.'[14]

It must be realised that very few of the ships steaming at full speed towards what they thought to be a superior enemy battle fleet that day in the sunlight, had ever operated in each other's company before. The ships of Force D indeed, were not privy to Somerville's detailed battle plans, nor had the two light cruisers of the 18th CS served with Force H before. Of the same class, speed and armament the *Manchester*, *Newcastle*, *Sheffield* and *Southampton* might have been, and a brave sight they made ahead of the fleet, but, as the captain of the latter states, their reactions were instinctive rather than planned.

My recollections are confined to that of an individual captain of a cruiser filled to overflowing with soldiers and civilians, one could almost say an integral part of the convoy. This was to become the first occasion that these four 6-inch cruisers had met as a fighting force. As we met as we met! You must, and probably do, realise that in battle a Captain is fully occupied in fighting and manoeuvering his own ship with or without knowledge of the general plan.

In the Mediterranean the planning was done between Winston Churchill, James Somerville and Andrew Cunningham and the greatest secrecy was observed. The individual captains had to 'Play it off the Cuff', under the direction of The Great Enigma and two great and self-willed sailormen with almost nothing in common. Fun while it lasted, but for none of us did it last long afloat![15]

Meanwhile, at 1207, Admiral Campioni ordered the concentration of all his groups at 1210 on a course of 90°, giving time for the *Pola* to launch yet a fourth seaplane, and then told the cruisers to increase speed to effect this concentration without further delay; the cruisers at that time were already making 25 knots. Further signals continued to come and go between Campioni and Supermarina; the Italian admiral advised them of his decision and Supermarina headquarters in Rome, more out of touch with the fast-developing scene, asked for his detailed reasons. These were not resolved until 1256 when Campioni was able to convince them that he was hotly engaged with superior forces.

A further misfortune had affected the Italians at noon, when the destroyer *Lanciere*, part of the escort for the *Trieste* Division, the most southerly and exposed of the Italian units under Admiral Sansonetti, developed defects in her engines and, as she was the leader of the 12th Destroyer Squadron, her compatriots were left steering slightly off course and behind their consorts for a while.

The bulk of the other Italian ships were complying with their instructions to return to their bases (Naples in the case of Sansonetti) and steering to resume contact with their C-in-C. At 1215, on the southern edges of these cruisers, the four unfortunate destroyers, steering to resume their screening positions, sighted what they took to be a cruiser bows-on. They only caught a brief glimpse of this vessel before it vanished in the distance.

Two minutes later however they signalled to the *Vittorio Veneto* that, at 1216, the destroyer *Alfieri* of the 9th Squadron, had sighted several cruisers to the south of her, at a range of about 3,000 metres; then one battleship and three cruisers were reported by her, on a bearing of 180°. Campioni informed Supermarina that the enemy group was in contact and that he was continuing to withdraw to his bases on a route of 90°.

Almost at the same time the captain of the cruiser *Pola* sighted at 200° a cruiser, which he correctly identified as being of the Cumberland class. It was of course the *Berwick*, with four smaller cruisers all heading north at high speed. He could also detect the presence by its smoke, of at least one battleship astern of them and perhaps two.

From the British side the point of contact was equally dramatic. It was at 1207 that puffs of smoke were observed from the bridge of the *Renown* far off on the horizon, bearing 006° and the leading British cruisers sighted both masts and then ships across their northern horizon. These leading cruisers were by now disposed on a line of bearing of 075°-255° in order from west to east, *Sheffield*, *Southampton*, *Newcastle*, *Manchester* and *Berwick*, but the *Newcastle* was dropping steadily behind the others as her defects began to tell, and in fact never got fully into line.

Nor was that the end of the cruisers' misfortunes for the *Berwick* also was feeling the pace. She reported that her best speed was limited to 27 knots and informed Somerville that in view of this she was falling back to take station with *Renown* astern. Vice-Admiral Holland, sensing that the action was about to become hot, wanted his only 8-inch ship to stay in line if she could and ordered *Berwick* to join him but by that time *Berwick* had made her turn and by the time she came round again she had lost a lot of valuable ground. Urging the best from her fading engines she eventually took station on the *Manchester*'s starboard bow but soon dropped back again.

The eager destroyers at this time, nine in all, a full flotilla, were still moving into their positions five miles 040° from the *Renown* in the classic position to be able to counter-attack any torpedo assaults by enemy destroyers on the two British battleships.

Further signals continued to be relayed from *Ark Royal* to *Renown* from the Swordfish patrols. One, timed at 1147, finally reached Somerville at 1213. It stated that the enemy fleet consisted of two battleships and six cruisers. It did not however put Somerville's mind at rest as to the location, or existence, of the other group reported by the Sunderland further to the westward of him. The final plot as the fleets came into action then, showed the situation as the British saw it as follows:[16]

A western group of three cruisers and some destroyers was visible between 340° and 350°, eleven miles off, hull down and steering north. An eastern group of cruisers and destroyers, further away and to the right, steering 100°. No sign of the two reported Italian battleships nor the other cruiser group (which was in fact non-existent) reported by the Sunderland.

The *actual* Italian dispositions at this time were as follows:

The *Pola* and the 1st Division were in line ahead at 28 knots on a course of 90°. These were the so-called Eastern Group. The 3rd Division was also steaming in line ahead on the same course, at 25 knots waiting for their destroyers to catch them up. This was the Western Group. The two battleships were some 24,000 metres left of *Pola*'s force (bearing 60°), again on course 90°, at a speed of 25 knots.

For the second time in five months Admiral Campioni found his fleet in contact with the Royal Navy against his wishes or desires. On the first occasion his destroyers' smoke screens had saved his bacon. How would he fare in this second encounter?

CHAPTER EIGHTEEN

'Run, Rabbit, Run'

As the two forces hove in sight of each other the position of the 3rd Cruiser Division on the Italian side was unenviable. They had already fallen behind during the change of course ordered by Admiral Iachino at 1101, and were indeed, as British pilots reported, in some state of confusion following this incident which was caused by the incorrect interpretation of what course to steer made by the captain of the *Trento*. As we have seen, this led to all sorts of trouble and by the time they had sorted themselves out not only were they left behind, but were themselves out of order with the flagship *Trieste* in the centre of the column instead of leading it.

Despite this it was the Italians who commenced firing first. Admiral Campioni had just signalled all his forces 'Do not, repeat, not, engage in battle',[1] when, at 1220, Admiral Matteucci ordered his own division from the *Fiume*, to open fire. He judged that the situation, not visible from the Italian battleships, more than justified this command, a decision which was later upheld. Much as Campioni adjudged the position to be unfavourable for combat it was now largely out of his hands and the Italian cruisers had no choice but to defend themselves from the fast approaching British ships.

All the Italian cruisers took up the firing in quick succession to each other. The distance that the first salvos were fired were 22,000 yards from the 1st Division and 21,500 from the 3rd Division, and the opening Italian shots were extremely good and highly accurate, achieving instant straddles on the flagship of Admiral Holland, the *Manchester*, and on the *Berwick* which was then still just holding her own alongside.

The general course of the opening cruiser duel, and indeed of the subsequent action, lay in a north-easterly direction, and the ranges varied considerably from each Italian squadron engaged, from 22,500 down to only 18,000 yards for the *Trento* and 17,000 for the *Fiume*, which was lagging slightly with engine difficulties. The fall of shot was almost exclusively centred on the rear of the Italian fleet and the advance guard cruisers of the British.

On the Italian side the intensity of fire was at its peak in the opening minutes of the combat until 1242. It became intermittent between that time and 1249 owing to the attentions of the British torpedo bombers which made their attacks; then it reached a new intensity between 1240 and 1253, and slowed down until 1305 because the ranges were becoming extreme. By 1315 the range was estimated to be 26,000 yards and the Italian 8-inch ships were not able to reach the enemy and fire was ceased.

From the British side the flashes of the enemy guns heralded the opening of the action at 1220 and the 8-inch shell splashes were uncomfortably close to the *Manchester*; they were exact for range but about one hundred yards out for line. The British ships returned their fire at once, but only the *Berwick* could match the ranges of their opponents. Nevertheless the twelve-gun salvos from the four 6-inch ships made a bold display and the Italians were almost immediately observed to be making smoke and turning away. In the odd intervals when they became visible through the clouds of smoke it was observed that they were making frequent alterations of course. As they zig-zagged away through the smoke they sometimes appeared almost end-on to the pursuing British gunners, sometimes almost broadside but they were engaged, largely ineffectually, whenever they could be seen.

At 1223 Somerville signalled the news to Cunningham, that he was engaged with the enemy battle fleet and at the same time two strange ships were sighted at extreme visibility steering a course between the two opposing battle lines. At first they were thought to be the long-awaited Italian battleships but it was later realised that they were more cruisers of the so-called Eastern Group.

Aboard the *Firedrake* a watching journalist set the scene:

Closer and closer – they were shouting the ranges now from the director, long strings of figures that meant only that the enemy was still too far for us to tackle.

Closer and closer – the wind that whipped our signal flags seemed now more eager, vigorous. The tiny streamers of grey haze which showed from the funnels of the cruisers seemed to whip back more furiously.[2]

The *Renown* and *Ramillies* were now pounding up in support of the cruisers.

I was on the bridge of *Renown* when the first enemy reports came in. Action Stations were soon sounded off and I went to my surface station which was in the after 15-inch control position. As Second Gunnery Officer I had charge of the AA armament in AA action but in surface action I was placed in the armoured after control position – this was a very antiquated method of fire control and my job was therefore to take over only in the event of the main forward control position being knocked out.

I mention this because the view from the after control was restricted forward between 30 degrees on either bow. 'Y' Turret was similarly restricted – or almost so as we found to our discomfort in the action off Norway earlier when we could almost hang our caps on the muzzles of 'Y' turret![3]

At 1224 the *Renown* came into action, taking as her first target the right-hand ship of the Western Group at a mean range of 26,500 yards. She loosened off six salvos at this cruiser before it vanished into the smoke haze. Two minutes later the *Ramillies* commenced firing at extreme elevation to see if she could reach the enemy. Two salvos were fired but despite her best efforts her straining engines could not achieve more than 20.7 knots and she was soon left astern.

Meanwhile it was hot work with the cruisers leading the assault. The *Manchester*, *Newcastle* and *Sheffield* all chose as their target the right-hand ship of the Western Group. The *Berwick* opened fire at the same squadron (the 3rd Division) but selected the left-hand ship, while the *Southampton* engaged the left-hand ship of the Eastern Group (the *Pola*'s division).

We turned to line ahead and manoeuvered to close the enemy and opened fire on targets indicated by the Admiral, difficult to distinguish in the smoke. I had no idea of the identities of the captains of the two cruisers we were in line with at this time.[4]

I remember the Town class cruisers of the 18th CS making a fine sight just before *Renown*'s starboard beam as they rushed into action firing very heavily. They were under fire themselves but the enemy spread of their fall of shot was very large at this time and I don't think that they were hit – but I believe the County class cruiser *Berwick* received one hit at around this time. I didn't actually see this.[5]

As Somerville later recorded:

No concentration of fire was ordered owing to the speed with which the situation changed and to the large selection of targets available.

Moreover, as Vice-Admiral Commanding, 18th Cruiser Squadron, states in his report, it is doubtful what the results of an attempt at concentration would have been, as ships of the 18th Cruiser Squadron had not been in company for a considerable time and assembled on the battleground from Rosyth, Reykjavik, Malta and the vicinity of the Azores.[6]

The *Manchester* was deluged with the spray from near misses and was very fortunate indeed to escape being hit, but her luck held. Both she and the *Sheffield* continued to engage their initial target in unison until 1236 and 1240 respectively, but *Newcastle* switched target to *Berwick*'s cruiser after firing 18 broadsides, while the *Southampton* ceased firing when her ship was lost in the murk, and took on a destroyer instead. She fired on this concentrated salvos at this ship for eleven minutes and claimed to have scored one hit on her at least. This was the unfortunate *Lanciere* and she was indeed hit twice, as we shall see.

Other targets were thought to have been hit. The *Faulknor* at 1227 and the *Newcastle* six minutes later reported seeing a cruiser of the Western Group hit, by a large calibre shell, but this was not observed by the *Renown*.

In return the accuracy of the enemy's opening fire was soon seen to be falling off, especially so when the Swordfish commenced their attacks on them, but the Italians were rewarded when, at 1222 an 8-inch shell hit *Berwick* on Y turret. The turret was put out of action and the turret crew suffered heavy casualties, mainly of the Royal Marine gunners inside.

We saw on *Berwick* suddenly a red flash that was not gunfire. Simultaneously splashes hid her after-part. As she drew clear she trailed a thin brown smoke behind her that was not gun smoke. She seemed to hesitate a moment, opening away from the other ships. Then she came back, firing again – three turrets only.[7]

They say war is glamorous, but I was there when they opened up Y turret, and I don't want to see the like again.[8]

By now 1234 the principal targets were fading in the smoke. The Western Group vanished completely and Vice-Admiral Holland directed his ships to switch to the still visible cruisers of the Eastern Group. As they did so, the *Berwick* was hit again by an 8-inch shell from a cruiser of this group. This shell again struck her aft, damaging officers' cabins and destroying the port after breakers room, but fortunately this time she escaped casualties. Apart from the loss of Y turret her fighting capabilities were completely unimpaired by these two hits, but her engines still continued to fail her and she dropped steadily out of the action. Nonetheless the impression given by Bragadin in his account is a completely misleading one. 'Soon after the *Berwick* received a damaging hit, and then was hit a second time so badly that a little while later she had to retire and proceeded slowly towards Gibraltar.'[9] In fact she did no such thing, nor was her withdrawal from the fight in any way attributable to these shell hits.

The *Renown* also, had been forced to switch targets due to the poor visibility on the battlefield. She altered course to starboard in order to lessen the distance between her and the reported Italian battleships and to bring the Western Group of cruisers broader on the bow. She was duly rewarded with a fleeting glimpse of the centre ship of this division, which she duly engaged with two salvos. To open up A arcs and give Y turret a chance to come into the action a further alteration in course was made to starboard and the left hand ship of the same division was then engaged with a further eight salvos as she bore 356°, but, by 1245, she too was lost in the haze.

> A and B turrets opened fire right ahead at extreme range – I don't think that Y fired very much. I could see nothing of the result but I don't think our fire was very effective. Visibility was good but there was a lot of smoke about and I doubt if any one expected much result – the action did not last very long and we were not fired at ourselves.
>
> I remember seeing the *Ramillies* pounding up astern, trying rather unsuccessfully to keep up and firing her forward turrets at their maximum elevation – she would have been about two miles astern of *Renown* and I remember thinking that she must really be out of range.[10]

There was still always the fear that one group of the Italian cruisers might take advantage of the smoke and work their way round ahead of the British ships to get at the convoy. Vice-Admiral Holland anticipated any such move by altering the course of his squadron from north to 090° thus placing the Eastern Group of the enemy, that furthest ahead, on to his port bow. The Italians had no such intentions of course, and continued to race eastward. As they crossed across the front of the British force it appeared that an attempt was being made to cross the 18th Cruiser Squadron's T, so they changed course southward again. Almost immediately that this was done the

enemy were observed making off again at high speed to the north-
east and it was clear that they had no such meaningful
considerations on their minds but were concerned solely with flight.
The 18th Cruiser Squadron thereupon came about again back to
070° at 1256 and 030° at 1258, but more ground had been lost.

At the time of this jostling for positions of advantage observers on
the leading British cruisers, *Manchester, Newcastle* and *Southampton*, all
reported seeing one of the enemy cruisers, the rear ship of the line,
heavily on fire aft and between 1252 and 1259 this vessel seemed to
be losing speed before again picking up after the others.
Unfortunately no report was made to Somerville of this incident by
the cruisers until after the action had terminated. In fact this was the
destroyer *Lanciere* and to see what the true position was on the other
side of the smoke pall that blanketed Somerville's north-eastern
horizon we shall once more revert to the Italian fleet.

Almost as soon as the action commenced, the *Fiume*, closest to the
British and at some risk due to her engine trouble, requested the 4th
Destroyer Squadron to lay down a smokescreen, and this curtain of
fog was at once effective. It was soon noticed how the accuracy of the
British salvos, and their intensity, began to fall off once they had
done their work. As at Calabria, the Italian destroyers' smokescreens had been put down both quickly and accurately and
probably saved the *Fiume* at least from destruction. Thereafter the
British could only engage at intervals in the main part, although a
particularly heavy concentration of fire on the 3rd Division was
noted at 1240 before they switched targets to the 1st Division, clear
of the smoke.

The superior speed of the Italian heavy cruisers soon began to
make itself felt with the 1st Division under Iachino, working up
quickly from 27 to 34 knots. The older Trieste class ships could not
match this but were still able to outpace the British vessels, and
would likewise have drawn clear very quickly had they not been
handicapped by their various misfortunes earlier: their destroyers'
accident, the handicap of the *Fiume* and the damage done by
Southampton to the *Lanciere*. Consequently it was on the 3rd Division
that the bulk of the British fire fell while *Pola* and her consorts
quickly reduced the gap between themselves and their C-in-C, thus
gaining the advantage of the covering fire of the two Italian
battleships. Iachino himself had ordered, at 1252, his own screen to
lay down their own smokescreens if necessary and their pall of smoke
soon blanketed their withdrawal.

Campioni meanwhile had been pressing eastward at 25 knots with his two heavy ships. The C-in-C could observe the rapid approach of the *Pola* group bows on to his flagship, as they closed the remaining distance, but it was observed that the 3rd Division had been forced to steer north to avoid the concentration of enemy fire and was thus in danger of falling even further behind, perhaps even of being cut off completely from the rest of the Italian fleet and destroyed in isolation. In order to give a measure of support to these hard-pressed units Campioni ordered his battleships to turn in a complete circle and this was commenced at 1227. As they turned back and round, the *Vittorio Veneto*'s own seaplane confirmed by signal the presence of at least two British battleships in the pursuing force. As the two Italian battleships completed their turn and stood off to the north-east, once more the leading British cruisers came into view at extreme range and, at 1300, the *Vittorio Veneto* opened fire with her main armament of 15-inch guns at the enormous range of 25 miles.

As Campioni reported: 'Quickly the distance between us dropped to 26 km (the maximum range of the older *Cesare*'s 12.6-inch main armament) and we engaged in an artillery duel with the leading enemy cruisers.[11]

However, as the two Italian ships completed their circle the range soon opened up again and the heavy ships were only engaged for about ten minutes before the British cruisers were seen to turn away.

Meanwhile, far astern the destroyer *Lanciere* was struggling after her pasting by *Southampton*. She, it will be remembered, was the squadron leader of the Italian flotilla screening on the most exposed side of the 3rd Division and Captain D'Arienzo reported that his ship was deluged with near misses before, inevitably, a 6-inch shell hit her and penetrated her after boiler room and exploded, almost immediately bringing her to a halt. Luckily the Italians' destroyers were built with two separate sets of machinery fore and aft and the forward engines managed to get her going again and she worked up to 23 knots while D'Arienzo ordered his two compatriots to shield him with smoke. Five minutes after the first hit, at 1240, while *Lanciere* was struggling north to pass across wakes of the 3rd Division cruisers to seek safety, a second 6-inch shell hit her on her port side, amidships. This projectile passed through the ship without exploding or else she would have been lost for certain. Then she reached the protection of the smoke.[12] But even as she entered its welcoming shroud a third shell from the *Southampton* landed hard alongside her. Again this shell failed to explode and her side plates were not pierced and no water entered the ship. The magnificent shooting of Captain Brooke's command was therefore nullified by faulty ammunition and *Lanciere* somehow survived her ordeal.

She was still in a desperate situation however, crippled, with her consorts vanishing fast and only her two loyal flotilla mates in company as the British fleet drew closer to her protecting smokescreen. Again she slid to a halt and lay dead in the water awaiting her fate.

As if this were not enough, the *Ark Royal*'s aircraft now began their attacks against the Italian squadron. It will be recalled that eleven Swordfish had been launched from the carrier, and they had now struggled to cover the distance between the *Ark Royal*, far astern of the main action, and the speeding enemy. As their own best speed was something less than 90 mph fully laden, and the enemy were retiring at speeds in excess of 30 knots, it was a considerable time before they could firstly locate the Italians, and then get into suitable positions to make their attacks. When they arrived over the battle zone they were able to make out that the Western Group were steering north-east, 'in a somewhat scattered state', and that the Eastern Group were steering south-east at high speed in line ahead. As the distance between the *Pola* group and the battleships was being rapidly reduced it was not long before the Swordfish could see these great vessels also, and they watched as Campioni's heavy vessels made their complete turn to take the pressure off the cruiser divisions. The Swordfish then manoeuvred to get up-sun from their targets and this took further time. The aircraft were of No 810 Squadron and led by Lieutenant Commander Mervyn Johnstone.

The whole eleven determined to attack the battleship force and the leader led them in over the destroyer screen, which they estimated at seven ships, towards the Italian flagship, which they correctly identified as one of the Littorio class. The Swordfish strike leader overshot this vessel in his approach and had to engage instead the Cavour class ship astern of her. Braving flak, which was not heavy, the remaining ten torpedo bombers made their assaults on the *Vittorio Veneto*, dropping at ranges between 700 and 800 yards from their giant adversary. They reported that as they passed the Italian cruisers they had fired heavy flak bursts into the air to attract the battleship's attention to the impending British aerial assault, even though the aircraft were well out of AA range, but that this ruse failed in its intentions and that, in their opinion, the Italian battle fleet had been caught by surprise. Flak was not opened by the battleships until the leading Swordfish had dropped down to about 1,500 feet and when the Italians did open intense fire with close-range weapons it was ill-directed.[13]

Despite this none of the British torpedo bombers scored a hit on either battleship, although they incorrectly claimed one hit on *Vittorio Veneto*. Immediately after the attack, during which the old biplanes had passed so close that they were able to machine-gun the battleships' bridges, both units started turning, the leading battleship violently north and the second ship passed ahead of her, but the retiring British torpedo bombers had to report that no loss of speed was obvious from either of their targets and clearly the first attempt by *Ark Royal*'s aircraft to influence the course of the battle had failed utterly. Once again then the torpedo bomber had failed to live up to its pre-war evaluation (and to its post-war inflated reputation). The fact that many historians have since claimed that the intervention of the Swordfish turned the tables and forced the Italians to flee is just so much nonsense, for, as we have seen, Campioni was determined on that course of events as soon as he realised he might have to face two British battleships and long before he was even aware that the *Ark Royal* was in the area.[14]

As the Swordfish retired from the scene they again passed close by the Iachino force of cruisers which engaged them with both heavy and accurate AA fire at 1245. Fortunately all escaped damage and were able to land on their carrier safely. At once frantic preparations were underway to make ready a second striking force. However it was clear that this would probably be too late and in any case would have to be made with far smaller forces than the first. Although Campioni stated that their attacks were 'carried out with resolution', it seemed that all hope of slowing down the Italians had now evaporated completely.

Meanwhile the *Renown* had lost sight of the enemy for a time and was seeking further targets. At this moment of high drama at the crescendo of the naval action a note of farce was introduced into the proceedings by the Vichy French. Two large ships were sighted from *Renown*'s bridge, steering resolutely between the fleets from out of the banks of smoke to the north. Could these be the Italian battleships come to offer combat? At once the 15-inch turrets trained round on this new bearing and prepared to open fire. Fingers trembled over firing keys and breeches closed on six one-ton projectiles in readiness for blasting them out of the water, when, at the last moment, word came that they had been identified as three-funnelled French liners, busy about their own mysterious affairs and not allowing a little thing like a battle to stop them! They passed on their haughty way, only one or two of the destroyers trying ranging shots on them for practice and for their cheek.

While this little incident was taking place Somerville decided that, as action against both Italian battleships was likely at any moment, it would be wisest for him to concentrate his own heavy units and commenced a turn back towards *Ramillies* to effect this. Just as this order was given however the Eastern Group of cruisers appeared again beyond the murk and the *Renown* swung back to 070° to engage them once more. A spouting whale was at first thought to be an Italian submarine, which forced a temporary check to these plans while *Renown* turned away and at the same time further reports reached Somerville that the Italian heavy ships had been sighted by Vice-Admiral Holland's cruisers ahead. Within a short time the first salvos of 15-inch shells from these were pitching into the water close by the *Berwick* and *Manchester* and *Renown* abandoned her concentration plans with *Ramillies* and moved up in support of the 18th Cruiser Squadron's ships. At 1311 she again opened fire on the left-hand vessel of two ships on the horizon, thinking them to be the enemy battleships, but they were in fact heavy cruisers of the 3rd Division. Both salvos from *Renown* fell short of these targets and the range was seen to be opening up once more.

When Vice-Admiral Holland first sighted Campioni's ships at 1300 they were still making their turn and the two groups were on rapidly converging courses. The British cruisers therefore turned back to work round the flank of their mighty opponents and close with *Renown*, but, as they did this the Italians completed their own circle and were soon observed heading off north-east once more and the 18th Cruiser Squadron resumed their pursuit on a course of 050°.

Somerville made to Holland at 1308: 'Is there any chance of catching cruisers?' The reply was a regretful: 'No'. Holland estimated that the Italians had at least three knots excess speed over his fastest ship. Nothing now could be seen of the enemy from *Renown*'s bridge in the smoke.[15]

A Question of Priorities

Admiral Campioni had already made his main decision, made it indeed before ever the two fleets had come in sight of each other, and despite subsequent events he held to that decision absolutely. He had requested the Regia Aeronautica to provide fighter cover for his units, none had arrived. He had requested them to bomb the British fleet, well within its range. Although he didn't know it for certain at the time, this request, too, had not yet been complied with. His orders from Supermarina were clear enough, he was to avoid a battle unless he had a decided superiority. This, from reports from his scouting planes and his recent ordeal by fire, he did not have. He was clear in his mind then that his decision to return to base at the best speed he could and evade any further embroilment with Somerville's ships was the correct one.

However he was a sailor of a fighting force first, and however painful his decision may have been to him personally he was determined to bring his ships out of battle quickly. He would not, however, completely abandon his damaged units to the enemy. Although he was determined just to avoid contact with his main force the situation behind him called for some decision on their fates. In fact it was upon his second-in-command, Admiral Iachino, that the main decision rested in the event and he rose to it.

It was the *Lanciere*, stopped and damaged, which was the catalyst of this new development. As soon as word reached the C-in-C of her fate it was decided to order the 3rd Cruiser Division back to try and help her if it was at all possible. This would obviously involve those ships, with the limping *Fiume* as a further handicap, in considerable danger. Admiral Sansonetti was not prepared to risk his whole squadron needlessly and without specific instructions, but he expressed the wish to save his valiant little escort if he could. On learning that she was under tow by the *Ascari* he realised that it would mean exposing his cruisers to the risk of being overtaken by the British battleships and wiped out. Accordingly he signalled for further instructions to Iachino, ending with a determined plea to be allowed to attempt a rescue, at 1326. 'Demand permission to go back for *Lanciere*.'[1]

Iachino knew the feeling his fellow Admiral had, but he, likewise, knew it would be folly to risk a whole cruiser division for the sake of one destroyer. He replied to Sansonetti accordingly: 'Approve your return to *Lanciere*. On *no* account become engaged with superior enemy units and, if necessary, abandon *Lanciere*.'

Iachino also passed on the decision to Campioni and asked that the C-in-C should repeat the requests of air cover for the squadron. This was duly done, and, eventually, but too late to affect the issue, the fighters arrived only for them to mistake the Italian division for the enemy and commence straffing attacks on them. While the 3rd Division fought off their own aircraft further angry signals buzzed back to Sardinia calling them off. Truly the Italians were handicapped by the complete lack of understanding by the Regia Aeronautica of events at sea, a similar problem shared by all naval commands when dealing with land-based aircraft throughout the war.

Although overuled in their requests to send the heavy cruisers back, for a time the 3rd Division's course served to cover the withdrawal of the crippled destroyer as she struggled north to Cagliari and safety under tow of her flotilla mate. By 1246 however, it was clear that she had won clear and Sansonetti crossed her wake and turned north-east to follow the rest of the Italian fleet back towards Naples. *Lanciere*'s troubles were still not quite over however as we shall see shortly.

How was it that these ships remained unscathed during this period? For that we have to return to the bridge of the *Renown* and the situation as it appeared at the time.

At 1315, the brief exchanges between the 18th Cruiser Squadron and the Italian battleships had petered out and all the enemy units were out of sight or drawing rapidly away from the field of battle. Firing had practically ceased and the huge pall of smoke across the northern and north-eastern horizons obscured all attempts to ascertain if any damage at all had been inflicted upon the enemy. The Italian battleships were withdrawing at an undiminished pace which the *Renown*, let alone the *Ramillies*, could not hope to equal. Somerville was therefore faced with an agonising decision, which he summarised later thus:

In view of our rapid approach to the enemy coast I had to decide whether a continuance of the chase was justified and likely to be profitable. The arguments for and against continuing the chase appeared to be:

For Continuing the Chase:
(i) The possibility that the speed of the enemy might be reduced by some unforeseen eventuality.
(ii) He might appreciate that his force was superior to mine and decide to turn and fight.

Against Continuing the Chase:
(i) There was no sign that any of the enemy ships and especially his battleships had suffered damage, nor was there reasonable prospect of inflicting damage by gunfire in view of their superior speed. Unless the speed of the enemy battleships was reduced very materially he could enter Cagliari before I could bring him to action with *Renown* and *Ramillies*.
(ii) I was being led towards the enemy air and submarine base at Cagliari and this might well prove a trap. His appearance in this area appeared to be premeditated since it was unlikely that this was occasioned solely by the information he had received the previous night of Force D's presence in the Narrows.
(iii) The extrication of one of my ships damaged by air or submarine attack from my present position would certainly require the whole of my force and must involve leaving the convoy uncovered and insufficiently escorted during the passage of the Narrows.
(iv) The enemy main units had been driven off sufficiently far to ensure they could no longer interfere with the passage of the convoy.
(v) A second T/B attack could not take place until 1530 to 1600 by which time the convoy would be entirely uncovered and the enemy fleet could be under the cover of the AA batteries and fighters at Cagliari. I entertained little hope that the attack would prove effective as I knew that the second flight was even less experienced than the first.
(vi) I had no assurance that the cruisers reported to the north west might not be working round toward the convoy and *Ark Royal*.
(vii) It was necessary for contact to be made with the convoy before dark to ensure the cruisers and destroyers required for escort through the Narrows should be properly formed up. It was also necessary to provide the fullest possible scale defence against T/B and light surface attack at dusk. To effect this a retirement between 1300 and 1400 was necessary.[2]

These were the pros and cons weighed on the *Renown's* bridge that November day. The natural wish to continue the headlong chase of a flying enemy was very strong in the fleet generally. The frustrations of the First World War, when the Grand Fleet were unable to come to grips with an equally coy German opponent, were still a dominant memory among the officers of the Royal Navy, most of whom had served as juniors at that time. Their tails were up and the men themselves were full of self-confidence. But Admiral Somerville had to fight these natural desires and temper them with what he judged best for the whole operation, and that, in his viewpoint, was the safe arrival of the convoy. He had made that clear before the operation started, and, like his Italian opposite number this day, he stuck to his decision no matter how unpopular the outcome might be to the public at large.

He had no doubts in his mind that the correct course for him to adopt was to break off the chase and rejoin his convoy as quickly as possible, and in this decision he had the fullest support from his staff. One officer wrote that: 'James Somerville was so adored by all those in the Force that I think there would have been a near revolt had it been known that his judgement was being questioned!'[3]

Another wrote:

Everyone in Force H had great faith in James Somerville. At our final staff meetings before our 'Club Runs' James asked anyone who wanted to put forward his suggestions. At the end of the meeting James summed up and laid down exactly what we would do. I can only say that – as a highly critical staff officer – I never came away from those meetings without feeling quite certain that he had chosen the best of all alternatives.[4]

Somerville himself was to write to his wife of how he felt at making that decision:

I have no ambition, as you know, and, unlike Nelson, I don't crave for glory. All I want to do is the best I can to help the country as *I* see it. I have an urge to throw caution to the winds and take a chance on things but I stifle it when I feel that to do so would not be the right and best service I can do the country. I don't suggest that my judgement is infallible but where that judgement leads me I go and don't think of personal consequences.[5]

He added, with some bitterness:

For that reason I'd really much sooner be doing some useful but more obscure job where my rights or wrongs don't matter so much. Occasionally I get a bun from Their Lordships but usually it is carping criticism and I feel that if they don't feel that I'm the right one for this job then they'd better get rid of me.[6]

Bragadin's judgement is far more scathing, and more uninformed. He wrote, for American consumption, that:

> Admiral Somerville also gave no sign of wanting to continue the battle, though he had reasons to feel himself in a more advantageous situation than really was the case, for his torpedo planes claimed to have scored hits on the *Vittorio Veneto* and three Italian cruisers. At any rate he made no offensive move shortly afterwards when the Italian 3rd Cruiser Division returned to the aid of the *Lanciere* ...[7]

The Fleet Air Arm pilots only claimed *one* hit on the Italian battleship, nothing more, and the quoted Italian signals make clear what the 3rd Cruiser Divisions instructions were should the British re-appear, but this is ignored by Bragadin.

Nonetheless Somerville's resolution was put to the test shortly after the decision to call off the chase. At 1335 another air sighting report came in which stated that a damaged enemy cruiser was about thirty miles away, ten miles from the Sardinian coast. It was a tempting target and Somerville gave serious consideration to finishing off this straggler. There was no question of turning the heavy ships back that close to the Italian air bases but the practicality of detaching two fast cruisers to do the job *was* considered. Again there was discussion on the *Renown*'s bridge.

From his five cruisers Somerville had to decide which two to send off on this mission. The *Manchester* and *Southampton* were ruled out because of their passengers, his most experienced ship, the *Sheffield*, was the only one fitted with radar and this he needed to provide early warning for the convoy against the expected mass air attacks. This left only the *Berwick* and *Newcastle* and both had unreliable engines. Again Somerville's own report summarised the careful reasoning:

> I considered this most carefully but decided against such a detachment for the following reasons:
> (i) It would involve my main forces remaining in a position to support these cruisers and prevent them from being cut off by enemy forces.
> (ii) Action as in (i) would cause an unacceptable delay in rejoining the convoy.
> (iii) Isolated ships in such close proximity to the enemy coast would be singled out for air attack. *Berwick* was most vulnerable to this form of attack and her disablement would have involved all my force to effect her extraction.
> (iv) There was no evidence to indicate that the damaged ship would remain stopped and she might well effect an escape before she could be overtaken.

A subsequent air search failed to locate this cruiser, so it appears that the stoppage was, in fact, only temporary.[8]

In fact Somerville's decision was doubly correct, for the 'damaged cruiser' reported by the aircraft was of course, the crippled *Lanciere* before she was taken under tow, and to risk two cruisers to finish off one destroyer was an obviously stupid thing to have done. But once again unreliability from spotter planes could have led to a serious situation if taken at face value.

In the event Somerville called off the cruisers from their shadowing of the retiring enemy battleships, ordering Holland to take *Manchester* and *Southampton* to rejoin the convoy itself while the other three cruisers concentrated on the British battleships. *Ark Royal's* second striking force was allocated the mission of locating and finishing off this disabled 'cruiser' as soon as they could mount their assault, but at 1410 the carrier flew off seven torpedo bombers to comply with the earlier request for a final strike at the main Italian forces.

This force duly sighted first Iachino's 8-inch cruisers with the destroyer screen, some twelve miles off the south-eastern coast of Sardinia steering eastward at high speed. As they drew closer they also sighted the two Italian battleships, some eight miles ahead of the cruisers and surrounded by ten destroyers. Naturally the battleships were the prime target and were given as the torpedo-bombers' main objective. But the leader of this flight had been given full liberty to change his targets to lesser vessels if, in his considered judgement, his reduced striking force stood no chance against the battleships in prevailing conditions. This option he chose to exercise, bearing in mind that in the complete absence of clouds in which to take cover prior to making their assault, their only chance of achieving the surprise their slowness required was to attack from out of the sun. If they tried to achieve this position against the more distant battleships, the cruisers between them and their target, would no doubt give ample warning to Campioni well before the Swordfish got there. It was therefore decided to attack the *Pola* group without further delay.

Again it appeared to the Fleet Air Arm Pilots, that surprise *was* achieved; the Italian cruisers only had time to get off two salvos against them before the torpedo drop positions were reached, but an emergency turn to starboard was undertaken by the Italians and many of the new pilots were unable to adjust to this in time and their strikes went wide. Flak now erupted from the Italian squadron with a vengeance, but it was wild shooting, even the main 8-inch guns were loosing off in every direction and they narrowly escaped hitting their own ships in the confusion; one heavy calibre shell was seen to smack into the water close to the rear cruiser while the light AA shells were churning up the water all around the squadron. Nonetheless, although a few Swordfish made good drops, and claimed hits on both the leading ship and the rear ship of the column, none in fact actually hit their target at all and again the Italians emerged unscathed.

Two of the Swordfish were hit however, but the shrapnel bursts failed to bring them down and all seven eventually got back to the *Ark Royal* safely. Nor was the third and final striking force more successful than its fellows. This comprised seven Skuas which were flown off from the carrier at 1500 to search for the cripple reported earlier. The Blackburn Skua was a dive-bomber that had achieved some notable success off Norway earlier that year, and it also doubled, not so successfully, as a fighter from time to time. It was a modern aircraft but not very fast and armed with a 500-lb bomb. Despite their searches they failed to locate any damaged cruiser, which was not surprising for there was none, but they did make dive bombing attacks on what they reported later to be three Condottieri class 6-inch cruisers steering north off the south-west corner of Sardinia. They chose the rear cruiser for their target and claimed two near misses on her which might have caused some damage. In fact there was none but they did manage to intercept and shoot down the *Vittorio Veneto*'s RO43 seaplane which was trying to land back at Sardinia after completing her mission with too little fuel to rejoin the flagship. This was the Fleet Air Arm's only success from their three air strikes that day. Their targets had been the 8-inch ships of Sansonetti's division.

After this, all contact was lost with the enemy by Somerville, and, at 1615, the last reconnaissance report received on their whereabouts put the two battleships steering north up the east coast of Sardinia at 25 knots, with a cruiser squadron astern of them on the same course. The second cruiser force were not sighted again after the Skua attack, although Iachino's group were known to have detached one of their ships to Cagliari, and this led to speculation that it might have been damaged by 6-inch shell fire. But, as we know, this was the *Lanciere* and she safely reached port after the attentions of the Sunderland flying boat had proved abortive.

The retirement of the Italian forces proceeded after that without further impediment, save for the continued flow of out-of-touch signals from Supermarina in Rome. The battleships and the *Pola* Division finally entered harbour at Naples between 1325 and 1440 on the 28th November. The 3rd Division arrived back at Messina at 2035 on the same day. No further effort was made to dispute the passage of the convoy through the Narrows by any major surface units. The damaged *Lanciere* struggled into Cagliari and later sailed under her own power to La Spezia where she underwent repairs and was soon back in full service again. She finally met her end in March 1942 during another attempt by the Italian battleships to intercept a British convoy to Malta, this time from the east, when she foundered and sank in a storm after the Battle of Sirte. It is ironical that she should survive so much punishment at the hands of her enemy only to succumb to the natural elements on her own back doorstep.

It was now left to the Regia Aeronautica to dispute the passage of the convoy and Force H. Frequent appeals had been made during the battle for such an intervention, but it came very tardily.

Somerville's main force was steering back towards the convoy at a steady nineteen knots when, at 1407, *Sheffield*'s radar detected the approach of enemy aircraft. Immediately the British heavy ships staggered their lines to present a less rigid target to the enemy and all AA positions closed up in readiness. This formation consisted of ten three-engined Sm79s in their altitude bombing role, escorted by 5 CR 42 biplane fighters.

The *Ark Royal* had seven Fulmar fighters in the air to meet this attack and they intercepted this force before it reached the fleet carrying out several attacks. According to Italian records one of their defending fighters was shot down and they, in turn claimed to have destroyed one Fulmar, but this was not so. The bombers held on through this assault, despite casualties and delivered their bombing attacks on the main units of Force H with some skill. The fleet's guns now took over defence of the ships in a controlled barrage and an emergency turn was made. As a result most of the bombs from the immaculate Italian formation fell well clear of the big ships and among the destroyers out on the screen. Somerville later wrote that:

> I had a bad moment during the afternoon just before the air attack came in and I had to decide which course to turn to to bring all guns to bear. Well, the best one put *Defender* on the side the attack was coming from and I felt rather unhappy and then kicked myself for allowing any such

consideration to enter my mind. After all, just before the action started in the morning I nipped down to my sea cabin to say a good dibby for you and the Bo and myself, so the whole matter was in better hands than mine.[9]

In the event no ship was hit, although some of the destroyers had close shaves from the towering bomb splashes. The Italian bombers retired having suffered damage to eight of their aircraft, two being badly knocked about, from the combined attentions of the Fulmars and the ships' gunfire.[10] There followed another short lull before the next wave came in.

The second bomber formation also consisted of ten Sm79s in two vics of five aircraft. This group was without any fighter escort whatsoever so short were the Sardinian airfields of this type of aircraft. Therefore the Italian pilots had to brave the attacks of the swarming Fulmars completely unaided. It is to their credit that they did so, holding a steady course without flinching despite hits and casualties.

This assault commenced at 1645 and the airmen concentrated their attentions solely on the *Ark Royal*. She was busy flying off and landing on aircraft and was therefore bereft of any support from the massed guns of the fleet, as such she was a tempting target and she was lucky to survive. Despite the fact that nine of the ten bombers involved were damaged by the Fulmars, two of them so badly that they had to jettison their bombs prematurely, they held again their rigid disciplined formations and bombed with great accuracy.

As one destroyer skipper recalls: 'The Italians bombed from a great height but with extreme accuracy. They were really very unlucky not to have achieved better results.'[11]

This particular attack was described by Somerville as 'a stinker'. The *Ark Royal* was completely hidden by bomb splashes, two of which fell within ten yards of her great wide and unarmoured flight deck. For brief seconds as she vanished behind the great gouts of water and spray watchers from the fleet thought she had been hit. Then her blunt nose appeared again, all her guns hammering away and they knew she had pulled through yet again. This graphic demonstration in accurate bomb aiming left the Italians without a single hit to compensate for their losses as they droned away. It marked the last serious attempt to dispute the battlefield, and Force H was left in solitary command of an empty sea and sky.

The courage of the Italian pilots, although unrewarded, deserves attention. Indeed Somerville himself commented on it in his Official Report thus: 'The complete failure of either fighter attack or gunfire to break up the formation flying of the Italian squadrons was most noteworthy.'[12]

At 1700 the *Renown* had the convoy in sight once more. There remained little else to do. At dusk the heavy ships turned back according to custom, while the convoy made its way through the Narrows in the darkness, met and reinforced by the 3rd Cruiser Squadron from the east. Apart from two abortive attempts by the submarines *Dessié* and *Tembien* on the night of the 27/28th to attack this unit, the Italian response was zero and all merchant ships and naval vessels reached their destinations unscathed.

Although failure to bring the enemy to account rankled somewhat in Force H nobody was particularly downcast and all felt that they had done the best they could in the prevailing circumstances. The failure of the Fleet Air Arm to slow down an enemy intent of evasion was the major blow, but again there were good and valid reasons for this as we have seen. Inexperienced pilots and observers made mistakes in the heat of battle, as do even fully trained crews, but their bravery and determination were beyond question.

On the surface side of the battle the lessons learnt were not new either; the fact that our ships were, in the main old, or had not worked together before whereas the Italian units were from squadrons and divisions used to acting in company was accepted as part of the normal price for world-wide responsibilities of the Royal Navy. Conversely the Italians had only to dominate waters within one day's steaming of their own home ports and were always able to select the time best suited to themselves to attack, to accept or reject battle, and with the, in theory anyway, full weight of their bomber units at their back. Moreover they had ample submarines to back them up, minefields that only they knew of and were not handicapped by having a convoy under their wing.

Despite all these advantages it had been Somerville with his smaller squadron, and his older ships, who had carried the fight to the enemy and it had been Campioni who had withdrawn. Both men believed they were carrying out the wishes of their superiors in acting the way they did. Both men were to receive a sharp lesson as a result of this battle that the wishes of their superiors were far more flexible than their own genuine interpretations.

CHAPTER TWENTY

An Unprecedented Judgement

That Force H had acquitted itself well in the battle was doubted by nobody in the Mediterranean as ships once more hove in sight of Gibraltar at the end of their return from the central basin. One young midshipman recorded in his journal:

> At a given signal all the ships in the advance force, consisting of *Renown*, *Berwick* and *Sheffield*, made smoke and the resulting spectacle was fine to see. We all flew our largest ensigns the band played 'Run, Rabbit, Run' as we entered harbour and we were, to our gratified surprise, cheered by an envious *Royal Sovereign* and destroyers.[1]

Signals of congratulations and good wishes came from Sir Dudley North, from Vice-Admiral Malta and from Sir Andrew Cunningham with the main fleet. And yet, gratified as he was with all this jubilation, and satisfied as he was in his own mind that he had acted correctly, Somerville himself was beset by grave forebodings. He had sent two brief signals to the Admiralty of what had taken place and was working hard with his staff, on a full and detailed report in the customary way. Yet he was uneasy. He had already confided these fears to his wife in a letter: 'I shouldn't be surprised if some of them at the Admiralty don't argue that I should have continued the chase.'[2]

How right he was to be, but the loudest growls of discontent came from much higher up than the Admiralty. Once again Somerville had aroused the wrath of the Premier, and this time Churchill was confident that he would find grounds to get rid of his outspoken critic at the Rock once and for all.

It was the day after their triumphant return to harbour that the blow fell. A signal arrived from the Admiralty[3] giving the amazing news that a Board of Enquiry, led by Admiral of the Fleet the Earl of Cork and Orrery, *had already started* on its way to Gibraltar to enquire into Somerville's conduct of the battle.

It was unprecedented in the history of the Royal Navy for such an action to be taken when the full facts had yet to reach the Board of Admiralty. Little wonder then that Somerville should have felt victimised and that someone, either at the Admiralty, or beyond, was determined to remove him come what might. In fact as in the case of North, but with far less justification, it was Somerville's 'offensive spirit' that was being questioned in Whitehall and there can be no doubt whatsoever, just who that prime mover was. As Captain Roskill has revealed, Admiral Sir William Davis, then serving in the Plans Division at the Admiralty and on the Joint Planning Staff, had no doubts that it was Churchill himself from whom the initiative came in sending out Lord Cork,[4] although Alexander, as First Lord, took the executive action in convening it.

The Premier was even determined on Somerville's successor. Having an overwhelming desire for 'men of action' he had selected Admiral Harwood, the victor of the River Plate action in 1939, as the man he wanted. And yet the River Plate was Harwood's sole claim to fame. He had been promoted to admiral from commodore on the strength of it, although previously passed over, and was then serving as Assistant Chief of Naval Staff (Foreign). He had never commanded anything larger than a small cruiser squadron in distant waters. Yet within days of receiving the first incomplete reports on Spartivento Churchill was minuting Alexander: 'Why not give Harwood his chance here?'.[5]

Alexander so shared the Premier's inflated opinion of Harwood that he was seriously nominating him for Force H's new commander with Pound's backing.[6]

The feeling in the Navy was one of indignation mixed with amazed disbelief that such a thing could be happening. Somerville wrote a letter to Cunningham that he was amazed to get such a signal, before the true facts were fully documented, which so reflected a 'lack of confidence in my leadership'.[7] 'Who', he asked with some justification, 'is playing these sort of games with the Navy?'[8]

Cunningham, not unfamiliar himself with this type of signal, was wrathful. 'I had thought this a most iniquitous action on the part of those at home, especially as the members of the Board of Enquiry were flown out to Gibraltar before the Admiral had sent in his report or even returned to harbour.'[9]

When Pound raised the point in a letter to the C-in-C, ABC was equally forthright in his rejoinder to the First Sea Lord:

You ask me if I was surprised at the Board of Enquiry on Force H's action south of Sardinia. You will wish me to speak out quite frankly and say that I was very sorry for the decision, more especially as the Board was set up even before Force H returned to harbour.[10]

Somerville's biographer commented on the feeling in Force H at the time the news broke:

Had Somerville not enjoyed an affection and respect from every officer and man of his Fleet, it would have delivered a blow at his leadership and their confidence in him which might have permanently shattered morale. As it was, his Captains and Staff were furious and indignant at the slight put on their Commander and on Force H and they went out of their way to make this clear. The wardrooms of the fleet were seething with indignation at the insult, they told him.[11]

Certainly those in the know could find no sense in it, although, contrary to the above, many did not know what was going on at the time.

As far as the subsequent Board of Enquiry was concerned – this was kept very secret and we did not know of it until very much later. I don't think therefore there was any 'feeling' in Force H at the time, as we just didn't know.[12]

Be that as it may, there was no doubt in the minds of many that a complete injustice was being done in suspecting Somerville of anything less than determination in the face of the enemy.

Somerville was the epitome of offensive action, equalling Cunningham in this respect. Any idea that he would in any way shirk action appeared absolutely ludicrous to the fleet. It was obviously Churchill who was gunning for him and Pound could not resist.[13]

Even in the choice of officers to conduct the Board of Enquiry Churchill's hand might well be seen. Lord Cork was a determined and 'offensively minded' officer right enough and Churchill's faith in him at this time was absolute. Already, during the Norwegian debacle, he had entrusted to him his confidences and even, as Captain Roskill had revealed, originated a whole string of signals direct to him which completely by-passed the C-in-C Home Fleet, Admiral Forbes, under whose command Lord Cork was. It may well have seemed that such a man would bring in the result that Churchill and the Admiralty obviously expected, and desired. If such were their feelings at the time they were underestimating 'Ginger', so-called because of his flaming red hair and equally flaming temper, who was first and foremost a seaman, not a diplomat.

Man of action he most certainly was. Appointed C-in-C Home Fleet aboard the *Nelson* in September 1933, 'Ginger' Boyle, as he then was, relieved Admiral Sir John Kelly. Kelly had been especially appointed as C-in-C Home Fleet at that time after the so-called Invergordon Mutiny to put lower deck affairs in order. In this Kelly had been brilliantly successful but such a task inevitably mitigated against the operational side of the fleet. On his appointment Admiral Boyle immediately took the fleet to sea on high speed exercises and rapidly restored the morale of the officers which had been somewhat neglected by concentration on lower deck affairs.

> Ginger Boyle was a strong disciplinarian and his occasional volcanic outbursts kept everyone on their toes. He took a particular interest in AA gunnery, presenting a trophy for competitions for award to the most efficient ship in this art. He was a good de-centraliser, leaving people to get on with their own jobs. After two years with the Home Fleet, Cork and Orrery became C-in-C Portsmouth. In 1940 he was given command of the naval forces to re-capture Narvik, which he successfully accomplished at the end of May in that year. It is a curious fact that he reached the highest rank in the Navy without ever serving in the Admiralty, except for a few months in 1940.[14]

Such a man was not likely to be swayed by policital influence in the job he was instructed to carry out at Gibraltar. His assistant on the Board of Enquiry was Admiral Sir George D'Oyly Lyon, a former England rugger player.

Meanwhile an already distasteful situation was aggravated by the Italian radio broadcasts which boastfully claimed to the world at large that Somerville's force had run away from Campioni's fleet and suffered heavy casualties. This rubbish was broadcast frequently and its echoes still reflect in some post-war histories. 'The conduct of the British commander was considered in London to have been so unsatisfactory that when he returned to Gibraltar he found himself an "interested party" before a board of enquiry, before which he had to justify his not having carried on the engagement more energetically.'

Coming after the wholesale flight of the Italian fleet such comment is of course a complete travesty of history, but similar comments were being made at the time, and Churchill, no mean propagandist himself, was quick to see the dangers. He wrote to Alexander and Pound of his fears on this score, still without relenting in his prejudgement of the Enquiry.

> Admiral Somerville had clearly lost the confidence of the Board – it is quite sufficient to tell him to haul down his flag and relieve him by Harwood without giving any other reason than we think a change necessary on general grounds. This is in fact true because even before these two episodes (by this he meant Spartivento and either Oran or the escape of Force Y) confidence in him had largely departed ...[15]

He added that it would be better if Cork were not now sent to Gibraltar after all. But it was too late for that now for Cork was on his way and Somerville knew it. Moreover such a decision would give the Italians more detailed food for their broadcasts and confirm in the eyes of the world that their claims were correct instead of complete falsehoods. Alexander also warned that such action might entitle Somerville himself to claim he had been unfairly treated. The Enquiry therefore had to go ahead anyway. Churchill and the Board were therefore well and truly hoisted on their own petard.

Churchill refused to concede defeat on this issue, writing: 'Should the Court of Inquiry consider the Admiral blameworthy and unless facts emerge which are very different to those on which we have rested, I hope the relief will take place *this week.*'*[16]

However, as MacIntyre records, the Board of Enquiry was not to produce the results expected in fact, 'it acted as a boomerang on those responsible'.[17]

Indeed it did for what the Board concluded at the end of their exhaustive study of the operation was as follows: 'The conduct of the action that ensued was correct and spirited and its success ensured the attainment of what had been selected as the primary object of the operation, viz – the safe and timely arrival of the convoy at its destination, and this in the face of a superior force.'[18]

They also made clear that they considered Somerville's reasons for breaking off contact when he did, the one point that stuck in his critics' throats more than any other, was the entirely correct thing to have done.

Such a conclusion was nothing more or less than a complete vindication of the Commander of Force H and refuted absolutely the

My italics.

criticisms levelled at him. Churchill was forced to accept it but not until after the bombardment of Genoa in 1941, did he mellow towards Somerville in any way and give up his campaign to have him removed.

Lord Cork wrote a frank letter to Somerville after it was all over, hoping no doubt to clear the air:

> I hope, after what passed yesterday, that you do not feel I have not sympathised with you in the position in which you have been placed after your successful action of last week. I have, very much. It is possible, however, that you take rather too harsh a view of the Admiralty action for the following reasons. There are always critics ready to raise their voices and suggest what might have been done although they are quite ignorant of what really happened or of the prevailing conditions. These people, impatient for results, exist both in and out of the Admiralty and in high quarters (I speak from personal experience), and no doubt have raised their voices on this occasion and the most expeditious way of silencing them has in this case been adopted.[19]

That he was referring to Churchill and that Pound's way of silencing him was the Board of Enquiry there can be little doubt. Vice-Admiral G.C. Royale, at the Admiralty, was even more specific: 'These damned politicians who know nothing of the real difficulties are responsible for these *stunts.*'[20]

Somerville himself had no illusions; he blamed Admiral Tom Phillips and Churchill for these snipings over the months and understood Cork's situation. He wrote to Cunningham stating that he believed that Cork 'considers the whole thing a bloody outrage'.[21]

Cunningham replied that he didn't think Pound was at the bottom of it but that 'he allows himself to be talked into these things, by W.C. and others'.[22] In his own memoirs he stated in his usual blunt manner that: 'At the time I thought it intolerable that a Flag Officer, doing his utmost in difficult circumstances, should be continuously under the threat of finding a Board of Enquiry waiting for him on his return to harbour if his actions failed to commend themselves to those at home who knew little or nothing of the real facts of the case.'[23]

Whatever the rights or wrongs of the case, and the absolute right of the Admiralty to criticise, and if necessary, replace, any officer has already been acknowledged as indisputable, as in North's case, it was the *manner* that the whole thing was handled at Churchill's insistence, that left the bad taste in the mouth afterwards. Nor did

Their Lordships accept the findings of the Court with anything but bad grace. They replied to Somerville, after hearing the Board's findings and reading his own full account, that: 'No opportunity must be allowed to pass of attaining what is in fact the ultimate object of the Royal Navy – the destruction of the enemy's forces whenever and wherever encountered.'[24]

It is hard to fault them in their wish to achieve the destruction of the enemy in this manner after the frustrations of the Great War, but, had they given some pause, the attainment of that objective was ultimately achieved, if not through glorious combat on the High Seas, in a more complete and permanent manner than any battle had ever achieved when the German fleet scuttled itself in Scapa Flow. A parallel was to occur in this war, for three years after the incidents related here the entire Italian Fleet steamed out to surrender to the Royal Navy in a like manner. But in the dark days of 1940, with the whole world either against us or indifferently neutral, it would be a hard person to judge either Churchill or the Admiralty too harshly in their wish to get to grips with at least one Axis partner decisively, in the only element in which we still enjoyed a superiority of experience and numbers. All criticism should therefore be set in context. Nonetheless the whole episode was badly handled and reflected little credit on those in London at the time.

And so Cunningham, Somerville but not North, survived their ordeals by trial. The nation was blessed with two of the most resolute and brilliant officers of their day in command of their fleets in the Mediterranean at this time. It would have been nothing less than a tragedy had either of them fallen foul of the Premier's ire and been replaced by a lesser man. With the hardships and heavy losses an over-optimistic strategy was to impose on their commands in the years to come, their strength and endurance alone brought the fleets through, unbroken in spirit if nothing else and on to final victory.

Admiral Somerville went on to greater achievements; what of his unfortunate opposite number, Campioni? If Somerville considered himself harshly treated by his superiors then Campioni's fate was all the more severe. Like Somerville he had believed he was doing what was best for his country, preserving what remained of their heavy ships after Taranto in order that they might fight again when the odds were more favourable.

In the event his fate was even harsher than that meted out to Somerville. He was replaced as Fleet Commander in a general re-shuffle that took place on 10th December, after six months of continued disasters at sea for the Italians. His passing was swift, but, because it was merely part and parcel of a general reorganisation, not so painful as North's ordeal. Moreover Campioni took his punishment quietly. The blow was softened for him by his appointment as Deputy Chief of Staff in place of Admiral Somigli.

In his new position Campioni served well enough; in fact during the bombardment of Genoa by Force H the following February, it was he who ordered the sailing and concentration of the Italian fleet north of Sardinia and in so doing came the closest to achieving a major naval victory that the Italians ever got. That same operation restored Somerville in the eyes of Churchill but it was a massive gamble that very nearly did not come off. Later in the war Campioni was appointed Governor of the Aegean Islands and he held that post in the critical days of the Italian surrender. Hitler was determined to hang on to that area come what might; Allied response was weak and piecemeal. Campioni, loyal to the new Italian Government, and hopeful of receiving help from the British, delayed things as long as he could, but the Germans were too fast and too powerful and at the end of their successful campaign took a cruel revenge on the Italians who had defied them.[25]

Taken as a prisoner Campioni was incarcerated by the Italian group loyal to Mussolini, and after being put on trial for high treason by these, was put against a wall and shot in April 1944 at Parma. He deserved a better fate.

His successor as Fleet Commander was Admiral Iachino, who had commanded the II Division from *Pola* in both the Calabria and Spartivento battles.* We have seen that he was a man in the same mould as Campioni, strict adherence to orders marked him for a similar fate. We have also seen how he was a sailor first and a politician second. His readiness to send back the 3rd Division to succour one crippled destroyer showed his feelings for his men. It was his basic humanity that was to lead him, and his fleet, into one of the greatest defeats they ever suffered at the hands of the Royal Navy. This was at Cape Matapan in March 1941. His old division, *Pola* and the rest, had suffered damage from torpedo bombers in the opening exchange of this combat. Again the Italian Fleet had strict orders to disengage and Iachino in *Vittorio Veneto*, led his ships back to harbour at high speed. As at Spartivento they would all have escaped save the

---

* These battles were known to the Italians as the Encounter off Punta Stilo and the Encounter of Cape Teulada respectively.

crippled *Pola*, his old, and much-loved, flagship, but again Iachino was loath to leave such a vessel alone and unaided. Let down yet again by his air reconnaissance, who informed him the British fleet under Cunningham was far astern, he sent back the heavy cruisers to help her, and, under cover of darkness, they ran slap into the three battleships of the British line and were pulverised.

Nor was Iachino ever able to rectify the position. At the second battle of Sirte he approached a British convoy with the battleship *Littorio* and an overwhelming strength in cruisers and destroyers. Facing him were a few small cruisers and some destroyers but this time it was the British who made the fullest use of the smokescreen, and they proved themselves to be equal to the Italians in its application, so much so that the Italians were forced to break off the battle and retire frustrated. Iachino himself was later replaced, in turn, as Fleet Commander by Admiral Bergamini.

History has not treated him kindly either. The judgement of one of his allies was this:

> The repeated failures of the Italian Fleet led to a change of command. At the beginning of December 1940, Admiral Riccardi replaced Admiral Cavagnari as Commander-in-Chief of the Navy. Admiral Iachino, hitherto commanding a cruiser division, was appointed C-in-C afloat. He was aged fifty-one, and his reputation stood high. Having been Naval Attaché in London from 1931 to 1934, he knew the British Navy. Either he acquired too much respect for his opponent, or maybe he was just unlucky, but the fact remains that in his new command he achieved even less than his predecessor.[26]

The British commanders had distinguished careers. Cunningham, after the victories of 1940 and early 1941, had to endure the tragedies and defeats of Greece and Crete, brought about partly by Churchill's instigation, before leaving the Mediterranean, whereupon Harwood took his place. This latter quickly proved himself out of his element and Churchill rapidly became disillusioned and had him removed as harshly as North had been. Cunningham became our greatest sailor, rising to the top of the service but he never stood any nonsense from the Premier.

Somerville, after a further successful period with Force-H, was appointed as C-in-C East Indies in 1942 at a time when our defences had crumbled before the Japanese onslaught. Given a hotch-potch collection of mainly old ships his unenviable task was to try and halt the Japanese spread westward. It was an impossible task but one to which he applied himself with vigour. He was extremely lucky to escape a major defeat in April in the Indian Ocean, but fortunately the Japanese then turned back east into the Pacific and his command withered and died. He was appointed to Washington where he was a great success and went on to an honourable, but brief retirement post-war.

Only Admiral North of the trio who earned Churchill's displeasure in 1940 remained, a lonely old man, fighting to clear his name on into the 1950s long after his two more distinguished colleagues had passed on and the issues that had raised such passions in 1940 were all but forgotten.

Source Notes

CHAPTER ONE: Against the Odds

[1] Ciano, Count Galeazzo, *Ciano's Diary, 1939-43*, (Heinemann, 1947). Section I of this book is full of the schemes and plots in which the Italian Foreign Office was deeply enmeshed at this time.

[2] Roskill, Stephen, *Naval Policy between the Wars, Vol 2, The Period of Reluctant Rearmament, 1930-1939*, (Collins, 1976), is a rich field of sources on this aspect.

[3] Fraccaroli, Aldo, *Italian Warships of World War II*, (Ian Allan, 1969), is a good basic guide to this period of Italian naval expansion.

[4] Roskill, Stephen, *Naval Policy between the Wars, Vol 2, op cit.*

[5] 'Forbes, Donald', *Two Small Ships*, (Hutchinson, 1957), gives a thoughtful pre-war comparison between the two navies' attitudes and thinking.

[6] Marder, Professor Arthur J., *From the Dardanelles to Oran, Studies of the Royal Navy in War and Peace, 1915-1940*, (Oxford University Press, 1974), of which Chapter III, *The Royal Navy and the Ethiopian Crisis of 1935-36*, is a good guide to the heartsearching that took place on this issue.

[7] Chalmers, Rear Admiral W.S., *Max Horton and the Western Approaches*, (Hodder & Stoughton, 1954). Chapter III 'Mare Nostrum 1935-37', shows how high a pitch of training the 1st Cruiser Squadron had reached pre-war.

[8] Clare, Mr D., to the author, 4 May 1979.

[9] Parker, Commander J.P., to the author, 16 April 1979.

[10] Cunningham of Hyndhope, Admiral of the Fleet Viscount, *A Sailor's Odyssey*, (Hutchinson, 1951). (Hereafter noted as Cunningham, *Odyssey*)

[11] Ufficio Storico della Marina Militare, *La Marina Italiana nella Seconda Guerra Mondiale, Vol IV, Le Azioni Navali in Mediterraneo, Dal 10 Giugno 1940 al 31 Marzo 1941*, (Ufficio Storico, 1976). (Hereafter noted as *Ufficio Storico, Navy, Vol IV*)

[12] *Aerei Italiani nella 2ª Guerra Mondiale, Bombardieri, Vol 4* (Edizioni Bizzarri, 1972), gives details of the SM79 and its units.

[13] Cunningham, *Odyssey, op cit.*

[14] Power, Admiral Sir Manley GCB CBE DSO RN to the author, 4 August 1978.

CHAPTER TWO: Opening Moves

[1] *Ufficio Storico, Navy, Vol IV, op cit.*

[1] Cunningham, *Odyssey, op cit.*

[3] Principal documentation on the British side is contained within PRO files ADM199/1048, M.03152/41, dated 29 January 1941, and M.05369/41 dated 29 January 1941, which cover MA.5 viz:

    1 Orders for Operation MA.5.

    2 C-in-C Mediterranean's Narratives: (a) Operation MA5. (b) Action off Calabria.

   3 Vice Admiral (D) Mediterranean's narratives of Operation MA5.

   4 Rear Admiral 1st Battle Squadron's narrative of Operation MA5.

5 Vice Admiral (D) narrative of Calabria.
6 Commander (D) 2nd Destroyer Flotilla narrative.
7 Captain (D) 10th Destroyer Flotilla narrative.
8 Captain (D) 14th Destroyer Flotilla narrative of Calabria.
9 CO HMS *Warspite* narrative.
10 CO HMS *Malaya* narrative.
11 CO HMS *Eagle* narrative.
12 CO HMS *Neptune* narrative.
13 CO HMAS *Sydney* narrative.
14 CO HMS *Gloucester* narrative.
15 CO HMS *Liverpool* narrative.
16 Signals
17 Summary of bombing attacks on ships during Operation MA5.
4 Power, Admiral Sir Manley, to the author, *op cit.*
5 See ADM199/1048, *op cit.*
6 Cunningham, *Odyssey, op cit.*
7 *ibid*
8 Mackenzie, Mr E.B., to the author 16 April 1979.
9 *Official Australian Navy History, R.A.N. Ships Overseas June-December 1940*, pp 174.
(Australian National War Memorial).

CHAPTER THREE: Closing the Enemy

1 *Official Australian Navy History, op cit.*
2 Power, Admiral Sir Manley, to the author, *op cit.*
3 *Ufficio Storico, Navy, Vol IV, op cit.*
4 Murray, Commander John B., RN, to the author 23 May 1979.
5 Cunningham, Admiral Sir Andrew B., KCB, DSO, C-in-C Mediterranean
station, *Despatch*, dated 29th January 1941, issued as a *Supplement* to *The London Gazette*, dated 27 April 1948.
6 Cunningham, *Odyssey, op cit.*

CHAPTER FOUR: 'Enemy Battle Fleet in Sight'

1 De Winton, Captain F.S., RN, to the author 1 July 1978.
2 *Official Australian Navy History, op cit*, quoting from Gerard, F., *Malta Magnificent*, (1943), pp 35.
3 Power, Admiral Sir Manley, to the author, *op cit.*
4 *Ufficio Storico, Navy, Vol IV, op cit.*
5 Parker, Commander J.P., RN, to the author, 3 April and 16 April 1979.
6 Griffin, Mr L., to the author, 6 April 1979.
7 Power, Admiral Sir Manley, to the author, *op cit.*
8 *ibid*
9*ibid*
10 *ibid*
11 Mackenzie, Mr E.B., to the author, 16 April 1979.
12 Clare, Mr D., to the author, 4 May 1979.

CHAPTER FIVE: A Single Shell

1 Cunningham, *Odyssey, op cit.*

² *Ufficio Storico, Navy, Vol IV, op cit.*
³ *ibid*
⁴ Cunningham, *Despatch, op cit.*
⁵ *ibid*
⁶ Power, Admiral Sir Manley, to the author, *op cit.*
⁷ *Ufficio Storico, Navy, Vol IV, op cit.*
⁸ Cobb, Commander G., OBE, RN, to the author, 11 May 1979.
⁹ *Ufficio Storico, Navy, Vol IV, op cit.*
¹⁰ Murray, Commander John B., RN, to the author, 23 May 1979.
¹¹ Power, Admiral Sir Manley, to the author, *op cit.*
¹² Marder, Professor Arthur J., *From the Dreadnought to Scapa Flow, Vol 3; Jutland and After, May 1916 – December 1916* (Second Edition, Oxford University Press, 1978), contains a detailed analysis of this tactic.
¹³ *Official Australian Navy History, op cit.*
¹⁴ Cunningham, *Despatch, op cit.*

CHAPTER SIX: Bombs, Bombs and More Bombs

¹ Clare, Mr D., to the author, *op cit.*
² Ufficio Storico; Santoro, General Giuseppe, *L'Aeronautica Italiana Nella Seconda Guerra Mondiale, Vol 2* (Edizioni Ease, Rome, 1957).
³ Cunningham, *Despatch, op cit.*
⁴ Santoro, General Giuseppe, *op cit.*
⁵ *Ufficio Storico, Navy, Vol IV, op cit.*
⁶ *ibid*
⁷ Ciano, *Diary, op cit.*
⁸ Cunningham, *Odyssey, op cit.*
⁹ *Official Australian Navy History, op cit.*
¹⁰ Power, Admiral Sir Manley, to the author, *op cit.*
¹¹ Parker, Commander J.P., RN, to the author, *op cit.*
¹² Cunningham, *Odyssey, op cit.*

CHAPTER SEVEN: Aftermath

¹ Bragadin, Commander (R) Marc' Antonio, *The Italian Navy in World War II*, (Naval Institute Press, Annapolis, 1957).
² Ciano, *Diary, op cit.*
³ Ruge, Vice Admiral Friedrich, *Sea Warfare 1939-45*, (Cassell, 1957).
⁴ Cunningham, *Despatch, op cit.*
⁵ Pound, Admiral Sir Dudley, to Premier, July 1940.
⁶ Power, Admiral Sir Manley, to the author, *op cit.*
⁷ Cunningham to Pound, July 1940.
⁸ Power, Admiral Sir Manley, to the author, *op cit.*

CHAPTER EIGHT: A Loss of Confidence

¹ Monks, Noel, *That Day at Gibraltar* (Frederick Muller, 1957), pp 2. (Hereafter referred to as Monks.)
² Plimmer, Charlotte and Denis, *A Matter of Expediency* (Quartet, 1978), pp 20-21. (Hereafter referred to as Plimmer). 'The Gibraltar post – inexplicably – was not considered particularly sensitive.' In November 1939 it was probably one of the most 'insensitive' positions going, there is nothing inexplicable about it; very few

persons would at that time have forecast the collapse of France and the loss of their Navy to the overwhelming Allied sea strength in the Mediterranean.

[3] Roskill, Stephen W., *Churchill and the Admirals* (Collins, 1977), pp 160. (Hereafter referred to as Roskill, *Churchill*).

[4] Litchfield, Captain John, *Review of Operation Menace* (*Naval Review*, April, 1976) pp 181.

[5] Monks, pp 5. '... Admiral North would have reached the great heights his colleagues predicted for him and become First Sea Lord, with a Viscountcy in addition.' Again on pp 11 he quotes from a letter Mountbatten to North, 26 Feb. 1941, thus: 'Everyone in the Service regarded you as a certainty for First Sea Lord,' ... What in fact Mountbatten wrote was that he was regarded as a certainty for 'First Lord and Principal', which is navalese for the Senior Naval Aide-de-Camp, a position which North well indeed might have qualified for after his long service to the Royal Family. Monks misquoted this (Mountbatten to Marder, 18 Sept 1974) but the original is no longer on file.

[6] Marder, Arthur J. *From the Dardanelles to Oran* (Oxford University Press, 1974) pp 137. (Hereafter referred to as Marder, *Dardanelles*).

[7] Marder, Arthur J. *From Dreadnought to Scapa Flow: Volume II: The War Years: to the eve of Jutland* (Oxford University Press, New Edition 1966) pps 266-296.

[8] Grenfell, Russell, *Main Fleet to Singapore* (Faber, 1951) pps 214-219.

[9] Litchfield, Captain John. Letter to *The Times*, 18 Nov 1977.

[10] Roskill, *Churchill*, pps 296-299. Also correspondence in Roskill Archives at the Archives Centre, Churchill College, Cambridge, under references ROSK 5/124 and ROSK 5/125.

[11] Operations Division, Naval Staff, Admiralty, 'Pink List', corrected to 4 pm 1st November, 1939.

[12] Rogers, Colonel H.C.B., *Artillery through the Ages* (Seeley Service & Co, 1971); Lewendon, Brigadier R.J., Royal Artillery Institution, Woolwich, letters to the author 13 Oct 1978 and 24 November 1978; Buckley P., Army Historical Branch, Whitehall. Letter to the author 4 Oct 1978.

[13] Operational Record Books of No 202 Squadron, AIR 27/1181 and Operational Record Book of No. 3 Anti-Aircraft Co-Operation Unit, AIR 29/45. Group Captain T.Q. Horner, RAF, to the author, 5 March 1979.

[14] Cunningham to North, 15 Nov 1939, North Papers, NRTH 2/3.

[15] Admiralty to C-in-C, Mediterranean Fleet (Pound), 1 Sept 1938, ADM 1/9543. After Munich progress was better and six meetings of British and French Staffs took place in London and one in Paris between 30 March and 3 May 1939, AGC(J) 74, dated 8 May 1939. CAB 29/160. Cunningham had established relations with Esteva at Oran during the Nyon Conference patrols in September 1937. Cunningham of Hyndhope, KT, GCB, OM, DSO, *A Sailor's Odyssey* (Hutchinson, 1951) pps 185-86.

[16] Cunningham and Esteva resolved the main points of Allied naval co-operation at a further meeting at Bizerta on 30 April 1940. Cunningham, *Odyssey*, pp 225.

[17] Marder, *Dardanelles*, pp 181.

[18] *ibid.* Pound had once expressed the opinion that the French Navy was '... not worth a hatful of crabs'.

[19] Admiral J.H. Godfrey to Admiral Cunningham, 7 May 1959: 'I reached the conclusion in May that Holland's judgment about French affairs had become gravely impaired and was, in my opinion, useless ...'

[20] Captain De Winton to the author, 31 July 1977.

[21] Captain R.E.D. Ryder VC to the author, 22 Nov 1978.

[22] North Atlantic Command War Diary, 1940(7601) (ADM 199/654).

[23] Brigadier R.J. Lewendon to the author, 24 Nov 1978.

[24] War Diary of 4th Heavy Battery, RA, WO 176/189; War Diary of 26th Heavy Battery, RA, WO 176/190; War Diary of 27th Heavy Battery, RA, WO 171/191.

[25] Brigadier G.G. Wainwright, RA to the author, 27 Oct 1978.

[26] Hogg, Ian V., *British and American Artillery of World War 2* (Arms & Armour Press, 1978) pps 196-98.

[27] Brigadier Wainwright recalls: 'No high speed target practice. Just a rather slow towed target. Guns could traverse east I think but certainly west towards Algeciras.' *Ibid.* Captain De Winton stated 'I remember a few rounds being fired from the guns (9.2") on top of the Rock during the more or less quiet period, about March, 1940. I suppose they must have been at a towed target.' Captain De Winton to the author, 22 Aug 1978. Rear Admiral J.H. Walwyn, CB, OBE, at that time a gunnery officer aboard *Renown*, stated: 'I do not know much about the shore batteries but I imagine that they would have been pretty effective – after all that was what they were there for ...'. Rear Admiral Walwyn to the author, 8 Oct 1978.

[28] Maurice-Jones, Colonel K.W., DSO, *The History of Coast Artillery in the British Army* (Royal Artillery Institution, 1959) pps 215-16 and 251.

[29] Pound to North, 3 Jan 1940 (Copy in ROSK 4/32).

[30] Roskill, Captain S.W. *Dudley Pound: A Balanced View*, typescript for article contained in ROSK 5/124. Captain Roskill was to later temper this viewpoint somewhat in the light of subsequent research and conclude that, '... whilst one may respect his humility it is none the less possible to doubt whether he was a big enough man for the job.' Roskill, Stephen, *Churchill and the Admirals*, (Collins, 1977) pps 296-99.

[31] A.M. 1724/24, dated 28 June 1940 (ADM 1/19180).

[32] Roskill, *War at Sea, Vol 1, op cit.*

[33] Macintyre, Captain Donald, DSO**, DSC, *Fighting Admiral* (Evans, 1961) pp 56. (Hereafter Macintyre, *Fighting Admiral*)

[34] Viscount Alexander of Hillsborough, Lords Debate, 26 July 1954. Hansard 5th series (Lords), clxxxix, col 96.

[35] Layman, Captain H.F.H., DSO*, *The Admiral North Case: A Personal Record*, copy of memorandum sent to Professor Arthur J. Marder 11 Jan 1974, and kindly made available to the author by both parties.

[36] See *Führer* Directive No 18, issued on 12 November 1940 on the German plans in this respect, particularly Phase III, 'Undertaking Felix'. Trevor-Roper, H.R., *Hitler's War Directives 1939-1945* (Sidgwick & Jackson, 1964). Also Irving, David, *Hitler's War* (Hodder & Stoughton, 1977) pps 165-171 for background details.

[37] Acting Captain R. Brockman's minute to Pound, dated 22 Jan 1941 (ADM 205/11).

[38] Pound to Admiralty 4 July 1940, received at Admiralty on 9 July 1940 (AVAR 5/4).

[39] Alexander Memo to Eden, 28 June 1940 (AVAR 5/4).

[40] Ciano, Count Galeazzo, *Ciano's Diary 1939-1943* (William Heinemann, 1947) pp 274.

[41] Alexander minute to Churchill 17 July 1940 (ADM 1/19177).

[42] Alexander minute to Pound 15 July 1940 (ADM 1/19178).

[43] Alexander minute to Churchill 17 July 1940 (ADM 1/19177).

[44] Churchill minute to Alexander 20 July 1940 (ADM 1/19177).

[45] Alexander of Hillsborough to Sir John Lang (Secretary of the Admiralty), 9 Aug 1953 (AVAR 5/16) (5/16/9(a)).

[46] Admiralty to FOCNA 17th July 1940 (ADM 1/19177).
[47] Alexander of Hillsborough to Premier Harold Macmillan, 27 May 1957 (AVAR 5/16) (5/16/9(a)).
[48] The Memo from 10 Downing Street, undated and unsigned reads as follows:

In October –	Forbes	–	Plymouth
	Philips	–	Home Fleet C-in-C
	North	–	the beach
	Max Horton	–	VCNS or ACNS(A)
	Blake	–	the beach
	Tovey	–	Gibraltar and N. Atlantic Force 'H'
	Harwood	–	2nd in C H.F.
	............?	–	VAS

[49] North to Admiralty 6 Aug 1940 (ADM 1/19177).

CHAPTER NINE: An Ill-Defined Relationship

[1] AM 2005/4/7/40 Admiralty to all commands.
[2] AM 1400/5/7/40 Admiralty to VA Force H, FOCNA etc. (ADM 1/19180)
[3] FOC North Atlantic 2014/5/7/40. (ADM 1/19180)
[4] AM 0226/6/7/40 Admiralty to FOC North Atlantic repeated SO Force H. (ADM 1/19180).
[5] War Office to GOC Gibraltar WO 75489/4/9.
[6] FOCNA 1644/6/7/40 (ADM 1/19180).
[7] AM 0012/7/7/40 Admiralty to FOCNA repeated VA (H) ADM 1/19180).
[8] AM 1357/8/7/40 Admiralty to Home and Abroad. (ADM 1/19180).
[9] AM 0241/12/7/40 Admiralty to FOCNA and others (Force (H) not listed in addresses). (ADM 1/19180).
[10] AM 2326/12/7/40 Admiralty to General Home and Abroad. (ADM 1/19180).
[11] FOCNA to Consul General Tangier, 1846/13/7/40.
[12] For a fuller account (to be taken with a grain of salt) of the setting up of BETASOM and descriptions of the passages of the Straits by Italian submarines at this time see Cocchia, Admiral Aldo, *Submarines Attacking* (Kimber, 1956) pps 17-37. Fuller details are to be found in Ufficio Storico, Rome, *La Marina Italiana Nella Seconda Guerra Mondiale:* Vol XII-I Sommergibili Negli Oceani (U. Mori Ubaldini), (Ufficio Storico, Roma, 1966).
[13] AM 1738/28/6/40 Admiralty to SO Force H, repeated to FOCNA (ADM 1/19182).
[14] De Winton, Captain F.S., to the author 31 July 1977.
[15] North Atlantic Command War Diary, 1940 (7601) (ADM 199/654).
[16] Stuart, Lieutenant Commander C.Mc.D., *Midshipman's Journal, 1939-41,* kindly loaned to the author.
[17] *Report of Proceedings of Force H for the period 4th to 10th September, Inclusive.* Vice-Admiral, Flag Officer Commanding Force H (ADM 199/392).
[18] *ibid.*
[19] *ibid.*
[20] Churchill, Winston S., *The Second World War, Volume II: Their Finest Hour* (Cassell, 1949) (Hereafter cited as Churchill, *II*)
[21] See for example, Marder, Arthur J., *Operation Menace* (Oxford University Press,

1976); 'Mordal, Jacques' (Hervé Cras) *La Bataille de Dakar* (Ozanne, Paris, 1956) and Roskill, Captain S.W., *The War at Sea, Vol 1, The Defensive* (HMSO 1954). (Hereafter cited as Marder, *Menace*; Cras, *Dakar*; and Roskill, *I*, respectively).

22 Crozier, Brian, *De Gaulle: The Warrior* (Eyre Methuen, 1973) pp 105.

23 Telegram from M. Masson, Governor of the Gabon, to General de Gaulle, 29 August 1940.

24 Churchill, *II*.

25 North to Roskill, 22 Jan 1951 (ROSK 4/32).

26 *Report of Proceedings of Force H for the period 11th September 1940 to 14th September 1940*. Flag Officer Commanding Force H, Letter No 60/8 dated 17 Sept 1940 (ADM 199/392). It also mentions, '... action taken by us at Dakar,' so the exact destination was also known.

27 North to Richmond, 27 Oct 1945 (RIC 7/4).

28 North to Roskill, 8 May 1950 (ROSK 4/32).

29 Naval Attaché, Madrid to Director of Naval Intelligence, Admiralty, 1842/5/9/40 (received by North on 6 Sept).

30 North to Secretary of the Admiralty, 6 Oct 1940 (X.224/465) (ADM 1/19180).

31 North to Roskill, 3 Nov 1951 (ROSK 4/32).

32 Somerville, *Report of Proceedings, 11 Sept-14 Sept 1940*, as note 26 above.

33 North Atlantic Command, War Diary, *op cit*. There is *no* report of any previous French convoy passing the Straits in either direction prior to the movement of 7 September.

34 This is important, especially so since various previous accounts create a totally false impression that these convoys were a regular feature *prior* to 11 September. They were *not*. Monks, *op cit*, pp 11, states: 'For many weeks now, the sight of French warships escorting convoys east and west through the Straits had been a common one that excited no unusual interest'. This is completely untrue. Likewise Heckstall-Smith, Anthony, *The Fleet that faced both ways* (Anthony Blond, 1963), (hereafter cited as Heckstall-Smith) pp 135.

35 Captain De Winton was still based ashore at this time, he still embarked from time to time for special operations, using *Gallant* as his 'Leader' and leaving the two senior officers, Colvill and Layman, to command their respective divisions for normal routine work. *Gallant* was in dockyard hands at this time. Captain De Winton to the author 31 July 1977.

36 Operational Record Book No 202 Squadron (AIR 27/1181) Night Order Book, HMS *Hotspur* kindly loaned the author by Captain H.F.H. Layman.

37 Commander E.N. Walmsley DSC to the author 10 Oct 1978.

38 De Winton, Captain F.S., *The Passage of Force Y*, a copy from the personal reminiscences of Captain F.S.De Winton, RN, loaned to the author 7 Aug 1977.

39 Captain H.F.H. Layman to the author, 22 Aug 1978.

40 DNI Admiralty 1928/5/9/40.

41 Consul General, Tangier to Admiral Gibraltar (repeated to Foreign Office 340. 1824/9/9/40).

42 Churchill, *II*, pps 425-6.

43 Hist. (A) 2, *The Dakar Operation, August and September 1940*, Brigadier R. Chenevix-Trench. pp 12 (ADO 199/ 07).

44 After the war this was brought to North's attention by Sir Rudolph Burmester in a letter dated 9 Dec 1949. (NRTH 2/1). He quoted from the biography of Lord Reith (*Into Wind*, pp 400), where the BBC Chief described the long journey necessary to reach the basement air raid shelter and how they were once told by Churchill when talking about this arrangement that, during the Dakar operation,

'... a signal giving warning about the French cruisers passing through the Straits of Gibraltar had not been dealt with in time owing to the FO staff having retired to this basement.'
[45] Naval Attaché, Madrid to Staff Officer (Intelligence), Gibraltar (repeated, for information, to DNI, Admiralty. 1809/10/9/40). (ADM 1/19180).

CHAPTER TEN: The Mission of Force Y

[1] The highest rank in the French Navy had hitherto been that of Vice-Admiral. However as Chief of Naval Staff Darlan promoted himself to a new, specially-created rank of Admiral of the Fleet after an unfortunate incident at the Coronation of King George VI when protocol deemed that, due to seniority, he was seated '... behind a pillar and a Chinese Admiral', at Westminster Abbey.
[2] Churchill once described him as '... one of those good Frenchmen who hated England', and the knowledge that one of his ancestors was killed at Trafalgar was still supposed to rankle. He was also unimpressed with the British Admiralty thinking that it lacked the offensive spirit, although no doubt he realised his error in that respect after Mers-el-Kebir!
[3] Due to vacillation on the various naval treaties Britain's new battleships were equipped with the 14-inch gun while France's now giants carried the 15-inch weapon and were ready almost a year earlier. Italy and Germany went for 15-inch, America for 16-inch and Japan 18-inch guns, leaving Britain in an unenviable position.
[4] The French word *contrôle* caused most of the confusion being taken by many in Britain to mean control, with all that applied, when in fact its meaning was a softer option than this.
[5] The only points gained from this by the Axis were a few propaganda leaflets showing a French battleship blowing up, but in the main the Germans did not take the advantage they could have done from the affair.
[6] *Not*, it should be noted, from Metropolitan France itself, despite Churchill's repeated assertions to the contary.
[7] Transmitted in clear language to all units from Darlan on 4 July 1940.
[8] Transmitted in clear language to all units from Darlan on 0718/5/7/40.
[9] Count Ciano for example recorded in his diary that the Duce was contemplating the occupation of Corsica. 'He is right. If we don't get there the British will, and from Ghisonaccia the Royal Air Force will attack Italy.' Ciano, *Diary, op cit*, 24 Sept 1940.
[10] Captain Claude Huan to the author, 7 Sept 1978.
[11] Cras, Hervé, *Dakar, op cit*.
[12] Diary of Admiral D'Harcourt, Casablanca. Copy kindly loaned by his son to the author. Entry dated 4 September 1940. (Cited hereafter as D'Harcourt, *Diary*)
[13] DCT, *Divisione Contre-Torpilleur*, the equivalent to the British Destroyer Flotilla. These large destroyers were rated as *Contre-Torpilleur's* in the French Navy which has no exact British equivalent. Literally it means destroyer of torpedo boats, which is the same designation originally given to British destroyers (*viz*: Torpedo-Boat Destroyers, or TBD's). The British had dropped the first part in 1924, about the same time as the first *Contre-Torpilleur's* were being built in France. These ships were much larger than normal destroyers at that time, and were envisaged therefore as 'Destroyers of Destroyers'. The French and Italians both built such vessels between the wars copying a large German type built in World War I. When first built they

were rather special on account of their size and armament causing some confusion of their appropriate designation compared to other nations' ships. This has led many historians to claim that they were in fact light cruisers, and the fact that for a period of two years in their twenty year lives the Navy so classified them has complicated matters. But in fact by 1939 most nations were building destroyers almost as large, and during the war Germany built destroyers larger with heavier guns and they were still called destroyers. Post-war the French Navy classed them as destroyers and so the oft-used title 'Super-Destroyers' for these ships is by far the most appropriate one and will be so used in this book. Of course claims that they were 'cruisers' is part and parcel of the pro-North faction in building up the considered odds against him had he have ordered intervention, as we shall see, but their merits as warships will be gone into later.

[14] *Führer Conferences on Naval Affairs 1940. Report of the Commander-in-Chief, Navy to the Führer on the afternoon of 6 September 1940,* Berlin, 6 Sept 1940. US translation from Naval Historical Center, Washington, DC pps 95-96.

[15] Telegram French Admiralty to all stations, Tgm No. 21 1520/25/30/8/40.

[16] The Italian Armistice Commission was represented at the highest level by the following: Count Galeazzo Ciano (Foreign Minister), Marshal Pietro Badoglio (Chief of General Staff); Admiral Domenico Cavagnari (Chief of Naval Staff); General Francesco Pricolo (Chief of the Air Staff) and General Mario Roatta (Military Attaché, Berlin).

The senior German naval representative was Captain (later Admiral) Wever, former German Naval Attaché, Paris, who was President of the Marine Section of the Commission. He was later killed in France at the end of the war, despite his having been strongly sympathetic to the French Navy between 1940 and 1945.

[17] *Waffenstill-stands* Commission Report, (Admiralty File PG/33636-7). Also-ix.61 *Documents on German Foreign Policy, 1918-45,* Washington, D.C.

[18] Huntziger to Stülpnagel, Letter No. 346 IEM, dated 5th Sept 1940.

[19] D'Harcourt diary, entry for 4th Sept 1940, *op cit.*

[20] D'Harcourt diary, entry for 5th Sept 1940, *op cit.*

[21] Darlan to Admiral Commanding 4th DC Message No. 5536, 1656/3/9/40.

[22] Admiral Jean Broussignac to the author, 9 Oct 1978.

[23] Admiral Jean Broussignac to the author, 26 Nov 1978.

[24] Captain Alan Hillgarth to Admiral North, 4 Jan 1947 (ROSK 4/32). The fact that Hillgarth was being used, to some extent, as a mouthpiece for the Vichy Government's viewpoints was valuable, but may have influenced Alexander among others, to distrust much of what he passed on as being propaganda put into his mouth by Darlan. It would help explain Alexander's distrust of his influence.

[25] Darlan to Delaye, Nrs A.5559-5563, 1106-1129/6/9/40.

[26] Rear-Admiral Rambert Delaye to the author, 2 October 1978.

[27] Hillgarth to North, 4th Jan 1947, *ibid* (ROSK 4/32).

[28] In his memoirs, Hoare, (then Lord Templewood), relates that he was given this information on 11 September. This is an error however for by then the French squadron was far out into the Atlantic. Templewood, Lord, *Ambassador on Special Mission,* (Collins, 1946), pp 85. (Cited hereafter as Hoare, *Ambassador*). This is not the only example of muddled memory with regard to this incident displayed by the Ambassador!

[29] Hoare, *Ambassador, ibid.*

[30] Hoare, *The Case of Admiral North,* (article in *Sunday Dispatch,* 30 May 1954).

[31] Marder, *Menace,* pp 72.

[32] Cras, *Dakar, op cit.*

[33] Ministry of Marine to Admiral *Sud*, Dakar, repeated Navy HQs Algeria, Morocco, Admiral 4th Cruiser Squadron. 1400/8/9/40.

[34] *Situation des forces navales au Maroc à la date du 12 Septembre 1940 à 0800 h.* (Marine au Maroc-Etat-Major No. 820 E.M. 3), dated 12 Sept 1940.

[35] That the French knew early on that the bulk of Force H had left Gibraltar is indicated by a signal of 6 September, thus:- 'My attention has been drawn to abnormal activity in the harbour of Gibraltar. Increase vigilance to avoid any surprise.' Ministry of Marine to Force Y, Tgm No. 5569. 1655/6/9/40.

[36] *Kriegstagebuch; Seekriegsleitung : 1. Abteilung – Teil A : Heft 13 vom 1. – 30. September 1940.* Entry dated 8 Sept 1940.

[37] Churchill, *II*, pps 425-27.

[38] *ibid*, pp 433.

[39] *ibid*, pp 436.

[40] Prime Minister to Prime Minister of Australia, Sir Robert Menzies, 29 Sept 1940.

[41] Aron, Robert, *The Vichy Regime 1940-44* (Putnam, 1958), pp 210

[42] Mengin, Robert, *No Laurels for De Gaulle* (Michael Joseph, 1967), pp 123

[43] Warner, Geoffrey, *Pierre Laval and the Eclipse of France* (Eyre & Spottiswood, 1968), pps 162-63 Footnote 1. He is quoting Bouthillier, Yves, *Le Drame de Vichy, Vol 1. Face à l'Ennemi, Face à l'Allié* (Plon, Paris, 1950).

[44] James, Rear Admiral William, KBE, CB, RN, *Ark Royal 1939-41* (Rupert Hart-Davis, 1957), pps 200-201.

[45] Muselier, Vice Admiral Emile Henri, *De Gaulle contre le Gaullism,* (Edition du Cherie, 1946) pp 80.

[46] Admiral Force Y to Darlan, Signal No. 5585, 1729/7/9/40.

[47] Ministry of Marine to Admiral Force Y, Signal No 5586, 1732/7/9/40.

[48] Ministry of Marine to Admiral Force Y, Signal No 6562, 1435/10/9/40.

[49] Ministry of Marine to Admiral Force Y, Signal No 04088, 1727/10/9/40.

CHAPTER ELEVEN: 'Bon Voyage'

[1] Captain Hillgarth to Professor Arthur Marder, quoted in Marder, *Menace*, pp 72.

[2] Admiral North to Admiral Sir Herbert Richmond, *Extracts from a letter from Admiral Dudley North*, undated, *circa* 1945. (RIC/7/4)

[3] *ibid*.

[4] North to Churchill, 4 March 1947. (NRTH 2/2)

[5] North to Captain Roskill, 8 May 1950 (ROSK 4/32)

[6] Admiralty Memorandum, 1957, quoted in Marder, *Menace*, pp 213.

[7] ACNA to ships on patrol; repeated *Hotspur* and *Wishart*. 0215/11/9/40.

[8] Operational Records Book, No 3 AACU, 11 Sept 1940. (AIR 29/45)

[9] Operational Records Book, No 202 Squadron, 11 Sept 1940. (AIR 27/1181)

[10] Captain Layman to the author 12 Oct 1978.

[11] Captain Layman's Memorandum, *The Admiral North Case: A Personal Record, Narrative* dated 11 January 1974. Copy loaned to the author by Captain Layman with Professor Marder's blessing.

[12] There are no entries in the ships' logs of the French squadron to indicate that they sighted any British warships until after daybreak.

[13] *Hotspur* to ACNA, 0445/11/9/40.

[14] Captain Edward W.J. Bankes to Captain Layman. Captain Bankes served in the Admiralty Signals Division at this time. Layman to the author, 28 Nov 1978.

[15] Captain Layman to the author, 12 Oct 1978.

[16] Captain Layman to the author, 18 Sept 1978.

[17] *Hotspur* to ACNA, 0525/11/9/40.

[18] Rear-Admiral John Lee Barber to the author, 25 Sept 1978.

[19] Captain E.V. St.J. Morgan to the author, 18 Nov 1978.

[20] ACNAS to *Hotspur*, 0555/11/9/40.

[21] Layman, *Personal Record, op cit.*

[22] Layman to the author, 12 Oct 1978.

[23] ORP No. 202 Squadron, *op cit.* (AIR 27/1181).

[24] Monks, *op cit*, pp 13.

[25] *Report of Proceedings of Force 'H' for the period 11th September, 1940, to 14th September, 1940*, No. 60/8, dated 17 Sept 1940. (ADM 199/392) (Cited hereafter as Somerville, *R-of-P*)

[26] Note 20 above.

[27] ACNAS to Admiralty, 0617/11/9/40.

[28] ACNAS to Admiralty, 0711/11/9/40.

[29] Monks, *op cit*, pp 29

[30] Captain Layman to the author, 13 Nov 1978.

[31] Roskill, *War at Sea, Vol 1, op cit.*

[32] Group Captain T.Q. Horner to the author, *op cit.*

[33] *Le Fantasque* to *Georges Leygues*, 0630/11/9/40. Log Entry.

[34] *Georges Leygues* to Force Y, 0630/11/9/40. Log Entry.

[35] 'Jacques Mordal', (Captain Hervé Cras,) to the author 20 Oct 1978.

[36] Admiral Jean Broussignac to the author, 9 Oct 1978.

[37] Rear Admiral E.N.V. Currey to the author, 29 Sept 1978.

[38] ORP 3 AACU, entry for 11 Sept 1940 (AIR 29/45)

[39] Log entries, *Georges Leygues*, '0736 – Speed 27 knots.' *Wrestler* resumed her normal beat, the other destroyer, *Wishart*, was on its way east to join Layman's group, hunting submarines, in order to relieve *Griffin* who was returning to Gibraltar early to refuel.

[40] Lieutenant Commander Charles Stuart to the author, 26 Sept 1978.

[41] Captain M.J. Evans to the author, 19 Oct 1978.

[42] Rear Admiral J.H. Walwyn to the author, 8 Oct 1978.

[43] *Renown*, Deck Log. Entries 11 Sept 1940. (ADM 53/113076).

[44] Log entries, Force Y, 0800/11/9/40.

[45] Captain Gabriele Rebuffel to Captain R.G. Mackay during a lunchtime discussion on Sunday 5 May 1946, during the Paris Conference. As recalled by H. Emmet in a letter to Captain Roskill, 27 July 1950. (ROSK 4/32). Confirmed, Admiral Rebuffel to the author, 8 Dec 1978.

[46] ORP No 3 AACU and No. 202 Squadron, *op cit.*

[47] Force Y to Ministry of Marine, Signal No 217, 1530/11/9/40.

[48] Reports of No 202 Squadron, 11 Sept 1940. (AIR 27/1181).

[49] Admiral D'Harcourt, Diary entries, 11 Sept 1940. *op cit.*

[50] *Kriegstagebuch: Seekriegsleitung, op cit.* Entry dated 12 Sept 1940.

[51] Hillgarth to Professor Marder, 28 Oct 1973. (Marder, *op cit*, pp 209)

[52] Admiralty to FOH 1239/11/9/40.

[53] Admiralty to FOH 1347/11/9/40.

[54] Admiralty to FOH 1429/11/9/40.

[55] Admiralty to FOH 1546/11/9/40.

[56] Heckstall-Smith, *op cit*, pp 138.

[57] Admiral Somerville to Lady Somerville, 12 Sept 1940. (SMVL 2/8).

[58] HMS *Renown, Deck Log*, entry for 11 Sept 1940. (ADM 53/113076).

[59] Somerville, *Report of Proceedings, 11th/14th Sept, op cit.*
[60] HMS *Hotspur*, Night Order Book, entry for 11 Sept 1940, *op cit.*

CHAPTER TWELVE: The Stange Silence

[1] Hillgarth to Marder, see Marder, *Menace*, pp 72, *op cit.*
[2] See above, pp 42.
[3] Marder, *op cit*, pp 73, states that Bevan received the de-coded message at about 12.30 a.m., 11 September. Bevan himself stated he got it at 0600 which is confirmed by Roskill, *Admirals, op cit*, pp 167.
[4] Roskill, *Admirals, ibid*, pp 167.
[5] Marder, *Menace, op cit*, pp 73, footnote.
[6] Churchill, *Vol II, op cit*, pp 426
[7] Pound, *Points which Admiral North Has Made*, minute 24 Jan 1941 (ADM 1/19187).
[8] Captain Roskill to the author, 13 Oct 1978.
[9] Admiralty to Bevan, 4 Oct 1940 (*Prem* 3-71)
[10] *Hansard*, 5th ser., Commons, Vol 365, cols 298-301, give the full text of Churchill's speech. Lord Halifax made a similar speech to the House of Lords at the same time.
[11] North to Lady North, 10 Oct 1940, (NRTH 2/3)
[12] Churchill to Alexander, 19 Oct 1940, Minute M. 213 (*Prem*-3-71).
[13] Alexander to Churchill, 23 Oct 1940, (ADM 199/1931)
[14] Churchill to Alexander, 23 Oct 1940, (ADM 199/1931)
[15] Pound to Alexander, 25 October 1940, (ADM 199/1931)
[16] Alexander to Churchill, 25 Oct 1940 (Prem 3-71)
[17] Churchill to Alexander, 27 October 1940 (ADM 199/1931)
[18] *Plimmer, op cit*, pp 76.
[19] Roskill to Acheson, 13 Aug 1954 (ROSK 4/32)
[20] Roskill, *Churchill, op cit*, pp 168-9.
[21] Grenfell to North, 26 Sept 1951 (NRTH 2/5)
[22] Grenfell to North, 1 Oct 1951 (NRTH 2/5). No other evidence appears to remain. Unfortunately any papers or documents that Grenfell may have assembled, or any statements he may have obtained from Bevan (and others) on this matter, seem to have vanished. They are not in the Grenfell papers box held at the Churchill College Archive Centre, for I made a diligent search. Captain Roskill informed me that: 'To the best of my recollection when he died I asked his widow to let us have all his papers which had survived, and she sent them to the College. They had rather an unsettled life, often moving house, and I think a lot must have got lost in the process.' Captain Roskill to the author, 11 Nov 1978.
[23] *War Cabinet Meeting, 247th. Conclusions. Minute 5. Confidential Annex.* 11 Sept 1940. 12.30 p.m. (*Cab/15 WM(40) 247th.*)
[24] *ibid*
[25] Heckstall-Smith, *op cit*, pps 139-140.
[26] Marder, *Menace, op cit*, p 76,
[27] Pound to Alexander for Churchill, Minute dated 4 Oct 1940. Annex 'K'. (ADM 1/19180).
[28] *ibid*
[29] Marder, *Menace, op cit*, footnote pp 78
[30] North to Admiralty, 20 Jan 1941. (ADM 1/19187)
[31] D'Harcourt diary, *op cit*. Entries for 11 Sept 1940.
[32] *ibid*
[33] Admiral Sud to *Sybille, Amazone, Amphitrite*, 1830/11/9/40.

[34] D'Harcourt to Darlan, Report No 850 E.M.3, dated 17 Sept 1940. *Departure of the Force Y from Casablanca on September 12th 1940.*

[35] *ibid*

[36] *Mission Report of the Milan,* No 833 E.M. 3 dated 14 Sept 1940.

[27] AdmiralBroussignac to the author, 12 Dec 1978.

[38] Mordal, *Dakar, op cit.*

[39] For numerous accounts of *Renown's* patrol off Casablanca which make little or no mention of the events related in Chapter 13 the reader can consult the following:-;:- Roskill, *War at Sea, Vol. 1 op cit,* pps 312-313; Marder, *Operation Menace, op cit* pps 77-78; Rohwer & Hummelchen, *Chronology of the War at Sea, Vol. 1* (Ian Allan, 1974) pp 53; MacIntyre, *Fighting Admiral, op cit,* pps 80-81; Monks, *That day at Gibraltar, op cit,* pps 33-34; Heckstall-Smith, *The Fleet that faced Both Ways, op cit,* pps 141-2; Churchill, *Their Finest Hour, op cit,* pps 425-7; Patrick Cosgrave, *Churchill at War; 1939-40 Alone* (Collins, 1974), pp 314; James, *Ark Royal 1939-41, op cit,* pps 200-201; Vader, John, *The Fleet Without a Friend* (New English Library, 1971) pp 118; Poolman, Kenneth, *Ark Royal* (Kimber, 1956) pps 136-138, *et al.* Only Mordal, *The Battle of Dakar, op cit,* mentions the events that took place, in a footnote. Perhaps the historians' silence is as strange as any other silences on this affair to date.

CHAPTER THIRTEEN: Clash by Night

[1] CO HMS *Vidette* to FO Commander Force H, *Encounter with French Destroyer,* dated 12 Sept 1940. (ADM 199/392).

[2] *ibid.*

[3] Commander Walmsley to the author, 10 Oct 1978.

[4] *Vidette* to FOCH, *op cit.*

[5] Mission Report of *Milan* to C-in-C French Maritime Forces, *op cit.*

[6] *Vidette* to FOCH, op cit.

[7] *Vidette* to FOH, 0305/12/9/40.

[8] *Vidette* to FOH, 0307/12/9/40.

[9] Mission Report *Milan* to C-in-C, *op cit.*

[10] Walmsley to the author, *op cit.*

[11] Mission Report *Milan* to C-in-C, *op cit.*

[12] D'Harcourt to C-in-C, *Departure of Force Y, op cit.*

[13] Somerville to CO *Vidette,* 16 Sept 1940. (ADM 199/392-Appendix).

[14] Mordal, *Dakar, op cit.*

[15] *Report of Proceedings Force H, op cit.* (ADM 199/392).

[16] D'Harcourt to C-in-C, *Departure of Force Y, op cit.*

[17] Marder, *Menace, op cit,* pp 77-78.

[18] Heckstall-Smith, *op cit,* pp 142.

[19] Plimmer, *op cit,* pp 79.

[20] *Report of Proceedings, Force H, op cit,* (ADM 199/392)

[21] ORP No 202 Squadron, dated 12 Sept 1940, *op cit,* Entries in Squadron Log for same date, *op cit* (AIR 27/1181.)

[22] *ibid.*

[23] *Report of Proceedings Force H, 16 September to 20 September 1940,* dated 20 Sept 1940. No. 63/8 (Copy also in SMVL 7/4).

[24] D'Harcourt to C-in-C Navy, *op cit.* Also Mordal, *Dakar, op cit:-* 'At about 0745 a large convoy was sighted accompanied by torpedo boats, 60 miles west of Cape Cantin, in advance of Force Y which did not round this cape until about 1100, but very close inshore.'

[25] *Report of Proceedings Force H,* dated 20 Sept 1940, *op cit.* (Signal time at 2015/11/9/40.)

[26] *ibid*

[27] *ibid*

[28] Addressed to French Admiralty, Admiral South, Force Y, Dakar Marine: 1805/12/9/40.

[29] Cras, *Dakar, op cit.*

[30] Log entry at 2050/12/9/40. *Georges Leygues.*

[31] *Departure of Force Y, op cit.*

[32] Log entry at 2115/12/9/40. *Georges Leygues.*

[33] *Report of Proceedings, Force H,* dated 20 Sept 1940, *op cit.*

[34] Commander Walmsley to the author, 10 Oct 1978.

[35] *Departure of Force Y, op cit.*

[36] D'Harcourt Diary, *op cit.*

[37] Arthur Marder to the author 2 June 1978.

[38] 202 Squadron Diary and ORP's, *op cit* Entries of 12 Sept 1940.

[39] *Report of Proceedings Force H, op cit.* Timed 0905/12/9/40.

[40] *ibid* Timed 1110/12/9/40.

[41] *ibid*

[42] 202 Squadron Diary and ORP's, *op cit.*

[43] *Report of Proceedings, Force H, op cit.* Signal F.O.H. to Admiralty 1643/12/9/40.

[44] Somerville to Lady Somerville, dated 26 Sept 1940 (SMVL 2/8).

[45] D'Harcourt Diary, *op cit.*

[46] *ibid*

[47] *Parliamentary Debates (Hansard),* 5th ser, Commons, Vol 365, *op cit.*

[48] Hervé Cras on the French side confirms this: 'In fact Mr Stokes was wrong. The English press had not printed before 11th Sept any announcement of the departure of the French ships for the Straits.' Mordal, *Dakar, op cit.*

[49] *Departure of Force Y, op cit.*

[50] D'Harcourt Diary, *op cit.*

[51] Log entries *Georges Leygues,* 13 Sept 1940.

[52] Heckstall-Smith, *Fleet that faced both ways, op cit,* pp 141.

[53] *ibid,* pp 142.

[54] *Report of Proceedings, Force H, op cit.*

[55] *ibid.*

[56] 202 Squadron Diary and ORP's, *op cit.*

[57] *Report of Proceedings, Force H, op cit.*

[58] *Journal de Marche Groupe de Chasse 1/5, 27-8-1939 to 20-12-1940*; S.H.A.A. Archives, G.129. Entries for 14 Sept 1940.; *Engagement avec un hydravion anglais*; Report by Contre-Amiral D'Harcourt a l'Amiral de la Flotte, Secrétaire d'Etat-à la Marine, Commandant en Chef les Forces Maritimes Francaises (FMF 3) Hôtel due Heldeir, Vichy, No E.M.2/668.; *Mote-rendu d'interrogaire d'aviateurs anglais;* Le Capitaine de Corvette Simon, *Amazone,* à Monsieur le Contre-Amiral Commandant la Marine au Maroc, dated 15 Sept 1940.

A subsequent telegram from the Consul General, Tangier, timed at 2020/15/9/40, was received by North on 16th September giving the full facts. It reads as follows: 'Addressed Admiral Gibraltar(R) Foreign Office. Your 0950/15. Following to 200 Group, RAF. Begins..

Flying boat was shot down near Casablanca by French fighter for having flown over forbidden zone and opened fire first. (2) Corporal Simpson (Fractured Fibula) was picked up trom raft. Aircraftmen Graham and Marshall picked up by French

Submarine. Latter two in good state. Ends.'
Copy of telegram loaned to author by No 202 Squadron Archives.
⁵⁹ *North Atlantic Command, War Diary, op cit.*
⁶⁰ Group Captain T.Q. Horner to the author, *op cit.*
⁶¹ Somerville to Lady Somerville, 12 Sept 1940 (SMVL 3/22)
⁶² 'Jacques Mordal', *The French Fantasque Class 1930*, (*Super Destroyers*, Warship Special 2, Conway Maritime Press, 1978). pp 31.
⁶³ VANAS to Admiralty 1645/15/9/40.
⁶⁴ Admiralty to VANAS 0145/16/9/40.
⁶⁵ *North Atlantic Command, War Diary, op cit.*
⁶⁶ (CAB 65/15) COS Meeting 250th. Minutes. Dated 1200/16/9/40.
⁶⁷ General instructions given following the incident of 19 Sept 1940. Message No. 5729. Darlan to Navy Toulon, Admiral 2nd Light Squadron, Volta, Admiral, South, Commander Bizerte, Oran, Algiers, Navy Casablanca, Dakar, Beyrouth, Marseille. Timed 1132-1137/20/9/40.
⁶⁸ *Points which Admiral North Has Made*, Admiral Pound, 23 Jan 1941. (ADM 1/19187).
⁶⁹ Admiralty Memorandum dated 1957 quoted as footnote in Marder, *Menace, op cit*, pp 261.
⁷⁰ Pound to North, 20 Sept 1940.
⁷¹ Admiralty to FOCNAS, 1800/27/9/40.
⁷² ADM1/19180.

CHAPTER FOURTEEN: Squaring the Circle

¹ Cunningham to Fraser, dated 30 Dec 1949 (Roskill, *Churchill, op cit*, pp 320)
² Fraser to Cunningham, dated 5 Jan 1950 (*ibid*)
³ Memorandum to First Lord, dated 30 April 1953 (published in *The Times*, issue dated 8 June 1954)
⁴ Macmillan to Alexander, dated 22 May 1957 (AVAR 5/16/16)
⁵ *Hansard*, Commons, Vol 570, cols 1401-4.
⁶ *The Times*, issue dated 25 May 1957.
⁷ *The Times*, issue dated 24 May 1957.
⁸ Cork and Orrery to North, dated 24 May 1957 (NRTH 2/1)
⁹ Cunningham of Hyndhope to North, dated 27 May 1957, (NRTH 2/3)
¹⁰ Cunningham of Hyndhope to Roskill, dated 2 June 1957 (ROSK 4/32)
¹¹ *Daily Mirror*, issue dated 25 May 1957.
¹² *Daily Mail*, issue dated 24 May 1957.
¹³ Macmillan to Alexander, dated 24 May 1957 (AVAR 5/17/14)
¹⁴ Alexander to Macmillan, dated 27 May 1957 (AVAR 5/17/14)
¹⁵ *Hansard*, Lords, *cciii*, col 1178.
¹⁶ *Daily Mirror*, issue dated 24 May 1957.
¹⁷ Marder, *Menace, op cit*, pp 262.
¹⁸ Rear-Admiral Walwyn to the author, dated 8 Oct 1978.
¹⁹ Captain A.W. Gray to the author, dated 15 Nov 1978.
²⁰ Captain John Osborne, to the author, dated 10 Oct 1978.
²¹ Plimmer, *op cit*, pp 68.
²² Mengin, *op cit*, pp 123.
²³ Cosgrave, *op cit*, pp 314.

[24] Walwyn to the author, *op cit.*
[25] *ibid*
[26] Admiral Currey to the author, dated 22 Aug 1978.
[27] Captain Layman to the author, dated 18 Sept 1978.
[28] Captain De Winton to the author, dated 22 Aug 1978.
[29] Lieutenant Commander Stuart to the author, dated 26 Sept 1978.
[30] Walwyn to the author, dated 8 Oct 1978.
[31] See ADM 1/9416
[32] Walmsley to the author, dated 9 Nov 1978.
[33] Commander Hugh Haggard to the author, 8 March 1979.
[34] Stuart to the author, dated 26 Sept 1978.
[35] Captain Claude Huan to the author, dated 31 Oct 1978.
[36] Hervé Cras ('Jacques Mordal') to the author, dated 20 Oct 1978.
[37] Commandant Costet to the author, dated 1 Nov 1978. Also Admiral Rebuffel to the author, dated 8 Dec 1978.
[38] *Extracts from a letter from Admiral Dudley North*, circa 1945, (RIC/7/4)
[39] Captain Evans to the author, dated 19 Oct 1978.
[40] Captain C.P.F. Brown to the author, dated 6 Oct 1978.
[41] Captain Layman to the author, dated 28 Nov 1978.
[42] Lord Fraser of North Cape to the author, dated 29 Oct 1978.
[43] Rear Admiral E. Sinclair to Captain Brown, dated 4 Oct 1978.
[44] Captain Brown to the author, dated 6 Oct 1978.
[45] Captain Layman to the author, dated 28 Nov 1978.
[46] Captain Evans to the author, dated 19 Oct 1978.
[47] Captain Litchfield to the author, dated 12 Dec 1978.
[48] Admiralty Investigation Memorandum 1957, quoted in Marder, *op cit*, pp 225.
[49] Lord Altrincham to North, 1953 (NRTH/2/1).
[50] Roskill, *Churchill, op cit*, pps 164-165.
[51] Juniper to the author, dated 4 Oct 1978.
[52] Osborne to the author, dated 15 Oct 1978.
[53] Evans to the author, dated 19 Oct 1978.
[54] Group Captain T.Q. Horner to the author; *op cit.*
[55] Walmsley to the author, dated 9 November 1978.
[56] Layman to the author, dated 28 Nov 1978.
[57] Gairdner to the author, dated 3 Nov 1978.
[58] Ryder to the author, dated 22 Nov 1978.
[59] Litchfield to the author, dated 12 Dec 1978.
[60] *Battle Cruiser Orders, No 38*, Sir David Beatty, 1916.

CHAPTER FIFTEEN: A Calculated Risk?

[1] Somerville, Vice Admiral Sir James F., KCB, DSO, Flag Officer Commanding, Force H, *Despatch*, dated 18 December, 1940, published as a Supplement to *The London Gazette*, dated 4 May 1948.
[2] *ibid*
[3] Somerville to Admiralty, quoted in MacIntyre, *Fighting Admiral, op cit*, pp 88.
[4] Maclean, Rear Admiral J.G., to the author, dated 19 September 1979.
[5] Walwyn, Rear Admiral J.H., CB, OBE, to the author, 14 September 1979.
[6] *Le Anzioni Navali in Mediterraneo, Vol IV*, (Ufficio Storico, Rome, 1976), pps 271-271.

[7] Somerville, *Despatch, op cit*, and information from Naval Library, London, 20 July 1979 and 2 August 1979.
[8] Cunningham of Hyndhope, *A Sailor's Odyssey, op cit* pps 292-93.
[9] Divine, A.D., *Destroyers' War*, (Muller, 1942), pp104.
[10] Somerville, *Despatch, op cit*.
[11] *ibid*.
[12] MacIntyre, *Fighting Admiral, op cit.*, pp 89.

CHAPTER SIXTEEN: Divide and Conquer

[1] *Le Anzioni Navali in Mediterraneo, Vol IV, op cit.*
[2] Bragadin, Commander (R) Marc' Antonio, *The Italian Navy in World War II*, (USNI, Annapolis, 1957), pps 49.
[3] Information from Commander Eugenio Cocchi, *Ufficio Storico*, Rome, to the author, dated 19 September 1979.
[4] See Bragadin, *op cit*, pp 50, and Rohwer, J. and Hummelchen, G., *Chronology of the War at Sea, 1939-1945, Vol 1*, pp 67, for examples of this error.
[5] Somerville, *Despatch, op cit*.
[6] Divine, A.D., *Destroyers' War, op cit*.
[7] *Le Anzioni Navali in Mediterraneo, Vol IV, op cit*, pps 278-279.
[8] Somerville, *Despatch, op cit*.

CHAPTER SEVENTEEN: Rendezvous Effected.

[1] Somerville, *Despatch, op cit*.
[2] *Le Anzioni Navali in Mediterraneo, Vol IV, op cit*, pp 279.
[3] *ibid*.
[4] Somerville to Lady Somerville, quoted in Macintyre, *op cit*, pp 94.
[5] Divine, *Destroyers' War, op cit*, pps 108-109.
[6] Gray, Captain A.W., to the author, dated 8 Sept 1979.
[7] See Smith, Peter C., *Hit First, Hit Hard*, (William Kimber, 1979) pp 157.
[8] Somerville, *Despatch, op cit*.
[9] *Le Anzioni Navali in Mediterraneo, Vol IV, op cit*, pp 283.
[10] Bragadin, *The Italian Navy in World War II, op cit*, pps 50-51.
[11] *ibid*.
[12] *Le Anzioni Navali in Mediterraneo, Vol IV, op cit*, pp 284.
[13] Somerville, *Despatch, op cit*.
[14] Gairdner, Captain J.O.H., OBE, to the author 13th July 1979
[15] Brooke, Vice Admiral B.C.B., CB, CBE, to the author 18 August 1979
[16] Somerville, *Despatch, op cit*.

CHAPTER EIGHTEEN: 'Run, Rabbit, Run'

[1] *Le Anzioni Navali in Mediterraneo, Vol IV, op cit.* pp 286.
[2] Divine, *Destroyers' War, op cit.* pp 110.
[3] Walwyn, Rear Admiral J.H., CB, OBE, to the author 16 July 1979.
[4] Brooke, Vice Admiral, *op cit*, to the author 18 Aug. 1979.
[5] Walwyn, Rear Admiral, *op cit*, to the author 16 July 1979.
[6] Somerville, *Despatch, op cit*.
[7] Divine, *Destroyers' War, op cit*, pp 112.

[8] C.P.O. Horstead, Jack, to the author. (This, the author's uncle, witness served aboard the *Berwick* during this battle and has described many incidents of this commission)

[9] Bragadin, *The Italian Navy in World War II, op cit.* pp 52.

[10] Walwyn, Rear Admiral, *op cit*, to the author, 16 July 1979

[11] *Le Anzioni Navali in Mediterraneo, Vol IV, op cit,*, pps 289.

[12] *ibid.*

[13] Somerville, *Despatch, op cit.*

[14] See for example Connell, G.G. *Valiant Quartet*, (Kimber, 1979), pp 138, '... the threat of torpedo air strikes drove off a superior enemy force'. This is just not so.

[15] Somerville, *Despatch, op cit.*

CHAPTER NINETEEN: A Question of Priorities

[1] *Le Azioni Navali in Mediterraneo, Vol IV*, pp 291.

[2] Somerville, *Despatch, op cit.*

[3] Walwyn, Rear Admiral, to the author, *op cit.*

[4] Evans, Captain M.J., to the author, 23 July 1979

[5] Somerville to Lady Somerville, November 1940.

[6] *ibid*

[7] Bragadin, *The Italian Navy in World War II, op cit*, pp 53.

[8] Somerville, *Despatch, op cit.*

[9] Somerville to Lady Somerville, *op cit.*

[10] Santoro, General *L'Aeronautica Italiana Nella Seconda Guerra Mondiale, Vol 2, op cit.*

[11] Layman, Captain H.F., to the author, 10 August 1979.

[12] Somerville, *Despatch, op cit.*

CHAPTER TWENTY: An Unprecedented Judgement.

[1] Stuart, Charles Mc D, Lieutenant, *Midshipman's Journal*, entry for 29th November 1940.

[2] Somerville to Lady Somerville, *op cit.*

[3] Admiralty Signal 2348/29/11/40.

[4] Roskill, *Churchill and the Admirals, op cit*, pp 170(footnote).

[5] Churchill to Alexander, dated 19 October 1940 (*AVAR 5/4/68(a)*).

[6] Pound to Alexander, (undated, probably October 1940), (*AVAR 5/4/72*).

[7] Somerville to Cunningham, quoted in Roskill, *Churchill and the Admirals, op cit*, pp 320 (Source note).

[8] Roskill, *The War at Sea, Vol 1*, pp 304.

[9] Cunningham, *A Sailor's Odyssey, op cit*, pps 202-294.

[10] *ibid*

[11] MacIntyre, Donald, *Fighting Admiral, op cit*, pps 98

[12] Walwyn, Rear Admiral, to the author, 16 July 1979

[13] Layman, Captain H.F.H., to the author 10 August 1979.

[14] Layman, Captain H.F.H., to the author, interview 16 October 1979.

[15] Churchill to Alexander and Pound 2 December 1940, and 3 December 1940.

[16] *ibid.*

[17] MacIntyre, *Fighting Admiral, op cit*, pp 98.

[18] *ibid*, pp 99.

[19] Cork to Somerville, *ibid.*

[20] Royale to Somerville, *ibid.*

[21] Somerville to Cunningham, *ibid.*
[22] Cunningham to Somerville, *ibid.*
[23] Cunningham of Hyndhope, *A Sailor's Odyssey, op cit*, pp 294.
[24] Admiralty to Somerville, Roskill, *Churchill and the Admirals, op cit*, pp 171.
[25] The only complete and detailed account of this campaign is to be found in *War in the Aegean*, by Peter C. Smith and Edwin Walker, (Kimber, 1974).
[26] Ruge, Vice Admiral Friedrich, *Sea Warfare 1939-45*, (Cassell, 1957), pp 115.

Index